Marketing and Promotion for Design Professionals

Marketing and Promotion for Design Professionals

John Philip Bachner & Naresh Kumar Khosla

 VAN NOSTRAND REINHOLD COMPANY
NEW YORK   CINCINNATI   ATLANTA   DALLAS   SAN FRANCISCO
LONDON   TORONTO   MELBOURNE

Van Nostrand Reinhold Company Regional Offices:
New York   Cincinnati   Atlanta   Dallas   San Francisco

Van Nostrand Reinhold Company International Offices:
London   Toronto   Melbourne

Manufactured in the United States of America

Published by Van Nostrand Reinhold Company
450 West 33rd Street, New York, N.Y. 10001

Published simultaneously in Canada by Van Nostrand Reinhold Ltd.

15 14 13 12 11 10 9 8 7 6 5 4 3 2 1

Library of Congress Cataloging in Publication Data

Bachner, John Philip.
   Marketing and promotion for design professionals

   Includes index.
   1. Design services—Marketing.   I. Khosla,
Naresh Kumar, joint author.   II. Title.
NK1504.B3   1977   658.8'09'74544973   76-57975
ISBN 0-442-20478-7

For Barney and Lissa
JPB

For my mother and father; Valerie and Shanon
NKK

PREFACE

For our purposes, marketing can be defined as that group of business practices designed to provide management with as effective a tool as possible for controlling the short-, mid-, and long-term development of its business organization. There is no question of whether or not a business has marketing. Rather, the question is to what extent does it have marketing and how effectively does it work.

Architects, engineers, and other design professionals, practicing on an independent basis, traditionally have followed marketing practices that by their very nature are counterproductive to the concept of controlled development. Few ever have undertaken the steps necessary to determine which markets they should be in. The promotion required to facilitate and sustain growth generally has been limited to word of mouth. As a result, the direction of the firm's development has more often than not been established by fulfilling the needs of those who happen to knock on the door. While this marketing method may sometimes bear fruit during periods of economic expansion, it falls far short of the mark during periods of relative or absolute recession.

There are, of course, numerous exceptions. And almost universally, those exceptional organizations are the ones that are leaders in their respective fields. They did not get there by accident. In almost all cases management undertook painstaking research to define areas of opportunity and to pursue plans and policies designed to turn potential business into bottom-line profits.

We realize, of course, that not all design professionals want to see their firms become leaders in the field, which is all the more reason why effective marketing is essential. With proper application, marketing can help you achieve whatever particular business goals you may happen to set. As it is now, however, relatively few design professionals have ever bothered to set down in writing what their particular business goals may be, let alone develop the planning required to achieve them. Nor can design professionals really be faulted for this omission.

Those entering the design professions are educated as designers—not businessmen. They further what marketing strategies they may have not through conscious marketing efforts, but rather through upgrading their own professional status. This is not to say that a high degree of professionalism is alien to the marketing concept—in fact, it is essential to it—but to strive for professionalism, and to rely on that effort as the primary marketing tool, is to put the business function out of balance. In essence, upgrading one's professional capabilities is a matter of doing one's utmost to improve service—the product—without considering the client's or prospective client's continuing need for the product, what other products may be saleable, or the ways and means of letting others know that the product even is available at all. In other words, the vast majority of design professionals regard their businesses solely as professions. As a result, many tend to overlook the business aspects of their professions, and their marketing strategies have developed accordingly.

There are those design professionals, of course, who hold that professionalism, by nature, precludes active pursuit of marketing tactics. It must be assumed that those who advocate such a position have no concept of what marketing really entails. As presented in this book, at least, even the most aggressive marketing program can and should be conducted well within the confines imposed by a rigidly-applied set of professional ethics. What misconceptions do exist probably stem from confusing marketing as a concept with promotion as a marketing tool. For example, introduction of a new consumer product usually involves a barrage of promotional activity in all media. Unfortunately, good taste is frequently sacrificed in the rush to get attention focused on the new product. When such attention promotes discussion of the new product—which is what it is intended to do, in part—comments often will relate to the "new marketing program underway." Thus, for many people, marketing and marketing programs have become synonymous with extensive, highly visible promotional activity geared to getting attention at any cost.

In fact, marketing involves far more than promotion alone. The uninitiated could not be expected to understand this, however, because so many of the other tasks are undertaken completely without fanfare or public visibility. Moreover, the specific type of promotional approaches selected relate strictly to the needs of the organization involved, not to the needs of marketing *per se*. Accordingly, promotion undertaken as part of one firm's serious marketing effort may be as conservative as another's is exhibitionistic.

Promotion, of course, is often considered to come under the separate discipline of public relations. For our purposes, however, promotion and PR are considered marketing tools. In fact, as you will discover, there are a variety of different subjects that we have placed under the marketing umbrella, which others—particularly practitioners of the various disciplines involved—will protest. To spend time splitting hairs really is not very productive, however, especially over matters of semantics.

One semantical point that must be clear, however, revolves around the term "marketing your services," a catch phrase often used in connection with books, articles, seminars, and manuals directed toward design professionals. More often than not, when such a context is involved, the word marketing is nothing more than a euphemism for "selling," a word that—for some reason—seems particularly abhorrent to many design professionals. In fact, marketing and selling are not at all synonymous words or identical functions. Selling is merely the tip of the marketing iceberg. To "market one's services," or sell, without learning how to develop a true marketing program, is like learning how to sail but not how to navigate. Your expertise would be sufficient for a while, but, once out of sight of land, watch out!

The practice of marketing, or the application of the marketing concept to your firm, first and foremost, means the establishment of overall company goals. Once goals are known, it is possible to establish the specific objectives whose attainment will help ensure achievement of each goal. Once objectives are specified, it is possible to identify the strategies needed to achieve each objective. Once strategies are known, the tactics required to achieve each can be identified and applied.

This approach requires an extensive amount of research, discussion, soul-searching, and planning. It isn't easy, but anything that proffers great rewards seldom is accomplished with little effort.

One of your first tasks will be to shuck just about all preconceived notions related to marketing and the way you think your organization should be run. If in reconstructing your thoughts in order to implement the marketing concept your preconceived notions are shown to have been valid, fine. If not, do not fret about the past. You can't change it. But you can, by doing things right, have far greater control over what the future will bring.

In that you are reading this book, it is relatively safe to assume that you are at least interested in marketing, and you may be thinking of taking some kind of substantive step to develop a program for your own firm. Be advised that one does not undertake a marketing effort simply by establishing a director of marketing and providing him with an office so he can "do his thing." In fact, application of the marketing concept to an organization means permeation. The organization must be concerned about marketing from top to bottom, front to back, because, in fact, marketing affects or is affected by everything that goes on in your firm.

Originally marketing was far less complex. It meant producing a product or developing a service and then, through promotion, selling it to the customer. Thus the expression to "market" your product.

Experience showed that this sort of marketing concept did not bear too much fruit when the product itself was not saleable, or not saleable enough, or when too many others sold the same or a similar product or service. Thus came the need for development of market or marketing research, a program of intelligence-gathering to determine who comprised the market for a given product or service, what their attitudes were, who already was involved in providing it, and so on. The idea was to overcome the problems of the original concept so the firm could be in a better marketing position. While marketing still was being used as a synonym for selling, the marketing function itself, because of research activities now connected with it, developed more status within the organization. As a result, the marketing function either was taken out of the hands of salesmen or, as more usually was the case, certain salesmen were made directors of marketing and then given new responsibilities.

This approach worked all right for a while, but it tended to overlook another set of problems.

First, because the emphasis primarily was on clients, prospective clients, and the competition, there was a tendency to overlook in-house capabilities and requirements. Thus, in many cases, firms entered some very lucrative markets, but did not really have the ability to do what they knew had to be done.

Second, because the emphasis primarily was on what was happening now, far too little attention was paid to the future or to the chameleon-like nature of public opinion. It is to be assumed that Ford stylists and engineers read market data carefully before designing the Edsel (once described so magnificently as an "Oldsmobile sucking a lemon"), but by the time it reached the marketplace public fancy had changed.

As a result of these lessons learned, it was realized that marketing also had to develop an introspective look. That is, in addition to other factors, it had to consider what the firm was capable of doing now and the ways and means its capabilities could be modified to accommodate change, the rate at which change could be made, and so on. Also, it was realized that marketing had to take the short-, mid-, and long-range future into consideration on a continuing basis so the future would not catch the company unprepared.

All of these changes in the marketing concept changed the function of marketing within the firm. It was recognized that marketing no longer could be an isolated function. It is concerned with too much that is going on.

Because of its obvious complexity, the full scope of marketing seldom is explained in a brief, didactic manner. After all, it is far easier to say, "Determine what your goals are and then . . ." rather than provide information on exactly how to go about determining what your goals are or should be. Nonetheless, this book goes, or tries to go, directly to the heart of the matter by providing you with the discussion and tools required for you to conduct a full-scale, comprehensive marketing program without having an extensive marketing background. This is accomplished through presentation of numerous forms that you should use per instructions provided. We don't particularly like forms. They are even more tedious to develop than to use. Nonetheless, there is no ready alternative.

Make no mistake. The authors do not labor under the impression that this book is the be-all and end-all, or that it represents "the only way." We present suggested methodologies. At a minimum, they should make you aware of the many factors that marketing must consider and so provide you with a launching pad for your own thoughts. If you disagree with what we suggest, so be it, just as long as you can determine why you disagree and so have the basis for establishing what you believe is the correct approach.

The organization of the book presented particular problems. After numerous attempts it was decided that it was simply impossible to make everything unfold in a 1–2–3–4 . . . sequence. Accordingly, we offer this suggestion for using this book. Read it through from cover to cover at least once. Make notes as you go to give yourself an overall grasp of the many factors that must be considered. By applying these factors to the particular set of circumstances unique to your firm, you will then be able to determine the order in which certain tasks must be undertaken. Be sure to consult the index for full discussion of any given element.

One last word. An initial skimming of this book may tend to indicate that the authors are writing primarily for larger organizations. This is not at all the case. We have tried to bring into the discussion factors that affect organizations of all sizes. As such, some material will relate only to larger organizations, while other material will relate only to smaller outfits. For the most part, however, the basic considerations advanced relate to all organizations regardless of size. Larger firms will have more work to do to fill in the blanks, so to speak, while smaller firms will have less work to do. But the basics still are basics, necessary if you are to enjoy a degree of control over the destiny of your firm, which, when you get right down to it, is what marketing really is all about.

John Philip Bachner
Naresh Kumar Khosla

CONTENTS

THE GMA, ITS SEGMENTATION, AND THE MU

As a design professional, you can define your market as the sum of those individuals and organizations who need and/or want services such as you provide and are willing to pay for them. Since most design professionals offer services that are relatively similar, however, those who need and/or want them usually will consider proximity of the provider to be a basic criterion in selection. Thus, for practical purposes, a market can be spoken of as a "geographical marketing area," or GMA, from which a design professional will draw the majority of his business. Because most design firms are relatively small, they have relatively small GMAs, frequently extending no farther than a given metropolitan area.

There are exceptions, of course. Firms that provide highly specialized services or have unique experience generally will have very large GMAs, often regional or national, sometimes international. In most cases, however, the population of such a GMA, in terms of prospective clients, is relatively sparse. Another exception is the firm with satellite operations, be they branch offices, affiliated firms, associated firms, or whatever. When satellite operations are involved, however, it usually is best to think in terms of each office or firm having a GMA of its own, rather than the full GMA provided by all offices as a whole.

Given that the GMA is one's marketplace, where one sells his services, it stands to reason that the more one knows about it the more able he will be to sense change and opportunity and so be able to take advantage of them. Unfortunately, the depth of understanding required cannot come about through experience alone. While experience is a good teacher, it is limited.

By definition, it is unable to provide us insight about something with which we never have had contact. Thus, the degree of familiarity required can be gained only through a program of research and analysis. At one time such an undertaking would have been numbingly tedious, but thanks to new marketing tools, research and analysis now can be performed relatively quickly and with far more productive results.

The tool advocated for GMA research is called segmentation. Through its application, one divides the GMA into segments, each of which can be divided into subsegments, which, in turn, can be segmented still further. In essence, it's like disassembling a complicated machine into its component systems, then taking the systems apart, so the person performing the work—once he puts the machine back together—is intimately familiar with all the various pieces, how they fit together to form systems, and how these systems interrelate to form a working whole.

For our purposes, the prime segment relates to user categories. Thus, a GMA can be broken into commercial, industrial, residential, institutional, and governmental segments. Within each of these segments there are numerous prime subsegments. In the commercial segment, for example, there are enclosed shopping malls, strip shopping centers, high-rise office buildings, etc. Each of these prime subsegments can be defined more precisely in terms of secondary subsegments. Thus, high-rise office buildings can be divided between speculative and owner-occupied, by new or existing construction, by general location within a GMA, and by size of fee involved for design.

In practice, however, taking the general segmentation effort beyond two or three stages seldom serves any useful purpose. Thus, speaking in terms of prime segment and subsegment usually is all that is required. If your circumstances are such that closer definition is necessary, however, you obviously have the means to make such closer definition possible.

The parameters you set to bound your segmentation effort result in definition of marketing units, or MUs, a term that will be used extensively throughout this book. If you decide to disassemble your GMA in terms of prime segments and subsegments, commercial/enclosed shopping malls, commercial/strip shopping centers, and commercial/high-rise office buildings each would become a marketing unit, or MU. If additional specification is required, something like commercial/high-rise office building/$150,000 may become a typical MU. Do bear in mind, however, that the more elements an MU must take into consideration, the more MUs you will have to deal with. Since proliferation of MUs is something that will occur even when the most general MU definition is employed, it is advised strongly that full segmentation be employed only when absolutely necessary.

As will be seen, use of the MU concept is not at all limited to application to your GMA. In fact, you also will be using it to analyze, among other things, the experience of your firm and its personnel. Thus, by using the MU concept in this manner, you will be able to assay your firm's capabilities in market-oriented terms.

2

BASIC ORGANIZATIONAL RESEARCH

Many elements of past and current business operations must be covered through organizational research. Because the purpose for obtaining some of this information will become apparent only in conjunction with other marketing activities, or only after certain other types of research have been performed, discussion here will be limited to what we call basic organizational research: identification of MUs in which your firm has actual or potential capabilities.

In analyzing these capabilities, it is likely that a somewhat paradoxical situation will come to light, namely, that it is sometimes easier to promote a capability you don't have rather than one you do possess.

A firm's capabilities are the direct equivalent of the capabilities of the persons who comprise the organization and the interrelationships between these persons, which result in crossfertilization of ideas and concepts upon which the design function relies. Thus, if the firm has on staff three architects who, within the past five years, have had responsible charge for the design of four hospitals, the firm obviously has a capability to design hospitals. If each of the three performed these design functions while with other firms, however, and the firm itself has not had experience in hospital design, it will be relatively difficult to promote hospital design capabilities. Conversely, if the firm, within the past five years, has designed three suspension bridges, but has since lost the key personnel primarily responsible for the design aspects, and no similar experience is represented on staff, the firm will have lost its capability in that field. Nonetheless, it will be relatively easy for the firm to promote its suspension bridge design "capabilities." And so the

4

paradox. It should not be taken to mean that firm experience gained solely through the experience of staff members while they were with other firms should be discounted. Far from it. It could be one of your most valuable assets when it comes time to establish planning for the future. Accordingly, it is essential that you become familiar not only with what your firm has done as a firm, but also with what your firm has done as a collection of specialized individuals, and this is what basic organizational research is all about.

2.1 FIRM EXPERIENCE

To undertake a thorough analysis of your firm's experience, it is necessary to initiate research activities relating to past and current projects. Obviously, those projects performed ten or more years ago will have little relevance to today's market unless they truly were outstanding, but even then their usefulness to the marketing effort is limited primarily to promotion rather than basic organizational research. For the purposes of identifying current capabilities, therefore, we suggest that research be limited to those projects undertaken during no more than the past five years. Even then the amount of work involved, as you read about it in the next few pages, will seem extensive. Nonetheless, the results it can provide—even if your marketing effort goes no farther than this particular step—should prove the effort worthwhile.

Project Analysis

Begin your effort by analyzing each project undertaken by the firm within the past five years. To do this, utilize a Project Analysis Form, as shown in Figure 1. Bear in mind that the form shown is one that covers only the specific MU elements and related factors with which this text is most concerned. Similar forms can be created easily to identify or highlight those particular factors with which you or your firm are most interested, or to take into consideration MUs of greater or different magnitude.

The factors covered in the Project Analysis Form shown are:

1. *MU:* As discussed, the MU being used throughout this book comprises two elements only: primary segment and primary subsegment. If more segmentation is required it can be included but, for the most part, other MU-type factors already are covered on this form.

2. *Date of Project:* The date you attach to a specific project could refer to the date the contract was signed, or work began, or work was completed, or the project was constructed. While we favor either the date the contract was signed or the approximate date when work began,

PROJECT ANALYSIS FORM

1. MU: Segment _____ Subsegment _____

2. Date of Project _____

3. Name of Project _____

4. Name of Client _____

5. Location of Project/Client:

   GMA Project/GMA Client _____

   Non-GMA Project/GMA Client _____

   GMA Project/Non-GMA Client _____

   Non-GMA Project/Non-GMA Client _____

6. New Construction _____ Existing Construction _____

7. Size of Project: A   B   C   D   E   F

8. Size of Fee: A   B   C   D   E   F

9. Services Provided: A   B   C   D   E   F

10. Profit (Loss) $_____

11. Percentage of Profit (Loss) _____%

Figure 1. Project Analysis Form.

the choice is yours. In all cases, however, the dating methodology
you establish here should be used consistently for other similar tasks
discussed later.

3. *Name of Project:* The name of the project should be the one referenced consistently throughout your materials. In other words, if your
   files refer to what ultimately became the "Smith Building" as "Office
   Building at Main and Second," the name of the project should be
   noted as "Office Building at Main and Second." This makes it that
   much simpler for other researchers working with or after you.

4. *Name of Client:* In addition to identifying the client's name, include—
   typically where interprofessional work is involved—the name of the
   owner or "indirect client."

5. *Location of Project/Client:* Although we are concerned primarily
   with your market as a GMA, there is a possibility that a decision to
   expand or otherwise affect your current GMA may be made. For
   this reason GMA information as covered in item 5 is necessary.

6. *New or Existing Construction:* Information on the project in terms of new or existing construction can provide direction, later on, in determining not only what kind of projects to seek, but also in developing strategies to obtain them.

7. *Size of Project:* In terms of current replacement value, it will be up to you to designate the ranges indicated by the various letters. For example, A may indicate "Up to $500,000"; B, "$500,001 to $1 million," etc.

8. *Size of Fee:* Utilize a category coding (e.g., A = up to $5,000) most suitable to your firm. Also, insert total actual billing for the project.

9. *Services Provided:* Determine typical types of services your firm provides. Typical categories would include, for various types of firms, design, field work, construction inspection, feasibility studies, energy conservation, economic analysis, as-built drawing, etc. These, too, are referenced by code.

10. *Profit:* The net amount involved. This usually is computed by calculating costs of personnel time, materials, general and administrative expenses, and overhead, and subtracting them from fee. Do not overlook later expenses such as liability losses resulting from costs of defense, settlements, awards (plus costs of personnel time involved), or bad debts.

11. *Percentage of Profit:* Net profit divided by total contract value for your services.

You may find it most expedient, once you have gathered this information or whatever information you seek, to develop a computer program to store and retrieve the data required for the following operations. In most cases, however, this will be most practical only for larger firms that have undertaken 200 or more projects within the past five years.

Annual MU Analysis

The next step is to group projects by years and, for each year, by MUs involved. Once this is done, utilize an Annual MU Analysis Form, as shown in Figure 2, to analyze, among other things, the profitability of projects on a factor-by-factor basis. The items in question are as follows:

1. *Year:* The year involved.

2. *MU:* The MU involved.

3. *Amount of Projects:* The total number of projects undertaken in the

ANNUAL MU ANALYSIS FORM

1. Year _____

2. MU: Segment _____ Subsegment _____

3. Amount of Projects _____ Average % of Profit (Loss) ___%

4. Location of Project/ Client, Amount of Projects

   GMA Project/ GMA Client _____

      Average % of Profit (Loss) ___%

   Non-GMA Project/ GMA Client _____

      Average % of Profit (Loss) ___%

   GMA Project/ Non-GMA Client _____

      Average % of Profit (Loss) ___%

   Non-GMA Project/ Non-GMA Client _____

      Average % of Profit (Loss) ___%

5. Amount of Projects New Construction _____

      Average % of Profit (Loss) ___%

   Amount of Projects Existing Construction _____

      Average % of Profit (Loss) ___%

6. Amount of Projects at Size and Average % of Profit (Loss)

   A _____ ___% B _____ ___% C _____ ___%

   D _____ ___% E _____ ___% F _____ ___%

7. Amount of Projects at Fee and Average % of Profit (Loss)

   A _____ ___% B _____ ___% C _____ ___%

   D _____ ___% E _____ ___% F _____ ___%

8. Number of Projects for Which Services Were Provided

   A ___ B ___ C ___ D ___ E ___

Figure 2. Annual MU Analysis Form.

9. Most Common Service Combinations

Combination	Number of Jobs	Average % of Profit (Loss)

10. Total Value of MU Projects (Gross Billings) $_____

11. Total Profit (Loss) $_____

Figure 2. (*Continued*)

given MU for the given year, and the average percentage of profit. (Average percentage of profit is obtained simply by averaging Project Analysis Form item No. 11 responses.)

4. *Location of Project/Clients:* Indicate the number of MU projects that conform to each of the four project/client location possibilities. Indicate percentage of profit for the projects so listed. For example, if review of Project Analysis Forms for the MU involved shows that the firm has undertaken four non-GMA projects for non-GMA clients, with respective percentages of profit of 8%, 8.5%, 9% and 10%, average profit indicated would be 8.875%. Obviously, if you find that working with non-GMA clients on non-GMA projects is highly profitable, on the average, it would be an indication that you should perhaps attempt to get more of this work in the MU involved.

5. *New/Existing Construction:* Indicate the amount of projects that involved new construction and the amount that involved existing construction and, in each case, the average amount of profit for the jobs involved.

6. *Project Size:* The number of projects at the various sizes you have designated, and the average percentage of profit for projects in each of the categories.

7. *Fees:* The number of projects at the various fee ranges you have established, and average percentage of profit for each category.

8. *Services:* Indicate on how many projects each of your designated services or service categories were provided.

9. *Service Combinations:* Through review of Project Analysis Forms, establish which service combinations were provided most frequently. This includes the "combination" of one service only, most typically design services. Indicate what the average percentage of profit was for jobs representing the five (or more) most common service combinations.

10. *Total Value of MU Projects:* This is a simple summary of gross billings of all projects in the given MU for the given year, as well as its percentage of the firm's gross billings for all projects indicated as having been undertaken during the year.

11. *Total Profit:* The total amount of profit for projects in the MU for the year.

Trend Review

Once you have performed an analysis of MU activity for each year under review, begin review of each MU for each of the five years involved. In other words, examine each MU on the basis of what changes have been noticed from year to year. What has happened to each factor? Has the firm steadily been increasing the number of projects performed within the GMA for a GMA client? Have highly profitable factors from one year increased their profitability? Maintained it? Have service combinations changed? Wherever you note any significant change of one sort or another, attempt to determine why the change took place. If no answer is readily apparent, be sure to write the question down for further study and review, perhaps while performing market research and analysis later on.

Obviously, if it can be shown that you are obtaining less of a given type of work simply because there is less of that work in your market or GMA, there is no cause for alarm. If the amount of work in your GMA has not been decreasing, however, it means that your market share is eroding. That is cause for alarm and you must do your best to determine why. Is the quality of your work declining? Have you become too tied up with clients who are doing less of the work for whatever reason? Is the competition increasing its share? These and numerous other questions must be answered. Finding the answers will help you hone your business and marketing strategy to ultimate precision and so help provide even more definite direction for the company's future. To obtain even more detailed data about trends, utilize an Annual MU Trend Analysis Form, such as the one shown in Figure 3.

ANNUAL MU TREND ANALYSIS FORM

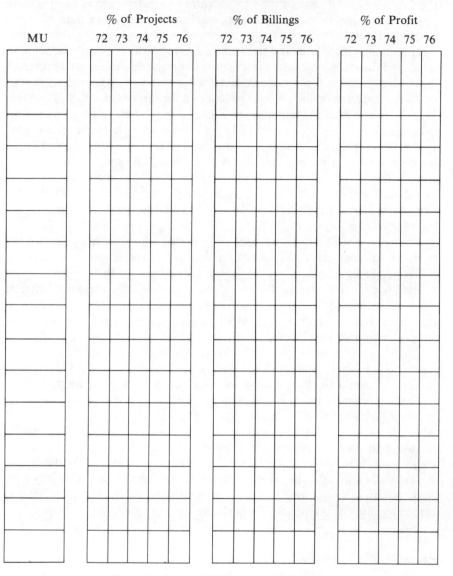

Figure 3. Annual MU Trend Analysis Form.

To use the form, first compute the number of projects the firm has handled, the firm's gross billings, and the firm's total profits for each of the past five years. This information can be obtained easily be totaling data on your Annual MU Analysis Forms.

To complete the Annual MU Trend Analysis Form, list all the MUs in which the firm has been active in the past five years down the left-hand margin, under "MU." If five years ago the firm did nothing in a given MU, blanks or "NAs" (not applicable) would be left in appropriate spaces. If, however, four years ago the firm had 100 projects and four of these were in the MU in question, the figure 4% would be inserted under the appropriate year in the "% of Projects" heading. Likewise, if these four projects accounted for $100,000 of gross billings, and if the firm's gross billings for the year were $3,000,000, 3.33% would be placed under the appropriate year in the "% of Billings" column. If the four projects brought in $5,000 in profits, and the firm made $100,000, 5% would be entered under the appropriate year in the "% of Profit" column.

An analysis such as this not only shows you what has happened in the past, but also can serve to present an indication of the future. For example, if the percentage of firm projects represented by a given MU steadily increases over a five-year period, you could assume—for the time being at least—that they will continue to grow. Of course, if the percentage of projects for the MU is on the increase while percentage of profits is in decline, such growth obviously is not worthwhile unless something can be done to change the profitability picture. Just as this trend analysis can give you indication of what is happening within your firm, so, too, does it serve, at least to an extent, to show you what is happening in your market.

Analysis such as this also can raise questions. In many cases, however, reviewing trend analysis data for a given MU will enable you to understand what forces have caused shifting relationships among MUs. And again, the more you can understand about these relationships, the more you understand your firm, a basic requisite to developing direction for the future which is anchored to the realities of today. In essence, it's relatively easy to determine where you want to be, but in order to map a strategy to get you there you must know precisely where you are right now.

Periodic MU Analysis

Once you have performed trend review, you are ready to establish periodic MU analysis. This is nothing more than summing up the various annual MU analyses for each MU for the various years involved. The period under review, in this case, is five years. Since the Periodic MU Analysis Form (Figure 4) is essentially similar to the Annual MU Analysis Form, no further descrip-

PERIODIC MU ANALYSIS FORM

1. Years _____

2. MU: Segment _____ Subsegment _____

3. Amount of Projects _____ Average % of Profit (Loss) ____%

4. Location of Project/Client, Amount of Projects

    GMA Project/GMA Client _____

       Average % of Profit (Loss) ____%

    Non-GMA Project/GMA Client _____

       Average % of Profit (Loss) ____%

    GMA Project/Non-GMA Client _____

       Average % of Profit (Loss) ____%

    Non-GMA Project/Non-GMA Client _____

       Average % of Profit (Loss) ____%

5. Amount of Projects New Construction _____

       Average % of Profit (Loss) ____%

    Amount of Projects Existing Construction _____

       Average % of Profit (Loss) ____%

6. Amount of Projects at Size and Average % of Profit (Loss)

    A _____ ____%   B _____ ____%   C _____ ____%

    D _____ ____%   E _____ ____%   F _____ ____%

7. Amount of Projects at Fee and Average % of Profit (Loss)

    A _____ ____%   B _____ ____%   C _____ ____%

    D _____ ____%   E _____ ____%   F _____ ____%

8. Number of Projects for Which Services Were Provided

    A ____   B ____   C ____   D ____   E ____

Figure 4. Periodic MU Analysis Form.

9. Most Common Service Combinations

Combination	Number of Projects	Average % of Profit (Loss)
_____	_____	_____
_____	_____	_____
_____	_____	_____
_____	_____	_____
_____	_____	_____

10. Total Value of MU Projects (Gross Billings) $_____

    % of Total Firm Billings ____%

11. Total Profit (Loss) $_____

Figure 4. (*Continued*)

tion of it is necessary. In reviewing the data it contains, however, realize that it is summary information. As such it should be reviewed with MU trend data in mind. While a periodic summary may show that a given MU has been the most profitable for the past five years, it is feasible that during the past two years it was among the least profitable. For this reason a periodic MU analysis has relatively limited application, being used primarily for analysis by ideal comparison, which in many cases answers some of the questions established through annual trend analysis.

Analysis by Ideal Comparison

Based on data contained in the Periodic MU Analysis Form for each MU, you are able to identify the profitability of various project factors. As you can see, there are five categories comprising a total of twenty-three factors, as follows: location of projects (4); new construction/existing construction (2); project size (6); fee (6), and service combinations (5). To establish an ideal project within a given MU, therefore, one first must rank the various factors in descending order. Thus, if the highest percentage of profit listed is for projects undertaken for non-GMA clients within the GMA, "non-GMA client/GMA project" would be listed first. If the factor showing the next highest percentage of profit is a given service combination, that particular combination would be listed second, and so on. An MU Profit Analysis Form such as shown in Figure 5 can be used.

MU PROFIT ANALYSIS FORM

In descending order, factors that contribute most to profitability:

1. _____
2. _____
3. _____
4. _____
5. _____
6. _____
7. _____
8. _____
9. _____
10. _____
11. _____
12. _____
13. _____
14. _____
15. _____
16. _____
17. _____
18. _____
19. _____
20. _____
21. _____
22. _____
23. _____

Figure 5. MU Profit Analysis Form.

To establish an "ideal" project, or one that statistics say should be most profitable, establish which factors relating to the five categories established have resulted in the most profit. As an example, consider Figure 6, an MU Profit Analysis Form completed for a hypothectical set of factors. (The firm involved had no experience with non-GMA projects/non-GMA clients, projects sized F, or projects with size F fees.)

As can be seen, the five categories of factors (location, new/existing construction, size, fee, and service combinations) are covered in the first six items listed. Accordingly, the ideal project for this particular MU would be: one located within the GMA and undertaken for a GMA-based client; new construction; size C; fee B, and involving service D (or feasibly AC).

Once this ideal is established, review the Project Analysis Forms for the MU involved, and identify all those projects that involve projects relatively

MU PROFIT ANALYSIS FORM

In descending order, factors that contribute to profitability:

1. Service D
2. Size C
3. New Construction
4. GMA/GMA Client
5. AC Service Combination
6. Fee B
7. GMA/Non-GMA Client
8. BD Service Combination
9. Size A
10. Existing Construction
11. Non-GMA/GMA Client
12. Fee C
13. Size B
14. Fee D
15. AF Service Combination
16. Size D
17. Service F
18. Size E
19. Fee A
20. Fee E

21. _____

22. _____

23. _____

Figure 6. MU Profit Analysis Form. The data shown are hypothetical.

close to the ideal. How does profitability compare to other projects within the MU for the different years involved? According to the statistics you have developed, such projects should have a much higher than average rate of profitability. If they do, you have an obvious indication of exactly what kind of projects you should be going after within the MU involved. If these projects do not show significantly greater profitability, or if they show less than average profitability, try to determine why. Who was the client involved? Was it a new client or one of long-standing? If it was a new client, you should not usually expect to make a significant profit—unfamiliarity with the client's ways of doing business often results in unforeseen developments that can erode profit—but do check subsequent jobs performed for that client. They should show gradual improvement of profitability. If not, why not? Is there something about dealing with that particular client that makes working with him difficult? If so, what is it and how can you compensate for it? If the client is one of long-standing, what was the cause for low profit? Examine other projects done for him. Was that particular one a fluke, or do all projects with this particular client return a low rate of profit? If so, why?

If profitability on an ideal project was low, also determine who served as team captain or responsible charge. Check into other projects in which that person served in the same capacity. If his projects consistently show a low level of profit, you obviously have a personnel problem and should take steps to identify it precisely and take corrective action.

In other words, by analyzing actual projects that have "ideal" characteristics, you should be able to determine whether or not the ideal actually exists and if not, why not. Moreover, you also will gain insight into the factors that, when present, result in least profitability. As a result, you can start from the bottom of your list and work up. Returning to Figure 6, the least profitable project supposedly would be one located outside the GMA performed for a GMA client: existing construction; size E (or feasibly D or B); fee E (or feasibly A, D, or C); and service combination F (or feasibly AF). Once again review the project analysis forms to find the "ideal losers." In fact, have they shown low profitability? If not, why not? And if they do, try to determine if the cause relates to something inherent within the MU or something inherent within the firm.

Inherency often can be established by reviewing the ideals (both good and bad) for other MUs. For example, if it can be shown that you continually do not do well with projects that are relatively large and involve large fees, regardless of the MU, chances are your firm is not staffed to handle them, perhaps losing too great an amount of profit through overtime or unsuitable management techniques. In such a case there would be an inherent problem within the firm that may or may not be correctable. If the firm has no difficulty with large projects in other MUs, however, it may indicate that there is something inherent in a particular MU that results in low profits, perhaps relating to the nature of the client or owner involved. For example, much of the work performed for religious facilities results in low profits because ownership often is represented by a committee, which all too often changes its collective mind, something incompatible with what usually is a low budget.

Through such analysis, therefore, you can not only gain good insight into each MU and the MU as it relates to others in which your firm is active, but also into the specifics of which clients are better than others; who among staff may not be doing as good a job as would be desired, and so on.

MU Summaries

The next step is to prepare a written narrative summary of information for each MU the firm has been involved in for the past five years. Indicate trends within the MU, its relationship to other MUs, and related information. Include for each MU questions that still require answers, as would be uncovered through trend analysis, possible situations (as with clients or staff members) that require looking into, and so on.

Once the summary is complete, prepare the following information in list form to be utilized, along with the summaries, at a later date:

1. Listing of MUs in descending order of profitability based on overall periodic data.

2. Listing of MUs in descending order of profitability based on trend data. In other words, the MU that shows the most trend toward increasing profitability would be listed first, and so on.

3. Listing in descending order of MUs that show the most trend toward growth in terms of number of projects undertaken.

4. List of clients for whom you have performed work during the past five years.

5. List of indirect clients for whom you have performed work during the past five years.

2.2 PERSONNEL EXPERIENCE

The other element of firm experience, as already noted, is experience of members of the firm, including principals and excluding those clerical and technical personnel below the level of engineer, architect, designer, or whatever other categories may exist.

BIOGRAPHICAL QUESTIONNAIRE

1. Name: _____

2. Education:

    a. College Attended: _____

        From _____ To _____

        Course of Study _____

        Degree Received _____

        Awards Received _____

    b. Postgraduate University Attended: _____

        _____

        From _____ To _____

        Course of Study _____

        Degree Received _____

        Awards Received _____

    c. Other Educational Activities (include nature of courses, such as workshops, seminars, etc., dates attended, etc.; use additional paper as necessary):

        _____

        _____

        _____

        _____

        _____

3. Employment Experience:
Indicate below those by whom you have been employed, the location of the organization involved, the dates of employment, name and location of each employing organization, and the title that you held or that best describes your capacity with the firm involved. Use a separate piece of paper if necessary.

    a. From _____ To _____ _____

        _____

        _____

Figure 7. Biographical Questionnaire.

b. From _____ To _____ _____

_____

_____

c. From _____ To _____ _____

_____

_____

4. Project Experience:
   Complete the following form to identify work you have performed as project captain or responsible charge within the past five years while with another firm. (Duplicate form as necessary.)

   a. General Type of Project (e.g., commercial, industrial, etc.) _____

   _____

   b. Specific Type of Project (e.g., high-rise office building, hospitals, schools,

   etc.) _____

   _____

   c. Name and Location of Your Employer at the Time: _____

   _____

   d. Nature of Services Provided, e.g., feasibility study, HVAC design, value

   analysis, etc. _____

   _____

   e. New or Existing Construction? _____

   f. Name of Client for Whom Project Undertaken _____

   _____

   g. Name of Owner (if different from No. 5) _____

   _____

   h. Year Project Begun _____

   i. Location of Project _____

   j. Project's Approximate Replacement Value _____

Figure 7. (*Continued*)

5. Professional Organizations:
   List below all organizations to which you belong (e.g., AIA, NSPE, etc.) and dates and identification of any officerial or committee posts you have held.

   _____

   _____

   _____

6. Registrations:
   List below states where you are registered and respective registration numbers.

   _____

   _____

   _____

7. Other:
   List below any special capabilities you possess that you feel would benefit the firm, such as abilities with a certain foreign language, acquaintance with certain prospective clients, etc.

   _____

   _____

   _____

   _____

Figure 7. (*Continued*)

In smaller firms, where turnover of personnel is relatively low, it will be unnecessary to undertake any comprehensive program. If a larger firm is involved, however, or if, in any case, we are talking about a firm that has on staff individuals in key positions who have joined only recently, it would be necessary to undertake a comprehensive staff survey to establish background information useful to the marketing approach.

The survey we are talking about involves key staff members completing a detailed biographical questionnaire. If this has not been done previously, it should be undertaken now. If it has been done previously, and the extent of information uncarthed is similar to what is suggested, it necd not be performed again for purposes of basic organizational research. However, on a periodic basis, annually or semiannually, the form should be given to all employees for review and updating as necessary for purposes of promotion.

The questionnaire we favor is shown in Figure 7. Much of the information relates to data that would be utilized in preparing brief or extensive résumés to be given to current or prospective clients to indicate the background of those who would be working on a specific project. Much of the data can also be used to identify MUs in which your firm has capabilities by virtue of experience of certain staff members (while with other firms). This information can be developed through question No. 4 relating to project experience. Certain other information can be very useful when the time comes to develop new clients. For example, knowing what organizations your key people belong to can be essential if you wish to initiate some contact through a shared association activity. That will be discussed later, however.

Employee Project Experience

For our immediate purposes we are concerned most with responses to item No. 4, project experience. The information given should be summed up in one master form for each MU as shown in Figure 8, to obtain the following information:

1. *MU:* By segment and subsegment.

2. *Amount of Projects:* The number of projects undertaken in the MU involving staff members while with other firms.

3. *Project/Client Location:* In terms of your firm, not in terms of the firm your personnel were with at the time. Consider branch offices of clients. For example, if the client for whom your staff member performed work was lcoated outside your GMA, but has branch or affiliate operations within your GMA, indicate that a GMA client is involved.

4. *New/Existing Construction:* Amounts of projects for each.

5. *Size:* Project sizes.

6. *Services:* Indicate services that a staff member has provided in the past, but that your firm may not be providing now, or may be providing only incidentally or occasionally.

7. *Total Value:* Total current replacement value of buildings, etc., for which services were performed in the MU involved. This can be useful in promotion, be it an MU you are not in now or one in which you are established.

From the information derived from this analysis, and where MUs are the same as those already covered, summarize data and include the summary as an addendum to MU summaries already prepared. Where the MUs involved are not ones in which you currently are or previously have been active,

STAFF PROJECT EXPERIENCE FORM

1. MU: Segment _____ Subsegment _____

2. Total Amount of Projects _____

3. Location of Project/Client, Amount of Projects

   GMA Project/GMA Client _____

   Non-GMA Project/GMA Client _____

   GMA Project/Non-GMA Client _____

   Non-GMA Project/Non-GMA Client _____

4. Amount of Projects New Construction _____

   Amount of Projects Existing Construction _____

5. Amount of Projects at Size

   A _____   B _____   C _____   D _____   E _____   F _____

6. Services Provided (Other Than Those Provided by Firm)

   _____   _____   _____   _____   _____

   _____   _____   _____   _____   _____

7. Total Value of MU Projects $_____

Figure 8. Staff Project Experience Form.

prepare separate summaries, held distinct from those prepared to date. In addition, prepare the following information for use later:

1. List of MUs in which key personnel (but not firm) have been active, in descending order, MUs in which most other projects have been undertaken listed first.

2. List of services not provided by firm, in descending order, those listed most times (regardless of MUs involved) listed first.

3. List of clients for whom work was undertaken.

4. List of indirect clients not included in No. 3 above.

3

BASIC MARKETING RESEARCH

The purposes of basic marketing research are to identify additional MUs in which your firm has potential interest, and to evaluate the way in which past, current, and likely future conditions probably will affect all MUs under consideration.

The effectiveness of basic marketing research is largely proportional to the time and effort you are willing to accord to it. It is somewhat more complex than basic organizational research because you will not have available any easily tabulated data. To a great extent you will be working with hearsay, seasoned opinion, and best-guess estimates, almost all of which are subject to interpretation. For this reason information or market intelligence must be gathered from many sources so that those opinions that relate to any given MU can be evaluated as a group to develop what looks like a consensus. Obviously, the more you are willing to dig, the more accurate the picture of any given MU is likely to be.

To be sure, basic marketing research is not an easy undertaking. It is necessary, however, if you are to have an effective marketing plan.

There are several ways of limiting the work entailed in basic marketing research.

First, and especially if yours is a relatively small firm, it would be possible to work with several other firms in developing intelligence. This can be done on a private basis, that is, in conjunction with firms with which you frequently work on an interprofessional basis, or it can be done more publicly, by making it the function of an association or a section or committee of an association.

Second, you can hire someone to do all or part of the work for you. This approach would be limited to larger firms that could afford this luxury, or to groups of smaller firms willing to pool their financial resources. Because the costs of hiring such a firm are sometimes very substantial, and because the nature of their work is so important, we provide below some guidance on selecting a marketing research organization.

Research Organization Selection

To obtain a competent research organization, begin by identifying firms involved in the field of marketing research. This can be done through contact with friends and acquaintances who have used (and were satisfied with) the efforts of certain firms, and/or by obtaining *Bradford's Directory of Marketing Research Agencies* (50 Argyle Avenue, New Rochelle, New York) which lists firms, their principals, number of employees, and a description of the work they do.

Once you identify firms that you believe have the capacity for handling your assignment, request the additional information required to narrow down the list and open negotiations. The process is not dissimilar from that suggested for selecting and retaining a design professional. The information you need relates to:

1. Organizational Experience
   a. length of time the firm has been in business
   b. length of service of key staff members
   c. listing of clients served within the past two to five years
   d. case histories of typical projects undertaken, the date such projects were undertaken, names of clients involved, etc.

2. Organizational Capabilities
   a. education, training, and experience of principals and key staff members
   b. growth of the organization's business volume
   c. recognition and awards received from professional organizations
   d. comments from clients on satisfaction with services received, the nature of the work performed, accuracy of work, etc.

3. Organizational Progressiveness
   a. organizational and individual membership in professional and trade organizations
   b. use and/or development of new marketing research techniques and tools
   c. writing, teaching, and speaking activities of key staff members

4. Organizational Suitability
   a. experience with projects of a similar nature and scope
   b. specialization in particular fields of research related to your requirements
   c. capabilities and experience of staff members who would be assigned to your project
   d. experience with, and current activities performed for, your competition

5. Adequacy of Facilities
   a. location of offices as they relate to your offices and areas where research would be performed
   b. adequacy of reference library facilities and tabulating and communications equipment
   c. general impression of the firm and its image as it would impact upon past, current, or prospective firm clients with whom researchers would come into contact

If specific undertakings are envisioned, such as development and utilization of a questionnaire, investigate the firm's specific capabilities and methods. Also consider the proposal that should be forwarded to you on request, the clarity of wording, business methods proposed, and so on.

In selecting a firm, do not allow cost alone to make a decision for you. Select the firm you believe is best equipped to do the job you want done at a price that seems reasonable and fair. To select a firm simply because it promises to do the work for a low fee is to risk basing a substantial part of your future efforts on beliefs not supported by all the data which should have been collected and analyzed.

3.1 TOOLS OF BASIC MARKETING RESEARCH

We advise strongly that you become familiar with the many different tools of marketing research before selecting those you intend on use for any specific purpose. In this way you will be able to establish a marketing research plan by identifying your research objectives and then determining how each tool will or could have an impact. In many cases there will be overlap. For example, specific books or articles may concern themselves with matters affecting the entire market and all MUs contained, while others may be concerned primarily with one or two MUs specifically within your GMA. As already mentioned, however, much of what you will be covering does not rest on hard-and-fast data. Thus, obtaining a variety of information on each MU will result in your being better able to define what is happening now and what is likely to take place in the future.

A. Publications

Most of the information you, or even a highly specialized marketing research organization, need to develop solid basic research data is readily available in numerous different publications. The following discussion identifies some of the many printed sources to which you should refer, including those—such as library catalogues and publications indexes—that can lead you to still more.

Publications Directories

Publications directories comprise one of the most useful sources for identifying specific sources of market intelligence. Some of the more useful directories include:

Library catalogues: The subject index of you local library's catalogue probably will be one of your most valuable research tools. Simply refer to the subject with which you are concerned—including "publications directories"—and take it from there.

Indexes of publications of bureaus of business and economic research: Published by many different such bureaus, state universities, et al. Frequently kept on the reference shelves of local libraries, they are also available from independent groups, such as the National Bureau of Economic Research, Inc., 261 Madison Avenue, New York, New York 10016.

Ulrich's International Periodicals Directory (R. R. Bowker Co., 1180 Avenue of the Americas, N.Y., N.Y. 10036): Lists U.S. and international marketing periodicals.

The Marketing Information Guide (Hoke Communications, Inc., 224 Seventh Street, Garden City, New York 11535, $10 per year): Formerly published by U.S. Department of Commerce, it lists and describes 100 or so books, articles, and other publications per issue (monthly) relating to marketing and market developments, domestic and foreign.

Statistical and review issues of trade and business periodicals: Typically issued annually by various business-related publications.

Ayer Directory of Publications (Ayer Press, 210 West Washington Square, Philadelphia, Pennsylvania 19106, $49): Lists virtually all periodicals in U.S. and possessions by state and city. Indexed by alphabet and subject. A vital publication for any public relations or publicity effort. Also can be used to locate magazines by trade, etc.

U.S. Government Publications

The U.S. Government is the world's largest publisher. In fact, experienced market researchers know that a very high percentage of much of the raw data they need is readily available from Uncle Sam, if you happen to know where to find it. The search sometimes is so arduous, at least three books have been written to help you look, namely: *Government Publications and Their Use* (Brookings Institution, Washington, D.C., $8.95); *A Popular Guide to U.S. Government Publications* (Leidy, Philip W., Columbia University Press, N.Y., N.Y., $12); and *Subject Guide to Major U.S. Government Publications* (Jackson, E., American Library Association, Chicago, Ill., 1968).

There are several ways of obtaining U.S. government publications. One of the easiest is to have someone who specializes in the field do it for you. One such organization is Bernan Associates Government Publications Service (4701 Willard Avenue, Suite 102, Washington, D.C. 20015). Your specific one-time or ongoing needs can be discussed with this and similar firms and, chances are, they can supply you with exactly what you need.

Another method of obtaining publications is to contact the department or agency involved and request that a catalogue be forwarded to you. For example, a Bureau of Census catalogue can be obtained directly from the U.S. Department of Commerce (FCAT Br., Room 6880, Washington, D.C. 20230). Material on how to find out what you want to know is provided in monthly updates, quarterly cumulative indexes, and an annual cumulative index. The cost for the whole "shooting match," on an annual subscription basis, is only $14.40. You also may wish to subscribe to "Center for Building Technology News," available free from Center for Building Technology (Program Planning and Liason, Room B266, National Bureau of Standards, Washington, D.C. 20234).

Still others ways of obtaining information about U.S. Government publications include:

contacting national associations with requests for information about publications that provide specific types of data;

watching association and trade publications for news of new government publications and what they are about;

reading marketing books and periodicals that mention new government publications, including such publications as *The Marketing Information Guide; Business Service Checklist* (U.S. Department of Commerce, FCAT Br., Room 6880, Washington, D.C. 20230, weekly, $9.70 per year, check payable to U.S. Superintendent of Documents); *Professional Services Management Journal* (Box 11316, Newington, Connecticut 06111, $54 per year), which also provides some excellent marketing tips for design professional firms, and similar publications;

contacting the U.S. Superintendent of Documents (U.S. Government Printing Office, Washington, D.C. 20402) to request catalogues and specific recommendations for publications, and contacting your local Small Business Administration office or Department of Commerce field office to request specific assistance.

Some of the governmental publications you will find valuable include those listed below. Unless otherwise indicated, they can be obtained from the Superintendent of Documents, U.S. Government Printing Office, Washington, D.C. 20402, or directly from the department, agency, etc., responsible for the contents.

Statistical Abstract of the United States: Published annually. Presents statistics on industrial, social, political, and economic organization of the nation. Contains selections from most significant governmental and nongovernmental reporting agencies. Sections on population, education, geography, environment, communications, power, transportation, manufacturers, construction, and housing. Excellent background information affecting all MUs.

Census of the Populations: Provides information on the number of individuals in U.S. by state, county, city, metropolitan area, and census tract. Also includes information on age, sex, race, citizenship, country of birth, family status, education, employment status, and income. Highlight reports available for specified geographic areas can be utilized to identify population shifts that affect your GMA and your market. For example, movement to certain areas or certain types of areas can indicate the need for additional housing, municipal facilities, etc. May serve to indicate certain areas where new branch offices may do well.

Census of Business: Published in three parts, retailing, wholesaling, and selected service trades. Retailers classed under 100 different headings with data on number of stores, total sales, sales by commodity, employment, and ownership. Wholesalers classed under 60 different headings with data on sales volume, sales by type of customer, sales by commodity, expenses, number of establishments, etc. Service trade data presented in a similar manner. County and city breakdowns provided. Can provide general information on extent of competition in different areas, locations in which wholesale and retail operations are expanding (indicating favorable economic conditions), specific types of activity being undertaken (through kinds of goods and services being provided in various areas), etc.

Census of Manufacturers: Covers 500 industries and 7,000 commodities detailing number of establishments, quantities and specific products produced, value added by manufacturer, cost of materials and equipment, etc. Provides an indication of economic trends in general, as well as specific industries that are expanding operations and likely to require expanded facilities.

Census of Housing: Head count of dwelling units, number occupied and unoccupied, year built, mortgage value status, types of structures, condition, fuels used, etc. Specific publications available for metropolitan areas of 50,000+ population. Excellent source material for those involved in housing and energy conservation. Coupled with data on population shifts etc., can serve to indicate areas where housing stock needs additions, replenishment, or refurbishment.

County and City Data Book (Statistical Abstract Supplement): Data on population, labor, housing, finance, government, retail and wholesale trade, industries, agriculture, and services for all U.S. counties and every city with a population of 25,000+. Excellent tool for investigating sites for future GMA expansion.

Commerce Business Daily (U.S. Department of Commerce, FCAT Br., Rm 6880, Washington, D.C. 20230, $75 per year, check payable to U.S. Superintendent of Documents): Daily publication listing federal and some international design project requirements, as well as research projects and undertakings that many design professionals would be capable of undertaking. For purposes of research, review back issues (including contract award sections) to determine which government agencies seem most active; where significant activity is taking place; types of jobs involved and types of firms obtaining contracts, etc., valuable information on competition. Excellent source for obtaining new business or determining which firms have the experience to make an association, joint venture, consortium, etc., worthwhile.

Project Reports (National Technical Information Service, U.S. Department of Commerce, P.O. Box 1533, Springfield, Virginia 22151): Reports on federal and state government-funded research including construction research. Data provided by research firms, trade and professional organizations, educational institutions, etc. Excellent for information on new products and techniques that may affect your areas of practice.

Association Publications

There are literally thousands of national, state, and local trade and professional associations in the United States, most of which produce at least a regular newsletter. Many produce other materials such as journals, research reports, manuals, etc. You probably are familiar with many of the organizations that relate to your particular practices, such as American Consulting Engineers Council (ACEC), American Institute of Architects (AIA), etc. There are other organizations related to your concerns that you probably have never heard of, just as there are numerous organizations related to your clients and their areas of concern. The materials available through these various organizations can be most valuable. For example, ACEC's *Directory of Members* (from ACEC, 1155 15th St., N.W., Washington, D.C. 20005, $25) lists some 3,000 consulting engineering firms, their location, principals, number of firm personnel, activities, etc.

Most other organizations have similar directories that can serve to indicate at least a portion of the competition, where larger firms are locating branch offices (an indication of what their marketing research has suggested), where the potential clients are, etc. To establish which associations you should be interested in, consult the *Encyclopedia of Associations* (Gale Research Co., Book Tower, Detroit, Michigan 48226) or similar publications (there are several), and use the subject index. You obviously should contact those involved with your profession; service organizations in general; small business in general, etc., as well as those related to areas of client or prospective client interest, including specific types of manufacturers, utilities, housing, government officials, and so on. Ask each organization contacted to furnish you with a publications index, and obtain those publications that are of interest. (It is illegal for a nonprofit association to refuse to supply nonmembers with most publications.) In addition, if you have specific research inquiries, direct your questions to the executive director or other staff member of an association. The worst that can happen is that the organization will be unable (or unwilling) to give you a response.

Trade Publications

A complete listing of trade publications can be found in the *Ayer Directory of Publications* by subject. You definitely should be subscribing to those periodicals that concern themselves with your practice and the industries and trades of your clients. Excellent information can be obtained on firms' expansion plans, new developments, etc., often in greater detail than supplied through association journals.

Reporting Services

There are numerous reporting services that provide information on upcoming projects and projects under development. Current issues are valuable for identifying prospective clients. Back issues can prove especially useful for spotting trends relating to types of construction being used, areas of growth, firms that are getting design business, and so on. In other words, these publications can provide some exceptionally valuable information if you are willing to review them and extract meaning from somewhat raw data. The best known of these reporting services is McGraw-Hill's *Dodge Reports*, which can be obtained for specified geographical areas. Other reporting services include, but are not at all limited to:

Engineering News-Record (McGraw-Hill, 1221 Avenue of the Americas, New York, N.Y. 10020, $10 per year), a weekly publication that contains "Pulse," a listing of the week's significant projects.

Million Dollar Project Planned List (Live Leads Corp. 369 Lexington Avenue, New York, N.Y. 10017, $540 per year): Lists projects of more than 50,000 square feet and/or $1 million in cost while in the planning stage (often before an A-E is selected). Projects broken into building types: commercial, educational, housekeeping, nonhousekeeping, residential, medical, and government. More than 5,000 projects reported yearly.

Industrial Project Planned List (Live Leads Corp., 369 Lexington Avenue, New York, N.Y. 10017, $540 per year): Similar to above. Covers projects in industrial, manufacturing, warehousing, and engineering.

Herb Ireland's Sales Prospector (712 Prospector Building, 751 Main Street, Waltham, Massachusetts 02154): Comprehensive information on who is doing what in terms of who is buying land and to what purpose they intend to put it, what companies contemplate adding to existing facilities, and so on. Fourteen regional editions: $49 annually for first region; $39 annually for each additional region; $345 annually for all regions. Samples available. Money-back guarantee.

BIDS Jobletter (Building Industry Development Services, 1301 20th Street, N.W., Suite 104, Washington, D.C. 20036, $100 per year): Lists some projects, names of contacts, etc., plus general copy on certain sources, who to contact for information, corporate contacts, etc.

Foreign Projects Newsletter (Richards, Lawrence & Co., P.O. Box 2311, Van Nuys, California 91404, $150 per year): Information on non-U.S. projects in planning and procurement stages, contract awards, foreign industry programs, U.S. industry programs in other nations, etc.

NBN Weekly Report (National Building News Service, Inc., P.O. Box 647, Ridgewood, New Jersey 07451, $625 per year): Lists projects over $1 million in planning or bidding stages in U.S. and Canada.

Medical Facilities Planning Report (National Building News Service, Inc., P.O. Box 647, Ridgewood, New Jersey 07451, $200 per year): Monthly report of medical facilities (hospitals, nursing homes, etc.) planned for development, expansion, or both. In most cases architects have been selected.

Educational Facilities Planning Report (National Building News Service, Inc., P.O. Box 647, Ridgewood, New Jersey 07451, $275 per year): Monthly report on educational facilities (elementary, secondary, colleges, junior colleges, etc.) plans for development, expansion, or both. In most cases architects have been selected.

NBN Architects' Monthly Building Report (National Building News Service, Inc., P.O. Box 647, Ridgewood, New Jersey 07451, $75 per year): Monthly report (compiled from *NBN Weekly Report*) of U.S. and Canadian projects ($1 million and up) for which architects have not as yet been selected.

Service World International (Institutions Magazine, 205 E. 42nd Street, New York, N.Y. 10017, Complimentary): Publisher, on request, provides readers with leads on construction/expansion plans of various organizations.

Federal Research Report (P.O. Box 1067, Silver Spring, Maryland 20910, $32 per year (22 issues)): Reports names, addresses, dates, and deadlines of research and development funding sources. Esentially, a capsulized review of more than 100 government publications.

In addition McGraw-Hill publishes annually the *F. W. Dodge Construction Outlook*, which analyzes changes taking place in various market segments and forecasts next year's construction contract value by building type, market, and market segment. A similar service is provided through *Standard & Poor's Industry Surveys* (345 Hudson Street, New York, N.Y. 10014), which analyzes trends in construction, utilities, retailing, transportation, etc.

Legislative Reports. News of federal legislation vital to you and your clients' interests can be found in trade and association periodicals and publications, not to mention local newspapers, national news publications, etc. News of what is happening in your own state government and in various local jurisdictions also is relatively easy to obtain through state and local chapters of national organizations. An excellent source for learning more of what is happening in other state and local jurisdictions is *From the State Capitals* (321 Sunset Avenue, Asbury Park, New Jersey 07712), which produces publications on subjects such as airport construction and financing, institutional building, school construction, sewage and waste disposal, urban transit, etc.

General Business Publications

There are numerous general business publications that report not only overall general economic trends, but also specific developments planned by various organizations for which your services could possibly be required. These publications include *The Wall Street Journal, Barrons, Business Week, Nation's Business*, and *Forbes*.

In addition, there are many journals devoted to management practices (these are published by almost all graduate schools of business), as well as magazines devoted to specific business trends for given areas or regions. Also, there are business sections in various general news publications, including national news magazines (*Time, U.S. News and World Report, Newsweek*, and *The National Observer*) as well as nationally prominent newspapers (*New York Times, Washington Post, Los Angeles Times*, etc.)

Local Publications

Many local publications can provide useful information about events taking place in your GMA, including trends relating to business, population, environmental concerns, taxes, etc. For this reason you should read various local newspapers (including weekly publications) as well as materials put out by local Chambers of Commerce, magazines about a given city (*New York Magazine, Washingtonian, Philadelphia*, etc.) and so on. Materials relating to MUs in which you are or may be interested or notes relating to such materials, should be kept in appropriate MU files.

GMA Government Records

Records on file with the various local governments within your GMA can prove to be an excellent source of valuable information. Typical documents to review include master plans, which indicate kinds of development that probably will be taking place; zoning exception requests, denials, and grants, which also serve to indicate types of development taking place and attitude to government to exceptions to overall master planning; construction permits issued; sewage treatment facility expansion program reports, which often will cite statistical research data that suggest development one way or the other, etc.

B. Other Research Techniques

Other research techniques are those that relate to extracting information from people who have insight into areas of concern. These techniques and tools should not be overlooked. In many cases they can provide up-to-date data unavailable from publications, or rumors, feelings, hearsay, and gut reactions, all of which a researcher may choose to ignore.

Casual Interviews

Casual interviews—casual because the person being interviewed does not realize that an interview is taking place—can be an excellent way of picking up both general and specific information on subjects ranging from what an individual sees for a given MU in the months and years ahead to what he has planned in the next few months, what he heard someone else has planned, etc. Interviews such as this seldom are planned. In other words they are held on a catch-as-catch-can basis and should under no circumstances be relied upon as a sole tool to extract information from various individuals.

Structured Interviews

A structured formal or semiformal interview is the tool most often relied upon to obtain specific types of information related to your areas of interest and concern.

To establish an interview program, first determine what information you need and then determine who can provide it. In most cases more than one person will be involved. For example, let us assume that you have identified fifty specific areas of inquiry, some general—relating to all or most all MUs— and some specific—relating to one or two MUs in particular. In some cases (see Figure 9) the information sought will cut a vertical swath, concerning

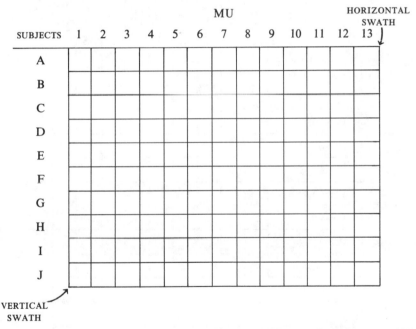

Figure 9. In some cases you may wish to broach one subject applicable to many MUs, and so cut a horizontal swath. In other cases you may seek to direct inquiries to various questions concerning just one MU, and so cut a vertical swath. Either approach is usable. The approach selected should be one that best fits the information that the person being interviewed is in a position to provide.

itself with one particular MU from top to bottom; that is, with all the different concerns that relate to the given MU. In other cases the information will cut a horizontal swath, covering one subject as it affects different MUs. Thus, any one individual can be selected to discuss numerous different issues affecting one or many MUs. Once you have established your areas of inquiry, therefore, determine whom you can talk to to learn more about the subject at hand. To do this, we advise you to develop a simple form, such as that shown in Figure 10, listing names or types of source persons on the vertical axis and areas of inquiry on the horizontal. By completing the form you know whom to contact and specifically what subjects could be addressed.

Once that is done, contact the source persons one at a time or have the contact made by that firm member best known to the source person.

Inform each that you are conducting market research and that you would

		Areas of Inquiry									
		Subject 1	Subject 2	Subject 3	Subject 4	Subject 5	Subject 6	Subject 7	Subject 8	Subject 9	Subject 10
	Person A										
	Person B										
	Person C										
	Person D										
Source Persons	Person E										
	Person F										
	Person G										
	Person H										
	Person I										
	Person J										
	Person K										
	Person L										

Figure 10. Sample form for use in determining whom to contact and what specific type of information should be requested.

like to meet with him to "pick his brains." Usually a luncheon meeting will suffice. Before meeting with any individual, however, be certain that you:

A. prepare a list of specific questions you want answered,

B. prepare a list of specific materials that could possibly be provided to you, and

C. bring a notebook and ball-point pen (or two).

Some of the persons for whom such a structured interview would be applicable and the kinds of information that could be extracted will be discussed below.

Private Owner Clients. In this category we include private owners (or builders/developers) who are direct clients or clients of an interprofessional client. This category also would include your contacts (owner representatives) from larger organizations, including industrial concerns, institutions (including such governmentally-owned institutions as vocational schools, junior colleges, colleges, universities, etc.) Typical information that could be obtained includes:

A. Projects planned or envisioned; time frame involved.

B. Other MUs in which the person or organization is active (MUs other than those in which you work with him).

C. Projects planned by others he knows of.

D. Impact of financial, legislative, and other conditions upon planning ("What would happen if . . . .").

E. General outlook for various specific MUs.

F. Plans regarding existing facilities in terms of expansion, modernization, energy conservation, etc.

G. Satisfaction with the services provided by your firm and any areas of dissatisfaction (ask him to be as candid as possible).

H. Factors he considers most important when retaining design professional organizations, including retention/selection methods he intends to use in the future (bidding, negotiation, etc.)

I. General trends he sees developing within a specific GMA.

J. Services that would be utilized if you had them available.

Especially when larger industrial clients are concerned, determine if you could obtain corporate marketing reports (assuming they exist) that indicate trends important to the company involved. Reports on future planning and projects and related materials also could be very helpful.

Government Clients. There are three distinct kinds of persons who should be interviewed as representatives of the agencies, offices, and departments that comprise government clients: the contracting officer, the project officer, and the department head. The contracting officer usually has broad responsibilities for a variety of projects from numerous different offices and departments. As such, he may be short on technical data relative to specific projects, but he is in a good position to give you information on the number of projects planned by the various offices and departments, budgets envisioned, and other such information. The project officer, by comparison, has the primary responsibility of seeing to it that everything the contract calls for is carried out, usually to the letter. As such he is technically competent with the subject at hand and so can provide in-depth information about his projects, many of which he or his office may have initiated. The department head, who may be more difficult to contact, can give you generalized (but still very valuable) insights into what the future probably holds in store, from the point of view of contracting procedures, to new kinds of projects he has in mind. Overall, the three should be able to provide both general and specific answers to questions relating to:

A. New projects planned or envisioned; time frame involved; budgets; whom to contact.

B. Tax increases, bond issues, etc., which would be required to implement planning and impact if events do not occur as planned.

C. Planning as it relates to existing facilities in terms of expansion modernization, energy conservation, etc.

D. Satisfaction with the services provided by your firm and areas of dissatisfaction (ask him to be as candid as possible).

E. Design professional selection/retention policies likely to be used in the immediate and short-term future.

F. Factors he considers to be most important in choosing a given firm (assuming he is in a position to choose or advise those who do).

G. Other services the agency or department requires and the frequency with which they are required.

Interprofessional Clients. When discussion of interprofessional clients comes up, we usually are talking about engineers' relationships with architects or with other engineers. Accordingly, since the kind of market research we are talking about relates virtually equally to all design professionals, the field of inquiry is as broad as basic marketing research itself. Particular areas of interest include:

A. Prospects for clients' business in general in the upcoming months.

B. Discussion of GMA and outside GMA business MU by MU.

C. Discussion of business in terms of owners or client's clients.

D. Satisfaction with service provided and areas of dissatisfaction (ask for frankness).

E. Primary factors utilized in selecting another professional to perform work in a joint venture.

F. Reaction to changes in contracting arrangements you may have in mind.

G. Reaction to what you see as developments in various MUs, GMAs, etc.

H. Changes within client's firm that could have an impact on your own.

I. What the client is doing by way of marketing, development of clients, promotion, etc.

Contractors. Contractors (generals and subs) who could be interviewed include those with whom you have worked in the past and/or who are known to you personally. Typical information they could supply would relate to:

A. General outlook for specific MUs, including names of those who are likely to be undertaking projects.

B. New contracting methods that may be used, such as joint venturing for turnkey contracts.

C. New types of work to be undertaken (such as modernization, energy conservation, etc.,) for which design professional services may be required.

D. New techniques and technologies affecting the specific trade and trends foreseen.

E. Financial conditions affecting ability to do business (insurance, bonding, financing, etc.).

    F. Information on other design professionals offering services such as you provide, regarding (in particular) clients for whom work is performed, services offered, clients' apparent satisfaction with services, etc. (We realize that certain design professionals may consider this line of questioning as bordering on the unethical. If so, do not pursue it, but do resort to other methods to determine information on the competition, as by reviewing *Dodge Reports*, etc.)

    G. New construction practices being demanded or desired by owners, such as construction inspection, etc.

Manufacturers' Representatives, Suppliers, Distributors. Manufacturers' representatives, suppliers, and distributors can comprise an especially valuable source of information because they maintain continuing contact with owners, design professionals, and many others with whom you are concerned. Besides that, they often are willing to give you their time because, to a great extent, it's part of their job. Do realize, when dealing with them, that your competition may be doing the exact same thing. Particular areas of concern would include:

    A. Business activity within specific MUs in the GMA and forecasts for the future.

    B. Owners who have made inquiries regarding products used for retrofitting, expansion, modernization, new construction, etc.

    C. Activity and personnel levels within competing firms, as well as specific new projects and/or clients with whom competing firms are working, financial conditions, etc. (Again, if ethical considerations suggest that such questions are improper, do not ask them.)

    D. Technical developments (general and specific) that will have an impact on various construction types.

    E. Marketing changes being used or considered by the manufacturer, distributor, or supplier involved.

By all means, ask the representative to provide you, if possible, with marketing and related reports that may have been produced by his company or companies with which he deals.

Employees. Do not overlook employees, especially relatively new employees, as sources of marketing information. Typical questions that could be asked relate to:

    A. Other projects that clients may have planned as reported by clients' representatives, contact at association meetings, etc.

B. General opinions about the future of various MUs and the reasons why such opinions are held.

C. Information about services, management methods, marketing methods, clients, etc., of the firm with which the person previously was employed. (Do not ask such questions if you feel it is not ethically correct or if you believe the employee will see it as ethically improper.)

Government Officials. There are numerous government officials with whom you can speak, whether they are concerned with international trade or developments in a given town. At the very least you should have on hand a complete list of the various governmental agencies, departments, etc. within your GMA that become involved in work requiring design professionals, including the agencies of various given jurisdictions, school boards, sewer authorities, government utilities (such as water, gas, or electric), and so on. For each of these you should attempt to obtain information such as that requested from those government officials who have acted as clients in the past. Note that it may be improper to take such a person out to lunch, even if he buys his own.

Interprofessional Subcontractors. Interprofessional subcontractors include those to whom you provide work (architects to engineers, engineers to engineers, etc.) Typical questions would include many of those asked of interprofessional clients. Also query satisfaction with contracting methods, actions that could improve the relationship on projects, better action for quality control, etc.

Owners. It will be relatively difficult to contact and question owners who are other than clients, past clients, or clients of clients, unless they happen to be known to you on a personal basis or, perhaps, known to another firm member.

Others. There are many others with whom one could speak to obtain valuable information, including mortgage lenders and bankers, union officials, association executives, utility representatives, and so on. It cannot be stressed strongly enough that the more you are able to contact and interview, the better your base of information and, thus, the better your planning can be.

Questionnaire

Questionnaires are used frequently as a basis for interviews as well as "survey instruments," usually sent through the mails. This latter approach has several drawbacks. First, it usually can be used only by larger firms dealing with large client organizations—public or private—that have personnel able and willing to respond. Second, even when a questionnaire is circulated among large client organizations, it can be ignored easily. Third, it usually is very structured and does not easily permit full elaboration of comments. Nonetheless, a questionnaire can enable some coverage of a very large and diverse prospective respondent group that ordinarily could not be covered through face-to-face interview techniques. Further, it easily can be expanded to more than just clients, in some cases creating contacts for use in a market entry program.

Vital to the success of the survey is the design of the questionnaire itself and the selection of the respondent group.

In most cases, the design should enable as rapid a response as possible, preferably through multiple-choice questions, and leave space for comments or "other" responses. Questions should be designed to concentrate on areas of primary and secondary concern. Respondents should be those who are involved in your various key MUs. The broader the coverage, of course, the more returns you will receive, and the more definitive your data will be. The people from whom information can be gleaned include virtually all those with whom you have come into contact in your business operations.

Casual Observation

Casual observation is a marketing research technique that involves little more than driving through various areas of a GMA to establish such things as the condition of buildings, where new construction is taking place, and needs for modernization. Notes can be written or, preferably, comments can be spoken into a tape recorder on the scene for transcription later. This technique obviously is practical only for small GMAs and, in particular, when you are relatively new to the GMA involved. In some cases the information gathered can be mentioned to clients and prospective clients to provide information on potential for new development, modernization, and related activities.

3.2 PUTTING THE TOOLS TO WORK

Now that you are at least passingly familiar with the tools of basic marketing research, the time has come to indicate generally what types of market intelligence must be gathered. It will be your job to establish the specific kinds of market intelligence required and, accordingly, to identify the tools required to gather it.

The first step in the process is to itemize the various MUs in which your firm is or should be interested. Once that is done, you must do further research to ascertain what has taken place in each MU in the past and what is likely to happen in the future. Numerous different issues must be considered, and any given source may be able to provide information on many of them. As a result, it is essential that you develop a basic marketing research plan, that is, an overall outline that indicates specifically what type of market intelligence must be gathered and the sources most likely to provide the information.

Research, of course, is a cumulative effort. The more you learn the more questions are raised. For this reason we suggest that you first become familiar with written research materials. As you move from one to the other, questions probably will arise that will require you to return to materials already read to look for different angles or to ferret out different types of information. It is difficult to do that through an interview process. It not only can be time-consuming but, given the press of business, it is highly unlikely that those interviewed would consent to being reinterviewed four and five times. Thus, by using published materials and casual interviews you should have a fairly compehensive background on the subjects to be discussed with a source person, and should be able to bring up many of the items of which you are uncertain. In other words, to make the most of an interview, be well grounded in the subjects at hand so you can follow answers with more questions. At the very least this will help you ascertain the validity of a source person's comments. For example, if your research shows that there is a marked shift in your GMA toward multifamily housing, yet a source person indicates that in his opinion the single-family housing market will gain considerably in strength, you will be able to confront him with your facts and so obtain the reasoning for his opinion, despite what appear to be contrary facts.

To reiterate, your ability to direct your firm toward a profitable, active future depends on the effectiveness of your marketing effort. The effectiveness of your marketing effort depends substantially on the accuracy of basic marketing research. The accuracy of basic marketing research depends largely on the amount of time you are willing to put into the basic research effort.

MU Itemization

The first step in your basic marketing research effort involves itemization of the various MUs in which you have at least passing interest. The importance of this step cannot be overemphasized. In many cases it will determine the direction of all subsequent research efforts and, as a result, virtually all subsequent marketing efforts.

You already have on hand a list of MUs. These include: MUs in which your firm has been active during the past five years, and MUs in which your key employees have been active in the past five years.

Client MUs. Now turn to the list of clients for whom you have performed work during the past five years. Using your research tools, especially reporting services, determine what other MUs clients are active in. For example, you may find that a client is giving you pickling plant design assignments, but he has a significant amount of standby power generation equipment design requirements that he is giving to some other firm. (Note that in a case such as this it may be necessary to amplify or further segment MUs to identify more precisely other areas of client activity.) (The purpose of this procedure, and other MU itemization steps following, will become more apparent later. Suffice it to say here, however, that if three clients are involved in an MU in which your firm is not involved, you obviously would have easy access to the MU, assuming you could gear up to handle its requirements.) To complete this step, add to the list those MUs in which you are involved with the clients and, on a separate piece of paper, indicate, after each MU listed, the names of the clients who are active in them.

Indirect Client MUs. As another element of MU itemization—and this one could possibly be optional, depending on the number of MUs that other efforts may identify or the size of the firm involved, contracting practices, etc.—review your list of indirect clients. Itemize the MUs in which they, but not your firm, are active. If you prefer, and after reading what else is said in this book on the subject, include only those MUs where you could conceivably go to the indirect client directly to offer services. For example, if you are a consulting engineer who has designed an HVAC system for an architect whose client was Smith, and Smith also is involved in modernization of an apartment building that he intends to convert to a condominium, you could list residential/condominium (existing) as an amplified MU (architectural services required by Smith would be minimal). In fact, it would be possible for you to obtain the contract directly and retain an architect, assuming that your design functions would be those most needed. Complete this step as you did the first by adding to the list of MUs those in which both you and the indirect client are active. Also, use a separate sheet of paper to indicate, for each MU listed, the names of those indirect clients involved.

Key Personnel's Client and Indirect Client MUs. Next in order is itemization of MUs in which former clients and former indirect clients of key personnel are active. In each case, use a separate sheet of paper to identify which clients or indirect clients are active in which MUs.

GMA MUs. Now prepare a complete list of MUs that exist in your GMA. You can do this easily by including those in which you already are active and those that common sense tells you exist. Further back-up can be obtained through *Dodge Reports* or similar publications. While the list does not have to be fully comprehensive, the more complete it is, the better.

Once you complete this last list, evaluate each MU in terms of services that the firm currently has the capability of providing, including those that are available through previous staff experience, but not necessarily firm experience. In each case indicate whether or not your services could be applicable to the MU under consideration. In the case of a geotechnical engineer, for example, services usually apply across the board. There are very few things that can be put on or into the ground without first having a thorough soil engineering report on hand. In the case of an architect, however, applicable MUs usually are far less, as for engineering firms with just one or two specialties. Nonetheless, do not sell yourself short. For example, if you are involved in interior design and have been specializing in the single-family residential market, you may well be able to branch into executive office design for various commercial and industrial MUs. Likewise, a consulting engineer who performs energy consumption/conservation analyses primarily for multifamily and commercial high-rise structures probably could perform his services for nursing homes, certain light industrial structures, and the like. The important thing to note is this: do not discount any MU or your ability to enter it at this point. Other data to be developed may give you insights that could change your mind dramatically.

To complete itemization of GMA MUs, prepare a listing of all MUs—including those you are in now—that could be penetrated by virtue of services available.

Following review of all MUs in your GMA, you could have as many as seven separate MU listings, as follows:

MUs in which the firm has been active,
MUs in which key personnel have been active,
MUs in which your clients are active,
MUs in which indirect clients have been active,
MUs in which key personnel's clients have been active,
MUs in which key personnel's indirect clients have been active, and
MUs in your GMA to which your services can be applied.

As a final step, prepare one overall master list of MUs, listing each MU only once, a task required by the next procedure: MU research.

MU Research Methods

The basic goal of MU research is to evaluate each MU in terms of its current activity and potential. The two really cannot be separated. After all, looking at things from a somewhat philosophical viewpoint, the present is merely an ever-changing moment in time that serves to divide the past from the future. As a result, the bulk of your research efforts must center on examining the past to determine how various events and developments have impacted upon MUs; looking to the future to see what events and developments are likely to transpire; and evaluating how probable future developments will affect the various MUs. Obviously, if someone could predict the future with unerring accuracy, he would not be trying to eke out a living as a design professional. All of us can only guess; but the more research we do, the more we come to understand what is in and around the MUs, the more accurate our guesses are likely to be. From these guesses or predictions we then can develop a plan that says, in essence, "This is what must be done to take maximum advantage of events that are likely to transpire." And since one of the elements of plan implementation is constant feedback and continual gathering of market intelligence, we continually have the ability to adjust these plans. In that way it is possible to take into consideration new developments that suggest that what we think is likely to happen in an MU one year from now is different from what we expected would happen when we developed a plan last year and considered the period two years from that date. The more time and effort you put into this particular step, therefore, the more accurate your prognostications are likely to be. The task is challenging and, for many, very enjoyable.

Development of a research plan has already been touched upon. A plan definitely is needed to determine what kinds of information are needed for all MUs, what specific information is needed to fill in blanks presented by certain specific MUs, and where the information can be obtained. While it is possible for one person to develop and implement the basic research plan, you should consider involving several persons, provided that you are confident each can produce the quality of work required.

Where more than one person definitely is needed, however, is to determine what events are likely to transpire and what their effects will be upon the various MUs. While the research process involves one with the concepts and ideas of many different people, channeling all these through just one person's mind seriously limits the thinking that can be brought to bear. Simply put, the cross-fertilization of ideas that occurs when several people are discussing the same issues cannot be beat.

While much of the following discussion on specific research topics lumps together areas of past inquiry and projecting past events into the future, we really are talking about a two-stage process.

In the first stage of the process, we have collection of research, including projections that may be made by source persons. The second stage involves MU-by-MU analysis of what future events are likely to transpire and how they are likely to impact on the MUs. If several persons are used to gather research, these persons also would or should be involved in second-stage projections. Even so, the data and associated materials collected on various MUs can be given to others for review and digestion, thus enabling them to prognosticate as well.

Use of Meetings. In typical practice, it is likeliest that just one person will be performing the bulk of the research and will be providing research data to others for background. These others then will sit in on one or a series of meetings to put it all together and arrive at consensus opinions.

Of critical concern are the meetings themselves and the way in which they are handled to minimize, to as great an extent as possible, undesirable group behavior. One of the key ways to achieve this is to limit the number of persons who sit in at any given meeting. Usually no more than six to eight persons should be involved. This will allow each person time to speak his mind without having to resort to shouting to be heard, whispering to someone across the table, etc. Another item of concern is the determination of specifically which persons should attend. Obviously, you want persons who understand your business or at least the business of some or all of the MUs involved. They should not be afraid to speak their minds in a group setting. If you have among the group, for example, a supervisor and a "supervisee," the relationship between the two should be such that, at least for the purposes of a meeting, both consider themselves to be prognosticators and, as such, equals. If one is to use the meeting as a forum of one kind or another, or as an opportunity to polish someone's apple, or whatever, it just won't work. Accordingly, those you select should know the ground rules. If compliance will be difficult or impossible, consider having more than one group or perhaps head-to-head, one-on-one discussion as needed.

Here are some specific considerations to bear in mind.

1. *Approach:* You must develop an overall approach to the MU forecasting effort. Will certain people be given responsibility to research certain MUs, or will one person be responsible for the entire function? Whoever is responsible for research must be present at the meeting during which the given MU is discussed.

2. *Research materials:* Although those with research information should be present at the meeting during which such information is required, everyone attending should have at his disposal some written material, be it in outline form or narrative, that indicates past developments within the MU, including the basis for which the MU is being discussed, i.e., because the firm has been active in the MU in the past, or a key staff member has been, etc. Data also should be included, indicating past activity of the MU in the GMA or in other areas, trends that are likely to affect it, and so on. (These elements will be discussed in more detail later.)

3. *Meeting format:* You must have a format, which includes both the overall format, if more than one meeting is planned, and the format of each individual meeting. You may wish to discuss just one or two MUs at each of several meetings or perhaps many MUs at one or two longer meetings. The length of the meeting also is important. A long meeting could result in participants becoming restless or, conversely, it may result in participants warming to the subject and becoming more interested and so more able to think in terms of interrelationships as the day moves on. Of course, the practical matter of time and other responsibilities of the firm also must be considered. You may want to consider flexibility as a key. In other words, if people begin getting "into" the subject, keep the meeting going. If interest begins to ebb, stop the discussion or at least switch to another subject. Because continuity of thought and discussion is so important, everything possible should be done to limit interruptions, such as telephone calls. Ideally, the meeting should be held away from the office in a relaxed environment conducive to thinking about nothing more than the subjects at hand.

4. *Chairman:* The chairman of the meeting must be able to command the respect and attention of all participants. It would seem natural, in this case, to have the head of the firm or at least its highest ranking member at the meeting as chairman. However, because the chairman and only the chairman should have the ability say what he wants to say when he wants to say it, we think it best that the discussion leader be the one with the greatest amount of research data and understanding of the subject at hand. In that case, the highest ranking firm member at the meeting, even if it is the firm's president or board chairman, may not be suited for the assignment. Accordingly, the chairman—even though not the highest ranking firm member present—would have to be given the respect of his superiors who would have to recognize that the context of the meeting creates a different pecking order from the context of the firm. To help in the effort, the meeting should be run, at least partially, on the basis of *Roberts Rules of Order.* The chairman must not be afraid to cut off the digressive talk of someone who ranks higher than he, although it probably will have to be done with some degree of finesse.

5. *Record:* Keep a record of what is said. This can be done by means of a tape recorder for later distillation of key ideas, by having the discussion leader take notes, or by a combination of these or other methods.

Remote Group Methods. There are other ways of conducting this element of research as well; for example, one can use remote group methods. These usually involve supplying persons with questionnaires containing items relating to specific areas of inquiry. One such method is called the Delphi Technique, a system utilized to develop consensus opinions about future developments from those who have insight into the subjects at hand. Established by the Rand Corporation, the Delphi Technique takes its name from the Oracle of Delphi, a blind seeress. In this case, "blind" is the key word because those who participate do not know who else is participating; thus, bias, which sometimes results when one may say something just to be opposed to someone else because of a personality clash, is reduced. The person running the Delphi program, therefore, would select recognized experts in a given subject or subjects but would not tell any of them who else is participating. At the same time, he develops a questionnaire that allows quantitative responses. For example:

1. By what year will the nuclear fast-breeder reactor become a practical reality?

2. By what year will there be a single national building code?

3. When will energy conservation in all existing buildings become mandated by the government?

4. What will be the approximate dollar value of new electric utility generating facilities during each of the next four years?

In most cases, of course, the subjects selected will be somewhat more related than those given above.

When the experts receive the questionnaires they will complete them and return them to the sender. The sender summarizes responses to each question indicating medians. For example, responses to question No. 1 could have been broken down as follows:

1. By what year will the nuclear fast-breeder reactor become a practical reality?

25%	50%	75%
1985	1996	2005

In this particular case, 25% of the respondents felt that the nuclear fast-breeder reactor would become a practical reality by 1985 or earlier, 50% felt 1996 or earlier, and 75% felt 2005 or earlier.

Once responses have been so summarized, they are returned to the participants, who are asked to revise their estimates as they see fit. This usually will result in some adjustment to seek a consensus. Those whose forecasts still vary significantly from the others are asked to give a written explanation. When these written explanations are received, the package is sent out again to all participants, who are asked to make comments and/or adjustments as they see fit, still seeking a consensus. Obviously, given the sophistication of this methodology and the time and expense involved, it is an undertaking that usually is restricted to larger firms or groups of smaller ones.

One also must consider the very small firm that lacks the manpower even to hold a meeting. Obviously, those involved can either do it all themselves, risking the perils already noted, or, to obtain the benefits of group discussion, try to interest several others in the field to make it a group undertaking with the knowledge developed being used by one and all. As noted earlier, this can be done by contacting those with whom you have worked, more or less a design team called together for a different purpose, or it may be done on the basis of selecting those involved in the same general or specific disciplines. In this case a local organization, such as a chapter or committee of ACEC or AIA, may be an excellent tool, with the special meeting—probably best held at some site that affords a relaxed atmosphere—running over several days to allow freedom from business affairs and an ability to relax and think.

MU Research Topics

Now the major question arises: "How does one proceed?"

To begin with, concepts have to be adjusted somewhat. Each MU must be thought of not only as a given market unit, but also as a set of clients (or prospective clients) and a set of competitors. In this manner, you can begin to review certain types of developments that are likely to affect a given MU, and to think of developments not only as they are likely to affect the MU in general, but more specifically in what way the clients and competition will react.

The developments likely to occur can be assigned to seven categories: *physical, social, economic, technological, political, legal,* and *ethical.* In some cases the same particular issue can be discussed under two or more of these categories or their subcategories. For example, environmental concerns (a subcategory of "physical") may have an impact on energy concerns (another subcategory of physical) and are affected by "social" concerns as well. In other words, there is no easy analytical process whereby these various prognostications can be made.

Physical. The physical category has several major components or subcategories, key among which are environment, population, energy, and land.

Environment: A few years ago environmental issues were *the* issues. At the time of this writing (1976) they have been largely replaced by energy concerns. That they have been replaced hardly means that they have been forgotten. The government machinery that, to a great extent, was put into motion to meet demand still is functional and still is generating a great deal of business for many firms involved in water treatment, waste water treatment, sewage treatment, solid waste disposal, air pollution control, waterfront development, and so on. In making an analysis, therefore, one has to become familiar with the various kinds of existing environmentally-inspired projects, their likely growth and development in the future, where within a given GMA they would be applicable, what specific specialized services might transcend a local GMA, etc.

Other environmental issues relate to consumer protection against disruption of the natural habitat. This is affected somewhat by social values and will be discussed there, too. In this analysis, one must consider the degree of opposition that might be engendered in a given GMA for certain types of developments. In other words, if marketing research indicates a specific type of new development is possible, such as a refinery, to what extent would the development actually or possibly upset the environment in terms of gaseous, liquid, or solid wastes? In this regard technological factors also must be considered.

Also to be considered are the trade-offs involved in environmental concerns. While many people are concerned about the environment, to what extent would their concern diminish if it were a matter of choosing between clean air and a warm home? For example, are energy concerns such that environmental concerns would be given a back seat? If so, what would the impact be? Would it mean merely being willing to allow a utility to burn higher sulfur-content fuel? If so, would that make electric rates more attractive? Would it also mean more design of scrubbers and other equipment to help reduce the extra pollution?

Consider, too, impact on zoning. Given, for example, that industrial, commercial, and residential concentrations usually result in more vehicular traffic, thus more cars and more pollution, what is the likelihood that more of an effort will be made in urban or suburban planning to effect a degree of environmental control?

Given the impact of these various factors and others, how are clients and prospective clients likely to react? Will there be more need for local treatment plants? If so, who will get the work? What will be the effect on your competition? Assuming there will be more work, will competitors be able to take a significant portion of it? Will other firms open branch offices in your area hoping to get additional work? How have they reacted to opportunity in the past? If it's a matter of, perhaps, restricting growth of major residential complexes, what will be the clients' reactions? Will they look for work in other areas and, if so, would they want services of an organization from within your GMA or in the area of the new projects they plan? If from your area, do you or the competition have capabilities for on-site inspection of non-GMA sites and projects? Or will clients turn to modernization of existing facilities or perhaps expansion or conversion (as to condominium)? If so, what impact will this have on your firm? Would you be equipped to handle the new kinds of services required? What about your competition? What about the firms now doing work for the prospective client? How will they be affected? Will developments create openings for the services you provide?

Population: There have been marked changes in some population trends just as there has been steady reinforcement of other trends. For example, the postwar baby boom was just that—a boom. There was no sustained growth in the birth rate. In fact, statistics indicate that the birth rate in the United States is decreasing. As a result, the once-famous prediction that at some time in the late 1960s or early 1970s half the nation's population would be twenty-five or younger never materialized. This particular turnabout has had a significant impact on schools. In many areas of the nation, school building programs have been curtailed sharply simply because the number of students has dropped off so markedly. What is the situation in your area? To what extent are you involved in schools, and how are likely developments going to affect you? Also consider manpower factors. Where are your personnel going to come from? Are your regional schools of engineering, architecture, interior design, etc., still graduating as many people as are needed to fill requirements? What about housing? What are the trends in your area? Fewer newlyweds and younger people could mean lowered demand for rental housing. A general lack of manpower could mean slow rates of industrial growth in your area. Just what are the demographic breakdowns for your GMA? Who are the people? How old? What are their income brackets? These factors all must be taken into consideration.

One trend that has not changed to any significant degree is urban shift and development of the megalopolis. Cities have more inhabitants and suburbs are becoming more urbanized and so extend the city's metropolitan area. Part of this effect is being counteracted by new development in the city itself, as some persons seek a return to urban living. What is happening within your GMA? Is there now any indication of modernization of older buildings in the city? Are new buildings going up? Or is development most likely to be concentrated in the suburbs? If so, where? Where are people moving? What kind of people are moving? What kind of housing and health care will they need? Will population shifts result in growth of more commercial facilities? How would any of these or other developments affect the MU under consideration?

What about areas other than the United States that you may have under consideration or may actively be involved in? Assuming an underdeveloped nation, what is its birth rate? How will growth affect demand for housing and industry? What kinds of facilities will be needed first? (In many cases, especially when considering underdeveloped countries, the needs for everything are great, but final decisions often are governmental and, thus, political concerns become the key issues.)

How will population trends affect your clients? Will they become involved in modernization in urban areas? Will their programs for residential developments be cut back substantially? stepped up? What about industry? Will it be locating facilities downtown? in urban corridors? In general, what is happening to your GMA in terms of population? How will it impact on your competition and its clients? These, too, are questions that must be answered for each MU under discussion.

Energy: The energy issue is likely to be lively for many years to come. How is it affecting your area? What is the availability of natural gas, fuel oil, and electricity? What programs are set for the future? Discussions with utility representatives can give you the answers to many of these questions and will give you an indication of what they see in the years ahead in terms of population growth, etc. Given the local energy picture, how will it affect development? Will it cause more people to become involved in modernization of current facilities, or will there be enough energy available to support continued growth of new facilities, including those required by commerce, industry, and housing? Will there be a massive effort to make existing buildings more efficient? If so, how will this affect needs for changes to architecture, interior design, lighting, etc.? In other words, the energy problem will create changes, some of which are likely to be detrimental and others full of opportunity. How is the energy situation affecting your clients? How will it affect the competition? Does your current practice enable you to take advantage of the opportunities, or will you be subject to the pitfalls?

One thing does seem certain about energy. We will come to rely ever more extensively on electricity. This is so because America's domestic reserves of oil and natural gas are diminishing and—based on experience— we must reduce, if not eliminate, reliance on foreign sources for these two fossil fuels. Electric utilities can and do use coal—our most plentiful domestic energy source—for generating most electricity. At the same time, utilities are gearing up to rely more on nuclear energy. Fast-breeder reactors hold promise of a greatly expanded domestic nuclear fuel supply. Fusion reactors hold promise for a virtually infinite fuel supply. Moreover, electricity can be generated by just about any other energy source, including hydropower, tides, geothermal water/steam, wind, combustion (as from trash), solar energy, and chemical reaction. According to current estimates, electric utilities will spend as much as $750 billion or more on new generating facilities during the period from 1975 to 1990. Even if lower estimates materialize, due to problems now being encountered in nuclear development and weak capital markets, expansion still will be significant. Can your firm become involved? Discussions with representatives of one of the nation's larger utilities indicated a preference for local firms, including joint ventures. In many cases the expertise needed—at least for jobs such as designing scrubber installations—is not substantial. What contracting methods are used by your local utilities? Would they be interested in joint ventures? What about their plans for new office space? Will greater emphasis on electricity have an impact on your clients? Will they be looking for more expertise with electric heat and heat pumps? Will manufacturers be more concerned with expertise in electric process heat? Will some clients be looking for special abilities in the field of solar applications? Will greater reliance on coal mean a demand in your area for air pollution control, mining surveys, and related investigations?

Consider, too, the effect of energy on transportation. Will it mean less development of vehicular transportation facilities in your area with more emphasis on mass transportation? Is there likelihood of an urban mass transit system developing in your area somewhat similar to Washington, D.C.'s METRO or San Francisco's BART? If so, what would be the effect in terms of your ability to obtain such work? Would any of your clients be involved? Will there be extensive new development at proposed station sites? If so, who owns the land? To what extent should you expect an influx of major firms opening branch offices to get involved?

Land: The land issue is becoming increasingly important. While there are many concerns that whirl about it, such as environmental, social, economic, etc., one has to consider availability. Where is the open land now? Is there still room for development in the city, or are the majority of new projects built on sites of previously existing buildings, making development costs all the greater? If there is a suburban shift, in which direction is it heading? Is there enough land available to support growth? Will it require new sewage treatment facilities? new roads? new housing? Who owns the land? Clients? Prospective clients? To what extent are your services affected by the development of totally new facilities? Would it be necessary for you to open a branch office in another area? Learning more about these and related factors can result in developing an excellent prospect list, that is, the names of those who are likely to be developing in the future and to whom you might be of service.

Social. Social concerns, too, can be broken into a variety of smaller issues, but few are as significant in and of themselves as those discussed under physical considerations. Many of them do interrelate, however.

Attitudes toward growth: It is essential to learn what the area's attitudes are toward growth. In many parts of the nation there are strong groups of citizens who oppose the idea of growth and who often will grab at other issues to give their attitudes a more factual *raison d'etre*. Often used as legitimate excuses are lack of adequate sewage facilities, lack of water, traffic congestion, pollution, etc. While these various conditions can be real problems in and of themselves, many of them can be remedied through proper planning and action. Unfortunately, no-growth advocates frequently will attempt to stall such action—and often are successful—by raising numerous issues that require extensive study. In many cases these activities become embroiled in political considerations. A casebook example can be seen in the Washington, D.C. area. A sewer moratorium was imposed for lack of adequate facilities, but the planning required to remedy the situation was delayed literally years by studies, protests, hearings, meetings, etc., to the extent that new construction in the area all but dried up. What is the situation in your area? Are attitudes for growth or against it? If they are for growth, what planning has been undertaken to promote it? How do urban shift and environmental issues impact? These and other questions must be answered. If there is growing sentiment against growth it could mean a drying up of many MUs and perhaps an urgent need to shift either the location of your business or the nature of services offered. If no-growth attitudes indicate that more persons will be concentrating on existing facilities, what other factors affecting existing facilities will impact? What will be the effect on clients and competition? And if no-growth attitudes are prevalent in other areas, will it mean more firms coming into your area to obtain work?

Attitudes toward recreation: We see a growing need for facilities to support leisure-time pursuits: more golf courses, tennis courts, biking trails, boating facilities, ski resorts, and so on. To what extent are these attitudes prevalent in your areas of concern, and what impact will they have on clients and the competition? What kinds of facilities are needed, and how will they be supported? Who is doing the planning and building? Is it being done by speculative developers or by recognized firms, perhaps backed by such larger organizations as insurance companies and industrial conglomerates? How will national attitudes affect your area? Will manufacturers of leisure-time products need to expand their facilities? Will large tracts of land be used primarily for golf courses? Do population statistics suggest that recreational facilities will be those primarily enjoyed by families or by younger persons on an individual basis? How will economic and energy concerns spur or limit developments?

Other: Given local social concerns and related considerations, what will happen to the local birth rate? Will there be a need for more hospitals, nursing homes, or other medical facilities? Will there be a need for more suburban shopping centers to cater to those who prefer not to make the trip downtown? How are social attitudes likely to affect public policy, and how is public policy likely to affect you? Will there be a need for low-income housing in a given area, or is it likely that some attempt will be made to keep prevailing community make-up unchanged? By the same token, will agitation among minorities and the poor result in more or modernized schools, more low-cost housing, innercity renovation? These and many other questions must be applied to given areas for each MU to determine what impact traditionally has been in the past and what is likely to occur in the future.

Economic. Economic issues always are important and are influenced by numerous other factors. Two things are apparent, however. First, it is almost impossible to predict with any accuracy what will happen with economic issues. In many cases groups of well known, completely accredited economists will be diametrically opposed. Second, at all times there seem to be anomalies. When times are tough for many, there always will be those who do better than ever before; and when times are generally good, there will be those who for one reason or another go under. Thus, while we can only assume that there will be some economic growth and development in the future, we still can try to establish which MUs are most affected by hard times and which are not. For this reason, too, as will be discussed later, you will eventually want to establish a good MU mix so that a variety of MUs are involved. In this way, should one or more be affected adversely, not all will be. In hard times, those who have put all or most of their eggs into one basket find themselves holding an empty basket.

MUs that usually are very hard hit by a slow economy are those that require an extensive amount of borrowed capital for development, such as speculative commercial and residential housing. Those that often are least affected are governmental MUs or those basic industry MUs whose products are such that they are quickly expendable and in constant demand. While you cannot hone your entire approach to planning for the worst, you must consider the "what would happen ifs" in evaluating the future strength of a given MU, also considering the other factors involved, some of which may be offsetting. For example, speculative rental housing developments would be affected adversely by bad economic conditions, but a shortage of housing could be enough to offset these conditions.

Technological. Technological developments relate not only to hardware, but also to new design concepts and requirements, some of which relate to social or political demands.

Systems: It is wise to consider new systems technologies that are being developed. Key among these right now are those related to energy conservation. How will these new technologies affect a given MU? For a while it appeared as though systems building would have a significant impact on many types of residential and small commercial projects, which would have meant development of whole new specialties for many design professionals. The tide evidently has turned because of a variety of factors. But examine developments closely, and bear in mind that many technological developments can imply new design methodologies that could eliminate the independent professional. In the field of high-rise fire-safety and building automation, for example, there is evidence that many of the large organizations developing the systems demand that they perform their own design and in some cases their own installation, too. The same is occurring if the field of uninterruptible power sources, some sewage treatment systems, foundation systems, and so on. Therefore, you must be able to assess in your particular field what the technological developments will be and determine how you intend to deal with them to stay involved. Consider, too, the impact new kinds of systems could have on client demand. Does it present opportunities for retrofitting existing facilities and, if so, to what degree? Consider as many of the new concepts and actual devices as possible. Keep in mind what happened to the slide rule industry just a few short years after the introduction of the electronic calculator.

Services: As mentioned, some systems under development or actually in production affect services, but technological change in services themselves also is being felt. For example, there seems to be an increasing reliance on turnkey construction. The facts of the matter are, however, that many of the benefits of turnkey can be turned to good advantage by independent professionals who are willing to work as a consortium or team on a project, or who are willing to work with general contractors who are going after the business. How will the trend to turnkey help or hurt various MUs in your GMA? In fact, is there a trend at all? If not, could a team be developed and used to approach those clients or prospects who may be willing to utilize the concept? What inroads has the fast-track design concept made in your area? How successful has it been? Indications are that fast-tracking—starting construction before completing design—can lead to some rather difficult problems. Are you familiar with what they are? Have you consulted your liability insurance carrier about the effects of fast-tracking?

What about requirements for building inspection? There appears to be a growing attitude that design professionals should take more responsibility for how a building is built, in addition to responsibility for how it is designed. Is there such a trend in your area? If so, to what degree will you be able to take advantage of it? To what degree will it be detrimental to your practice? We also see trends to construction management. Does construction management exist yet in your area? Is it likely to? How would its development affect your way of doing business? your clients'? your competitions'? Is your competition offering some of these relatively new services and, if so, what successes have they had? You may not want to consider some of the breaks with tradition, but, if the trends exist, you may have to take action to ensure the continued existence and development of your own organization. If your competition is not yet involved, it could mean a profitable opportunity for you. If they already are involved, it could mean a change for operational necessity.

Political. Politics constitutes such a fuzzy gray area that the only way to approach the issue successfully is to rely on as many analytical processes as possible.

In essence, any self-governing political subdivision will be affected most by the decisions of local governing bodies and their attenuated bureaucracies. Thus, it first is essential to know how your local government works, how its members are elected, trends manifested in past elections, responsiveness of officials to the needs of various people and kinds of people or groups, and so on. In other words, you must do your best to ascertain how local government is likely to react to social, economic, and other developments. Recognize, too, that any self-governing local subdivision also will be affected by other layers of government, perhaps county government, then state government, then federal government. Accordingly, you must establish how these various governmental structures relate to one another, how they influence your GMA, and how they respond to local needs, either on the basis of meeting locally-expressed needs or on the basis of meeting national needs by developing or mandating local programs.

In the case of locally-elected governments where those elected act as more than just figureheads, to what extent will there be responsiveness to the needs of various groups to obtain reelection, and to what degree will there be responsiveness to the perceived needs of the community, regardless of the popularity of decisions? By getting a general feel for this, you can also establish a general feel for the way in which other concerns will be addressed. What is the general attitude of the various governments involved? Is it the kind of government that likes to be one step ahead in terms of developing new programs, and the kind that favors industrial growth? Does it try to foster programs with consumer interest in mind? These attitudes must be understood in developing answers to questions relating to political impact on such matters as develpment of public works projects, zoning, growth, design professional selection practices, building codes, innercity development, development of low- and moderate-income housing, environmental protection, schools, support of local businesses, landlord-tenant relations, condominium conversion, and others. You must consider how these and numerous other factors will have an impact on your clients and prospects, as well as the competition. And consider, too, the degree to which you or the competition are entrenched in area government and the likelihood of that penetration continuing in the event of political change. To what extent will the political involvement of competitors work in their favor or against it? By analyzing the various levels of government and by applying them to each MU involved, you are likely to bc able to deal with the subject with some measure of control. For example, if a group of citizens is strongly opposed to industrial development, the attitudes of polticians toward the need for industrial growth and the need to get reelected should supply an answer. What has happened in the past? If those who have opposed citizens' groups have not been reelected, chances are those now in office will take heed.

Legal. Legal developments are related closely to political developments in certain cases, especially in light of various local ordinances. Thus, you must be aware of all local ordinances that could affect your MU, as well as new developments that are likcly to have an impact. In certain cases these latter legal implications have been national in scope and have literally saturated the marketplace. For example, consider the impact of legal decisions on minority hiring practices and the degree to which minority firms have come into demand for numerous projects in the governmental sector. If yours is a minority firm, therefore, consider the various MUs in which you are active and the ones that hold potential. Do those MUs in which you now are active hold promise for the future by virtue of the fact that yours is a minority firm? Does the MU hold even more potential through joint-venturing or perhaps working with larger organizations who are looking for involvement with minority firms to help secure contracts? If yours is not a minority organization, what is developing within your various MUs? What are the attitudes toward the various laws that exist? Is an attempt to conform so extensive that minority presence outweighs certain quality criteria, or are quality critera still paramount?

The selection/retention process is something else affected by legal decisions. How have the various governments involved reacted? Is there an attempt to resort to more in-house work, or to select professionals more on the basis of a low bid? What about impact on clients? Are they utilizing traditional retention measures or are they also beginning to take pricing more into consideration?

In considering legal implications, one also must consider contractual relationships. Does your firm work mostly through interprofessional relationships or directly for the owner? The trend seems to be for more direct owner contact among all professionals through use of multiple or separate contracting techniques. How will this affect your practice?

Consider, too, the legal implications of liability problems, especially as they relate to third-party suits. Given a growing "let's sue" temperament among many people, what kind of projects in which MUs are most likely to be affected and to what extent? Are certain clients or prospects more prone to sue (for whatever reason) than others? Is it likely that the increasing complexity in a given sort of project will result in more law suits? At the same time, what industry efforts, either national or local, are developing to meet the growing number of liability cases? Are they such that problems will be minimized, as through development of a mediation/arbitration concept, industry councils, etc.?

Consider, too, what legal developments now in the works are likely to transpire. As an example, is there agitation now for development of laws governing the use of energy? The federal government already is getting such laws into shape, and in some cases local governments already have them on the books. What about laws that deal with pollution, environment, landlord-tenant relations, condominium conversion, zoning, etc.? What developments are taking place and what effects might they have? What about occupational safety and health laws? How will they affect your ability to work in certain types of projects in given MUs? How will they affect your clients and prospects? How will they affect the competition?

Ethical: A great many changes are occurring in the area of professional ethics. In general, one can say that there are four types of ethics: those that are "generally accepted standards of practice"; those that are enacted and enforced by associations; those that are legally enacted and enforced, and those that are subscribed to by the leadership of a given firm.

Generally accepted standards of practice or conduct are, to say the least, vague. Although referenced in the bylaws of numerous associations, they are largely undefinable and totally unenforceable unless they happen to be the same as those enforced by an association or official governmental entity. In other words, they are meaningless.

Ethical standards enacted and enforced by associations, in most cases, are just "this side" of meaningless. To a very real degree they usually are arrived at through extensive compromise and, thus, are very general in nature, except when backed by detailed standards of practice. In fact, there is excellent reason to believe that many of the specific prohibitions included in such ethics could be reversed by legal challenge. The matter of bidding is a perfect example. Even if an association is permitted to state that its members cannot submit bids, which is unlikely, the fact that more and more agencies and organizations and individuals are resorting to bidding or modified versions of bidding indicates that codes of ethics will have to be changed to keep up with prevailing conditions, or else membership will reach an extremely low ebb. By the same token, prohibitions against approaching someone else's client seem to be an apparent restriction on commerce, as do certain other prohibitions. In other words, as loose as some official codes of ethics already are, they are likely to get even looser to conform with new interpretations of the law and new sets of prevailing business conditions.

Legally enforced codes of ethics exist in two forms, the first of which is a set of laws. Thus, while it is unethical to do a certain thing it also is illegal. Stated another way, an ethical professional must be a law-abiding citizen. The second set of ethics concerns those enacted by design professional registration boards in various states. These have come into being primarily as a result of scandals that occurred in Maryland (a typical example of the illegal also being the unethical). In many cases, however, these codes are a combination of ethics and standards of conduct, stating that the professional has certain given things he must do and not do for certain situations. In fact, the only ethics a firm must abide by are those prescribed by law. If a firm or individual does not particularly like the code of ethics of a given organization, he simply does not join that organization.

Last on the list of ethics, and perhaps the most important type of ethics, are those to which the leadership of the firm subscribes. These ethics are bounded by extremes. At one end you have those who believe that anything goes, legal or otherwise. Every attempt should be made to put such firms, or at least their leadership, out of business. This "free-wheeling" approach will result in more and more constraints on the practice of architecture, engineering, surveying, land planning, interior design, and so on, plus the accompanying public black eye. At the other boundary are those whose ethics comprise unusually high standards, such as abstaining from any promotion other than an occasional report in a technical journal, no contact with others' clients unless client-initiated, no advertising of any kind except to obtain new employees, and, in general, promotion of nothing other than what is considered a "professional" image. There is nothing wrong with such attitudes, but it is interesting to note that those who abide by them usually are leaders of old, highly successful firms. To look down on others who do not abide by such high standards, therefore, is somewhat hypocritical. Obviously, newer, smaller, less experienced firms simply cannot afford to have such attitudes. If they did, they never would be able to achieve the position—in this day and age—of being able to adopt loftier ones.

The ethical attitudes of a given firm, for the firm is really where matters of ethics are decided, should be at least legal. Whether or not you wish to retain or adopt more rigorous standards can be decided only through consideration of what you have to do to stay in business and/or get ahead, and moral convictions that state, "Beyond this line ye shall not pass." It must be recognized that bidding certainly is not in the public interest. To select a firm on the basis of its fee is to overlook far more important criteria. Do recognize that simple cost bidding is not what is involved in most cases. The attitude now developing seemingly holds that selection and ranking procedures can be carried out in the traditional manner, except that the two or three firms ultimately ranked "most qualified" each will be asked to submit a cost figure, instead of being negotiated with individually until a satisfactory arrangement is found. Those who are willing to go along with this procedure when if first is introduced will be the ones most capable of working with it. Those who refuse to work in such a manner, sooner or later, will either participate or go under, unless their services are such that there just is no competition.

Another matter of ethical concern relates to interaction with someone else's client. In fact, just about everyone in a market is someone's client. To fail to go after new business because of an ethical proscription against it is, frankly, foolhardy. There still exists in the United States the intact vestiges of what used to be a fierce competitive spirit. To the extent that it exists today it still helps keep prices as low as possible and quality as high as possible for the dollar. Those codes of ethics that prohibit a person or a firm from trying to take business away from another firm were originally formed in a very self-serving atmosphere for, stated another way, such a code of ethics says that you won't try to take business from me. Our obviously hostile attitude to this type of ethical proscription should in no case be taken to mean that you should say bad things abut the competition, spread rumors, or do anything of that nature—such actions are reprehensible; but it does mean that you should do your level best to contact prospective clients—all prospective clients—to let them know what you can do. And while you may not like that approach, realize that others are doing it; that it long has been considered not only ethical in American business but essential, and to stay in business you'll have to do it sooner or later. Naturally, there are exceptions to the rule. For example, in interprofessional relationships, courting your client's client is, to an extent, biting the hand that feeds you: while it may not be unethical, it most certainly could be foolhardy.

Another element of ethics concerns the extent to which you are willing to obtain information on the competition. You should know what competitors are up to. You can obtain an excellent idea by talking with various people, including the competitor himself. You can read reports published by the competitor to learn more of his activities, as well as articles about the competing firm. In other words, there are abundant sources of knowledge that you should take advantage of to keep abreast of the other guy's activities. But there are limits. To hire someone from another firm purely or primarily to learn more about that firm, or to pirate his personnel, certainly borders on the unethical or immoral. It is being done, however, and it certainly is an effective business practice, in dollars and cents. Nonetheless, we do not recommend it, not so much for moral as for practical reasons. Simply put, the person who becomes known for this practice loses the respect and trust of his peers, assets that are difficult, if not impossible, to regain. Piracy may have little impact in the short term, but in the long run it can mobilize competition into opposition, and that could signal the end of a career. To be at the other extreme, however; to refuse to initiate any significant activity to determine what is going on across the street, is to bury your head in the sand.

Another question of ethics involves promotion. As already discussed, some firms are opposed to promotion of any kind. Most of these are opposed because they misunderstand or misinterpret what promotion really is. Others do understand what it entails and still feel it to be unethical. These latter are unlikely to be reading this book anyway, and probably are in positions at firms whose business has been established and active for so long that they can afford to abide by their archaic beliefs. In fact, promotion, as we define the concept, is nothing more than letting other people know what you're doing and how well you're doing it. Many firms already are doing some of this, but do not regard it as promotion. In those cases converts will be made easily for, to them, promotion means only redirecting efforts to ensure that what they are doing is communicated to people who should know about it.

One last word on ethics, this relating to international practice. In many areas of the world there are standards of getting things done that are relatively shocking when compared to ours. This is particularly true of such activities as graft, kickbacks, bribes, and so on. If such a standard exists in a nation that you're interested in, and it apparently is the only way to get anything done, including obtaining contracts, you obviously have a choice of either conforming or not getting the work. In making the decision you absolutely must let honesty (with yourself) hold sway. To use the excuse "I did it because everyone else was doing it" just does not hold water. To make a decision, perform an honest analysis of the situation as it exists. If everyone—literally everyone—is doing it to get business, or to get approvals and so on, if it is even standardized to an extent, if it is recognized to exist by government, which makes allowances for it (as is the case in some nations), then possibly it is the only thing to do short of looking for work elsewhere. If it exists less than universally, if just one firm states "This I will not do" and still gets work, then all others, by comparison, are dishonest. To be sure, it is not an easy evaluation to make. The decisions based on the evaluation are tougher still. Graft, wherever it exists, stinks. Nonetheless, in some cultures it is an accepted way of doing business and in such cases it may be unfair and unwarranted to make others subject to cultural, moral, and ethical values that they, as a nation or culture, have had no influence in molding. To sum it up, therefore, about the only advice we can give on an admittedly ticklish subject is this: if participation even in universally accepted activities in a foreign locale gives you feelings of guilt, causes you to worry about getting "caught," or forces you to lose sleep at night, or in any way makes you feel shoddy or unworthy of your profession or professional attitudes, don't do it. Business is important, but most important of all is the esteem in which you can hold your own actions. This applies as much to issuing a news release in this country as it does to giving gratuities in some other nation. In essence, self-respect is something that always can be sold, but once sold no amount of money in the world can ever buy it back.

Assuming that you have a handle on exactly what your firm's ethics are, the next step is to apply them to the various MUs. If there are no qualms about using the various promotional techniques discussed, then there is no problem. But do consider the ethics of the competition. Are they such that you should attempt to take safeguards? Are they such that you have excellent prospects? Consider, too, the ethics of general types of clients and specific prospects whom you may have in mind. What are their ethics? To what degree will you have to bend, perhaps in terms of bidding, to get work from them? Are they such that you do not want to be associated with them? This analysis, frankly, is relatively easy. The hard part is determining where the firm stands on ethics and, harder still, making adjustments consistent with requirements of business and the need for self-respect.

Once you have developed some basic indications of what the future has in store, you can begin undertaking some basic analysis. In this particular case, this means developing as good an idea as possible of what the future holds for each MU in terms of interrelating the various elements that affect it. Amplify written summaries of existing MUs and develop new ones. If at all possible, discuss these summaries at meetings, preferably by preparing and distributing them beforehand. See what others think of the way in which you have analyzed your various research undertakings and research into the future. To what extent is there agreement or disagreement? To what extent is it possible to identify more than one specific possibility that should be noted? This is not a simple process and should not be treated as one. The more you are willing to dig into it, the more likely its fruits will result in progress, growth, and profits.

GENERAL POTENTIAL EVALUATION FORM

MU	Physical		Social		Economic		Techno-logical		Political		Legal		Ethical		Total	Adjusted Total
	Weighting Factor	Total	Weighting Factor	Total	Weighting Factor	Total	Weighting Factor	Total	Weighting Factor	Total	Weighting Factor	Total	Weighting Factor	Total		

Figure 11. General Potential Evaluation Form.

To facilitate the undertaking, and to put the results of analysis in a form compatible with subsequent undertakings, develop a General Potential Evaluation Form similar to the one shown in Figure 11.

To use the form, first list each of the factors used in evaluating the future development of MUs. For purposes of illustration we have used only the general headings, i.e., physical, social, and so on. If you prefer, the more important subcategories (population, environment, energy, etc.) can be used in addition to, or instead of, certain general factors.

Once listed, each factor is weighted or ranked from 0 to 5. In this case note that the weight of a factor could vary from MU to MU. Thus, while political concerns may be of great importance in one MU, they may have no bearing on the future of some other MU. Accordingly, to complete the form for any given MU, first determine the relative importance of the various factors as they influence the future of the MU, and then indicate how favorable or unfavorable future conditions are likely to be, insofar as the particular MU is concerned. This latter indication is made on the basis of -10 to $+10$. A ranking of -10 indicates that research shows likely future conditions for the factor involved to be highly unfavorable to the MU under consideration. A ranking of 0 would indicate that conditions are neither favorable nor unfavorable. A ranking of $+10$ would indicate that conditions are highly favorable. For the purposes of this evaluation, do not take into consideration, unless unavoidable, the extent of competition, which is to be covered later. As an example of how to work with the form, consider the following:

For the MU concerned, physical factors are very important (5); social factors somewhat less important (3); economic factors, very important (5); technological factors, slightly important (1); political factors, slightly important (1); legal factors of no importance (0); and ethical factors, because of recent actions by several clients, somewhat important (2).

Physical factors indicate that the MU will be very active in the months and years ahead ($+9$); that social factors are somewhat mixed, but slightly positive ($+2$); that economic factors are improving ($+4$); that technological factors are such that the firm will be able to handle new developments with ease ($+10$); that political factors are relatively promising ($+6$); and that the firm will be able to adjust its ethics to meet the requirements of some clients in terms of giving an indication of cost along with other materials, as they require ($+10$). (Legal factors for this MU would not be listed because they are of no importance at all.)

The total number of points achieved by the MU in terms of its general potential is 107 $((5 \times 9) + (3 \times 2) + (5 \times 4) + (1 \times 10) + (1 \times 6) + (2 \times 10) =$

45 + 6 + 20 + 10 + 6 + 20 = 107). The adjusted total, or the total divided by the total of the weighting factors is 6.3 (107 ÷ (5 + 3 + 5 + 1 + 1 + 2) = 107 ÷ 17 = 6.3).

How you handle development of this particular form is up to you. What is considered the best approach, however, would be to give each person involved in basic marketing research and the various meetings a blank form for completion. Collect the completed forms and compare them. Hold a meeting to discuss the variations and to arrive at a consensus. The importance of this particular form when finalized cannot be overestimated. It will be used extensively as a tool to plot the future course of your firm.

4

MARKETING PLANNING THROUGH MU EVALUATION

To this point you have developed, among other things, materials that indicate MUs in which your firm has actual or potential capabilities and what the future is likely to hold in store for each. The fact that a certain MU may appear to hold far more promise than any other does not necessarily mean that you should immediately bend every effort to get involved in it, however. There are many other factors to consider, not the least of which are compatibility of MU activity with the goals of your firm's leaders, ease of entry or further penetration into the MU, and the impact of the competition. Only through consideration of these and other factors can you obtain a balanced view and so a better collection of data on which to base decisions. It is in this stage, too, that you will begin to consider what changes, if any, should be undertaken to enable pursuit of those MUs that are both compatible with organizational considerations and future prospects. For this reason, you will be evaluating the desirability of MUs in terms of the firm "as is" and as a somewhat changed entity. If analysis shows that you can plot a sound future course without change, so be it. If analysis shows that the desired future can be obtained only through change, however, you must be willing to make it.

Admittedly, change can present a somewhat frightening prospect. It can mean not only entering uncharted waters, but also entering them in an untried ship, captained by an individual not fully sure of himself. For this reason moderation is the key. The course must be plotted carefully and in great detail. The turns must be made gradually. In that way, if continuing feedback through ongoing marketing research indicates that something up ahead requires a different tack, it can be taken with minimal disruption.

4.1 MU EVALUATION PHASE I (NO CHANGE)

The first phase of MU evaluation is designed to determine the extent to which the firm can realize MU potential without adding new services or disciplines. (While there may be a need to add additional personnel, they would be used only to implement the services now available, not to create new ones.)

The Phase I evaluation procedure itself is relatively simple. All MUs covered are analyzed in light of three factors: goal compatibility, ease of MU entry/penetration, and impact of competition. In each case evaluation is made in terms of numerical coefficients that ultimately are weighted. The MU that achieves the highest "score" is the most important one to the firm.

Goal Compatibility

To evaluate an MU's compatibility with company goals, you first must determine what company goals are. This usually entails an additional element of basic organizational research. As mentioned previously, this particular task can be undertaken earlier. It is discussed here primarily to indicate how the information fits into the overall marketing program.

Establishing Goals

To begin with, the principals of the firm must agree on precisely what the firm's goals are or should be. For the purposes of planning, possible goals should be limited to growth, increased profit, increased rate of profit, and increased market (or GMA or MU) share.

Growth. Growth, the willingness to have the company expand its operations, is an operational necessity if the marketing effort is to bear fruit.

As mentioned previously, one of the key goals of marketing is to give the firm flexibility to change both short- and long-term direction in response to changed market conditions. This requires activity in a variety of different MUs so that efforts in any one of them can be increased or decreased as conditions demand. Without a willingness to grow, flexibility is severely limited. In addition, growth is the vital concomitant of the other three goals if they are to be achieved in a positive, effective manner. Still and all, there will be those principals who will prefer to have the firm retain its current size. It has achieved what they consider to be "idyllic" proportions and they don't want change. In most cases such an attitude stems from fears of inadequacy, many of which are well-founded. Design professionals, by and large, lack adequate business experience and training. They fear growth because they believe they lack the skills required to manage it. Therefore, if the principals of your firm are opposed to growth, it must be a priority undertaking to help them determine why they are opposed to it. If the opposition is grounded in fear, principals must be given the facts of business life. Key among these are that growth is essential to practically all business endeavors; that the future of the company depends on flexibility, which only growth or a willingness to grow can provide; that attainment of other goals requires a willingness to grow, and that growth can be controlled. Many persons, for some reason, imagine growth to mean doubling firm size overnight. This simply is not the way it happens. Through effective marketing operations one can establish where the growth will take place and to what extent. It thus becomes a gradual process. Accordingly, through self-improvement, increased experience, hiring of qualified personnel, and other techniques, one is able to increase management's capabilities to anticipate the increased requirements that growth will entail.

Increased Profit. This can be attained in two ways, either as a result of growth or as a result of increased rate of profit. We suggest strongly that, if increased profits are desired, you seek them primarily from growth. Not only will this help ensure the success of a marketing program (by permitting growth to take place), but it also will avoid the pitfalls that undue emphasis on increased rate of profit may create.

Increased Rate of Profit. This differs from increased profit in that increased profit refers to the actual amount of profit achieved, and increased rate of profit refers to the percentage of profit achieved. Thus, rate of profit may decline sharply while actual amount of profit increases. In fact, because growth often implies increased overhead and working with new clients, rate of profit often does decline, which is not to say that one should forget about increased rate of profit to attain growth, or that growth and increased rate of profit are incompatible. They are very compatible, providing each is pursued in a balanced manner. In other words, in seeking expansion, one should make every effort to concentrate on those MUs or those services that, according to experience or research, yield the highest rates of return. To concentrate solely on high-profit MUs or services could lead the firm into a box. The ability to react to market conditions demands flexibility. Concentration on a small set of MUs could result in disaster if, for some reason, these MUs begin to dry up. In short, increased rate of profit, just like increased profits, is an acceptable goal as long as it is considered an element of, and balanced with, growth.

Increased market (or GMA or MU) share. As a goal, this means taking an increased percentage of the business available in the market in general, in a GMA or, even more specifically, a given MU. It can be done to achieve a higher rate of profit or simply to become known as a specialist in a given area, perhaps to massage the ego of various principals. Be that as it may, such a goal is viable only when considered a component of growth. In this way, once again, you avoid backing the firm into a corner from which it is unable to escape when times become more difficult in the areas of concentration.

In asking principals to define their goals, one should not present the limited list of four. Rather, ask each principal to write down specifically what his goals for the company are. If possible, principals should be called together for a meeting where they can each discuss what the others have written to arrive at a consensus. Once this list is one hand, it is up to you to analyze perceived goals and translate them into one or more of the goals already discussed.

The six goals most commonly indicated by principals are:

1. to make enough money for principals to have a comfortable income;

2. to become known as the best firm for certain types of work in certain MUs;

3. to attract skilled, talented employees and keep them;

4. to become large enough to undertake large projects, but small enough to permit involvement of the principals in the design and client relations of all projects;

5. to have an interesting and challenging variety of projects and so avoid having firm practice limited to specialists in every field, and

6. to retain ownership of the firm among the current principals.

To make enough money to have a comfortable living often is a goal designed to duck the real issue at hand. In fact, how much is comfortable? We are told that expenditures rise to meet income. Does this mean that if a principal receives a greater income his standards of "comfort" will increase proportionately? Moreover, one must consider that inflation erodes the ability of a given income to meet even static requirements, while, at the same time, competitive pressures demand that as little of this inflation as possible be passed through. Therefore, while this particular goal cannot be discounted, it must be regarded as vague and, even then, it usually can be met only through increased profits and/or increased growth.

To become know as the best implies some degree of ego flattery just as it also implies, although secondarily, that a firm or individual will become sought out because of a recognized proficiency. There are several ways of achieving this goal. One is to concentrate efforts in a given MU. While such specialization certainly is possible, it should be sought only within the general context of an overall marketing program to enable activity in other MUs. In other words, specialization is an acceptable objective providing it is conducted within an overall framework of growth. Another method of achieving "best" status is to set high standards of quality. While high quality of work performance is an esssential of marketing—you can't get repeat business without it—it all too often is accomplished through principal involvement in almost all projects. This particular approach to attaining quality is not acceptable to a marketing program because it immediately implies restrictions on growth, that is, the number or scope of projects handled can in no case exceed the ability of principals to handle them. The approach suggested for maintaining quality and growth together involves development of an effective quality control apparatus and principals' delegation of responsibility, something fundamentally essential for growth. A third approach to attaining quality requires hiring top design professionals. This is somewhat acceptable providing it is compatible with other firm objectives and strategies. Attaining a top specialist is fine if you have enough work within a given specialty to keep him busy or if he has competence in disciplines or service beyond his specialty. In either case, it must be recognized that attaining top persons requires increased expenses that, in large part, can be borne only through increased income, which usually results from growth.

To attract a group of skilled employees requires that the firm have what it takes to keep them. This implies money, to be sure, but surveys have shown repeatedly that money is not the only thing. Employees look for opportunities for advancement, recognition, and challenging and rewarding work. Growth obviously will supply the money required, and it also will supply varied projects to which employees can apply their skills. It also will provide opportunity for making partnerships or junior partnerships available without jeopardizing the roles of principals within the firm, thereby providing opportunity for staff recognition and advancement.

To achieve ideal size by being large enough to handle large projects, but small enough to permit principals' activity in projects is an impossible dream. Feasibly such a size might exist for the brief moment when the given project mix within the firm allows it. For the most part, however, project mix is highly dynamic and firm size, by comparison, is static. The only way a firm will be able to achieve a size large enough to handle the very large projects, or several such projects at the same time, is through growth. Growth should in no way imply that the firm will handle only large projects, however. Through development of very basic management procedures it is a relatively simple matter to structure the firm so that a specific *project team* is assigned to each job. The team is as large or as small as project requirements dictate, but principals will not be able to be involved in all projects. Nor should they be, as already discussed, because such a goal limits growth. Their reasons for involvement can be met easily, however, through quality control and by their selecting the specific projects in which they want to become involved.

To have an interesting variety of projects is a goal toward which most creative persons strive. "Interesting" is a relative term, however, and so can be defined only on an individual basis. Accordingly, what may be of great interest to one person may be deadly dull to the other. To keep as many persons as possible happy, the firm has to have an effective project mix. This, of course, can be achieved only through growth or the willingness to seek it.

Retention of ownership is an understandable goal, but one not generally in harmony with growth. In essence, growth implies a need for more personnel, technical and management alike. The better qualified these people are, the abler the firm will be to achieve its goals. But to attract and retain qualified people, the firm must be willing to recognize accomplishment. In some cases this can be done only through allowing an individual to buy in. If that option is not given to a person, he may feel, and rightly so, that there is no room at the top, which could result in his opening his own firm. This would mean not only that you would be likely to lose some of your top people, but also that they will establish competing firms that, in some cases, will have a list of prospective clients that looks amazingly similar to your list of current clients. What many design professionals evidently fail to recognize is that buying in can be done in numerous different ways. Different types of stock can be issued. Ownership may be limited to only certain elements of an organization's operations and so on. In other words, allowing other persons to own a part of the firm usually is far more frightening in aspect than in fact, especially when one can relinquish at least a portion of ownership, but still retain control, which, in most cases, is the real heart of the issue.

Another factor must be considered as well, especially when smaller firms are involved. Research shows that professional service firms have a very short life expectancy past the first generation. One reason for this is the clients' preference for doing business with certain people, not necessarily certain firms. Once these people no longer are on the scene because of death or retirement, the client may look elsewhere. This translates directly into the value of the firm. In fact, who would be willing to pay anything for a firm when it is known that to keep it operational one would have to cultivate each client just as though he was beginning "from scratch"? To compensate for this situation, we advise strongly that principals bring new blood into the firm, either new partners or junior partners who can get to know the clients and begin to work with them while the original leaders still are at the helm. In this way, when command does change hands, the new person in charge already is familiar with the clients; thus the firm is a very valuable entity to its new leadership who will be willing to pay for the value involved. Once again we see that growth is the key, for only through growth can the firm support additional owners who, eventually, will be willing to buy out other owners to make the firm their own.

Although the list of goals above is relatively short, it should be sufficient to indicate how subjective goals can be analyzed and translated into one or more of the four general goals.

Once principals' goals have been translated, they should be brought back to the group for further discussion. If necessary, principals should be given a copy of this or a similar book to explain in extensive detail some of the issues involved and to ease their minds a bit if growth seems alien to their goals as stated originally.

Assuming that at least some degree of growth can be obtained to permit continuation of the marketing effort, and that all other goals have been translated into one of the four general goals, the next step is to evaluate MUs in terms of their compatibility with goals.

As can be seen in the Goal Compatibility Analysis Form, shown in Figure 12, ranking MUs on the basis of goal compatibility involves ranking the goals in terms of relative importance (weighting factor), and evaluating an MU's ability to meet specific goals.

Each of the four goals should be evaluated on a scale of 1 to 5. A goal deemed of great importance would be ranked 5; one of very little importance would be ranked 1 or 2; if a goal has no importance whatsoever, it should not be listed. Thus, each goal should have a weighting factor of 1, 2, 3, 4, or 5. Each can be given a different evaluation. All may have the same.

In evaluating an MU in terms of goals, consider how penetration (initial or continued) would affect the company and rank that MU on a -10 to $+10$ scale. A -10 ranking would indicate that activity in the specific MU would be totally counterproductive to attainment of the goal involved. A ranking of 0 would indicate that activity would in no way help or hinder goal attainment. A ranking of $+10$ would indicate that activity in the MU would be of great value toward attainment of the goal under consideration. Thus, penetration activity in a given MU may be of great value toward a goal of growth ($+8$), of some assistance in achieving increased profit ($+5$), of very little assistance in increasing the rate of profit ($+1$), and of more significant assistance in helping the firm attain a larger share of business generated by the MU ($+7$). Each of these numbers would be entered into the left portion of the column below each goal, then multiplied by the weighting factor. The total then would be entered in the right-hand portion of the column. List under the "Total" column the total (ranking $\times$ weighting factor) attained

GOAL COMPATIBILITY ANALYSIS FORM

MU	Growth		Increased Profit		Increased Rate of Profit		Increased Market Share		Total	Adjusted Total
	Weighting Factor		Weighting Factor		Weighting Factor		Weighting Factor			
	Rating	Total	Rating	Total	Rating	Total	Rating	Total		

Figure 12. Goal Compatibility Analysis Form.

by an MU for the total of the four goals. Divide that total by the total of the weighting factors to arrive at the final ranking. As an example:

> Assume that growth is rated 5; increased profit, 4; increased rate of profit, 2; and increased market share, 3. The MU under consideration is ranked 9 for growth (total = $9 \times 5 = 45$); 7 for increased profit (total 28); -2 for increased rate of profit (total -4), and 8 for increased market share (24). The total for this particular MU would be 93 ($45 + 28 - 4 + 24$). Its adjusted total for purposes of ranking and later consideration would be 6.6 (93 divided by $5 + 4 + 2 + 3 = 93 \div 14 = 6.6$).

By using this method one can calculate not only a given MU's importance to attainment of a given goal, but also the relative importance of the goal and, thus, the true value of the MU in terms of meeting the most worthwhile goals.

Ease of Entry/Penetration

The next step is to evaluate each MU in terms of the relative difficulty the firm will have entering it or, if already involved in it, maintaining or increasing penetration.

Perhaps the simplest method of establishing ease of entry and penetration is to review the various lists of MUs that have been prepared, including MUs in which the firm has been active, MUs in which the firm's clients have been active, and so on. These are indicated in abbreviated versions across the top of the Ease of Entry/Penetration Evaluation Form shown in Figure 13.

To use this form, the degree of activity in each MU for each of the seven categories should be rated on a 0 to 10 scale. For example, if the firm has been very active in a certain MU for the past three or four years, a 9 or 10 would be inserted in the "Firm" column. Personnel, it can be presumed, also would have been active, and so would be given a similar ranking. Likewise for clients and indirect clients. If there has been no activity in the MUs to which services could be applied, so indicate by inserting a 0. As another example, consider the MU in which the firm has been only marginally active (2); in which firm personnel have been somewhat more active (5); in which several clients are somewhat active (8); in which indirect clients are somewhat active (8); in which personnel's clients and indirect clients are active (7 or 8); and one that could be entered relatively easily through services now available (9). This MU also would achieve a high score, even though the firm itself has not been that active in it.

To finalize the form, total the score achieved by each MU. Establish an average by dividing by 7 (or the number of MU listings considered). The average will indicate the ease the firm should have in entering new MUs

EASE OF ENTRY/PENETRATION FORM

MU	Firm	Personnel	Clients	Indirect Clients	Personnel Clients	Personnel Indirect Clients	Services	Total	Average

Figure 13. Ease of Entry/Penetration Form.

or maintaining its position in, or penetrating further into those MUs in which it already is active. This, of course, does not take into consideration the impact of the competition (covered in the next step) and it assumes, to an extent, that promotional efforts can and will be marshalled to help assure entry and penetration. The form also does not consider timing of entry into new MUs. In some cases, timing can be critical, assuming, for example, that the firm possesses or can obtain specialty services that suddenly became needed by many prospects in a given MU. Much this situation occurred, for example, when acoustical consultants found their specialties in great demand following passage of the OSHA law. At this stage in development of a marketing plan, it is exceedingly difficult to "plug in" data relative to timing. Accordingly, timing decisions should be based primarily on those factors to be discussed below. As events transpire, indicating that timing of certain intended procedures should be changed, such changes should be made. In fact, this is one of the reasons why having a marketing plan is so beneficial.

Impact of Competition

The final factor to be evaluated is the impact of competition in terms of your firm's ability to enter or maintain or increase penetration of an MU.

The ranking basis is −10 to +10. As examples, if the firm is active in an MU in which there has been and probably will continue to be extensive competition, but the firm still has increased its penetration over the years, the MU would be given a ranking of 9 to 10. This would indicate that the impact of competition is minor. If, however, there are indications that certain competitors in an MU are taking a larger share of the market and your firm is taking a smaller share, impact could be rated at 4 or 3 (or perhaps lower), indicating a less favorable state of affairs. (If that is the case, incidentally, every effort should be made to determine why your company is losing business to the competition.) If the MU is one in which the firm has not been active, but in which several other firms are reasonably well established, a negative number may be used to indicate the situation. By the same token, if these competitors are seen as "lightweights," and if rapid penetration appears to be possible, the impact of competition would be minor and so could be rated at 4, 5, or even higher.

A form similar to that shown in Figure 14 can be used for ranking purposes.

Evaluating Overall MU Potential

The next step is to evaluate the overall potential of each MU. This is done simply by adding together the goal compatibility adjusted total, ease of entry/penetration average, and impact of competition ranking of each MU

IMPACT OF COMPETITION EVALUATION FORM

MU	Ranking

Figure 14. Impact of Competition Evaluation Form.

and then averaging the total. A Business Potential Summary Form, such as shown in Figure 15, can be utilized.

It must be recognized, of course, that we are here evaluating potential of the various MUs on the basis of the organization as it exists now. We are not talking about changing services or disciplines. However, we are assuming that a variety of management and promotional tools are available to enable you to change emphasis within the firm. That is, an MU that achieves a high rating, but in which the firm is not now active, could be entered and penetrated through utilizing resources that we know exist, such as clients, and so on.

The question now becomes, how do these MUs, rated on the basis of potential, compare with what basic marketing research has told us will be developments within these MUs in general.

To facilitate this phase of evaluation, utilize a form similar to that shown in Figure 16, which lists rankings achieved on the basis of business potential with rankings achieved on the basis of basic marketing research.

To complete the form, simply insert the MU rankings listed in the Business

BUSINESS POTENTIAL SUMMARY FORM

MU	Goal Compatibility	Ease of Entry/ Penetration	Impact of Competition	Total	Average

Figure 15. Business Potential Summary Form.

BUSINESS POTENTIAL/GENERAL POTENTIAL COMPARISON FORM

MU	Business Potential	General Potential

Figure 16. Business Potential/General Potential Comparison Form. Use this to compare business potential of an MU (from Figure 15) with general potential ascertained through marketing research (from Figure 11).

Potential Summary Form (Figure 15) under "Business Potential" and the MU rankings listed in the General Potential Evaluation Form (Figure 11) under "General Potential."

Compare the two sets of rankings. If those MUs that have the greatest potential for the firm are the same MUs that appear to have the rosiest future, chances are the firm does not have to alter the services or disciplines it provides to meet the changing conditions likely to occur. It must be the goal of marketing and the marketing director, therefore, to help ensure that MUs in which the firm is active are the same MUs that research indicates will be the most active in years to come. Put another way, the firm, if it is to grow and prosper, must continually hunt where the ducks are. If the firm has potential in MUs that have potential, the main concern is to develop the potential that exists. The ways and means of doing this are explained in later sections of this book that deal with management and promotion. Unfortunately, the likelihood of the firm being active in precisely those MUs that are likely to be most active are very remote. Thus, most will have to proceed to the next step, evaluation of change.

4.2 PHASE II—EVALUATION OF CHANGE

There are two fundamental changes a firm can make. The first is to change its service mix, that is, the number and types of services offered and the way in which they interrelate with one another and client needs. For example, provision of feasibility studies is a service applicable to most design professions and one easily added.

The second change involves alteration of the discipline mix, meaning the disciplines provided to the client and the way in which they interrelate. In many cases a changed discipline mix also implies a modified service mix. In changing disciplines, one usually adds new ones that are an extension of those already provided. As examples, a structural engineer or land surveyor could add soil and foundation engineering; an architect could add mechanical and electrical engineering; an interior designer could add lighting design or acoustical engineering.

The purpose of making change is to facilitate further penetration of MUs in which a firm already is active or entry into new MUs that will bring the company additional business, profit, and flexibility.

Many principals will be reluctant to undertake change or even consider it. It should at least be considered. To refuse to look at alternatives for the future is, bluntly put, childish. Reasons given for such reluctance often are similar to those advanced to support an antigrowth attitude. Root causes often are the same. To change implies entry into a sphere of activity in which principals are not fully competent. As will be discussed, however, there are numerous different ways of effecting changes, some of which have only slight impact on management's responsibilities but significant impact on business development.

Identifying Change Possibilities

To begin the process of change analysis and evaluation, first identify ways in which your firm could modify its service and discipline mix. Do not at this time consider how the changes will be made. Rather, assume that they can be made and proceed from there.

This particular process should not take too long. Begin by reviewing the list of services your company can or does provide. What other services do similar companies provide? List all those you do not now offer. In many cases these will be what we refer to as "secondary services," those that support or extend from basic design professional technical services. In some cases there may be a difference of opinion as to whether or not something new is a changed service or a changed discipline. For example, does construction management involve a new discipline or an extension of a service already offered? Whichever you think it is is right because, in essence, it doesn't really matter, nor is it a very profitable use of time to debate academic issues.

Once new services are listed, consider new disciplines that could be offered and whatever services they entail that are different from what is being offered now. In most cases the disciplines to consider are those that would be utilized prior to your getting work or those that would follow your performance. Structural engineers (or architects for that matter) could consider providing soil and foundation engineering services. A geotechnical engineer could consider structural engineering services. An architect could consider interior design, acoustical engineering, and lighting design. A consulting engineer could consider provision of architectural services, and so on. Remember: all we are doing right now is considering. No commitments are being made. Therefore, allow yourself scope and range in terms of changes being considered. At this point very little should be "out of the question."

Evaluation of Change

To evaluate change, utilize a Change Evaluation Form, similar to that shown in Figure 17. *Prepare a separate form for each change under consideration.* Evaluate what impact it will have on the various MUs in terms of goal compatibility, ease of entry/penetration, and impact of competition, the same factors utilized to evaluate business potential without change. In each case the evaluation should be made on the basis of −10 to +10.

To compute ratings for goal compatibility, simply reuse the Goal Compatibility Analysis Form shown in Figure 12, and recompute data on the basis of the firm having the additional service or discipline involved. Repeat this and the following steps for each particular change.

To evaluate ease of entry/penetration, refer to materials covered when forming the earlier evaluation on the basis of business potential without change. Rather than computing degree of activity among clients, indirect clients, and so on, consider what the impact of the change will be on the various clients, indirect clients, etc., and evaluate that change on the basis of −10 to +10. This particular assessment is of critical importance. For example, a consulting engineer who works extensively with architects as a subcontractor could consider the possibility of establishing architectural services in-house. Chances are the reaction among many clients, therefore, will be strongly negative. To simply write down a −10, however, would be

CHANGE EVALUATION FORM

Change: _____

MU	Goal Compatibility	Ease of Entry/ Penetration	Impact of Competition	Total	Average

Figure 17. Change Evaluation Form.

incorrect, unless all or substantially all clients are architects. Therefore, one must consider the current client/billings mix, that is, the percentage of clients who are architects and the percentage of billings that these clients represent. If it appears that these clients are becoming continually less active, and that there are enough owner clients who would be willing to utilize your architectural capabilities, then perhaps a weakly positive (1 or 2) rating would be in order. Otherwise, a negative rating may be appropriate. Undertake the same kind of considerations for former clients of personnel, and so on.

To evaluate impact of the competition, proceed much as you did before. This time consider the firm to actually have the change under consideration. In most cases you probably will find that changes will help you keep in step with the competition or go one step beyond them, resulting in elevated ratings in either case.

Go through this procedure *for each change* and develop averages much as you did before. Once done, utilize a form similar to that shown in Figure 18 to compare business potential in the various MUs on the basis of no change (Figure 15), general potential of the MUs (Figure 11), and business potential of the firm for each of the various changes considered.

Examine the effect on business potential caused by the various changes. Chances are that at least two or three of the changes will enable your firm to become more involved in those MUs that have the best general potential. One method of determining which have the most beneficial impact involves the following analytical process:

1. Compute the difference between business potential without change and business potential to be achieved in an MU for a given change by subtracting business potential from each change potential. Thus, if the business potential without change for a given MU is 6, and the potential for that same MU with change No. 1 is 9, the difference is +3.

2. Weight by multiplying the difference (in this example +3) by the general potential of the MU. Thus, if the difference is +3 and general potential is 8, the total is 24.

3. Sum the totals for all MUs.

4. Repeat the process for each change. The change that achieves the highest score is the one that has the highest level of positive impact on the most important MUs.

Now comes the question, "How will these various changes be implemented?" This is something which only you can answer, with the help of the following procedures.

MU	Business Potential	General Potential	Business Potential with Change Number:					
			1	2	3	4	5	6

Figure 18. Form to compare, for each MU, business potential without changing firm's service or discipline mix, general potential regardless of the firm, and business potential resulting from each of several possible alterations of the firm's discipline or service mix.

Change Methodology Evaluation

To consider the various ways and means by which change can be made, you first must be familiar with the various existing methodologies of change.

Change Methodologies

There are numerous ways of implementing change. Some require massive reorganization. Others require very little reorganization at all. The following change methodologies are considered to be among the most prevalent.

Maintaining Same Staff. It is possible to provide a new service if certain members of the staff have had extensive experience with it. Do realize, however, that assigning new responsibilities to someone already on staff usually means that someone else will have to take over that person's former responsibilities. Therefore, unless you drop someone's responsibilities somewhere down the line, this methodology will usually require hiring additional personnel.

Changing Manpower. It sometimes is possible to change the service or discipline mix simply by changing manpower, rather than increasing staff size. This can be done by reassigning responsibilities of persons already on staff, or by laying off some and hiring others who possess the specific expertise required. Before doing any laying off, however, examine staff members' backgrounds. Can in-house capabilities be put to better use? Can personnel be retrained? In either case it usually will be more beneficial to firm morale to retrain or reorient rather than to dismiss and hire, providing the level of capability, timing, etc., are compatible with objectives.

Expanding Staff. Expansion of staff is a change methodology used most often to facilitate growth. It also is used to expand services provided by the firm. It is not used as frequently to expand the firm's discipline mix, however, unless a particularly large firm is involved that can afford to hire top level professionals capable of directing a staff, which also would have to be hired. In the case of smaller firms, adding a discipline usually is achieved by adding principals and/or somehow establishing a relationship with an existing firm.

Merger. Merger occurs when two firms merge into one. Usually each firm gives up a share of its identity to form a new whole. This is an especially useful tactic for adding one or more new disciplines, as through merger of architectural and engineering firms, architectural and interior design firms, mechanical and electrical engineering firms, etc. In such a case each firm brings its clients who, in many instances, will use a full range of services from the resulting firm. Whenever two firms join together problems are likely to occur. There always is the problem of who is responsible for what. There also are problems relating to the laying off of certain staff members. In that merger often means economy of operation through elimination of duplication, one of the firm's bookkeepers or office managers, for example, may have to be let go. The question is, which one? Also to be considered are potential personality clashes. Occasional flare-ups in a marriage can be smoothed over because spouses usually are apart during the day. A business merger also is a marriage, except that a personality clash can create tremendous problems because it continues all day every day and often into other waking moments. Thus, if you consider a merger or any other kind of close alliance with some other organization, be certain to answer all questions before finalizing the relationship. There are many publications available on the subject, as well as many competent consultants.

Buy-Out. The outright purchase of one firm by another is similar to a merger except that, in many instances, the principal of the purchased firm often will not assume an ownership position in the parent company, or will remain only for a short while before retiring. Even if this is not the case, however, a buy-out usually implies that the firm doing the buying has the funds necessary to make the purchase. In a merger, or at least in some mergers, no cash changes hands at all.

Affiliation. In many cases affiliation will be used to establish branch operations. Numerous different kinds of strategies can be used. One can buy all or a portion of an existing firm, go into partnership with an existing firm, go into a partnership to establish a new firm, and so on. What it implies, in essence, is lowering the capital outlay required to establish a branch operation by bringing in an "outsider" while, in many instances, using the parent company's name to help provide instant identification. The parent also can make available on demand a manpower pool to meet any special requirements of a satellite operation. Affiliation also is a method that can be used to meet growth demands.

Branching. A branch office implies that a parent company is offering its regular services through a local office. Opening a branch implies that all expenses are borne by the parent company and that the manager of the branch is a member of parent company staff and, in some cases, is a principal. Branching, as with development of any kind of satellite operation, usually is accomplished easiest when the branch's GMA has a shortage of the particular service offered, lack of quality service, and/or when a major client has operations in the GMA so the branch can be opened with the prospect of immediate business. Branching also can be used to meet demands of growth.

Association. The association of two firms usually is a very loose arrangement wherein one firm agrees with another to refer to it a certain type of business. While the association of two firms involves very little risk, it does have drawbacks. Chief among them is the necessity of explaining to the client or prospect that some of the services available by association are not in-house services. Likewise, services provided through an association-based relationship often are not as cost-effective as others, due to duplication of effort, and so on. You also lose a degree of control and profit. Nonetheless, the establishment of an association between two organizations in a manner similar to joint venturing or forming a consortium can be of benefit to firms that are experimenting with change or growth, prior to making a more serious commitment. Association (and joint venturing and forming a consortium) also provide a very inexpensive method for observing closely the operations of another organization prior to considering merger, buy-out, affiliation, or similar moves.

Joint Venturing. Joint venturing involves two or more firms pooling their manpower for a given project. One simply assembles a team that can provide the services required and establishes who will be paid how much for what. While this permits flexibility from job to job, it does create some potential problems in terms of the way in which the various partners of the joint venture interrelate. While long-term joint ventures are possible, alternatives are usually more feasible.

Consortium. A consortium is, by and large, a flexible, long-term joint venture. Several firms, usually four or more, come together to form a new, separate firm, which has no technical capabilities per se. If work is obtained, a design team is assembled utilizing manpower as appropriate from each of the consortium members. This approach often is used by several smaller firms looking for work in other nations.

As your next step, list, for each change under consideration, the specific methodology that could be used to effect the change. By specific, we mean to name names wherever possible, such as "joint venture with XYZ Engineers" or "hire an experienced mechanical engineer," or "merge with XYZ Interior Design," etc.

Use a Change Methodology Evaluation Form, similar to that shown in Figure 19. List each specific change methodology across the top with the general changes (from Figures 17 and 18) listed down the vertical axis. Determine to what degree (0 to 10) each specific change methodology would help attain the specific change in question. Pay special attention to those change methodologies that have impact on more than one change. Through careful review of this form, you should be able to infer which particular change methodologies will have the greatest positive impact on specific changes and, in turn, which changes will have the greatest impact on the firm.

Obviously, some change methodologies will have far more impact than others. If you are considering entry into mechanical engineering, for example, "hiring a mechanical engineer" will not rate nearly as high as "buy out an existing mechanical engineering firm." Unfortunately, buying out a mechanical engineering firm in most cases is far easier said than done. Other problems aside (such as finding just the right firm), one must consider the financial aspects, which, in the final analysis, usually comprise the major problem.

CHANGE METHODOLOGY EVALUATION FORM

	Change Methodologies						
Changes (new services and/or disciplines)	A	B	C	D	E	F	G

Figure 19. Change Methodology Evaluation Form.

To begin the process of determining which changes are best and most practical for the firm, start by determining what the cost of the various changes would be. In most cases, costs can be broken into three categories:

venture capital,
physical modifications, and
payroll.

Venture capital is that amount of money required to initiate the change, that is, the amount of money required to buy an existing firm or effect a merger, etc. One also must consider other costs related to establishing a new venture, such as new promotional materials required, new stationery, publicity, etc. When a major move such as a buy-out is contemplated, these other costs are relatively minor. When a less dramatic venture is involved, such as joint venturing, these costs often are the only costs involved.

Costs of physical modification include any changes made to create additional space, whether through moving partitions or transferring to larger quarters. One also must consider the cost of any new equipment required, such as drafting tables, desks, typewriters, chairs, computer terminal, etc.

Payroll costs are those associated with having new staff members, including professionals, technicians, draftsmen, field personnel, secretaries, and so on. Don't make blue-sky estimates. Do a little research—just a few telephone calls often will do—to obtain realistic figures for estimating. Payroll costs also should include certain fringe costs as well, including those of health and life insurance, vacations, association dues, professional liability insurance, and so on.

Once you have evaluated the approximate costs of each change methodology, consider the ability of your firm to pay them. You may have to consider, among other things: amount of likely bad debts, amount of accounts payable, overall value of firm (needed primarily for merger purposes or as a basis for obtaining borrowed funds), likely increases in operating expenses during the next one or two years without change, amount of capital expense probably required in the next few years without change, and so on. In most cases the firm's accountants can help obtain data.

With cost and related information in hand, undertake the following steps.

Using your most recently completed year as the base (N), compute the gross billings of the firm for each MU. Do the same for each of the preceding four or five years. (See Figures 2 and 20.) Now assuming that the firm will alter its tactics somewhat to permit greatest penetration in those MUs that have the best future potential, indicate the MU-by-MU gross billings for the current year ($N + 1$) and the five subsequent years. Be realistic. While the firm probably will be able to make some alteration of its MU concentrations, a complete turnaround virtually overnight will be

MU	Year										
	$N-4$	$N-3$	$N-2$	$N-1$	N	$N+1$	$N+2$	$N+3$	$N+4$	$N+5$	$N+6$
Miscellaneous											
Total											

Figure 20. Form for use in recording past, current, and projected annual gross receipts of the firm on a per MU source basis.

impossible. Recognize, too, that the firm will probably have to lay out some funds for certain other activities covered later in this book, which must be borne in mind now.

Based on what you have prepared, and considering the firm's current financial condition, the amount of money required to carry it through slow periods, funds required to fuel promotional and other efforts, and so on, plus the amount of time required to bring the firm into a solid position (as through organizing for a marketing approach and promotional activity), consider when the first affordable, relatively high ranking change methodology can be implemented. Recognize that the particular methodology chosen need not be the best way to achieve the change. It is the best way for the money available. It could be considered the first step toward the long-term attainment of change, therefore, or it may be—as through merger—the making of a major change overnight. Obviously, we have now gotten completely out of the realm of daydreaming. We are completely serious about these changes, and they will become part of the overall organizational plan.

Review carefully what you have done. Is the change selected the best one for the funds that probably will be available? Will the firm be in a position to support the change at the time it is made? Could you have made a less significant change earlier? All these factors must be considered. Use trial and error, and do not be afraid to discuss the process through meetings. Nor should you limit yourself to one change or one change methodology. Are there several changes that could be made? (This may require your going back through change analysis. The combination of two changes actually is a new change in and of itself.)

Assuming, therefore, that you can achieve a target date by which a given change will be made, recompute estimates of MU-by-MU gross billings by virtue of previous evaluations that show how given changes will affect MUs and how specific change methodologies affect the changes. Be certain to consider the amount of business an addition may bring with it. For example, if you merge with an existing firm it will not only enable your firm to expand activities and gross billings in the MUs affected, but will also bring the gross billings for work being undertaken by the firm involved. When talking about adding just one or two individuals to staff, it is best to assume that little new business will be brought along, unless you have specific reason to assume otherwise.

Given the changed figures following implementation of a change methodology, when should the next change methodology be implemented? Is another one really needed? Could it be made optional? Will the change made be enough to get the firm on course in terms of its having the most potential? In other words, examine carefully when which changes should and could be implemented from now through the period five years hence.

Above all, do not commit yourself to change too soon. For change to be accommodated the firm must be prepared for it and market conditions must be able to support it. For this reason we suggest that you allow yourself at least six months and perhaps a year to get all your ducks in a row so that the changes made will be, to an extent, a natural outgrowth of activities you have undertaken for the six months or year previous. Of course, if market conditions are such that you simply cannot afford to wait that long, do your best to meet immediate needs immediately, and—assuming that immediate change does tide you over—continue to develop your marketing plan in a manner that allows for flexibility and control.

4.3 PREPARING THE PRELIMINARY PLAN

To this point you have identified those MUs you want to penetrate or penetrate further, and what changes to the organization must be accomplished to make the changes. You now have the ability to put assumed data on paper, and there are several reasons for doing this.

First, creating the plan by necessity forces you to think through many of the items that may be covered in numerous different notes or may be entrusted to memory alone. By having data on paper you can analyze them carefully to ensure that everything jibes. If errors or omissions have been made, they can be corrected easily.

Second, the plan itself generally includes comprehensive planning notes for the first and second year into the future, with less and less detail for subsequent years. The basic framework for latter years gives you something to build upon when the time comes.

Third, having the written plan enables you to monitor progress. You can determine what actions that were supposed to have been taken were actually taken and compare actual results of actions with those forecast. Likewise, it enables you to make changes in subsequent actions planned for when circumstances dictate, and so see how those changes interrelate with other plans and so suggest their change as well.

Company goals already have been established. The objectives required to achieve these goals also have been established, to an extent, by identifying the degree to which emphasis is going to be placed on various MUs.

Strategies required to implement objectives relate primarily to changes that will be made in the structure of the firm and various overall promotional techniques to be applied.

Tactics required to implement the various strategies relate to specific change methodologies to be employed, as well as specific promotional techniques that will be used.

Although we still have not covered promotional strategies and techniques, we still can create a basic marketing plan, that is, one devoid of promotional considerations.

One of the easiest ways in which to undertake creation of the plan is to list the various MUs in which you are now involved and those you intend to become involved in during the next five years down the left hand margin of a page and, across the top, years reflecting the fiscal year most recently ended, the current, uncompleted year, and each of the following five years. It may be necessary (or easiest) to use a large chart page or something similar.

A typical preliminary plan is shown in Figure 21, developed for a hypothetical mechanical/electrical consulting engineering firm, which relies primarily on architects for work.

For the purposes of discussion here, the plan was made relatively simple and somewhat optimistic. Nonetheless, it will serve to indicate what a plan itself can show.

Data shown for the year 1975 represent gross billings for the full fiscal year. Those for 1976 are estimates of year-end billings for the year currently in progress. Subsequent years reflect the results of marketing research, goal identifications, change analysis, and so on.

In overview, it can be seen that the goal of the plan is rapid expansion within the five-year period to be capped by conversion to A-E in 1981. Since the firm now depends primarily on architectural references, and because conversion to A-E likely will jeopardize relationships with architect clients, the firm's plan shows that the growth required to merit conversion comes about in areas that:

are logical outgrowths of services already offered;

do not jeopardize relationships with architect clients (in fact, enable architects to give interprofessional consultants an even larger volume of work), and

are centered in areas that permit development of contact directly with the owner. As such, when the firm converts to A-E (preferably through merger to enable pick-up of current clients) it will have an existing clientele to which it can propose services immediately. (This also assumes that the firm's ethics are such that, subsequent to conversion, it would not approach its indirect clients.)

Examination of the plan in some detail indicates that it perhaps is more subtle than initial appearances indicate.

The MUs in which the firm is active at present include: institutional/ secondary schools; institutional/colleges (and presumably government/ secondary schools and government/colleges); commercial/high-rise; government/high-rise; commercial/stores; commercial/malls, and residential/ high-rise.

MU	1975	1976	1977	1978	1979	1980	1981
Gov/Sec Schs	60,000	65,000	90,000	110,000	155,000	220,000	275,000
Gov/Colls	80,000	20,000	50,000	80,000	180,000	250,000	350,000
Inst/Relig	40,000	30,000	60,000	40,000			
Comrcl/Hi-Rise	150,000	175,000	280,000	365,000	365,000	500,000	450,000
Gov/Hi-Rise	50,000	75,000	110,000	140,000	200,000	220,000	300,000
Comrcl/Stores	20,000	15,000	65,000	90,000	125,000	175,000	175,000
Comrcl/Malls	30,000	10,000	40,000	125,000	160,000	160,000	175,000
Res/Hi-Rise	190,000	80,000	175,000	350,000	375,000	150,000	425,000
Comrcl/Warehouses			10,000	50,000	65,000	75,000	90,000
Comrcl/Prkg Facils			10,000	50,000	65,000	80,000	80,000
Comrcl/Airport Hangars				50,000	70,000	75,000	80,000
Comrcl/Airport Terminals					50,000	80,000	110,000
Comrcl/Stadia					50,000	90,000	80,000
Gov/N.C. Studies					25,000	50,000	40,000
		Changes	*Changes*	*Changes*	*Changes*	*Changes*	*Changes*
		Add strct. P. E. and two strct. d-men in September	Expand struct. component by June-2 designers (equit. position for P. E.?) add inspection as service by July. Add inspector by November.	Add acoust cons. component in July consider branches in four areas	Open branch (affil); staff up	Open second branch and staff; add CM	Merge w/arch firm in March

Figure 21. Preliminary marketing plan for mechanical electrical consulting engineering firm.

From the looks of things, the firm's GMA probably is mostly white collar and light industrial. Commercial/high-rise office buildings, government/high-rise office buildings and residential/high-rise construction seem to predominate.

In order to obtain a large percentage of the design dollar, the firm's first major management tactic is to add structural engineering capabilities. Impacts of the recession are considered in estimates for year-end 1976 gross billings. A substantial portion of billings probably is envisioned for near the end of the year to justify addition of a structural engineering component (through addition of personnel) near year's end.

The various MUs are forecast for expansion in 1977. By that time, the firm believes, its three key MUs will have expanded and it will be taking a relatively larger share of the design dollar through sales of its structural design services. Because of anticipated activity in the high-rise construction MUs, the firm believes that further expansion of the structural department will be required in 1977, so much so, that two more designers will be needed. (Expansion of established service departments is not indicated, but will occur.) To retain a top structural PE, it also is recognized that a piece of the business may have to be made available. It is anticipated, further, that structural capabilities will enable design (probably complete, including limited architectural requirements) to obtain design assignments in the commercial/warehouse and commercial/parking facilities MUs. Initial assignments obtainable during the year are relatively few, it is assumed, until a track record can be established. Nonetheless, it does provide direct contact and contracts with owners.

The firm also anticipates some expansion into construction inspection during late 1977. Since construction inspection primarily is an outgrowth of structural engineering, chances are the head of the structural department would be in charge, thus indicating another reason why he would be offered a principalship. Note, too, that construction inspection does not have to be limited to the firm's own projects, although performing the service for the firm's projects does, of course, foster easy entry into the field. Its expansion in the subsequent year will permit still more direct contact with owners, again, without stepping on architects' toes.

The year 1978, by and large, comprises a holding-pattern period, which enables the firm to soldify its rapid growth during the previous two years. Although the various MUs are expected to increase that year, the bulk of the firm's increased revenues will come primarily from its new services, not from a rapid increase in GMA construction activity. It also is anticipated that, during 1978, the commercial/airport hangars MU will be penetrated, probably due to an anticipated contract with the local airport, which, by that time, would need expansion. (By that time the firm will have become well acquainted with the various area government capital improvements planners, project, and contract officers.) Note, too, that 1978 represents the last year that the firm intends to maintain involvement in the institutional/religious facilities MU which, its organizational analysis showed, simply was not profitable.

The only new service that the firm believes it will add in 1978 is acoustical consulting. This will further capabilities for college projects (for auditoria of various types, theaters, etc.), government high-rise buildings (which generally are treated far more for noise control than private counterparts), malls, and some residential/high-rise structures (especially condominiums). Study of four possible areas for branching will be made in 1978 as, it would be expected, the size of the firm probably will then be at a maximum in light of what GMA business can sustain.

Expanding the various service categories and adding new ones will enable the firm to take substantial portions of the GMA's design dollar volume. By 1979, however, only the government and institutional MUs will continue to grow without let-up. The various commercial MUs will have started to slow down. What growth exists will be supplied primarily through expanded services. It is at this time that the firm believes the opening of a branch will be required, primarily to provide services to an area outside HQ-GMA. In this way the firm can bring in more business that, in part at least, will keep the headquarters staff busy. The branch will be created ideally through affiliation, that is, establishing (or perhaps buying out) a firm that would bear the same name (essentially) as the parent firm, but that would be owned only partially (probably in the majority) by the parent company. It is forecast that the firm in 1979 will be able to get the assignment for a relatively major airport terminal, primarily through its work in designing hangars, and its abilities in acoustical consulting, construction inspection, and so on.

Having the branch office and, by now, a fairly wide array of services and client types leads the firm to believe that 1980 will be a "banner" year. To support and sustain growth, the firm plans to add an additional branch during the year and to enter into the burgeoning field of construction management. The shift into this field probably will be relatively easy, especially after several years experience in structural engineering, construction inspection, and related endeavors. Having assignments such as warehouse and parking facilities also will enable the firm to get its feet wet with relatively small projects. It also will bring the firm additional direct contact with owners, and in a meaningful way.

The firm intends to go A-E in March 1981. The move itself will be accompanied by a drop in certain MUs due to loss of some (if not most) architectural clients. It should cause a spurt, particularly in the design of malls, of large projects to which all its services can be applied.

The above hardly contains all the observations that could be made based on the plan. However, it is sufficient to indicate what the plan encompasses.

Recognize that the plan should be reviewed at least annually, preferably every six months, and perhaps as frequently as quarterly. Any time that it appears an estimate is substantially off, the plan can be changed. Accordingly, by the time 1981 docs roll around, the firm may be off on an entirely different tangent. If major changes are required, however, they can be planned easily. Naturally, whenever plans do not materialize, some analysis of why not should be made.

In general, it should be noted that the firm will be expanding its project mix, services mix, and client mix. In so doing, should there be a recession in 1980, the firm will have the ability to retrench significantly—primarily into the most active MUs remaining. While its size compared to what was envisioned will be stunted, it will still be a substantial firm. Firms that depend primarily on one kind of client and a relatively narrow project mix usually are those hit hardest when times get rough.

Note, too, that the plan shown represents summary data only. For the first two future years, at least, specific items such as month-by-month business projections can be made. Also, MUs can be amplified greatly. For example, service segment elements can be added, so that residential/multifamily/high-rise/new and residential/multifamily high-rise/conversion-to-condo become two separate MUs. Energy conservation projects also could be set off from others, and so it goes. The more specific the planning is, the easier it will be to determine how the firm is doing and, if its progress does not match projections, where deviations occurred and why.

Remember, too, that this plan does not take promotional activities into consideration, and the general and specific tactics that can be planned on an annual and monthly basis. How to add such elements to the plan is discussed in the last section of Chapter 7.

As a last observation, note that the preliminary marketing plan also can be used as a goal plan. In other words, if it is projected that gross annual receipts from a given MU will be $100,000, the $100,000 figure could become a goal for which the firm and its sales personnel will strive.

If you do envision taking this approach, we advise strongly that you develop a separate plan to be used solely for the purpose of establishing company sales goals. This second plan would be essentially similar to the first with the exception that there would be, for each MU each year, three goals rather than one. The first would be the *minimally acceptable goal*, say 90% of forecast sales. The second would be the *desirable goal*, approximately 110 to 120% of forecast sales. The third would be the *optimum goal* of 180% of forecast sales.

The purpose behind this approach is relatively straightforward.

It is exceptionally doubtful that a sole sales goal will be achieved. While it must be realistic, it never can take into consideration all the eventualities that might occur. Set it too low and, once it becomes apparent that it will be achieved, there will be a let-down. Set it too high and, once it is viewed as impossible, no one will take it seriously. Contrast this with what happens with three sets of goals.

Sales personnel obviously will want to strive for the optimum goal, which will be very difficult to achieve. The minimally acceptable goal should be achieved but, as stated, it is the one minimally acceptable. Thus, if every effort is made and that is the best that can be done, so be it. The achievement was acceptable. If, however, this goal is surpassed during the year, there is another to strive for. And if for some reason that one also is surpassed, still another remains. In other words, having three distinct sales goals for an MU rather than just one overcomes the problems associated with setting a goal too high or too low, something that occurs almost always and can be ascertained only through hindsight.

MARKETING ORGANIZATION

The costs involved in making change must reflect the costs involved in re-organizing, which in many cases will be required even without change. This section, then, has two purposes.

First, it should be read to give you an overall idea of what may be required in terms of additional personnel even when no change in services or disciplines is needed.

Second, it should be read to indicate the procedures market planning requires once the basic five-year plan is developed.

When speaking in terms of marketing organization, we do not mean that office within the firm that has "Marketing" painted on the door.

Development of a marketing plan implies sensitivity to the needs of the client and the needs of the marketplace: needs that are always changing. While one can do his very best to predict what the changes will be from day-to-day or year-to-year, the changes are, in reality, largely unpredictable. All we can do, through diligent effort, is guess as accurately as we can and, when we are wrong, make adjustments as quickly as possible to stay in as advantageous a position as possible.

The ability to adjust and the degree of sensitivity required means that an organization—your organization—must be designed and developed in such a way that it will be as sensitive as possible to change and will be able to adjust quickly and well.

The organization mix shown in Figure 22 is not meant to imply an organizational chart and lines of authority. (If it did, we'd all be in trouble!) Rather, it is intended to show the interrelationships that should exist in

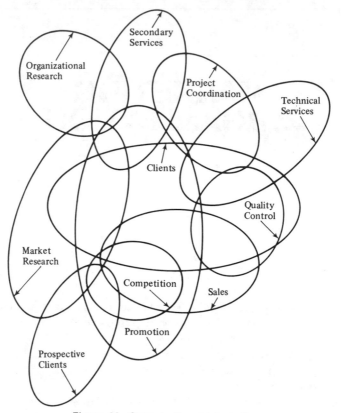

Figure 22. Organizational interaction.

a firm and show that, in fact, strict lines of authority do not have to exist. (More formalized charts will be shown later, so do not lose hope now.)

The chart is very complex, but analyzing it should help explain the way in which a firm should be organized.

Client

In the center of the chart are clients. Starting from the bottom and proceeding counterclockwise, we see that the client is affected by *business promotion*. The fact that a given person or organization is a client often is used in promotion. In many cases the client himself likes to know that the firm with which he is dealing is active and becoming better known.

The client also is affected by *sales and sales staff*. These are the people, often including principals, who are responsible for being the account executives. This does not mean that an account executive is the project manager.

He is not. Rather, he maintains contact with the client or his representatives throughout the course of a project to make sure the client is satisfied. To an extent, the account executive acts as an ombudsman for the client in the firm. Only by helping ensure satisfaction can a firm be somewhat assured that it will obtain repeat business, perhaps the most important business of all.

The client also is affected by *quality control*. In fact, quality control is essential within a firm. Without it there is too great a chance for error; error breeds dissatisfaction; dissatisfaction can mean loss of a client and loss of reputation, both of which are essentials.

The client, of course, is influenced by *technical services*, meaning such of the actual design work performed. *Project coordination* is involved as well, ensuring that the design team assembled for a given project is the one most suited. *Secondary services* interact with the client in terms of special services he may need, which the firm may have available. For example, there may be a need to perform an economic feasibility report or some other similar function. *Market research* bears on clients because, as noted earlier, what clients have planned for the future can shape the future development of the firm to a large extent.

The client also is affected, last but hardly least, by the *competition*. In fact, a firm must always look over its shoulder and keep in mind what the competition is doing. Its new programs or new developments may very well be geared expressly to offer a service package that the client you now have may be unable to refuse, unless you have something equally good or better. In other words, competition should act not only as a threat, but also as an incentive to offer services to a client in a way that would make his seeking similar services from another firm a waste of time.

Obviously, clients are those interacted with most; nor is the full extent of the interaction explained by the above. The other elements and the way way they interrelate and the reasons for the interrelationships also bear explanation.

Sales

Turning now to *sales*, we see that account (or sales) executives interact with *clients*. They bring clients in and, we all hope, keep them in. The sales staff also interacts with *quality control*, however. This is so because quality control is so important to the successful outcome of a project. While a sales executive is not necessarily responsible for the way in which quality control works, he should be involved at least to the extent required to ensure that it is operational and that all technical services, without exception, are reviewed carefully and closely.

Sales staff also interact with *market research*. Obviously they receive information from market research that provides indications of what kinds of business to look for, who in particular to see, etc. By the same token, sales executives should be in continuing touch with those in market research to relay information that may have picked up from meeting with individuals, attending conventions and association get-togethers, and so on. Also, those in the sales department (some of you may not like that term, but it is applicable) frequently are the ones in the firm who have the most "universal" view of the marketplace, client needs, new developments, and so on. Thus, they are the ones most capable of working with market research staffers to distill and extract information from market intelligence received.

Sales are also affected by the *competition*. The more aggressive the competition, the more difficult it is to make a sale. Sales executives also are in a position to learn about the competition from conversations with prospective clients and through direct dealings with the competition at various organizational meetings, etc. (We remark on one characteristic of the design professions based on our experience. Seldom is the relationship between competitors more cordial, more ethical, and more understanding. While it is to be expected that competitors want to know what the other guys are up to, in many instances each will tell the other and in some cases will offer help to one another in making their operations more efficient. The very fact that the various organizations of design professionals have been able to make such significant contributions to the design professions and to the nation, in fact to the world, stands in silent but eloquent testimony to the fact that competitors can cooperate to further the goals of their peers and to help protect the public welfare.)

Sales staff interacts with *prospective clients*, obviously, which in many cases should result in turning these prospects into clients. The fruit of this relationship, besides obtaining business, is the acquisition of more information that can be fed to market research. Last, sales staff interrelates with *promotion* and helps provide direction on what specific types of promotion are needed. As will be seen later, the promotion element of a firm also will help sales staff prepare specialized materials, such as proposals.

Quality Control

We see *quality control* next. Its relationship with *sales* already has been explained, and its relationship to *clients* should be well known. It is also essential in the field of *promotion*. Unless you have a good product, no amount of promotion in the world is going to keep you in business. When one promotes, even using strictly a low-key approach, he is, in essence, telling others how good he is. Unless you actually are good, promotion is a waste of time and, to an extent, it perpetuates a falsehood. Thus, quality control is essential to promotion, just as promotion is essential to quality control. (Without promotion there is little business; without business there is no design, and, thus, no need for quality control.) Later in this chapter we devote more attention to quality control because, when growth is involved, it is something that sometimes falls by the wayside. Typically, when a firm is small or relatively small, one of the principals will make quality control a personal responsibility. As growth forces him to divert attention elsewhere, he no longer can make the previous effort. By the time he does return to it, the volume of work is such that he cannot do it all. It is an admitted fact that when a principal is not directly involved in quality control of all projects it is likely that the quality will slip a bit, which only reflects human nature. But establishing a flexible, effective and rigorous quality control procedure can help offset the slight decline to a significant degree. In some cases it can actually elevate quality control above previous levels.

Quality control also is involved with *technical services* and *project coordination*. In fact, project coordination is an element of quality control. If you can assign to a given project a team of individuals whose capabilities, training, and experience are such that they are most suited to the project at hand, half the battle already is won.

Technical Services/Project Coordination

Technical services and project coordination have been explained. They both affect one another and in turn are affected by quality control. They also have an impact upon *promotion*. In fact, the better your services, the tighter your quality control, and the more promotion will take care of itself.

Secondary Services

We now come to secondary services. As touched upon earlier, these services include development of feasibility reports, economic studies, research of zoning laws that may affect the client, developing information on governmental programs, providing assistance in floating bond issues, etc. In many cases, the persons who perform this work are the selfsame persons entrusted with elements of organizational research, market research, and associated functions. If they're good enough to develop plans for your own organization, they certainly should be qualified to perform some services for clients.

Secondary services obviously are a part of *project coordination*. In fact, several larger and well-known firms have secondary service personnel sit in on all project development meetings to ensure that no stones are left unturned. In this way a secondary services specialist may suggest that perhaps part of the project could be paid for through grant monies, or perhaps that recent zoning developments may have an effect and, accordingly, that a basic set of plans should be developed immediately to take advantage of a zoning requirement that is about to be changed. In many cases, therefore, secondary services can have valuable input that not only can make the project run smoother, but can provide services that are of significant value to the firm and the client.

As mentioned, secondary services people are also involved in *organizational research* and *market research*. They not only can provide input, but, at the very least, they will be able to obtain information from these departments that can prove of value to the client and to the promotional effort.

Organizational Research

Still moving in a counterclockwise direction, we come to organizational research, which encompasses functions of office management, accounting, and so on, all of which lead to development of information about the status of the firm, much as was discussed under the basic organizational research section earlier in this book. The information developed obviously has bearing upon *secondary services* in terms of its interrelationship with *marketing research*. Organizational research also has a direct bearing upon the promotional effort. It provides information on the firm's developing capabilities, staff, volume of work, and so on, much of which is essential to promotion.

Marketing Research

Marketing research relates to *secondary services, organizational research, clients, sales staff, promotion, competition,* and *prospective clients.* It receives input from, and provides output to, *secondary services.* It receives output from *organizational research* in that it can take cues from the firm's capabilities in giving an extra amount of effort in those spheres of activity in the marketplace in which the firm, because of its make-up, most obviously is interested.

Market research involves *clients* because an effort must be made to determine what the client sees for the future, not only in terms of his own plans, but in terms of other MUs, the GMA, and the market itself. In some cases market research also will result in input to clients—through nontechnical services—by providing information useful to them.

Market research interacts with *promotion,* obviously, because it provides information on where the promotional effort should be directed and what particular aspects of the firm's activities (information gained from *organizational research*) should be stressed most. By the same token, market research interacts with *sales staff* and can provide them with insight on what approximations may be best in light of a given prospect's needs, or in light of generally developing trends. Likewise, of course, sales personnel are in a position to provide input to market research.

Market research relates to the *competition* because the competition is a very important part of the market. Accordingly, it is the responsibility of market research to learn as much about the competition as possible. Of course, market research also has an impact upon *prospective clients* in terms of the information provided to others in the firm who have impact upon prospects, as well as by identifying who the prospects are, what plans they have for the future, etc.

Competition

The competition, as already discussed, is a vital element of the overall organization. It is a concern of *market research* in that it affects advice developed for the future of the firm. Competition affects *clients* and especially *prospective clients*, as well as sales strategy and *promotional activities*. In other words, while clients and the competition cannot be shown on any organization chart, they are very much a part of the firm and have a substantial effect on what it does and what it plans to do.

Prospective Clients

Prospective clients come next. They are most affected by the competition because in most cases they are the competition's clients. It is up to *market research* to determine who the prospective clients are, what their needs are, and what they plan to do. It is also up to market research to help identify why a prospective client is someone else's client and not a client of the firm. From the information dervied by market research, sales strategies are planned. This includes both sales executives and those in charge of promotion.

Promotion

Next on the list, and already covered in depth, is *promotion*, yet to be explained in this book so still perhaps a dirty word to some readers. As can be seen, promotion becomes the infrastructure of the organization and is influenced by every other element of concern, which is the way it should be. Promotion cannot be used unless those involved in it know what is happening in all parts of the firm. Thus, promotional activity takes into consideration the needs of *sales executives* and the support they require; the *clients* being provided with service; the *quality control* so essential to producing a good product without which promotion is useless; the *technical services* that form the heart of the firm's ability to tackle a given design project; *project coordination*, so important to *quality control* and performing work swiftly and well; *secondary services*, which can help influence promotional strategies through insights into the market; *organizational research*, which develops much of the data used as promotional ammunition; *clients* who can be brought in at least partially through promotion, and whom promotion must consider in an effort to maintain ongoing programs to help ensure client retention; *marketing research*, which is essential for a well-directed promotional effort so the right thing is promoted to the right public in the right medium at the right time; the *competition* who will be watching the progress of your firm on the basis of your promotional efforts; and *prospective clients* who, to a significant degree, are the targets at which promotional guns are aimed.

Not shown is *planning*. In fact, planning should be visualized as a diaphanous overlay that takes everything into consideration. Planning should permeate the entire organization, not as a tool to stall action when it is needed immediately, but rather as a device to develop a picture of the future and from that to establish the specific goals, objectives, strategies, and tactics that can be used to help ensure the company a successful tomorrow. Planning should be such that, when changes occur, plans are changed accordingly so tomorrow cannot take the firm by surprise. And if immediate actions are required, decisions can be made immediately in light of plans for the present laid out months in advance and kept current through continuing review.

If yours is a smaller firm you probably have read through this section rather lightly feeling that the discussion was not meant for you. If so, you have some rereading to do. The structure involved applies to the one-man operation just as it applies to a 1,000-man operation. In fact, it's easier for one man because he probably is undertaking all these operations without thinking about their interrelationships. Yes: the graphic shown in Figure 22 could apply to a large firm with numerous departments, but the chart primarily is task-oriented in nature, showing how different functions interrelate with one another. Thus, it is applicable to large and small firms alike.

5.1   DEPARTMENTAL ORGANIZATION

Obviously, the lines of communication and organization of the firm itself cannot be shown as in Figure 22. Just as obviously, the interrelationships illustrated by the figure, which should exist in fact, cannot be shown by any typical organizational chart. For this reason we are providing only a division-by-division chart. The interrelationships that must exist between these divisions, departments, offices, and so on, can be shown through copy that spells out specifically who should be communicating with whom, reinforced through clearly written and defined job descriptions. Recognize, of course, that if one person holds down more than one position, a job description should be prepared for each position to ensure that the organization is function-oriented. To design organizational relationships on the basis of persons who may be on staff can result in organizational changes each time a personnel change occurs. In addition, realize that the following material comprises a suggested model. If it is acceptable for use in your firm, fine. If not, use it as a taking-off point for designing your own chart.

Division of Client Operations

The Division of Client Operations (Figure 23) is that group within the firm concerned primarily with preparing the product for the client. The Director of Client Operations, who should be a principal of the firm, has direct responsibility for four functions: project coordination, quality control, secondary services, and technical services. In the event that one individual is assigned several functions at once, be certain that he is not another's superior in one function and his subordinate in the other.

Department of Project Coordination

The Director of Project Coordination has two primary responsibilities.

First, he must be able to inform sales staff about the availability of qualified personnel to undertake a proposed project within a given period of time. Admittedly, this particular function can become somewhat difficult if several projects are being sought at the same time. Nonetheless, by at least having information on "what happens if," the necessary activities are far easier to undertake when some of these "ifs" turn into actualities.

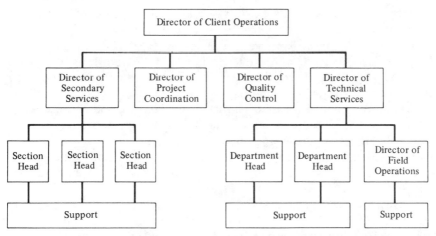

Figure 23. Organizational chart for Division of Client Operations.

Second, the Director of Project Coordination must be able to review a project, determine what is required, and delineate a precise schedule for various operations to take place. As conceived here, the Director of Project Coordination would also be involved in quality control to the extent that he would be responsible for organizing the technical team. However, if secondary services are required, the Director of Project Coordination also would have to schedule these services to coordinate the entire project.

The Director of Project Coordination in most cases will work with a Project Coordination Team, which provides more insight into each of the various operations that contract performance requires. This does not mean that the team should be limited to those whose services would be needed according to the client's specifications. Rather, each project should be reviewed from many different aspects if only to ensure that nothing has been overlooked. For example, would the client be eligible to obtain grant monies if certain changes were made? Would it be worth it to the client? Only direct contact can obtain the answer. Even if the client does not want to make the change, he cannot help but be impressed by the thoroughness of the firm, especially if the suggestion comes about as a part of a proposal.

Through general review of the project the Director will be able to establish a schedule that shows what tasks the specific project entails, how these tasks interrelate, and the order in which they must be performed. From this will stem the specific scheduling and, from development of a schedule, a monitoring process to help ensure that things get done correctly, within budget, and on time.

Department of Quality Control

The Director of Quality Control has the important responsibility of seeing to it that each project meets the firm's standards of quality. Positive impact on liability aside, quality control helps ensure that each design is "up to snuff" and that smaller fees mean less work involved, not less quality. The Directors of Quality Control and Project Coordination must determine, based on experience, where the interface of functions or tasks requires special care to avoid quality drop-offs.

Because quality control is so important to the firm, and because its implementation may cause or aggravate certain interpersonal relationships within the firm, the person who directs the operation must have an authoritative position, must see to it that all subordinates understand the need for quality control, and must be sure that actions related to quality control take on as few personal overtones as possible.

Because quality control is so important to the marketing function, every effort should be made to ensure that those persons who are involved in it are fully familiar with the way it should work. While the following guidelines should be reviewed and followed, they hardly can suffice. Published materials on the subjects should be read; worthwhile seminars should be attended; group discussions on quality control should be held. Both the growing problems of professional liability and the development of aggressive competition demand that a firm strive to maintain the highest quality service possible.

While in most cases quality control will concern itself with technical services, whose quality is relatively easy to determine, there is no reason why quality control cannot also be applied to secondary services. In such an instance, however, quality responsibility should rest with the Director of Secondary Services.

Note that the following items relating to quality control go beyond the specific responsibilities of the Director of Quality Control. Nonetheless, it is his responsibility to ensure that others do their jobs correctly.

1. Place Basic Agreements in Writing. For a variety of reasons, insurance liability among them, do not entrust basic understandings and agreements to memory. Put them in writing. There are some long-time clients with whom you probably have worked on a handshake basis, but that really isn't the point. What we're talking about is not a matter of personal trust; we're talking about communication. In other words, while a handshake agreement may work instead of a contract, only by having understandings in writing can you be sure that you both are shaking on the same terms.

Basic written agreements should discuss, among other things: general terms of business; services required and quality; reporting times; delivery dates; fee and payment dates; mutual responsibilities, and related items.

2. Prepare Concise Instructions. Turn the client's specifications into written instructions for your design department. Again, do not trust word of mouth or memory. Write down exactly what is required so there are no misunderstandings.

3. Project Coordination. Assign personnel, preferably on a team basis. The project manager or team captain must not only be technically competent, he also must have the ability to motivate, through techniques of interpersonal communication, those who will be working under him. Those most capable of handling individual aspects of a project should be assigned to the team. Where necessary, train personnel, hire additional manpower, or use an associate when current in-house capabilities will not suffice.

4. Confirm Understanding of Instructions. Meet with the entire team assigned to the project to ensure that everyone is fully aware of what instructions mean and who has responsibility for what. Where advisable, prepare additional instructions on an individual basis.

5. Provide Necessary Equipment, Materials, and Facilities. Be sure that the necessary tools, materials, and work space are available to enable the team involved with the project to function smoothly.

6. Plan the Project. The project manager and the chief designer must begin immediately to plan the project's progress on a step-by-step basis, selecting the exact work methods to be used as well as alternatives. Time-cost and production control factors must be considered before the best method is established and before actual work methods are specified. In this manner, problems associated with last-minute decisions should be avoided simply because last-minute decisions will be avoided. Also, planning will tend to minimize the necessity of overtime, which is not only costly, but usually inefficient. (Overtime work usually is more carelessly performed than that done during regular working hours, thus requiring even more time in the inspection process.)

7. Design with Quality in Mind. To design a system with quality in mind, the following steps, at least, should be taken:

a. develop design concepts based on client and/or end-user specifications;

b. prepare and evaluate alternative designs;

c. build models if necessary;

d. determine conformance with specifications and quality standards;

e. establish the preferred design concept and coordinate with other members of the in-house design team, as well as other designers involved with the project;

f. make necessary calculations;

g. perform value engineering analysis;

h. finalize design and prepare specifications;

i. prepare drawings and sketches for use by drafting personnel accompanied by precise, clear, written instructions, and

j. have plans reviewed by another firm member on the same level as the project manager or head of design. Reviewer should inspect plans in light of quality standards, reliability requirements, client specifications, and so on. Any problem areas should be discussed openly and frankly, but in a completely inoffensive manner.

8. Prepare Concise Specifications. Specifications must be written to provide prospective suppliers with a clear understanding of what is required to meet design criteria. Specifications should relate to, among other things: purpose, equipment, materials, system description, material procurements, method, workmanship, inspection, performance, control, installed system reliability, durability, dependability, guarantees, warranties, etc. When possible, products specified should be those that have been tested by the manufacturer under acceptable test conditions. A master-specifications-index approach is an excellent means to record and store specifications on magnetic tapes for computer usage. We also advise using the CSI standard specification format.

9. Establish Drafting Quality Norms. Quality norms should be established for drafting produced by the firm, with draftsmen being informed of criteria for accuracy and speed. All drawings should be checked prior to presentation to the clients for both accuracy and general quality, as well as performance time. Obviously, the better the quality of drafting, and the less time it takes to prepare it, the more likely the client will be satisfied, and at lowest possible cost.

10. Provide Information to User. The user of the end result of the project should be supplied with information vital to its smooth running. For example, he should be supplied with information regarding preventive and corrective equipment maintenance. Special effort should be made to provide as much assistance as possible during start-up.

11. Inspect Your Work. Work must be inspected when it is in the shop and in the field. In-house inspection requires inspection of the design work in progress. Before plans and specifications are released to the client, another member of your firm on the same level as the project manager or the design head should review all final drawings and specifications in light of written client specifications, design criteria, and drafting quality norms. He must not only ensure that the material developed represents the quality the firm wishes to be known for but, in the event it does not, must determine where the problems are occurring and why. Review findings should be placed in written form for general review at regular periods. Identification of areas of commonality will enable identification of persons or systems responsible for making things go right—or wrong.

Field inspection requires proper selection of the person(s) responsible for the job. Those selected must be experienced in field installation procedures, construction methods, and specification and design requirements. They must not make "quality trade-offs" to contractors responsible for installation of any portion of a specified system. Also, they must be instructed to report immediately any deviations from plans or specifications.

Establishing effective quality control, obviously, is not a simple matter. It takes time and a great deal of effort. Nonetheless, its establishment will boost your organization's efficiency, while also making the client happy.

Department of Secondary Services

The Director of Secondary Services is responsible for conducting secondary service operations required for a given job. This includes review of those factors that the client has not initially earmarked as requiring secondary services. In addition, the Director of Secondary Services usually is responsible for certain marketing operations, which already have been discussed. Again, recognize that while the person who directs secondary services may be the selfsame individual who directs marketing, or some other function, the functions themselves must be separated and considered in terms of functions, not people.

As shown, the Department of Secondary Services is broken into specific sections, each with a head, each drawing upon certain support personnel within the organization.

Department of Technical Services

The Department of Technical Services has been designed to facilitate the team concept in design, whereby resources are drawn from the different sections and offices involved to assemble a team that is competent for a given project. The team concept helps in scheduling and quality control; it enables appointment of a team captain who can maintain close liaison with the client and sales executive, and thus enables the firm to draw upon its many resources to relate to the client in a far more responsive manner. This is especially important for larger firms that often are accused, and too often rightly so, of being unresponsive to client needs because of an assembly line approach.

It should be noted that this configuration calls for the Director of Field Operations to be subordinate to the Director of Technical Services. This is so because, in many cases, field operations are used to support design functions. If, however, your firm is heavily involved in performing field work on its own, or in construction management, construction inspection, etc., to the extent that field operations are far more important, a modified relationship as shown in Figure 24(B) may be more appropriate. In the event that branch or similar operations are involved, the same organizational framework could be applied. In actually staffing the positions, however, it probably will be most economical to staff locally those positions that are used most commonly, with the more sophisticated positions being staffed by persons from headquarters operations or perhaps from some other satellite operation.

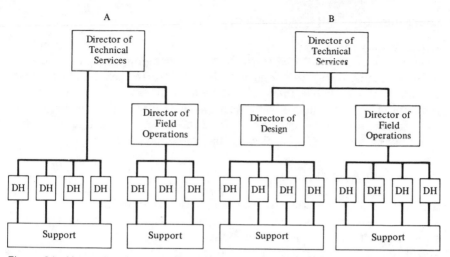

Figure 24. Alternative organizational charts for the Department of Technical Services.

Division of Organizational Services

The Division of Organizational Services is divided into two departments: office management and marketing. Marketing is a separate function, as shown in Figure 25.

Figure 25. Organizational chart for Division of Organizational Services.

Department of Office Management

Office Management comprises the personnel office, accounting, and related functions, as well as administrative services, including purchasing. This is a fairly routine department and requires little further explanation except to note that somewhere there should be an individual responsible for assembling data from these various sections and offices that can be utilized for organizational research. The information so developed figures directly into the marketing effort, as already discussed.

Department of Marketing

The Marketing Department has three basic components: marketing research, promotion, and sales. The departments of promotion and sales show support staff, primarily specialists in various editorial fields. These specialists can provide basic editorial needs, but, in most cases, outside consultants will be needed for more sophisticated undertakings or for those where an objective viewpoint is essential, if only for review purposes.

We already have discussed what marketing research entails, and we shortly will discuss in detail what promotion involves. However, some discussion should be given to sales executives, who also can be referred to as account executives, sales engineers, and so on. Few design firms would label these people salesmen although, like it or not, that is precisely what they are. Even if you are a sole practitioner, when you go out to call on a prospective client, no matter how many degrees follow your name; no matter how dignified or rarefied the service, you are selling it and so you are a salesman.

The person doing the contacting must be effective. In most cases, we are talking about a principal of the firm who typically has had no formal training in selling. If this is your situation, we advocate some sales training or at least reading on the subject.

If you are in a position where you are about to select someone from staff to act as a salesman, or bring someone new aboard, look for the following attributes:

1. *Education:* Depending on the kind of firm involved, the salesman should be a graduate engineer, land surveyor, interior designer, architect, etc., preferably with some practical experience.

2. *Adaptability/sensitivity:* The salesman must be sensitive enough to grasp quickly what the prospective client is looking for. In so doing, he must be able to adapt to the prospect and emphasize that part of his character that best relates to the prospect's.

3. *Appearance:* There are no set guidelines on appearance, except that the person should not be painful to look at. In terms of dress, precontact

research should indicate what is best to wear for any given sales call. In most cases, however, "middle-of-the-road" attire will be fine.

4. *Attitude:* A positive attitude is essential for any salesman. If a person is enthusiastic about what his company can do; if he relays this positive attitude, he in turn can engender enthusiasm in the prospect. If the positive attitude is lacking; if the enthusiasm is forged, then it will be seen for what it is—fake—and any chance of making a sale will be lost.

In many cases you will find that you have on staff certain persons who, with a little training, can make excellent salesmen of your firm's services. We also advocate that they act as continuing contacts with the client throughout and following a given project, serving to an extent as a client ombudsman.

In some cases you may wish to take on a specific kind of salesman to enter a certain MU, or even to attract a particular client. While this can work well, it often can have drawbacks if the goal is to present a false image. Remember, a salesman represents your firm. If the client's actual experience indicates that the firm itself is not at all as the salesman represented it to be, either explicitly or tacitly, it usually will work to your detriment.

In some cases the contact will *have* to be a certain person. For example, if the contact is made because a personal friend of the prospect suggested to a member of your firm that the prospect should be contacted, it would be best for that member to whom the suggestion was made, if possible, to pursue the contact. In this way, the contact can answer a question such as, "How long have you known our friend, Fred?" Even if the contact is not ideally suited, bear in mind that when it comes to time for a personal meeting, he can be accompanied by another member of the firm better suited to the job of selling.

Compensation of sales staff is something else that warrants at least brief discussion. In larger firms, sales personnel are often salaried (usually at a base $20 to 25,000) plus bonuses. The bonuses usually are somewhat problematical, especially when you consider that some projects may be brought in, at least partially, by other than salesmen. A relatively good approach to such bonusing, which also creates much-needed incentive, is to document how each new project or client was brought in, outlining who played what role. The memo or letter with the details should be sent to the head of the firm with copies to those mentioned. Then, at the end of the year (or perhaps somewhat more frequently), those who were involved in effective sales are given bonuses according to the degree of involvement and the value of projects.

Because you may not now have on staff people familiar with marketing and promotion, a few words of advice are offered here.

In selecting someone to head marketing functions, recognize that experience or even education as a design professional may not be that important. The structures of various businesses are much the same. The only major variable is the product involved. If the person knows anything about marketing at all, he can apply basic principles regardless of the product. If he makes errors due to lack of familiarity with certain technical problems, there should be enough technical experts on staff to review what he has to say and to provide a backstop. In the beginning, at least, it probably will be best to hire someone with at least a little experience in marketing, while also retaining a marketing consultant. As the staffer begins to come into his own, the consulting firm can be relied on less. In the case of smaller firms, a consultant can be used instead of a department head until such time as the size of the firm demands a change. Much the same is true for promotion. In almost all cases, however, it is wise to retain both a marketing consultant and a promotion consultant to provide objective points of view and a needed level of expertise for special assignments or problems.

The specific set-up of the Marketing Department should reflect the size of the firm. For relatively larger firms, an arrangement as shown in Figure 26 may be practical, where A, B, C, and D represent either geographical areas, types of MUs, or types of clients. In other words, if a geographical arrangement is desired, each sales manager would have his own "territory." If arrangement is on the basis of MUs, the territory would be defined by the types of MUs, such as industrial, commercial, etc. If type of clients is the nature of the division, one salesman would have responsibility for other design professionals, another for contractors, and so on. In any case, the A, B, C, D division should be consistent.

Very large organizations may be more amenable to the divisions shown in Figure 27. The major difference in this approach is that subdivisional

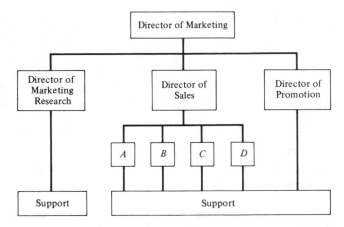

Figure 26. Alternative organizational chart for Department of Marketing.

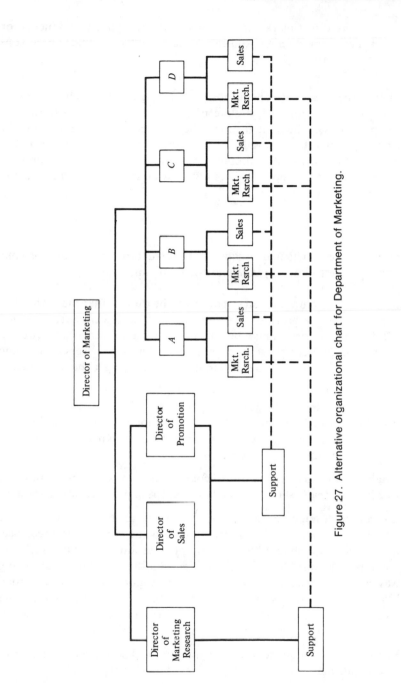

Figure 27. Alternative organizational chart for Department of Marketing.

heads have more direct marketing responsibility, and have components for specialized marketing research and sales, each of which would obtain support from headquarters.

Note. Large firms' satellite operations must be especially careful to ensure close coordination among all satellite personnel. In some cases branch or affiliate operations of the same firm may begin to compete with one another by submitting separate proposals on the same job. This obviously is not good for esprit de corps. More important, however, is the damage done to image. If a firm cannot coordinate its own sales efforts, how could one expect it to coordinate a project?

General

Regardless of what particular organizational structure you choose for your firm, consider the following guidelines for finalizing:

1. Base your structure on work that has to be done rather than what has been done in the past, or what your current staff is capable of doing. While every effort should be made to utilize current manpower to the maximum possible advantage, it simply may be necessary in some cases to replace certain staff members in order to get the job done.

2. Inventory all essential items of work required to reach goals. Identify those that are related for probable placement within the same organizational division. In most cases both supervision and individual job performance increase when work assigned requires skills and experience that are fundamentally similar.

3. Establish positions in relation to coordinative considerations. In other words, size of sales staff should relate to scope of production capabilities.

4. Use care in developing managerial staff functions. First, there should be an adequate number of supervisors to provide control required. Second, an attempt should be made to optimize supervisory talent. If too few report to one supervisor, his talent and his capabilities are being wasted. Too many reporting to any one supervisor will overburden him. Third, be precise when differentiating supervisory work from more production-oriented work. In most cases, when the two kinds of assignments are given to one individual, the supervisory tasks suffer.

5. Keep layers of bureaucracy to a minimum. The longer the chain of command, the more frustrating the work experience can be.

6. Determine the degree of responsibility, authority, and accountability incumbent upon each position, bearing in mind that the three must be in harmony if the position is to be kept filled. For example, one can expect only frustration if authority does not accompany responsibility or accountability in the proportions adequate to get the job done. Accountability, in particular, should be stressed, in order to develop and elevate personnel on the basis of performance criteria.

7. Indicate inter- and intradepartmental relationships required to facilitate communication, integration and maximization of effort, team work, and decision-making.

8. Establish a basis for sound short- and long-range planning to overcome the usually greater emphasis placed on day-to-day problems and deadlines.

6

PERSONNEL RELATIONS

While it may seem out of keeping to devote any substantial amount of time to personnel relations, we feel the subject is worthy of coverage here for two essential reasons, one philosophical, the other practical.

First, marketing depends extensively on the firm's capabilities and the firm's capabilities depend on those of its personnel. Because effective personnel relations help create open communication, team spirit, and loyalty, it is essential to keep those you want to keep, and so it becomes a marketing concern. Further, effective personnel relations can boost productivity and so help achieve organizational goals, while also assisting in transition as changes are being instituted within the firm.

Second, experience shows that many consulting engineers and architects have little awareness of what effective personnel policies are all about; consequently, they need as much basic guidance as possible.

Realize that this chapter is a capsulized discussion of a major concern. It is intended only to highlight some of the key elements of effective personnel relations. We hope it will inspire you to research the subject in greater depth and to institute programs and procedures to ensure that the capabilities that fuel the marketing program are there when you need them.

6.1 COMMUNICATIONS PROGRAMS

The most prevalent problems in personnel relations result from improper or inadequate in-house communication. Consider the following methodologies for improving communications.

Policy Handbook

Your firm is one of the most important elements of an employee's life. The satisfaction an employee derives from his work is a major determinant of the satisfaction he derives from life itself. How much you pay determines how well he lives. The promise you provide for the future helps determine the way he conducts himself each day, striving to turn promise into reality.

While many subjects will be covered during an orientation to the firm, others will not be. Even those that are explained frequently fall victim to quirks of memory. Too often important questions such as "What do you have to do around here to get a raise?" are answered by rumor. We suggest, therefore, that you develop a comprehensive employee policy handbook to let an employee know exactly where he stands and to answer as many questions as possible about his job, his working environment, and what he must do to advance himself and make his own life better. Developing the handbook also makes management think through its own policies and, in so doing, develop uniform policies.

Contents

Some of the items that should be in a policy handbook are discussed below.

Introduction. This is probably the most critical element of the employee policy handbook. Because most of the handbook will be worded very tersely to spell out rules and regulations, the introduction must serve to soften all that follows and illustrate management's genuine concern for the welfare of all employees. A typical introduction might be worded as follows:

> This policy handbook has been created to provide you with some basic information regarding employment at Smith and Doe Associates. Because much of what follows defines rules and regulations, it is written in what might seem to be a very abrupt, unfriendly manner. Unfortunately, there is no other way to write rules and regulations if they are to be spelled out clearly and exactly and be recognized as applicable to all employees in a fair manner. Please do not think that management is unfriendly or unconcerned about you. We feel that each employee is an individual, a human being like everyone else who walks on this planet. If you have problems with which you feel we can help, if you have questions that this policy handbook does not answer, or for whatever appropriate reason, the door is *always* open. Please come and see me and talk. Don't accept rumor or hearsay or gossip. We will try to do our best to answer your questions, to help when we can, and to make our relationship mutually rewarding and satisfying.
>
> John Doe

The Firm. The firm itself is a fit subject for a second introductory statement in the policy handbook. You should mention the history of the firm, expansion that has taken place over the years, business philosophy, ethics, responsibilities to clients and the public, etc.

Departments. Department information also could be included, describing how the firm is divided into departments and what responsibilities are carried out in each. An organizational chart can be shown. Stress how critical each department is to the overall operation of the firm.

As an Employee. This section can come just prior to the rules and regulations. Typical wording for such a section follows:

> As an employee of Smith and Doe Associates, you represent the firm. When speaking on the telephone, when talking with visitors or others who enter our offices, even when not on the premises, you represent our firm. What you say and do represents our firm. To a very real degree you are entrusted with our reputation. This is not to imply that you must be a model of virtue at all times when in our employ, but we do ask that you conduct yourself in a manner that reflects well not only on yourself, but on your place of employment. Just as an example, you probably were once treated rudely by an employee of some establishment and, as a result, you probably make it a point to avoid the establishment as much as possible. Actually, the establishment probably is good, but the actions of just one person, acting foolishly or without thinking of his or her responsibility to the place of employment, resulted in making you an enemy. So, we ask you to bear in mind that, as our employee, you are a member of our family. What you do or say can have a lot to do with what other people think of you, your fellow employees, and everything concerned with Smith and Doe Associates.

Rules and Regulations. For ease of reference, these should be itemized, as in the following suggestions:

1. *Work day and week:* Discussion should center on how many hours in the work day and week, when employees are expected to report, and so forth.

2. *Overtime:* Discussion of this subject probably is best carried out by differentiating between salaried and nonsalaried employees. Mention that as much advance notice as possible will be given and, when overtime is required, nonsalaried workers will receive appropriate compensation, detailing exactly what compensation is, such as time-and-

one-half. Salaried employees usually are not given overtime, and this, or whatever policy is used, also should be mentioned.

3. *Sick leave:* Discussion of sick leave information should include: when sick leave first is available, for example, after the first six months; how many days per year, per six months, or during whatever time division is established; whether sick leave can be accumulated from year to year, just during two years, or what have you; and how sick leave not used is reimbursed, or otherwise compensated, if at all.

4. *Leaves of absence:* Your firm should have a policy regarding leaves of absence, as for pregnancy, including how long leave is granted, whether or not the position is protected, and so on.

5. *Vacations:* Cover who is entitled to vacations; how much time is granted for vacation after varying lengths of service; how vacation time can be accumulated; how vacation time can be reimbursed if not used; how much notice must be given in establishing time for vacations.

6. *Holidays:* Discuss and list what days of the year are given as holidays.

7. *Insurance program:* Include what your firm provides in terms of health, life, and other insurance programs; how and when employees are eligible; and who pays for what, e.g., firm pays 100% for individual coverage, with employee paying extra for families.

8. *Pension and related programs:* Discuss pension and related programs, such as profit sharing, who is eligible, when eligible, and so on.

9. *Educational programs:* Discuss whether or not time off with or without pay is given for attending special educational programs, such as seminars, workshops, and actual courses; how the firm recognizes educational advancement; if educational loans, grants, or partial tuitions are available, and related items.

10. *In-house career development:* Include what the firm does by way of providing lateral mobility, so a person can move from a position in one department to a position in another, thereby increasing his overall knowledge and abilities.

11. *Promotions:* Detail what criteria are used in promoting a person; whether or not the attempt first is made to promote from in-house staff, and so forth.

12. *Other:* Other subjects you may wish to cover include annual bonus; policy in regard to snow; payment during jury duty, military leave,

and so on; payment for association dues or while attending conventions; reimbursement for use of personal auto; eating lunch at desk; use of the telephones; and so on. Every other year the Consulting Engineers Council of Metropolitan Washington (8811 Colesville Road, Suite 225, Silver Spring, Maryland 20910) publishes its *Business Practices Survey*, which includes numerous employee policy matters you may wish to consider. ACEC also has materials on policy handbooks.

Writing Style

Except for the introductory material, the writing style should be terse and easily understood. It can even be outlined if necessary. Make everything completely understandable to answer as many questions as possible.

Format

The simplest format for such a book is a typewritten page, inexpensively printed and bound. This allows for easy page changes or insertion of new material. Also, an inexpensive publication can be given to each employee, which is suggested.

Employee Council

The employee council is an excellent vehicle management can use to give employees a voice without having to resort to unionization. A council can represent the interests of employees through selection of a representative or two (other than department heads) from each department. The council could be consulted on matters such as development of an employee-of-the-month program, suggestion programs, bulletin board programs, and so forth. Further, it can be consulted on more substantive issues, including administrative rules and regulations. The comments of an employee council can be very worthwhile if a program that you otherwise would have begun would have resulted in bitterness and thinning of the ranks. Establishment of such an organization must be undertaken with the realization that any recommendation of the council can be ignored by management if it so wishes, but that most recommendations, particularly those unrelated to administrative rules and regulations, will be followed. Any recommendation that may be overruled should be discussed fully before it is overruled. Any overruling should be accompanied by a thorough explanation.

While a council has many benefits, there are some potential pitfalls to consider. First, while the program demonstrates management's willingness to have employee involvement in decisions concerning employee programs, it will backfire seriously if those items allowed for consideration are inconsequential or if council recommendations or decisions are continually overruled. Second, if the program is begun, but is dropped because of continual conflict between management and employees, it could lead to unionization. We advise, therefore, that any such program be undertaken with care and that complete guidelines be established regarding mutual responsibilities.

General Meetings

Where the number of employees warrants, or where an employee council does not exist, it makes sense to hold general meetings of all employees to discuss matters of mutual concern, such as productivity, reorganization, etc. You can use these meetings both to obtain employee involvement and enthusiasm, as well as to answer questions. Meetings should be kept short, and held at reasonably convenient times.

Clouds-on-the-Horizon Meetings

We suggest that once a month management hold a meeting with department heads. This get-together is called a clouds-on-the-horizon meeting, and is used primarily to discuss emerging situations within each department, what management has in mind for the future, and related items. In other words, those attending comprise a general planning unit, utilized to ensure continued smooth running of operations. Clouds-on-the-horizon meetings also serve to involve key employees with management, making them feel all the more part of the firm.

News in General

Employees should be the first to know about any major developments within the firm. If, for example, they first hear about a new department head by reading about it in a newspaper, they cannot help but feel overlooked by management. They can be kept informed in several ways: in meetings, through bulletins posted on a bulletin board, or through an employee newsletter. Use that vehicle which allows the speediest delivery of news.

In the case of significant changes within the firm, such as reorganization, the following three steps should be taken:

1. Before making any announcement, gather information to answer the questions who, what, why, where, when, and how.

2. Discuss changes with all employees at a special meeting. Cover specific changes with all affected employees personally. Let them get used to the idea and ask for their cooperation and suggestions. Other em-

ployees should be told, too, even if just to be assured that they will not be affected in any way.

3. Always stress positive elements of change.

Bulletin Board

An employee bulletin board provides opportunity for management-to-employee and employee-to-employee communication.

From management's point of view, a bulletin board is ideal for displaying memoranda concerning scheduling, policy changes, new employees, and related items. From the employee point of view, it provides a vehicle for announcing employee activities, posting items for sale, workshops and seminars for given occupations, and whatever other items employees deem appropriate.

To make a bulletin board program effective, remember the following points:

Location is essential: The bulletin board should be located in an area used frequently by employees.

Physical criteria are important: The board must be large enough to provide adequate space for the bulletins to be posted. If the board is always crowded, get a larger one.

Policy covering use must be established: It must be determined whether the board will be placed behind locked glass or will be open for anyone's use at any time. The former method limits access but ensures control, bulletins being placed only through the consent of whoever is in charge. The latter method allows for free access but also the possibility that some bulletins may be removed before they should be.

Control should be vested: The person in charge of the board should be selected by employees. He also should be allowed to establish most operating policies. Responsibilities should include seeing to it that outdated bulletins are removed and that those posted are appropriate. By having a control apparatus, the bulletin board program will have far more meaning and will be recognized as a viable means of communication.

Suggestion Box Program

A suggestion box program provides for meaningful employee-to-management communication. Carried out correctly, the program demonstrates to employees your belief in their having something worthwhile to say; it shows your willingness to reward interest and valuable ideas and, not at all to be overlooked, it provides potential for receiving effective, valuable suggestions.

Consider the following guidelines in establishing a suggestion box program:

Suggestion box: The box itself should be locked. Rules governing its use either should appear on the box or be posted nearby.

Rules: Rules concerning the program should include one stating that all suggestions, to be considered, must be signed. Unsigned suggestions should be discarded.

Policy: Management policy should be established ensuring that all signed suggestions will be considered and replied to, perferably by letter sent to the employee's home. Should you see the employee prior to his receipt of the letter, you can comment on his submission in person, but be certain to send the letter. The letter should say why the suggestion won't work or what has to be done to make it work. By itself the letter indicates that the suggestion was considered and that the thoughtfulness on the employee's part (in making the suggestion) is responded to in kind by management.

Rewards: Good suggestions should be rewarded by something commensurate with the value of the suggestion itself. It probably is best not to establish a standard suggestion-of-the-month award, simply because suggestions received in three consecutive months may be all but useless while in the fourth month there may be several good ones. Awards should be made when appropriate and in all cases when good, usable suggestions are received. You may wish to consider a "suggestion of the year" award.

Methods of Praise and Scolding

There will be occasions when certain employees, individually or as a group, will perform above and beyond the call of duty. Whenever this occurs, management should make it a point to offer praise. The first and most obvious vehicle is to seek out each person and compliment him in person. The second step should entail a personal letter sent to the employee's home. Should there be occasion for a general meeting of employees, take the time to make note of the fact that certain of them did excellent work and deserve praise.

There also will be occasions when certain employees deserve scolding. Reprimands should be made in private, never in public. By scolding in public you humiliate the employee and embarrass others who may hear. You come off all the worse, being regarded by those who hear you as thoughtless. Nor should a scolding be delivered in the form of a scolding. It should take the form of appropriate interpersonal communication. For some persons it may be wiser to state, "I was very disappointed in your actions," rather than, "You really screwed up yesterday." Put yourself in the employee's shoes. Deliver your message in terms that will produce the best corrective action and increased motivation, and that avoid creating hostility and continued counter-productive behavior, which will have to result in dismissal.

As a general rule, remember: praise in public; scold in private.

Handling Employee Complaints

There are times when an employee either will not bring a complaint to the attention of the person who should hear it, or will continue to complain even after he has made his gripe known. In either case, information about the employee's complaining should be obtainable through a clouds-on-the-horizon meeting or from other sources. In all cases, the employee should be called into the office. If he has an honest gripe and you have not done everything possible to resolve it, do your best to resolve it as soon as possible. If the complaint cannot be resolved, or if everything possible has been done, and the employee still complains, he should be told either to stop his complaining or look for work elsewhere (providing unions are not involved). If this action becomes necessary, it usually is wise to inform several persons why the staff member was dismissed to ensure that the word gets around quickly that everything possible was done. In all cases, act quickly to resolve the complaint or remove a chronic complainer.

6.2 RECOGNITION PROGRAMS

There are a variety of recognition programs available to your firm, each designed to further the concept that an employee is an individual and should be treated as such. Employees who feel they only are cogs in a wheel cannot be expected to have any strong ties to the firm, and will leave promptly when another job beckons. Nor can they be blamed for such action. Conversely, when an employee feels that he is known as a person, that his work is important and is regarded as such by others, then he has the beginning of a tie that will make him think twice before looking for work elsewhere.

Employee Identification

It has been said that nothing is so sweet to a person's ear as the sound of his own name. In terms of employee relations there are a variety of simple recognition programs worthy of note.

Memory Improvement. A good memory can let you know employees by name or nickname, a most valuable attribute. It's easy to feel no real bond to an establishment when those who run it don't even know who you are. However, when the boss sees you in the hall and says, "Hello, John, how are you feeling today?" it cannot help but make the person addressed feel comfortable and secure in the knowledge that he is recognized as an individual. Make an effort to know employees on sight. Take every opportunity to treat them in a cordial, friendly manner. If the task requires some instruction in memory improvement, as available through books and numerous short courses, we strongly advise that you take it. It will stand you in excellent stead, in many instances far beyond the value to be received in employee relations alone.

Business Cards. Business cards should be supplied to at least each department head. Even if used only on occasion, a business card is an ego-building device that has value only as long as the employee remains an employee.

6.3 EDUCATIONAL POLICIES AND PROGRAMS

Your firm should consider developing overall policies on employee education. The following are typical programs.

Lateral Development

In larger firms it is a relatively simple matter to develop lateral development programs that allow an employee to shift from one department to another without loss of pay. In this manner he is able to broaden his background and, in time, advance vertically.

Vertical Development

Guidelines should be established on promotional policies and should be included in the employee policy handbook. Every effort should be made to fill vacancies through promotion. Nonetheless, you should be aware of the "Peter Principle," which states, in essence, that many people are eventually advanced to a position of incompetence. In other words, if John Doe does excellently at Job A, he is promoted to Job B, where he also does well. Finally, he is promoted to Job C, which really is not his "dish of tea" and, as a result, he stays there, continually doing mediocre work in a job he really doesn't like. Lateral mobility enables persons who have reached a "level of incompetence" to work elsewhere, so they can once again start turning out excellent work and continue to advance vertically.

Education Leave

You should have a policy covering educational leave for workshops, seminars, two-week courses, night courses, even year-long college-level courses. In the case of long-term leaves, such as for a semester at college, try to guarantee that the student will have, when he returns, a job worthy of his increased education and abilities.

Scholarships and Grants

Develop policy regarding payment for educational courses. Will the firm grant leave with pay for day-long courses? Week-long courses? Will tuition be paid for courses that will improve the employee's work skills? Will it be paid in part? Will a low-cost loan be given? Will dues to associations be paid when membership provides job enrichment or improved skills?

Advancement

If the firm encourages employees to further their job-related education, how will such improvement be rewarded? Especially in cases where costs of additional training are not reimbursed by the firm, some attempt should be made to meet increased capabilities with increased pay, responsibilities, or both. Simply being interested in an employee's continued education is not enough. The proof of a firm's intentions is the extent of its willingness to meet an employee's initiatives with initiatives of its own.

Employee Library

As an adjunct to educational policies, you may wish to consider creating an employee library to consist of pertinent books and other publications on a variety of subjects germane to the various jobs in your firm. A 3×5 card index system can be used, as well as a simple withdrawal mechanism, which allows a person to know who has a book in which he may be interested. The library could be run by employees themselves. Costs should be underwritten by the firm.

6.4 FRINGE BENEFITS

The real cost of fringe benefits seldom is appreciated by employees because management seldom does enough to emphasize them or to develop very obvious ones. Here are suggestions to improve fringe benefits and to make employees more aware of them.

Cost Savings Program

If your firm has enough employees, several programs are available to provide them cost savings. An example of such programs is United Buying

Service or similar buying services that may operate in your area. These organizations contract with various distributors, particularly car dealers, to purchase an indeterminate number of items at a percentage above wholesale, splitting the profit when members of the service present a purchase order and buy. There usually is no cost to join and cost savings can be significant. For example, United Buying Service makes most American cars available to members at $100 above wholesale. Similar programs should be investigated, including a credit union; having the firm's accounting personnel prepare income tax returns for employees at reduced rates; and so on. For the most part such programs cost your firm little or nothing, but can become very important benefits of working for you. In some cases these programs are provided through chapters of AIA, ACEC, and other organizations.

Employee Tips Program

Probably not a day goes by when you do not read some periodical or hear of an incident that can result in some sort of tip or cautionary advice for others. Around income tax time, for example, many tax tips appear in newspapers or can be supplied by your firm's accountant. Many of these can be geared for employees. Similarly, we hear tips about the dangers of mixing radial and nonradial tires, how to save on heating bills, and *ad infinitem*. Save these tips. Put them into the form of memoranda or pay envelope stuffers and pass on such usable advice to employees. The cost of running such a program is practically nothing. The good will established can be priceless.

Letting the Employee Know

Many employers complain that employees seldom realize the enormous difference between what they make and what management actually pays. In fact, fringe benefits and related payments often cost one-quarter to one-third more than actual pay. To inform and remind employees of these additional expenses, as for vacations, sick leave, holidays, insurance, and so on, prepare a special statement for distribution with a W-2 form at year's end, showing exactly how much the employee has received. You may wish to include typical examples in your employee handbook.

6.5 EXTRACURRICULAR ACTIVITIES

Another program devised to improve the employee's relationship with the firm involves development of social, athletic, and other activities whose enjoyment becomes unattainable the moment the relationship with your firm ceases.

Typical social functions include holiday parties for employees and their families, picnics, monthly birthday parties for employees, and similar social events. Sports activities also bear consideration, including bowling, softball, golf, and similar activities. Also to be considered are employee contests, such as technical brain teasers, bridge and backgammon tournaments, and so on.

6.6 NEW EMPLOYEE RELATIONS

The new employee must be treated in a distinct manner to ensure that he begins his relationship "on the right foot." If every effort is made in this regard, then a firm foundation for the future will be established.

Training

Much of the relationship with a new employee often involves training, a subject beyond the scope and purpose of this book. Suffice it to say that the employee must be trained sufficiently to enable him to perform his tasks correctly, for his sake as well as your own. An employee who cannot perform well is frustrated and of little value to management. It is imperative, therefore, to determine the effect of training, necessitating a monitoring process as well as a continuing program of encouragement based on the rules of interpersonal communication. Do not expect an employee to perform well at a function in which he has not been trained or in which your specific requirements have not been related.

Orientation

Another key element of new employee relations is orientation, which is a relatively easy task. Briefly, new employee orientation involves a tour of the facility with emphasis on the new employee's department and his co-workers there. Provide information that illustrates how his job is integral to the smooth operation of the entire firm. If the new employee does not already possess a copy of the employee handbook and a job description, he should be given one of each, along with any other pertinent material. The new employee should be introduced to as many other employees as possible (a task that is perhaps best handled by a long-time employee in the same department). News of the hiring could be made public through the bulletin board, newsletter, and other means, including a news release for key personnel. The new employee's superior, and even the superior's supervisor, should visit the new employee during his first few weeks on the job to ensure that he knows what he is doing and that he is happy with his work. In such a manner one lays the foundation for a solid relationship.

6.7 PROSPECTIVE EMPLOYEE RELATIONS

Proper hiring techniques are essential. It is imperative that the person hired be suited for the work involved. If not, he will become disgruntled or will be unable to perform assigned tasks. He will eventually leave or will continue to do subpar work. Given the rising costs of hiring, orienting, training, terminating, and associated functions, it is essential that some thought and consideration be given to hiring policies. While much information on this subject is available from other sources, at least some food for thought is contained below.

Job Descriptions

Writing good job descriptions is a necessary and crucial task. You may think you know what the job entails, but you may not be correct. To hire a person based on only an educated guess of what really will be required of him jeopardizes an investment of time and money and also risks irritating what is obviously a prospective ambassador of good will.

A job description should be prepared for each job category in the firm. To prepare a job description, we suggest that you write down exactly what you believe the job entails. Have several others do the same, including the head of the department in which the vacancy exists, and perhaps the immediate superior or co-workers. Compare the several job descriptions and note any discrepancies. Meet with those who have written the descriptions to discuss the issue and determine precisely what is and is not required. Once this is determined it is a relatively simple matter to proceed to general attributes that the job requires.

Personal Characteristics Checklist

Once the job description is complete, you should meet with those people who will be working most closely with the new worker to determine what other-than-job-related characteristics may be important. For example, given the character of vital members of the staff who would be working with the new worker, it may be essential that the new staffer be capable of maintaining a cheerful attitude. When selecting an employee, try to avoid co-worker conflicts that may appear inevitable. A checklist of desirable or undesirable attributes should be kept confidential.

Requirements/Quantity List

A requirements/quantity list states which abilities and/or characteristics are most important, which second most, etc. For example, if the person, to do the job, must have talents A, B, C, D, and E, the quantity checklist would indicate the relative importance of each. You can use a 1 to 10 scale so that quality A, most important, would rate a 10, with quality B a 3, quality C a 5, and so forth. During or after the interview rank the prospective employee's characteristics in terms of quantities possessed using the same scale. By using this method you may find, for example, that an applicant may possess all five qualities required, but they may be in unfavorable proportions. A secretary who can take dictation and type may be what you are looking for but, if you hire a person who cannot take dictation too well but can type very quickly, when in fact dictation is the key element, you have made a costly mistake. The requirements/quantity list can help minimize the chance of error.

Tour

A tour of the facility, similar to the one given as a part of orientation, should be given to all prospective employees. Pay particular attention to those areas where the applicant would work.

Employee Handbook

An employee handbook either should be given to the applicant for review at his leisure or for study while in your firm. The former approach is considered best, providing enough are available.

6.8 FORMER EMPLOYEE RELATIONS

This section possibly should be retitled "About-To-Be-Former Employees." It concerns primarily those employees who have decided to stop working for you. In the case of amicable partings, we advise that you maintain contact, keep the person on the mailing list for your newsletter if you have one, and invite him to appropriate functions. In this manner you keep close contact with those who might help when you are in dire need, or when you least expect it.

In cases where the leave-taking is not so amicable, where the person leaving clearly is dissatisfied for one reason or another, we recommend strongly that an exit interview be performed to help determine what went wrong. The information gained from such an interview can be very important. In many cases it can indicate problems in your hiring mechanisms. It also may point out some problems with personnel or policies that you knew nothing about. A frank talk is the best kind. Draw out the truth if at all possible.

Emphasize that your reasons for knowing result from a desire to improve the situation so it will not happen again. In some cases it could mean giving the employee a chance to blow off steam, which might turn a potential enemy into someone who is at least neutral. You also may be able to take immediate corrective action and perhaps keep the employee through mutual consent.

7

PROMOTION

Like many others, we use "promotion" as synonymous with public relations. We do not use the term "public relations" much because, although it is accurate, it is subject to numerous different interpretations. Conversely, although promotion is not as accurate for our purposes, it is better understood and so we use it.

As you may be aware, there exists a running debate between PR and marketing people as to which is subservient to which: where does marketing end and PR begin? Since this debate is mostly academic, suffice it to say that PR can be, and for our purposes is, an element of marketing. Certain PR and communications skills are discussed in this chapter. Other, similar skills and techniques will be covered later.

Before getting into the specific skills, it will be worthwhile to spend a few moments on the nature of PR and image development. If one can obtain a grasp of the theories involved, implementation becomes mostly a matter of common sense.

7.1 PR AND IMAGE DEVELOPMENT

Definitions of public relations abound. There is no more accurate definition, however, than "public relations means relating to your publics."

Relating. Relating means communicating. Communication takes place whenever a person becomes aware of someone or something else. In other words, whenever someone or something impinges on one or more of a person's (receptor's) five senses, communication has taken place. The specific kind of communication is determined by the sense that is impinged upon. Thus, if a receptor is made aware of a surface because it is much smoother or rougher than he would expect, the communication is tactile (sense of touch). If the receptor is made aware via the spoken word, the communication takes place through the sense of hearing. The important thing to realize is that such communication can be deliberate or inadvertent. In fact, many people are not aware of the many different ways in which they communicate. For example, during a face-to-face meeting with a prospective client in your office, you and your firm would be communicating not only by what you say, but perhaps also by the way you are dressed, the cologne you are wearing, the design and condition of your office, and other factors.

Publics. A public is defined as a group of people who have one or more interests in common. A common interest can be generic or vested. For example, home builders in your area have a generic common interest because they have something in common, i.e., building homes. Those who comprise your public of prospective clients, however, have something in common *only from your point of view*, i.e., they all are prospective clients of your firm. You, therefore, have vested a commonality in them.

An ability to identify publics is essential in the contemporary business world because communication is based on very brief contact. For the communication to be successful, the communicator must be on the same "wavelength" as the receptor. By being able to identify publics, you perforce identify the commonality or common interest. Therefore, you should be able to conduct communications in light of a public's concerns. This does not mean that you say what you think your public wants to hear. Rather, you communicate information in which your publics are interested. Obviously, the more narrowly you can define your publics, the better you can identify interests and the more specific you can be in your communication. For this reason establishing publics also involves a process of segmentation, whereby you can identify subpublics, subsubpublics, and so on, all of whom can be identified just as "publics" without the "subs." For example, within the prospective client public you have the prospective owner client public, the prospective contractor client public, the prospective government client public, etc. The prospective government client public can be segmented into the prospective local government client public, prospective state government client public, etc. In most cases you will want to identify only your primary publics and rely on segmentation to develop more specific communication when the need arises, such as to inform a certain prospective client public of a specific kind of project you have just completed.

Image Formation

Understanding how an image is formed is essential to developing a PR/ communications program. By way of explanation refer to Figure 28 and the following comments.

Image formation begins with communication from the *source*. This communication is labeled *output* and can take many forms, as already discussed.

The output, once it is perceived, becomes *input*. Input and output are not necessarily one and the same, however. For example, you probably are aware that bulls are color blind. Thus, when the matador waves his red cape, the bull sees a blue cape. In similar manner, a compliment given by one person can be taken by the receptor as mild sarcasm. In other words, the communications output as perceived by the communicator and the receptor may be two entirely different things.

The perceived input also is subject to the *prejudice* of the receptor, shown for our purposes as a combination of past experience and attitude toward the experience. If there is something about your communication that elicits the memory of a given experience in the receptor, there is an excellent chance that the receptor's attitude toward that remembered experience will be evoked and applied to your communication. If, for example, while making a presentation, you happen to hit upon certain points that had been made before to the receptor, and had impressed him favorably, his attitude toward the past experience will stand you in good stead.

Still another element of the image formation process centers on the context involved. This goes right back to the reason for identifying publics. Most communications experiences have a context of some kind. If you are standing next to a person in an elevator and guess at his occupation because of his attire, the context is most general and, accordingly, you probably won't give the person observed much second thought. When purposeful communication is involved, however, the context becomes far more important. Thus, when you are making a proposal to a prospect, everything you communicate is utilized to establish an image in light of the context involved,

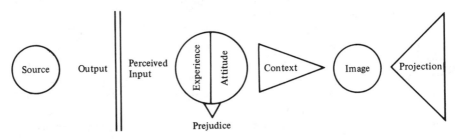

Figure 28. Basics of image formation and projection.

namely, your ability to do the job. If you ramble on about this and that and make a generally poor presentation, you probably will not get the job unless the receptor's prejudices indicate that such an approach is favorable. In all cases, therefore, you must keep the context in mind when you communicate purposefully and attempt to provide information, both verbal and nonverbal, in direct and honest support of the image you wish to convey.

The actual development of the *image* comes next. In essence, an image is a way of referencing something by a kind of shorthand. It is a mind's eye picture that can be recalled at will, something needed in this day and age of mass communication. In some cases the image may be as general as positive or negative, or as specific as prolonged contact or an active imagination will permit. In most cases, however, it is a general image that is stored and then retrieved and fleshed out when further consideration is necessary. Of course, some communications, because of insignificant context or impact or brief exposure, may not result in image development and memory storage. Nonetheless, if pressed, an individual still could develop an image. For example, the next time you speak with someone unknown on the phone, try to guess at his age, height, weight, general overall appearance, etc. You probably could come up with answers to all these and more questions, thus forming a very specific image where none existed before. Of course, every answer you give may be wrong, but that really is not at issue for, until you learn differently, that is the image that will stand.

Still another element of image formation is *image projection*, wherein the image developed can be projected to any other context or to much greater proportions. For example, if you receive a letter from a firm offering to provide services to you, and the letter is filled with typographical errors, you probably will develop an image of the typist as sloppy, and of the sender as careless for not reviewing the letter before signing it. And if the firm involved has a lot of competition, chances are you will ask competitors for the service. Why? Because you have projected the image of the typist and the signatory onto the entire company. After all, if the letter is representative of the typist and executive, the typist and executive are representative of the company. Therefore, the information that is really communicated in this case—typographical errors—becomes the basis for the image of an entire organization.

PR in Practice

What all the foregoing indicates is this:

1. You communicate whether you want to or not, usually in more ways than you realize. In essence, therefore, you are relating to your publics whether you want to or not, and you have public relations whether you want it or not.

2. The communications you transmit possibly may be perceived as different from what were sent.

3. The perceived communication is subject to bias.

4. The perceived communication will be applied to a given context determined by the receptor.

5. The image developed from something insignificant can be projected to typify an entire organization of fifty people or more.

Given that you have public relations whether you want it or not, and given that even the smallest bit of inadvertent communication can be used in whole or in part to develop an image of your entire organization, it is obvious that the more you can control what and how you communicate, the more you can control the image developed, i.e., what people think about you. And this is what a PR/communications/promotional program is all about: *control*. By establishing an effective program you can control as many elements of your communications as possible, leaving little to chance. Moreover, you will be able to see yourself as others see you, and you can consider the many possible repercussions of any given action.

In all cases, of course, the image you want to develop should be honest. To attempt to create a false image usually results in untold difficulties. Although it is relatively easy to design an attractive and appealing bookcover, it will be regarded as false and misleading if it does not jibe with the contents. Books eventually get read. For this reason, for example, you should not attempt to convince someone that you have extensive expertise in an area where your expertise is limited. If you do get the job, chances are you will bollix it and then lose all the client's work.

Honesty in image formation does not mean that you should show all publics the same image. To do so, given the limited time of the communications process, whould mean conveyance of a general image only. Given the specific interest of each public, and the context in which each views your communications, a general image would satisfy none. Therefore, you must establish the common interest of a given public and the specific context involved, and then proceed to communicate only those bits of information that are relevant. For this reason you do not show a prospective client a list of every project ever done by your firm and/or its key employees. Rather, you prepare a list of projects that should hold special interest for the prospective client, and perhaps a brief smattering of others to indicate related experience. In this light it can be seen that you and your firm have many images each dependent on the context involved. There is absolutely nothing wrong in this. Even the most uncomplicated person will have different images depending on the relationships he has—images of brother, son, father, uncle, employee, supervisor, and so on. And thus it is with any more complex person or organization: there will be many images. In each case, however, the image *must reflect what actually exists*, and it can be interpreted that way only when you establish an overall PR/communications *control* program designed to minimize the chances of misinterpretation.

Assuming that you now have a reasonably good fix on the kinds of clients you will be pursuing, you now must consider the specific overall image you want to present to them.

Your first step is to evaluate the client and prospective client publics. Taking them all into consideration, are there any particular images that would be good or bad to present? For example, would it be good to come on as ultramodern, ultraconservative, or middle of the road? Do not forget to consider, too, the evolutionary aspects of image. In other words, you should not attempt to portray an image of being competent to perform services that you probably won't be offering for another two or three years. Stick to reality, remembering that your firm's image will grow with the firm.

Once you have decided upon some of the general parameters of your image, the next step is to apply the image or type of image involved.

The first, and most obvious application, centers on printed materials. All should have good graphics, preferably developed by a professional who can interpret your image and supply you with a good logo, good type, etc. All printed materials should be unified, including letterhead, envelopes, business cards, bill forms, brochure, proposal cover, newsletter, etc., thus promoting firm identity.

The second application involves the firm's offices. In each office the reception area and conference room should be decorated along similar lines. For example, if you have contemporary furniture in the reception area, you should have similar furniture in the conference room, with the same theme being carried out in each branch office. You can elect either to hang graphics on the wall, or renderings of projects, licenses, registration certificates, etc. Where applicable, design should reflect specialty. For example, the offices of a firm that offers illumination design services should have good lighting. If you do not have competent, in-house interior design staff, utilize an interior design firm.

Executive offices within an office complex can be designed to reflect the overall design theme, the particular preference of the person occupying the office, or the general preferences of the clients most apt to visit a given office.

In all cases the firm's offices should look as professional as possible. All office space must be kept neat and clean. Calendars with cheesecake photos should be removed, and so on. It would be wise to have an independent source—such as a representative of a PR firm—evaluate your offices and turn in a detailed report on how he interprets what he sees from the point of view of a prospective client.

Bear in mind that everything associated with your firm—all the people associated with it, what they do and say, how they do and say it—can and will be used in developing an image. The more you can control your image the more you can help people see you as you really are.

7.2 SOURCES OF ASSISTANCE

The nature of promotional activity is such that many needs can be met completely or partially by in-house talent. Occasionally, relatively inexpensive outside talent may be used to supplement staff endeavors or, as in the case of such important pieces as brochures, to undertake most of the work to help ensure a top quality product.

The kinds of assistance you may need from time to time will depend on the specific projects you have in mind. The following discussion relates to all the various kinds of talent that may be involved.

Determining Need

The first order of business is to determine exactly what your needs are. Try to be as specific as possible and isolate each task. For example, designing stationery means designing letterhead, envelope, and second sheet, as well as business cards and billing forms. (For developing an image, especially one related to fast recognition, it is best to have all these elements appear as part of a "family," using the same basic design, paper, ink color, etc.) In this case, the task may involve development of a logo, selection of type, design of the materials, selection of ink color, selection of paper color, selection of specific paper, etc. Because of the frequency with which these materials would be seen, it would appear logical to obtain the best job possible. There are several ways of getting it, depending on what is available to you. For example, you could use a talented art instructor from your local high school, junior college, or university to design a logo, rely on the typesetter for choice of type, and rely on the printer for paper selection. Or you may prefer to have an advertising agency or PR firm do it all, whether through its own or associated talent. No matter which way you do it, however, you need good quality work, and it is doubtful that you could obtain it from in-house talent alone. Conversely, if you use this book to write a news release, but are not quite sure if your result is effective, you may ask a local college journalism instructor to review it quickly and make a few appropriate changes. In other words, it's a matter of identifying specifically what functions an individual task entails, determining all the different talents that could be applied to achieve the functions, and, from that, determining who to use to get the job done. Assuming that you know what talent may be required, you can ask friends or business acquaintances for references, and/or make some contact yourself from the various sources covered below.

Where To Find It

Before getting into specific sources of talent, consider these few general observations.

First, the quickest and easiest way of finding out about certain kinds of talent is to ask friends and business acquaintances for references. Chances are they use or know of individuals or firms that may be of service. Do not limit your prospective sources of talent to just those recommended, however. Also, use the Yellow Pages (writers, artists, etc.).

Second, try to find people who can be objective and who are not afraid to act as devil's advocate. A yes-man can ruin just about anything if he is afraid or unwilling to speak up when he sees something being conceived or produced in an incorrect manner.

Third, try to be objective about your own capabilities and those of your firm's personnel. Know the limits of your own expertise and the limits of those you employ. Try to avoid the "success syndrome," wherein a person who is successful and experienced in a given field believes he knows everything there is to know about that field. All too often credence will not be given to a person who has not yet achieved a high level of success, not because his idea is not good, but rather because he has not as yet "scored," i.e., "If you're so smart, how come you're not rich?"

Sources of Talent

In-house. Survey your own people to determine what talents they may have that could possibly be put to use in your PR program. These talents would include, for example, writing, public speaking, photography, art, publications design, and so on. If you have a drafting department, for example, chances are that one of the draftsmen may have some artistic talent. A department manager may be able to make a good presentation. A secretary may be able to follow established rules and issue some news releases. One of the best ways to obtain such information is to prepare a questionnaire for all employees, listing the various talents required. For all you know, you may now be employing someone capable of implementing 90% of your PR program. But you'll never know unless you ask.

Friends/Relatives. Friends and relatives also are a source of talent, but dealing with them often is problematical. A situation that arises because of business dealings can become complicated by personal relationships. How, for example, do you tell your brother that he's a lousy writer? What do you say to a friend who hands you what you consider to be an excessively large bill for services rendered? When you do consider hiring a friend or relative, therefore, be circumspect. Be sure to spell out clearly that "business is business." Of course, do not rule out using friends or relatives for certain functions whose success depends on honesty. For example, if you want an honest appraisal of the way your office looks from a prospective client's point of view, or an assessment of the quality of something you've written, it could be assumed that a friend or relative could give an honest answer, providing you stress the need for honesty and you respect his judgment.

Newspapers. Newspapers frequently are the source of many different sorts of talent, including writing, photography, illustration, advertising, paste-up, design, etc. In some cases you can contract directly with the newspaper to have the needed work performed. In most cases, however, you probably will be able to obtain the talent you need on a moonlighting basis. As examples, if you want some writing done, contact a by-lined reporter and ask if he does any free-lance work. Chances are he does. If you need photography, ask for the name of the staff photographer, if there is one, and determine if he is available for a little moonlighting. The switchboard operator also can provide you with names of advertising personnel, graphic illustrators, and so on. One of the benefits of working with newspaper personnel, of course, is the fact that it creates contacts for you. This does not mean that you should request to have items about yourself or your firm published. But it could result in your getting some insight into the kinds of stories the editor is looking for, and so on.

Magazines. Local magazines often can be a source of talent similar to that provided by a newspaper. Usually, but not always, a magazine employs more talented persons. The graphics usually will be better, as will be the writing. Do realize, of course, that newspaper and magazine styles are two entirely different things. By the same token, however, if your local newspaper has a feature section, or a local Sunday supplement, chances are such features producers would be equivalent to those who work on magazine staffs.

High Schools/Colleges/Universities. Schools can be good sources of moonlight talent. In colleges and universities you need only contact the appropriate departments, such as journalism, English (creative writing), art, and so on. In high schools your choice will be more limited. In either case, however, ask to speak with the appropriate teachers or professors to ask if they are willing and able to do the work. In certain cases, as for the news releases or art design, it even may be possible to have a student do the work for you.

Associations. Associations often can be the source of moonlight talent. If your local AIA or ACEC chapter works with a PR firm, chances are the firm would not be adverse to making a few extra dollars working with you on your program. Other associations to which you belong, including those such as Rotary or the Chamber of Commerce, may have PR directors or firms. And even if a group does not, chances are it does have someone on staff capable of preparing an adequate news release or performing some other tasks that involve writing. You also can check with the executive director to see whom he recommends for certain types of work.

Advertising Agencies. Advertising agencies usually have on hand talent for developing logos, other artwork, paste-ups, news releases, and performing similar tasks. Be cautious with an advertising agency when trying to obtain work that is more PR than advertising in nature, especially when it comes to preparing copy for brochures, developing employee relations programs, etc. In most cases, even though an ad agency will tack "Public Relations" onto its title, its PR capabilities will be strictly limited.

PR Firms. Some PR firms also perform advertising. Some do not. In many cases, however, PR firms have a variety of talent capable of performing most of the work you need done. PR firms can be located through friends and business acquaintances, Yellow Pages, and organizations such as the Chamber of Commerce. You also may call a local newspaper and speak with a member of editorial staff to determine if he can recommend or at least identify some local PR firms.

Art Firms. Firms specializing only in art work are relatively few and far between in other than urban areas. They can be most helpful when it comes to design of logos, letterheads, and so on.

Photography Firms. There are three distinct types of photography firms. One specializes in studio photography, primarily portraits. Another specializes in sensitive, posed photography as used in fashion photography, development of brochures, etc. A subspecialty is architectural photography. The third type is called a newsphoto photographer who specializes in getting the job done in a workmanlike manner, usually with little regard to tonal qualities, use of filters, etc. In some cases one firm may provide all the different types needed. In other cases you may find that a newsphotographer can provide you with a higher degree of sensitivity than you otherwise might expect. Make inquiries and look at examples of work to really find out what capabilities a given firm may have. Photography firms can be located through references, use of the Yellow Pages, etc.

Printer. A printing firm usually will have available certain in-house talent useful to you. This includes primarily art talent, which can help you with selection of type styles, measuring copy for type, overall design, and so on. A printer also will be able to provide you with a variety of samples of similar work that you may find of great help in determining what you want your product to look like, or not to look like. Chances are that a local printer also can be a good source of references for advertising agencies, PR firms, art firms, and so on. In many cases you will be able to obtain free assistance from a printer if the job on which you need help will be printed by him, or if you give him a good amount of work. Otherwise, there may be a charge.

Typesetter. A typesetter specializes in setting type. In most cases he will have a much larger selection of type faces than a printer, and often can do the job at the same or less cost. Of course, the amount of assistance the typesetter can provide will be limited. In most cases, he will have available minimal art talent, with greatest emphasis on pasting-up. He can be a good source of references, however.

How Much To Pay

It is difficult to state exactly how much you should be paying because of variables. For example, free-lance writers often ask $12 to $20 per hour, as compared to some PR firms that command $35 to $50 per hour. The $12 to $20 an hour is a bargain only if the writer can do the job well and if he works speedily. A simple news release usually can be written in half an hour or less. If the free lance charges you for two hours at $15 each, the "bargain" doesn't look too good if the PR firm charges you for half an hour at $40 per hour. The only way to determine how much to pay, therefore, is to obtain cost estimates from a variety of different sources, being sure that—when hourly rates are involved—you consider the amount of time that will be involved for a given task.

Making a Selection

In the case of a major project, or in the event that you wish to give continuing work to just one or two sources, rather than to make changes each time, it will be best to make a thorough selection to ensure that you have the best talent for the price. Chances are it will be most logical to use an integrated selection policy, in that you will be selecting, let us say, art talent from sources such as an art firm, a PR firm, and ad agency, etc., rather than just choosing one ad agency from ten, then one PR firm from five, and so on. Consider the following steps.

Determine Types of Work. Make a list of the types of work you will need to have performed. Indicate which of it will be ongoing and which of it will be one-time only. For example, development of a logo, letterheads, and related work will be one-time. Development of news releases will be ongoing.

Develop a List of Suppliers. Develop a list of suppliers for the different work you need performed, either one-time or ongoing. A free-lance writer may be useful for just preparing talks or developing news releases. A PR firm may be capable of meeting all needs. As such, segregate the list by tasks, and list each source under as many tasks as you feel it should be capable of performing.

Touch Base. Contact each supplier by phone, letter, or in person and ask for a meeting to determine exactly what capabilities the firm or individual has. Ask for samples and references. In the case of firms, obtain samples of each kind of work you have under consideration. Bear in mind, of course, that one sample may comprise examples of many different kinds of work. For example, a brochure can illustrate art work, overall design capabilities, copy preparation, editing, photography, etc.

Check References. Check all references supplied by each individual or firm. Determine exactly what kind of work was produced and the degree of satisfaction the client obtained. Also, if the sample was done for someone not used as a reference, check the company that the work was done for.

Rank. Examine the capabilities of each firm or individual listed for performance of each task. Rank them in order of most qualified, second most qualified, etc. For each task, consider the top three or four firms or individuals.

Reorient List. Reorient your list in terms of individuals and firms listed rather than tasks. For example, if you have a PR firm listed under five tasks, it now would be listed only once, with the tasks you are considering it for listed under it.

Discuss Price and Related Matters. In light of rankings and the reoriented list, meet with the various individuals and firm representatives you have under consideration. Describe as precisely as possible the work you have in mind; determine what fee arrangements could be utilized (lump sum, hourly, etc.); learn the amount of money that would be involved in performance of typical tasks; determine what turnaround time would be, etc.

Make Selections. Based on discussions, determine whom you would prefer to use for which types of tasks. Money should not be the sole criterion, which is why the selection method was set out as it was. If you consider cost along with quality and related matters, chances are you will bias selection. In most cases, you are talking about imagination and talent, rather than a doing-it-by-the-number approach. As such, you are looking for quality within a specified budget. Therefore, make decisions by quality first, then by cost. By keeping them separate, you can probably get a better product. If, of course, none of those you ranked for a certain task is able to do it within the cost you envision, either interview more suppliers or allow more money for the task to be performed. In some cases it may prove practical to utilize just one or two sources for a variety of tasks, rather than to give the work out piecemeal. Some firms, for example, even if they don't have in-house talent, have associates, free lance or moonlighters whom they use, and, thus, can act as a manager of the PR function for you. If, for example, a firm can handle one task best, and several others adequately, it may be best to give all the tasks to the one firm. Being familiar with your overall needs, they possibly can be more responsive to each of them. When just starting out with a firm or individual, do not make any long-term commitments. Also, when dealing with a firm, be sure to determine exactly who would be running your account. All too often you'll talk with the firm's top brass, but the actual work will be done by a "flunky."

Economizing

True economy results when you run a tight ship and do everything as efficiently as possible. Spending less money for something is not economizing if you wind up with an inferior product. Determining the most efficient way of doing something is not all that cut-and-dried, however.

In-house/Outside Talent Interface. One way to obtain economy in using outside talent is to utilize in-house talent to the maximum desirable degree before resorting to outside talent for finalizing. This requires that you be fully familiar with the capabilities of in-house talent, as well as the cost of their services. For example, let us assume that you need a talk written. You assign a member of your staff to perform the research and do the writing. Once done, you hand it over to an outside writer for polish. The cost for outside writing is $50. If the outside writer did it all, it would have cost $250. Did you just save $200? Yes, provided that the staff member who did the work had nothing else better to do and the time involved otherwise would have been wasted. Assuming that is not the case, and the staff member spent ten hours at $8 per hour, then your savings was $120, still sizable. What if the staff member had to spend 20 hours at $10 per hour? What if the staff member—to get the job done—had to put off completing a proposal or getting one in on time? Would it have been better to just produce an outline and spend $100 for the outside writer to do the writing, or perhaps just provide the research materials—such as three magazine articles—and then spend $175 on the talk? In other words, you have to make some decisions and use a little trial and error to find out exactly what methods will work best. It would be a mistake not to use some of your in-house talent if you possibly and conveniently can, but it would be just as big an error to use it if those involved could be doing something else that is more important, or if the outside talent will have to spend too much time undoing what in-house talent did wrong in the first place. Also note that, when an important item is involved, and you do plan to rely almost completely on in-house capability, turn it over to an outside source for critical evaluation before finalizing. By being able to see something you cannot, for whatever reason, a reviewer could wind up saving you a lot, in terms of money, and in terms of saving you from an error that could prove detrimental to your image or to the successful completion of the project.

Add-ons. A firm frequently will have out-of-pocket expenses for products or services obtained on your behalf. In such cases there often will be an add-on. If a printer has to obtain outside type, for example, chances are he will mark it up by 15% to 20%, or more. Before giving out work or awarding a contract for work, be certain to clarify whether or not add-ons will be used and, if so, why. If they will not be used, ask for copies of original statements for your review. If they will be involved, ask if you can contract directly with the outside source to save the add-on, or possibly pay for the work in advance to eliminate it.

Retainers. A retainer fee sometimes will be beneficial. In essence, it usually means agreeing to purchase X hours from a firm or individual each month, for a specified period, usually a year. The X hours usually are given to you for less than the "going" rate. This can be a bargain if you consistently use the X amount each month, or if you average that amount of use. If you use less, however, you will have wasted money. If you use just slightly more, you'll be charged, but probably at the retainer rate. If you have a retainer agreement with an advertising agency or any other organization that provides advertising for you, be sure to request that any commissions provided by newspapers or other media be counted as a credit to your account.

Contracts. A retainer usually is put into contract form, or in the form of a letter of agreement, which has the force of a contract. When it comes to long-term agreements of a year or more, be certain that everything is spelled out: exactly how much is to be paid; number of hours of work you are to receive;

what will be done about commissions received by the firm or individual as a result of placing your work; add-ons; etc. It also is a good idea to include a cancellation clause, whereby you could cancel the contract after thirty days notice. Chances are the firm or individual with whom you deal also will want a clause enabling him to cancel, often within sixty or ninety days. In the case of a one-time contract for performance of a given task, try to insert a penalty clause that holds the producer to a certain period of time for completing the work, allowing recognition for change orders, of course.

7.3 COMPANY IDENTIFICATION

We all are familiar with the initials RCA, GE, GM, and ITT. Each set is instantly identifiable. Each represents a giant of American industry. In fact, just about every product these companies manufacture has the company logo on it someplace. Letterheads have the logo. Business cards have the logo. So do advertisements.

The primary reason one responds instantly to these corporate signatures is the omnipresence of these companies, that is, hardly a day goes by when you don't see one of their products or advertisements. But consider this: what would happen if the logos themselves were not uniform? What would happen if RCA had a variety of different logos and at times called itself (for promotional purposes) Radio Corporation of America? What would happen if IBM at times promoted itself strongly as International Business Machines? In both cases, the impact that could be achieved through a program of corporate identity would probably be greatly lessened.

As a case in point, consider Lever Brothers. While many people have heard of Lever Brothers, how many can name five of the products they manufacture? In fact, they manufacture scores of different products, most of which are household names. Lever Brothers *per se* has no significant corporate identification program and, thus, the response to the name is not nearly as great as response to IBM or RCA, despite the fact that Lever Brothers is one of the nation's—in fact the world's—largest advertisers. In terms of marketing strategies, the difference between IBM and Lever Brothers is that the latter spends its money identifying brand-name products rather than the company itself. The same holds true for other giants such as Proctor and Gamble and General Foods.

In essence, then, what we're saying about company or corporate identification is this: uniformity is the key. The more consistent you are about your company identification, the likelier it is that any one element of your organization will communicate a much larger image. If the color and logo on a survey crew truck are the same as the color and logo on a letterhead, you will tend to think of the truck if you see the letterhead, or vice versa. In other words, they all interrelate. By contrast, if your trucks are painted a variety of different colors and if your letterhead is different from your business card, you can't put two and two together. Thus, the impact of your image is greatly lessened.

Establishing an Identification Program

Establishing an overall company identification program is part and parcel of establishing an overall PR/image program. In general, however, elements of the program can be geared to different publics. A logo and accompanying identification apply to all publics equally. Thus, in determining how you want to identify yourself, you must consider the image that is most consistent with what the company is really like and what your key publics are really like.

To begin, consider all those external (other than employee) publics to which you relate. Consider your top-rated public and the various individuals who comprise it. What are they like? Are they individuals who look for the new approach or do they prefer the traditional? In many cases you will find that government workers as a group are somewhat middle-of-the-road. Private developers, in many cases, are known for bottom-line analysis. They seldom are swayed by any image, *per se*, unless that image is one that reflects experience in the kind of project involved, reliability, and economy. That type of image is one that must be substantiated in fact. Architects often look for the new and different. Engineers also like to be in the vanguard of the new, but they tend to present themselves and their organizations in a relatively conservative manner. Recognize, of course, that generalizations never can substitute for firsthand experience. The decisions you make on this matter must be up to you and your own impressions.

For sake of argument, let's assume that you decide it best—in light of your current and prospective clients' preferences—to come across as a relatively contemporary organization that uses modern techniques and equipment, but is willing to keep costs down and perform quality work for reasonable compensation. The question then becomes, does this fit with what you actually are? To create a false impression is to lay the groundwork for a problem so significant that all your PR efforts could backfire. Therefore:

1. Determine which elements should be stressed to create the image most suitable for your most important clients and prospects.

2. Determine which elements of company realities jibe with ideal image elements.

3. Stress those elements of company realities that come closest to what most clients are looking for.

Assuming you can accomplish this task, the next step is to put vague generalities into specific purpose.

Logo

A logo is a company symbol. Ideally, everytime you see the logo you should think of the company. Thus, when you see the circular GE logo, done in its own distinctive way, you immediately think of General Electric.

Many individuals believe a logo adds a touch of class to an organization. If it is done well, it does, but adding a touch of class is not the real purpose of the logo. It should serve to help identify the company every time it is seen and, ideally, give an indication of what the company does.

In the case of GE, RCA, IBM, and so on, the logo does serve to provide corporate identity, but the fact of the matter is that if you spent as much on promotion as they did, your logo would be just as meaningful and recognizable. You can't spend that much, however, so your logo must be able to do more of the identifying job on its own, without the assistance of a big promotional/advertising budget. The questions then become, is it worth it to develop a logo, and, if so, how much does it cost?

Is it worth it? Yes. The company symbol can add a great deal of prestige to the company. It indicates, to an extent, that you have arrived, assuming that it is done well. Still, as mentioned, the fact that the logo can identify your company in a relatively small space and in a very brief amount of time is the key.

Cost is another matter. Some companies spend tens of thousands of dollars developing logos that are magnificent little symbols complete with swirls, angles, and so on, although, taken by themselves, they mean absolutely nothing to most people. They mean something only when the name of the company is placed next to them. In other words, they may indicate that the company has arrived, but as far as identification is concerned, they get lost in a sea of other symbols that look more or less alike. Open any consumer or trade publication and see what we mean. If you took the company's name away from the symbol, in most cases you wouldn't know which logo belonged with which company.

In developing a logo, then, the first question to ask is, "Will it identify the company?" IBM is fine for International Business Machines because everyone calls it IBM. What if you saw the letters WE? They could stand for Western Electric, let us say, but unless you saw the name Western Electric who would know? Thus, avoid the temptation to take the easiest route to logo design by taking the initials of your company and making a design from them, only to have to use the company name with the logo everytime to explain what the letters stand for.

Now consider, if you will, some of the other logos you may have seen, namely those that spell out the full or partial name of the company in a distinctive type style. What does this kind of logo do?

First of all, if done well, it looks handsome and distinctive. Secondly, and even more important, it spells out the name of the company. Thus the well-known SONY logo is nothing more than SONY spelled out in a distinctive typeface.

There are several ways that you can go about obtaining the graphic talent needed for development of a logo. Perhaps the best source will be a typographer who can show you literally hundreds of different typefaces to select from. Do not choose from just five or six (as often are available from a printer). Select from hundreds. If you do not have a typographer nearby, determine if a local printer has the catalogue of one of the larger "type houses," or if, perhaps, a graphic arts organization, PR firm, etc., could be of assistance. In any event, the costs involved should be relatively low.

Selection of type should be based on the image you want to convey. This requires a certain sensitivity. Some typefaces immediately connote "modern" or "contemporary." Others connote "traditional" or (to some) "old fashioned." Most typefaces come in different weights, that is, the width of the lines that comprise the letters in relationship to the height of the letters. Thus, some typefaces are thin while others are bold. A boldface contemporary type can connote that a firm is contemporary, somewhat large, and probably well-established. And so it goes. To get a feel for how typefaces in logos can have an impact and so help create an image, simply leaf through a few magazines and look at logos. Chances are you can say something about every single company just by determining what image is conveyed by its logo. Will you be right or wrong about your assumptions? That doesn't really matter. Without further contact, the logo gives the image that must be assumed to be correct, just as a voice on the other end of a telephone creates an image that stands until corrected.

Putting the Logo to Work

The question now becomes, "Where do you use the logo?" The answer, very simply, is everywhere you reasonably can. Still the logo is not the only consideration.

Letterheads. The keystone of most company identification programs is the company letterhead. The logo, depending on its size and shape, often will be placed about a half-inch or more from the top of the page either centered or placed on one side or the other. If the logo has the full name of the company, the only other element needed is the address and telephone number of your organization, often placed in relatively small letters beneath or to the side of the logo. If the logo contains only part of the company name (for example, "Smith-Doe" for Smith and Doe Associates, Inc.), the full name of the company also should be included in the small type.

The type selected for other than the logo should be compatible with that used for the logo. In other words, you should not use relatively old-fashioned type to spell out the address and the name of the firm, etc., if the logo uses a modern face.

The letterhead also seems, in many cases, to act as the dumping ground for numerous tidbits of information, such as membership in various organizations, date of the company's founding, and so on. To be sure, this type of information is relevant and important. The fact that your organization cares enough about professionalism to belong to AIA, ACEC, ASLA, etc., can be a big plus in many persons' eyes. Since this is the case, however, it stands to reason that you shouldn't merely dump the information onto the letterhead somewhere where it seems to fit. Rather, find a place where it can go well so the letterhead is uncluttered, for example, across the bottom of the letterhead. Contrast this neatness to those that have the logos of several groups and outfits scattered all around.

One of the major reasons for this scattering is that many letterheads are put together with very little thought about image impact. You must be concerned about appearance because all too often that is what you and your firm will be evaluated by. Another reason for the problem is this: the letterhead often is designed in terms of embellishing a blank page. But who ever sends a piece of stationery with nothing on it? Therefore, when designing a letterhead or having one designed for you, always insist on seeing how it will look with typing on it.

No matter what image you are trying to get across, always keep the letterhead uncluttered and organized, unless you want people to think that your organization is disorganized and perhaps fly-by-night.

Be sure to examine other firms' letterheads. See what you like about them and what you dislike. You probably have hundreds of different examples in your own files.

Second Sheets. Second sheets often are plain paper, unprinted. If you want to convey the image of organization and professionalism, however, consider having the name of your company or its logo printed in relatively small letters in the upper left- or right-hand corner of the second sheets.

Envelopes. Envelopes can be done up in many different ways: you can have the logo in the upper, middle, or lower left portion with the address on the back flap; you can have the logo and address on the front; you can print the address vertically up the left edge; to name only a few. The way you treat the envelope, regardless of the typeface used and logo, can make an impression, sometimes even more so than the letterhead.

Business Cards. Cards should be kept uncluttered. There are a variety of ways of doing them, but, again, the logo and typeface used should be the same as that used for the letterhead and envelope. This helps establish uniformity.

Other Printed Matter. Other printed matter includes billing forms, bulletins, news releases, newsletters, and so on. In each case, the special type that can be used (such as BULLETIN or NEWS FROM. . .) should be of the same "family" as that used for everything else. This heightens uniformity, which heightens company identification.

Trucks and Other Vehicles. Trucks and other company vehicles can be emblazoned with the company logo, especially on the doors.

Signage. All signage should have at least the company logo. This includes signs at job sites, signs at company facilities, and those "signs" that are painted on the facilities themselves. Some people will even have a special banner made bearing the company logo, and it will be raised in the morning beneath the U. S. flag or on a flag pole of its own.

Color

Another element of company identification centers on the use of colors. Many companies will choose a "corporate color," which will be applied to many of the things a logo is applied to, including vehicles. Realize that the color can be applied to just about everything. Let's say, for example, that you have selected a certain shade of red or a combination of colors as your "color." The printing on your letterheads and other printed materials can use inks in these colors. Trucks can be painted in these colors with the logo and other printing in other compatible colors, and the same for signs. Do bear in mind that you can also get typewriter ribbons of the same color (or close to it) used for printing. Likewise, recognize that you can obtain paper (for stationery) in colors other than white. These present only a small problem in terms of making corrections. Some paper manufacturers supply special correcting tapes with their colored paper. Also, you can obtain custom-matched correcting fluid from Liquid Paper Company (Dallas, Texas 75231) just by sending along a sample of your paper. Realize, too, that paper can be surprinted, that is, you can print a piece of white paper solid yellow except for the logo and company name, which then would appear in white, or whatever color the paper is.

Again, uniformity is the key. If you select a color, use it for as many things as possible.

Stock

Stock is the "official" name of the paper used for printing. While color can be a consideration, as discussed, recognize that there are numerous different kinds of paper stock in terms of composition, weight, and texture. Consider the image you are striving for. If you want to get across the idea that your outfit is an "old line" company, obviously a heavy "antique" paper will be best. Some specially textured papers often are useful to get across the feeling of modernity. Examine the different papers a printer has available. He should have hundreds to choose from and should be able to make recommendations based on the image you want to convey. Where practical, select families of paper. Thus, your letterhead, second sheet, and envelope should all be made of the same paper.

Some Tricks and Cautions

There are a variety of tricks of the trade or special effects that can be put to use when developing those items that bear company identification. Before utilizing them, however, be aware of what really may be involved.

High-quality Printing. There are a variety of ways to make a letterhead outstanding. Some of these involve embossing; using raised letters (ink that stands up from the page and appears glossy); hot stamping (printing through a metallic strip, which deposits a glossy film, usually silver or gold, but available in colors); screening (whereby the logo can be enlarged and printed at 25% of the strength of the ink, so it is faintly visible—especially without typing on the page), and other techniques. These are all well and good, and each has an appropriate application. Consider not only the cost involved, but also the image produced. Will using one of these techniques make too strong an impression? Will it create an impression that conflicts with other elements? If you do feel the urge to do something along that line, however, be certain to consult with a graphic artist of one type or another. Chances are he can channel your desires into something very striking and appropriate—for a price.

Special Stock. There are new types of special stocks on the market that some people are using for business cards in particular. Some of them create a three-dimensional effect. Others involve printing on clear plastic. Again, consider your overall image goals. The trick device that is highly unusual may be viewed with pleasure by some, but for others it can be a significant "turn-off."

Special Colors. Many logos can be designed with color in mind and, thus, can be made two-color, three-color or four-color. (Four-color printing results in your being able to have as many colors as you want by using the four primary colors independently and by mixing quantities of each to produce other colors.) While it is one thing to be able to reproduce a logo in more than one color, it is quite another thing to have the logo *dependent* on color for its effect and impact. In essence, it means that you have to print the logo with two or more colors every time it is used, which can result in a large printing bill.

7.4 TELEPHONE TECHNIQUE

Effective telephone technique is an essential communications strategy to which few firms give proper attention. To understand the importance of correct telephone technique, you first must understand what telephone communication implies.

The person speaking with a representative of your firm is deprived of four of his five senses. He must rely on his sense of hearing, so that his imagination works overtime in developing an image, which increases chances of misinterpretation of output.

This is of particular importance when you consider that a person's first direct contact with your firm often is by telephone; that first impressions often are lasting; and that you have only one chance to make that first impression. If the caller is impressed favorably, or at least is not bothered by the way he is treated on the phone, there should be no problem in follow-up. But if he is "turned off," his first, lasting impression may be negative—perhaps very negative—allowing little opportunity for correction of image.

If an organization offers unique services, it has little to worry about in terms of image. Given the competition in your field, the amount of ground work that is carried out by telephone, and the undeniable importance of first impressions, however, it becomes obvious that the necessity of correct telephone technique cannot be overemphasized.

Development of effective telephone technique is merely a matter of following a few simple guidelines, willingly adhered to once all personnel recognize that they are responsible not only for their own image, but also for that of your firm.

Here are the basic guidelines that, if observed, should help ensure establishment of a positive image by telephone.

Receiving Calls

Answer Promptly. The telephone should not be allowed to ring more than two or three times. Delays in answering can create an image of confusion or a generally unprofessional atmosphere.

Lift Receiver Straight Up. When the phone is answered, the receiver should be grasped firmly and lifted straight up. This minimizes chances of bumping it on the cradle or dropping it, either of which causes a loud, unpleasant noise on the other end of the line and creates an image of clumsiness.

Avoid Carryover. Whoever answers the phone must avoid carryover of conversation or mood. *Carryover of conversation* refers to someone's finishing a conversation or comment while lifting the receiver, so the first thing the caller hears is something like: ". . . and have it taken care of today. Hello." which can be totally unsettling to someone relying solely on his sense of hearing. *Carryover of mood* is sometimes worse and usually occurs when something has irritated a person immediately prior to his answering the phone, resulting in a terse, irritating, "Hello." In such cases, the person answering the phone should have the presence of mind either to compose himself before answering or have someone else answer.

Receptionist Needs Clear, Pleasant Voice. The duty of the person who is primarily responsible for answering the phone (receptionist) is to make a caller feel welcome. Her voice should be clear and should exude a cordial, competent, composed personality. Too often a receptionist will fall into "switchboard syndrome" so that her voice sounds like that of a robot, and instantly conveys a feeling of cold impersonality.

Receptionist Should Give Opening Salutation. When the telephone is answered by a receptionist, an opening salutation such as "Good morning" should be followed by the firm's name stated fully and distinctly. If the firm's name is relatively short, it can be followed by, "May I help you?"

In some cases a firm may have several different firms located at one address, typically the case when joint ventures are involved. In order to minimize expenses one phone will be used for more than one firm, and the phone will be answered with the last four digits of the phone number rather than a listing of all the firms on the phone. Some people can get the impression, when the phone is answered "Good morning, 4321," that the organization they're dealing with is perhaps somewhat "fly-by-night." If you feel this may be a potential problem, consider having separate lines installed for each company.

Modified Salutation for Nonclerical. When the telephone is answered by someone whose job usually does not entail answering the phone, such as a draftsman, the salutation should consist of the firm's name followed by the name of the person speaking, omitting the opening greeting. This is a simple method of letting the caller know that he is speaking with someone in a nonclerical position.

Handle Two Incoming Calls Correctly. If an incoming call conflicts with one already in progress, and if the receptionist cannot signal someone else to answer the incoming call, she should either transfer the first caller and then answer the incoming call, or ask the first caller's permission to be placed on hold ("Excuse me. The other line is ringing. May I place you on hold for a moment?") and answer the incoming call. The incoming call should be answered with the full salutation, not with, "Hold on please," or words to that effect. If the incoming call cannot be transferred immediately, and if the first caller still needs two or more minutes of attention, permission should be requested to call back the incoming caller immediately after the first caller is taken care of.

Use the Caller's Name. If the caller identifies himself, as he should, his name should be written down and referred to during the course of conversation, if only to say, "Just a moment, Mr. Doe, and I'll connect you." This shows simple courtesy and efficient attention to detail.

Do Not Screen Calls. Calls should not be screened. When they are, the caller immediately realizes that someone is judging him, determining whether or not he is worth being spoken with. Most consider that the time savings of such an approach is not worth the potential harm it may cause. We advise, therefore, that honesty holds sway and the following rules be applied:

1. If the caller has identified himself, and if the requested party is known to be available, the caller should be told: "Just a moment, Mr. Doe. I'll get him for you."

2. If the caller has identified himself, but the receptionist is uncertain of the requested party's availability, the caller should be told the situation:

   "Mr. Smith is in, Mr. Doe, but I don't know if he can come to the phone just now. I believe he's conducting an interview. Would you mind holding a moment while I check?"

   If the requested party cannot come to the phone, the caller should be told: "Thank you for waiting, Mr. Doe. I'm sorry, but Mr. Smith is still tied up. Is it something that someone else could help you with, or would you like Mr. Smith to call you back? He'll probably be free in about a half-hour."

3. If the caller has not identified himself, and if the requested party is known to be available, the caller first should be informed of the requested party's availability and then be asked for identification: "Mr. Doe is in, sir. May I tell him who's calling please?"

   Note: "May I tell him who's calling, please?" is the most acceptable identification request. "May I ask who's calling?" can place a caller on the uneasy defensive (it's the standard line used in a screen) or, in some cases, it can anger a caller who feels that the secretary does not have to know who's calling. "May I tell him who's calling, please?" immediately shows the reason for making the identification request, and very gently reminds the caller that he should have identified himself in the first place.

4. If the caller has not identified himself and if the requested party's availability is in question, the identification request should be made only after the caller has been informed whether the requested party can come to the phone. If he cannot, but if another party can be of assistance, an identification request should be made prior to the transfer. If another party cannot be of assistance, and if the caller requests a return call, then his name and phone number should be requested. A caller should not be asked what firm he represents, although it is permissible to ask: "Mr. Doe, does this call refer to an ongoing situation so I can have the file in front of Mr. Smith when he returns the call?"

Note: Some individuals attempt to screen calls by using a standard line such as, "Mr. Smith may have stepped away from his desk for a moment," prior to determining if the requested party wants to answer the call. While such a statement is permissible if true, realize that a "standard line" is recognizable as such the second time it is used on the same person.

Transfer the Call Correctly. When a call must be transferred from one office to another, the transfer process should be carried out in several steps:

1. The caller should be told why a transfer is necessary and his permission to make the transfer should be obtained: "Mr. Doe, I believe the best person to answer the question is Jim Jones. Would you mind holding a few moments while I see if he's available?"

2. Assuming he's in, the person to whom the call is transferred should be told who is on the line and why: "Mr. Doe is on line 28 about the Apex project."

3. The caller should be thanked for waiting and be told that the transfer can take place. In the event that the party to whom the caller should be transferred is not in, or is on another line, a call–back should be arranged or the person can be invited to hold for two minutes or so.

4. When the person to whom the call has been transferred picks up the phone, he should greet the caller, identify himself, and apologize for the necessity of the transfer (if appropriate): "Hello, Mr. Doe. This is Jim Jones. I hope you don't think we've been giving you the runaround."

Differentiate between Caller and Secretary. If a call is being placed by the secretary of a caller who will get on the line once the requested party is reached, the requested party should be told, "Mr. Doe's secretary (or office)

is on the line," not "Mr. Doe is on the line." Failure to make this differentiation could lead to embarrassment if the caller's secretary, and not the caller,
is the recipient of a particularly hearty or off-color greeting.

Time Limit for Hold. If a caller must be placed on hold while a requested
party is finishing another call, or while information is being gathered, or for
whatever reason, his permission must be asked first ("Would you mind holding a few moments, please?") and he should not be left unattended for more
than thirty seconds to a minute. At the end of that time he should be informed
of the status of his request, and status reports should continue at thirty-
second to one-minute intervals until three to five minutes have elapsed. At
the end of that time a call-back should be suggested.

Keep the Call-back Promise. If a caller has been promised a call-back at a
certain time, he absolutely must be called back at that time, if only to be told
that the party or information he requested still is unavailable.

Don't Leave Telephone Unattended. An unanswered phone can create a
negative image of your firm in terms of its ability to have sufficient personnel
on hand. If there are occasions when your firm's telephone may be left unattended during normal office hours, consider either an answering service
or an answering device. Select an answering service with care. All too often
the people employed by an answering service have switchboard syndrome
or are unfamiliar with good telephone techniques. In other words, they can
create a worse impression than no answer at all. One suggestion is to obtain
a list of at least several of the answering service's clients and call at times when
the answering service will respond. As far as answering devices are concerned,
the main drawback is that some people get annoyed at having to talk to a
machine. Accordingly, the recorded message you have is of utmost importance. We suggest such wording as: "Hi. This is Jim Jones. I'm sorry that no
one is here right now to handle your call personally, but please don't get annoyed at the answering device. If you leave your message at the sound of
the tone we'll do our best to get in touch with you as soon as possible." And
do get in touch, if only to inform the caller that you got the message.

Placing Calls

Prepare before Speaking. Prior to placing a call, the caller should have
before him: the name of the party being called; the complete telephone number of the party being called (if the caller is placing the call directly); if necessary, an outline or checklist of points to be covered during the conversation;
information pertinent to the call (files, etc.), and a reliable writing implement
and paper.

Determine Who Places the Call. While most in the field seem to favor an individual placing his own calls, others argue that it's a waste of time if the requested party is unavailable. The retort to that argument is that if the requested party is in, it is impolite to force him to wait while the caller comes onto the line. An acceptable compromise for those who do not wish to place their own calls is to have a secretary place the call and have the caller pick up the receiver as soon as the requested party's availability is ascertained.

Determine Alternatives Beforehand. Before a secretary places a call for her boss, she should know what is desired if the party requested is not in. Should a message be left? Should the party call back at his expense or your firm's? This saves time and mistakes.

Give the Correct Opening Salutation. If the caller places the call directly, he should say, after the opening salutation on the other end, "Hello. This is John Smith calling from Smith and Doe Associates. I'd like to speak with Bob Miller if he's in, please." (If the call is direct-dial, long distance, the transferring process may be speeded if the caller adds the location of his firm, e.g., "Smith and Doe Associates in Boston. . . .")

If the call is being placed by a secretary, the opening salutation can be modified to: "Hello. I'm calling for Mr. John Smith of Smith and Doe Associates (in Boston). He'd like to speak with Mr. Bob Miller if he's in, please."

General

Have Pen and Paper by Each Phone. A reliable writing instrument (such as a ballpoint pen), paper, and a telephone memorandum pad (which facilitates message taking) should be placed near each phone.

Minimize Background Noise. Background noise such as loud music, voices, paper rustling, running water, etc., should be kept to a minimum. The telephone can pick up such sounds and make it almost impossible to hear on the other end, not to mention the harm that can be done to image.

Speak with Nothing in the Mouth. No one should speak on the telephone with anything in his mouth, such as a cigarette, cigar, pipe, gum, or food. The telephone can amplify noises of smoking and mastication, thus creating an unfavorable image of the speaker.

Talk into the Mouthpiece. Speak directly into the mouthpiece of the telephone receiver. Some people have the bad habit of letting the receiver dangle so it picks up sounds more from the throat than the mouth, which makes conversation difficult and creates a negative image.

Use of a desk-top amplifier/microphone, which allows you to speak (and listen) without using the receiver, should be avoided. In most cases people sound as if they are speaking from the bottom of a well. In addition, it may inhibit the other party, who might prefer to use some strong language or pass along confidential information, but fears to do so lest he is overheard. Likewise, a lack of such an inhibition may cause embarrassment if there is someone else in your office. If it is for some reason essential that hands be free while speaking on the telephone, consider using a head set.

Hold the Phone Securely. The receiver should be held securely in order to avoid dropping it. If you prefer to cradle the phone between ear and shoulder, use a shoulder rest.

Speak Normally. People using the telephone should speak in a normal, conversational manner. Speaking too quickly results in a mumbling sound. Speaking too loudly can sound like shouting.

Use a Composed Voice at All Times. It is essential that a businesslike manner be reflected at all times through a composed voice that evidences cordiality and concern for the person on the other end of the line. If there is a situation that causes an obvious deviation from this norm (such as anger, impatience, depression, etc.), the speaker should either apologize and offer an explanation, or ask to return the call at another time.

Avoid Artificiality. Artificiality is often conveyed by overcheerfulness or overconcern, which can create an image of being false, hence, creating distrust.

Double Check Information. All information should be double checked prior to closing a call. Spelling, in particular, must be gone over carefully, especially when it involves, M's, N's, F's, and S's, which are easily distorted by the telephone. The best method for verifying letters is to use common words beginning with the letters in question, such as "M as in mother," "N as in never," etc.

Hang Up Gently. When a call is completed, the receiver should be cradled gently or cradled only after the other party has hung up. A heavy hand is easily misinterpreted.

Avoid Immediate Comments. Some people have the bad habit of making comments about a caller as soon as the conversation is ended. On occasion, a person with this habit will make a comment prior to cradling the receiver completely and the other party may overhear. If the other party happens to overhear a derogatory comment the result can be disastrous.

Implementing a Program

Providing staff members with the above rules can help improve telephone technique significantly. Nonetheless, it is suggested that additional steps be taken, specifically a seminar or workshop for employees conducted by a staff member or a representative of a public relations/communications firm or, in some cases, a representative of your local telephone company.

The main points that must be driven home center not so much on the actual techniques as the reasons why they are important. If staff members understand why something should be done a certain way, it is far likelier that the specific instructions will take root.

A most effective instruction technique involves tape recording a simulated, typical telephone conversation. Begin a seminar by dimming the lights and playing the tape. Ask those present to write down answers to questions relating to the persons in the conversation. Questions asked can include, "What sex are the persons?" "How old?" "Generally friendly or unfriendly?" "Really concerned or phony?" Also ask what type of firms the people represent. Large? Small? Well organized? Haphazardly organized? With little concern about who speaks on the phone and how they speak?

After playing the tape ask each attendee how many questions he answered. The point to be emphasized is not how the questions were answered, but rather that *just by hearing a voice people were able to answer some of the questions.* This indicates to them what others are doing when they call your firm. Once they realize what happens over the phone in terms of image formation; that they are being judged every time they speak on the phone and that in so doing they represent your firm and so invite it to be judged, they very often are eager to learn and carry out the specific do's and don't's.

7.5 WRITING

The ability to write is essential to the success of most promotion activities. While you almost always can obtain writing talent of a degree consistent with the nature and importance of the task involved, it usually is far simpler to obtain the talent needed from staff—including yourself.

Some people believe they have no writing talent at all. In many cases, however, the ability is there but has never been developed. Make no mistake. We are not talking about writing short stories or great novels; rather, we are talking about an ability to transmit an idea through the written word in a manner that will eliminate, or at least minimize, the possibility that the reader will misunderstand what the writer is talking about.

This section is intended to present some of the steps you should consider whenever writing something—whether a proposal, an important letter, brochure, bulletin, news release, magazine article, or whatever. There are several books available on the subject of effective writing. Any one of them may be a good source of additional assistance.

Know Your Subject

Know exactly what you are supposed to be writing about. Don't just "feel confident." Be absolutely positive. Numerous pieces have been written, and perhaps well, that have failed to meet the original intent simply because the subject addressed was not really the subject that was supposed to have been discussed. If, for example, you are writing a reply to a business letter be certain that you know *exactly* what questions or subjects the reply should address itself to. If you are writing a news release, have the vital information correct. If you are writing an article for a journal be certain that you know *exactly* what subject the editor wants to know about. By being absolutely positive about the subject, you can better develop your piece, especially when it comes to research. You will know what subjects can be mentioned only briefly or not at all, and which ones deserve special emphasis, if the subject is to be developed in the appropriate manner.

Establish Research Requirements and Collect Materials

If you know exactly what your subject is, you should have a reasonably good idea of what your research requirements are. Typical research items include old correspondence, magazine articles, files, and so on, as appropriate to the subject at hand and the writing medium involved. In many cases, if not most, the research materials needed will be immediately available to you somewhere in your office. Do not rely solely on your own research materials, however. Consider a trip to the library to utilize a good cross-referencing index; contact trade and professional associations to request copies of pertinent reference materials; use bibliographies of books or of other research materials that can provide you with sources for additional information. In some cases, especially when it comes to articles, you may even consider some original research, that is, interviewing persons for comments. This tactic may even be used in writing a letter, where you would say something such as, "I have spoken with John Doe about this subject and he shares my feelings completely." Do not rely on your memory alone. All too often someone will remember "exactly" how some event or series of circumstances developed only to discover later—and to his embarrassment—that his written account is incorrect. Always double check to help ensure that your facts are accurate and that everything pertinent has been covered.

Read Research Materials

Once you have gathered all your materials together, read them. As you read, make reflective notes. They should be general and subjective. Note what a given person has to say, as well as your own ideas, which gel as a result of forming your own opinions of someone else's thoughts. You may even want to make a note such as "Emphasize this point," which will provide guidance later when you start writing. In fact, you'll probably be taking many of these notes because, as you read, you probably will be able to sense the more important factors becoming apparent, suggesting ways in which the specific topic should be addressed. The more notes you take, the better. If the written research materials are such that you can dog-ear pages or underline, it will make note-taking that much easier.

Organize Research, Reread, and Take More Notes

When you have gone through all your research materials once you should have a feel for the subject at hand. You also should be able to tell whether or not you have covered everything that needs covering. If you are even the slightest bit hesitant about the adequacy of your research on any given aspect of the topic, perform more research until you feel comfortable with what you are talking about.

Gather all your research materials together. Assuming that you are familiar with them, group them by topic. If you are dealing with one topic with no subcategories, the task is simple—in fact it's no task at all. In most cases, however, there will be several subcategories or more. Reread your materials in terms of these subcategories, so that everyone's comments on the subcategory can be read in proximity to one another. Take notes on 3 by 5 or larger file cards. Notes, as before, can be reflective, but should also include reference notations that identify the topics covered and research sources. Only one topic or subcategory should be included per card.

Complete Research

Once you have gone through all your research a second time and have taken notes, start experimenting with the way in which you want your writing to unfold. You can try many different arrangements just by placing your cards in different orders. Once you arrive at an order you feel is somewhat in line with what the piece of writing needs, examine transitional areas. Do you have all the information you need to make the transition from one thought to the next? As you visualize the article, news release, or letter coming into focus, determine if you have all the quotations or facts needed to emphasize or factualize everything you have to say. If so, proceed to the next step. If not, perform more research.

Create the Outline

Creating an outline is a step that grows easily from the step before. There are several methods that can be used for establishing an outline, depending primarily on the nature of the writing involved. A news release, for example, moves from the most important item to the least important because of the unique requirements of news media. Many magazine articles follow a chronological order, that is, a report on what happened first, what happened second, and so on. Other items move on the basis of association of ideas, moving from one idea to another, as each leads to the development of the next. Assuming you can find the ordering that best fits your needs, develop an outline based on your notes. An outline of this section would look something like this:

    I. Introduction
       a. writing as a procedure

   II. Know subject
       a. must be positive
       b. writing to the wrong subject

  III. Research and Collect
       a. most materials available in office
       b. other sources
          1. library
          2. associations
          3. interviews

  IV. Read Research
       a. take reflective notes

   V. Organize and Reread
       a. getting a feel for subject at hand
       b. group materials by topic
       c. use 3 by 5 cards

  VI. Complete Research
       a. typical ways of organizing, based on medium

 VII. Talk Through
       a. getting familiar with overall work

VIII. Start Writing
       a. work with outline
       b. start where it's easiest; do tougher parts later on

  IX. Initial Review
       a. look for flow and transitions

X. Rough Editing
   a. check sentence structures
   b. pejoratives
   c. explanations

XI. Intro/Concl
   a. tell what you will tell; tell what you've told—check both with what you say

XII. Final Editing
   a. close review and elements of it

XIII. Devil's Advocates
   a. one for technical correctness; one for general comments

XIV. Rewriting
   a. as necessary only

Talk or Write it Through

The easiest and fastest way to get going with your writing is to talk or write your piece through once very quickly. You may find it helpful to use a tape recorder. If so, play back what you have said and take notes in terms of expanding one thought or another, revising your outline, or whatever. You may want to have your thoughts transcribed, or you may be happiest just writing the whole thing through, providing you can type somewhat quickly. Do not be wedded to anything developed in this attempt. The purpose of this exercise simply is to ensure that you are familiar with the subject as an integrated whole, and to try out in brief practice some of the ideas you may have been developing and noting. In many cases, the material developed in this step is looked at and then thrown away. But even so, it will have accomplished its purpose.

Begin Serious Writing

You should now be ready to begin serious writing, drawing upon your own skills and the work you have performed up to this point. Work with your outline. Do not worry about grammar or spelling. Say as much as you can in the best way you can. If you have difficulty with the introduction, skip it. Start writing that element of your story that you feel most comfortable with. Once done, go back and write those sections that are more difficult. By the time you are ready to return to them, you will have gotten sufficiently into your subject to handle them with ease. Once you have completed writing your first draft, check your outline. Have you included everything worthy of inclusion? Check your notes, too. Have you left out anything important?

If so, include it, even if it means writing a paragraph that right now fits nowhere into what you have written. Get everything possible in. It's much easier to delete materials later on than it is to add something, which probably will require extensive rewriting for it to be integrated into the rest of the work.

Perform Initial Review

Perform your initial review by determining whether or not your material flows in a good order, and whether major ideas or sections should be changed in terms of their ordering. Again, it is much easier to make these major changes now before final editing more or less "cements" what you have written into place. If you have new paragraphs or thoughts that require integration, put them in now, complete with transitional wording where needed.

Perform Rough Editing

Perform rough editing by checking transitions. Do ideas flow smoothly? Should sentences be added? Do you avoid repeating yourself? Are sentences short and to the point, or do they ramble on? Wherever possible, make sentences brief. It will make your writing that much more forceful. Try to make a passive voice active, that is, it is better to say "she did" rather than "it was done by her." Avoid pejoratives—words that inadvertently cast a shade of meaning on what you are saying because of an inherently negative quality. For example, the "only" of "only six" indicates that, in the writer's opinion, six is not enough. If you want to get in your own opinion, of course, leave the "only." Check your technical references. A certain kind of process may be very simple and understandable to you because you are around it all the time, but if a reader is not aware of the subject you may lose him completely. Therefore, be prepared to offer an explanation of a process, possibly including a real or hypothetical example.

Write/Rewrite Introduction and Conclusion

The purpose of an introduction usually is to tell people what you are about to say to them. The conclusion tells them what you have told them. Obviously, it is easiest to write either one after you've done the telling. Accordingly, review both in light of what you have written. Once you get into the writing you may find that your conclusions will be slightly different from those initially anticipated.

Perform Final Editing

At this point you should be ready to perform final editing. Go over everything. Check sentence structure, punctuation, and spelling (including spelling of names, places, etc.); double check facts and statistics, and the like. If at this point you are unhappy with the way something is ordered or the way an idea develops, resist the temptation to say "to heck with it." Rewrite as needed to make what you have written say precisely what you want it to say in the manner in which you want it said. In the case of major editing, which may be necessary, do not be afraid to cut out paragraphs and tape them into new locations, adding a few words or sentences here and there to ensure that the newly placed material is integrated into the rest of your writing. Once done, have what you have written final typed.

Devil's Advocates Review

The next step entails submitting what you have written to at least two persons: one to review for technical content, the other to review for general understandability. The technical reviewer should be able to give you comments about the accuracy of what you have said in terms of technical correctness. The other reviewer should comment in terms of how well the piece is written. In either case, consider the comments carefully. Do not be caught up in the "pride-of-authorship" syndrome, where you feel that because you have spent a great deal of time on something it must be good. By the same token, do not make changes just because of the comments. Consider what has been said carefully and evaluate it as objectively as possible. If you feel changes should be made, make them. If you feel they are not necessary, do not make them. If two people make the same kind of negative comment about a given sentence or paragraph, however, then it almost certainly needs changing. If the piece involves something to be given to a major public, as would be the case with a brochure, letter to the editor, or something else that is very important, you may wish to consider bringing in outside talent for review and comment or perhaps professional revision, which, at this point, would not be very expensive.

Rewriting

If rewriting is in order, perform it, and then resubmit to your devil's advocates. The extra work involved in perfecting a given piece—even though you may have thought it really was perfect before—often is well worth the time, effort, and aggravation involved.

7.6 TYPEWRITTEN CORRESPONDENCE AND RELATED MATERIALS

Business letters and other typed materials, such as reports and proposals, are often unremarkable forms of communication, except when negative elements call attention to themselves and so create an unfavorable image. There are several excellent publications available on what should and should not be done.

The following items are given to serve as reminders of key points.

Outline

As with any other kind of writing, first take notes on all items you wish to mention, organize them in terms of importance, and create an outline. When just brief letters are involved, the outlining process becomes established as a good habit and so is automatic.

Write

Work with the outline and write or dictate your material, assuming the tone called for by the message and medium involved. Keep sentences as short as possible. Try to make your point quickly. In cases of very important items, have a draft written first and edit as necessary.

Proofread Carefully

In examining the material before it is sent, especially proposals, proofread carefully. Putting your signature on a letter or binder of a report means you are responsible not only for what it says, but also the way it reads and looks. Check for misspellings and appearances, especially corrections. If there are more than one or two visible corrections, have the page retyped. Also, if you note one or two mistakes in terms of what you have said or the way you have said it, redo the letter. It is much better to take the time to create a more favorable impression. If you are forced to do this frequently, however, try to do a better job in the first place either by having a draft copy typed and/or by editing the draft more closely. The importance of proofreading reports cannot be overemphasized. Concerns of image aside, just a misplaced decimal point could result in a law suit.

Review Mechanical Procedures

It is good practice to review occasionally those secretarial practices relating to letter writing. You should obtain and review any one of several available secretarial handbooks covering the subject. A typical business letter can be seen in Figure 29; the parenthetical letters refer to the items below. Bear in mind that the following sample letter is but one of several acceptable possibilities.

November 8, 1976 (B)

Mr. Fred Miller
123 Second Street
Ourland, State 05432 (D)

Dear Fred: (E)

(F)

(G) I have received your letter of October 26 and am pleased to learn that Smith (C) and Doe Associates is one of the firms still under consideration for your project.

I believe it may interest you to know that we have added a new staff member, Mr. John Jones, who received a master of science degree in mechanical engineering from the State Institute of Technology in 1963. Following graduation he was employed as a design division engineer by the State Waterworks Administration, achieving the level of assistant division chief, until he resigned last week to become affiliated with Smith and Doe. As you can well imagine, his experience is extensive, and I believe he would be an asset to your project should we be given the opportunity to become involved with it.

Fred Miller   -2-   November 8, 1976 (I)

Also of interest, the XYZ Manufacturing Corporation has recently developed a new kind of boiler that I believe would be ideally suited for your project. According to information received from the company, it meets or exceeds performance criteria already established, yet it falls well within budget. I am enclosing herewith copies of correspondence and data sheets for your own review.

I look forward to hearing from you in the not too distant future and to working with you on your forthcoming project.

Sincerely, (H)

JD/emm (K)   John Doe, President (J)
Enclosures 2 (L)

Figure 29. Typical business letter.

(A) Typewriter characters should be clean. The ribbon should be in good condition. While slightly more expensive than a fabric ribbon, a carbon ribbon gives much better results. (This holds true for all type-written material.)

(B) The date can be placed in the upper righthand corner, three or four lines below the last line of the letterhead. In the case of a very short letter, the date, name, and address should be placed lower on the page.

(C) Leave at least an inch or so margin on either side.

(D) The name and address of the addressee is placed on the left of the page approximately two lines below the date. Do not use abbreviations for streets or states. In the case of a letter going to a particular company official whose name is unknown to you, add below the address, "Attention: Shipping Department," or whatever department is appropriate. Start the letter with "Gentlemen:" or a similar salutation.

(E) When corresponding with those whom you do not know on a first name basis, or for letters of which copies will be sent, the opening salutation should be formal, using the correct title. (A personal, handwritten note can be added to an original letter after copies are made if need be.) In the case of a woman whose marital status is unknown, it usually is best to use a Ms. rather than a Mrs. or Miss. If the letter is important, however, try to perform minimal research to determine the correct title. In the case of letters to congressmen and governmental officials, consult a dictionary to learn the correct forms of address. In most cases, the opening salutation of a business letter should be followed by a colon (:) not a comma (,).

(F) If you choose to indent a salutation, indent all subsequent paragraphs. Likewise, an unindented salutation, as illustrated, should be followed by paragraphs separated by an extra space or two, unindented.

(G) The opening sentence should refer to the material about which the letter is written, be it a letter, telephone call, personal visit, or whatever. In some cases it is appropriate to add a line to the right of and below the last line of the address, stating: REFERENCE: Our order No. 12404, or whatever specific item (other than a phone call or visit or similar general matter) is going to be discussed.

(H) If the letter is of such a length that a closing will have to be squeezed in at the bottom of a page, or if just the closing, signature and related material will have to appear on a following, separate page, retype the letter. Begin it lower on the page so at least three or four lines appear on the second page, along with the closing apparatus.

(I) At the top of the second page, and each succeeding page, should appear wording identifying the letter, such as the name of the addressee and the page number.

(J) Include your title with your name. Usually it is best to include it after your name, although others prefer it one line below. Also, some prefer to include the name of the firm below the name and title.

(K) The initials of the person dictating the letter should appear in capital letters, followed by a slash. The initials of the typist should be lower case.

(L) If there are enclosures, the letter should so indicate, followed by the number of enclosures in parentheses.

Copies

Include the full names of those persons to whom carbon copies (cc) or xerographic copies (xc) will be addressed. You may wish to mention in the body of the letter that copies are being sent. You also may wish to add a brief note to certain copies.

Blind Copies

A copy of a letter sent to a person not included among the recipients listed on the original should be marked bcc or bxc, indicating that the letter's addressee does not know that a copy has been sent. A letter of explanation usually should accompany a blind copy. Keep a list of blind copy recipients on the file copy of the letter.

When Not Reviewing/Signing

In some cases you will dictate a letter that you will be unable to proofread or sign. In such cases your secretary should sign your name, putting her initials in parentheses. You also may wish to have added at the bottom, below the typist's signature, "DICTATED BUT NOT READ."

Response Time

In all cases you should try to send a response as soon as possible. Consider having your secretary keep track of those letters or other items to which you must reply and, if they are unanswered after a week has passed, automatically type a letter stating that you are working on the situation and will reply shortly. All delayed responses should begin by apologizing for the delay. You also may want to consider using a short memorandum form or even typing or writing a reply on the original letter itself, if called for, stating something on the order of, "Please excuse the informality, but I felt you would appreciate the fastest possible reply."

7.7 INTERPERSONAL COMMUNICATIONS

Interpersonal communications is the term used to identify communications back and forth between persons, such as in a conversation, a series of correspondence, and other informal contact. This would contrast with one-way communications (advertising, public speaking) or most other forms of nonverbal communication.

We are not going to get too deeply involved in this particular topic because, first of all, it is the subject of numerous texts available virtually anywhere, and, secondly, it is subject to numerous theories and suppositions, many of which conflict.

What we are going to concentrate on is the practical application of interpersonal communications and how it can be used to benefit your PR program, your company, and yourself.

The practical application of interpersonal communications means, more than anything else, salesmanship. In this particular case, however, you usually are not selling a commodity; you are trying to sell an idea, concept, or other intangible. Nonetheless, while the product may differ from a suit of clothes or a car, the same techniques of good salesmanship apply. You must still determine how to present your product to increase the chances of selling it. In terms of your employees, for example, you must phrase comments in terms that are most likely to be meaningful to each.

For the sake of argument, let us assume that the productivity of a certain employee has slipped a bit and you want to give him an opportunity to improve it before calling him into the office for a chat. Rather than simply giving him an assignment or giving it to him with some stock comment such as, "Let's really try to move on this," consider whom you are talking to. You probably know him as an individual. You should be aware of some of his work habits and how he has performed in certain situations. Thus, if he seemingly has done best when working with short deadlines, you may make a comment such as, "Bill, we really have to haul it on this one. I want the work done by Monday, not Thursday, so we can get right on the Smith job. It's important. Do you think you can handle it?" In this way you present a challenge to him, which his past history indicates is what is needed to spark his own motivation. If working under pressure has seemed to bother him in the past, however, you may have to take an approach such as: "Bill, we're running into some difficulties on the Smith job, so we'll want to get it started about three days early. It's no big problem. See what you can do. Work out a schedule on paper and we'll go over it. I don't think we'll have any problems." In essence, both approaches, though entirely different, are geared to accomplishing the same thing. One is right for one person while the other is right for the other guy. The same applies to almost any situation. You must:

a. consider what you want the comment to achieve,

b. determine the character of the person you are communicating with, and

c. phrase your comment in terms of your own goals and the character of the person involved.

In essence, what interpersonal communication and salesmanship all boil down to is empathy—the ability to put yourself in the other guy's shoes. While some people are better at this than others, much of what is needed can be learned.

To begin, realize that there are certain concerns and interests that a person is likely to have because he occupies a certain position. For example, most employees like to feel that they are making a solid contribution to an overall effort, that they are appreciated, that they are recognized for their efforts, and that they are rewarded fairly. To make the employee happier, therefore, one usually has to reinforce somehow any one or more of these typical concerns, most of which are covered in personnel relations.

When dealing with a governmental project officer, you know that he is concerned about the quality of design, time schedule, and budget. Thus, if you address these issues in a positive manner, you are likely to have positive impact. For example, if work will be delayed by one month to ensure quality of design after discovery of unanticipated conditions, quality should be used to offset the negative impact of the delays.

In essence, you first must be aware of some of the general concerns that a given person has or is likely to have by virtue of his position, which is exactly what a sharp salesman realizes. If a person comes into the showroom looking at cars, the salesman knows that person wants to buy a new car. He doesn't have to encourage the person to buy a new car. Rather, he has to encourage the person to buy the particular brands of cars he sells. He will do that by trying to learn more about the individual involved, his likes and dislikes, and similar information.

The second stage of interpersonal communications, therefore, is to learn more about the specific individual involved. Insofar as your relationship with him is concerned, what makes him tick? Let's assume that you have been approached by an owner who is in the process of converting a rental property to a condominium. He was referred to you by another owner.

The first step you should take, of course, is to check his credit. If he has poor credit, or if he is notorious for slow payment, you would naturally avoid doing business with him or you would structure the contract in a manner that gives you certain guarantees.

In terms of interpersonal communications, your first step is to evaluate the accuracy of general assumptions. These general assumptions could include that the owner involved is a relatively shrewd businessman, that he may be interested more in initial costs than long-term costs, and that he probably will be taking informal bids from several firms.

Since you have not done business with the man before, you obviously will contact the person who referred him. At this time you will thank him for the referral, speak with him to determine how valid your general assumptions are, and obtain some secondary information, such as organizations the prospect belongs to, hobbies, etc.

Once you have this information, you are prepared to meet the prospect. Chances are you will chat a bit about areas of mutual interest. For example, if you are both members of an organization, you can discuss a few pending organizational matters (easily learned from the organization's most recent newsletter if need be). In going over the specific project, you will let him talk for a while to learn more about his own particular goals. Is he looking for the cheapest way of doing it, or would he prefer to add an element of quality perhaps to be used as part of the marketing effort? By acting in a professional manner, by asking leading questions, by being frank and open, you can impress upon him that you are completely knowledgeable in your field and have the diversity required to accommodate his objectives in an effective manner. In fact, you may even want to acknowledge that you anticipate his obtaining other estimates for the work, and you may offer some advice about certain pitfalls.

During your meeting, you obviously will have to take cues from the responses of the prospect. If it's obvious that he cares only about the lowest possible cost, you certainly would not want to waste time trying to convince him to upgrade. Among other things, he could take it to indicate that you are not really interested in obtaining the project if it involves something less than the best. By the same token, you want to be careful not to indicate that you specialize in "cheap" work. Rather, he should feel that you can do any kind of job well.

If it is obvious to you that the man is very busy, you do not want to spend too much time on unrelated talk. Get to the point quickly, in essence, gearing your approach to the prevailing situation.

You also will want to take cues from nonverbal communication, in particular, facial expressions, lifting of eyebrows, angle of head, and so on. These slight changes in many cases provide a far more accurate clue of what the person is really thinking than the words he may be uttering, which brings us to the subject of sensitivity.

By being sensitive to what a person communicates verbally and nonverbally, you should be able to adjust what you have to say to mesh with his attitudes. Consider, too, the way in which you phrase things that many people are sensitive about.

Should you say something inadvertently that hurts the other person's feelings, be certain to apologize—even if you have to call him the next day to do it. While business is business, recognize that people are people.

If at all possible, do some reading on the subject of interpersonal communication. One of the better books on the subject, believe it or not, is *Between Parent and Child* by H. G. Ginott. While it is geared for parent–child relationships, many of the observations apply to relationships between any two people. The book also discusses the language of "childrenese," which, essentially, suggests that negative comments should be "thing"-directed rather than person-directed. Do not discard the concept simply because Dr. Ginott suggest that it be applied to children. It works for everyone. Many of the needs of children are the same as those of adults. Another excellent book on the subject is *Games People Play* by E. Berne. In this book, Dr. Berne points out that the words people utter do not necessarily mean what a literal interpretation would indicate. In fact, a person in some cases may say one thing to imply the exact opposite of what he has said.

There are numerous other books available, too, some of them bestsellers, others more like textbooks. Since everything everyone does somehow involves people and interpersonal relationships, however, it stands to reason that the more you know about these relationships, the more you understand how people communicate, the more you are able to put yourself into the other person's shoes, and the more likely that you will be able to structure your interpersonal communications to control the situation. Control, to a very real extent, is what PR is all about.

7.8 BROCHURES

The need for a brochure, as for any other PR tool, must be evaluated in terms of an overall program designed to meet the goals of company leadership.

In essence, a brochure is a salesman for your company. It has an appearance (graphics) and it has a sales "spiel" (copy). Unlike other salesmen, however, it always dresses the same way and it always says the same thing. It is important, therefore, that the way it "dresses" and what it says promote exactly the image you want promoted. If you approach the job of developing a brochure in a haphazard manner, it is more than likely that the graphics will not be effective and that the copy may be confusing or disorganized.

Whenever that is the case, you do harm to your image everytime the brochure is seen, and you probably would be better off having no brochure at all.

As with almost everything else you do in developing a program of image control, you must be sure the image fostered by the brochure reflects actuality. If the brochure portrays your firm as a spit-and-polish outfit whose officers dress nattily, yet the person who calls on the prospect is dressed poorly, or the firm's offices are shabby, the person who reads the brochure cannot help but feel that it is promoting a false image and, accordingly, everything about the organization involved may be suspect.

While what follows is intended to provide you with basically what you need to produce a brochure in-house, it is advised strongly that somewhere down the line professional assistance be obtained if for no other reason than to provide devil's advocate opinions before anything is finalized. You may feel that what you have written and designed is excellent, only to have an outside, objective source point out serious flaws. If that is the case, be receptive. Do not be blinded by pride of authorship. Likewise, be careful not to make a change that you are not convinced is correct. (One of the main reasons for including so much information in this section—including information on techniques *not* recommended—is to give you as much competence as possible. Should worse come to worst, you will have the knowledge required to tell an outside source that his idea does not meet your requirements.)

A brochure is intended to represent the company. In that it represents an opportunity for an organization to describe itself, it obviously should be as flattering as truth and accuracy permit. It will be judged on its appearance and its content. Accordingly, you should make every effort—should you decide to develop a brochure—to ensure that what it communicates supports your firm and is consistent with the image conveyed by other factors.

The First Step

In most cases, developing a brochure requires the input of more than one person. Since it is a product of your company, it represents it. Accordingly, it should have the input of the company or at least those who form your firm's leadership.

We suggest that the first step be delegation of major responsibility to one individual, along with delineation of who will be involved in certain key processes, such as review and evaluation of research, review of copy, and other items discussed below. In addition, a group decision must be made regarding at least the audience involved (whom you are directing the brochure to) and the purpose of the brochure.

The audience, of course, is composed of prospective clients. But who are they? Are there certain basic characteristics of all or a majority of them? If so, what elements of the company best coincide with these characteristics? How are these elements to be conveyed via a brochure? What compromises will have to be made? For example, if a competent firm feels itself to be very modern, should it play up its modernity if the bulk of the reading audience is relatively conservative and traditional?

The purpose of the brochure likewise can be stated generally: to sell your company and its services. But is that really the case? Hardly. A brochure, more than anything else, should act as a teaser. It should be a best foot forward and that best foot should be wedged firmly "in the door." Accordingly, the brochure should not be too long. It doesn't have to say everything that can be said. Rather, it should say everything that needs to be said. If it is too long, the reader, probably a very busy person, simply will not take the time to read it. Remember: your firm will not be selected on the basis of its brochure, but a well done brochure can help ensure that your firm will be considered for further investigation. This, in essence, is what a brochure is for, and it does not have to be lengthy to get the job done.

Once you have decided who your audience is and exactly what your brochure should do, check other firms—those in your field and others—to obtain copies of brochures. Examine them. See what you like and what you dislike. The more you obtain, the better you can define what you want and don't want in your own.

Outside Talent

Many different skills are required for producing a brochure. Some of these skills may be available within your own company. Others will have to be obtained from outside sources. Before deciding which services can be obtained from staff and which will have to be contracted for, we suggest strongly that you read the rest of this chapter to become familiar with the tasks involved and skills required.

One of the main criteria to be considered is cost. But be sure not to confuse cost with cash outlay. Work performed in-house is never performed at "no cost," especially when time could be spent on income-producing assignments, or when work results in failure because of unfamiliarity with the task involved.

One way to keep down both cost and cash outlay is through proper utilization of outside talent. This requires determination not only of what type of talent is needed, but when it is needed. In most cases you will find that the more work you can do in-house and present to an outside consultant for review, or what have you, the less expense is involved.

Another consideration in use of outside talent is determination of where to obtain it. There are two general sources: firms that specialize in the types of services you require, and individuals who work on a free-lance or moonlighting basis. Use of a free lance or moonlighter generally implies less expense, but also potential pitfalls, especially if the person moves from the area, takes a job, does poor work, and so forth. On the other hand, use of a firm implies higher cost, attributable to overhead and related factors, but also some assurance that the firm will take full responsibility for the work it produces to ensure your satisfaction and possible future business.

In either case, the selection procedure should be about the same. For each category of service prepare a list of possible providers whose names you know or have obtained through references from others who have produced brochures, business and social acquaintances, Yellow Pages listings, and other sources of talent. Invite the provider of a service to come into your office to discuss capabilities, provide samples of previous work, lists of previous clients, and so on, as well as to discuss the basis for pricing and estimated costs. Examine the work samples closely. Be certain to check references, asking them, if desired, how close estimated costs were to actual total billing. Final selection should be based on factors you consider most important, such as quality of work performed, versatility, willingness to provide "polishing" only, cost, etc.

For your own protection, consider having the supplier of a service prepare a letter of agreement or contract that specifies the exact nature of the work to be performed, pricing basis, estimated overall cost, responsibility for errors, and similar items. Be wary of an open-ended agreement that states an hourly rate but does not include a "not to exceed" clause.

In most cases you will be able to obtain a significant amount of assistance from your printer. Because cost is an element in selecting a printer, obtain price bids from several using a standard hypothetical example such as:

Brochure, 12 pages plus cover. Size $17\frac{1}{2} \times 11\frac{1}{4}$, fold to $8\frac{3}{4} \times 11\frac{1}{4}$. Saddle wire. Strathmore Beau Brilliant 65-pound cover and 80-pound text. Ten half-tones. No bleeds. One-color cover. One color throughout text. Text color different from cover color. Covers No. 2 and No. 3 unprinted. Quantity 500.

The lowest price does not guarantee the best value.

Size

One of your first decisions concerns the size of the brochure. Below we discuss some of the most typical sizes, their virtues, and their drawbacks.

$8\frac{1}{2} \times 11$ Inches. The $8\frac{1}{2} \times 11$ brochure is probably the most typical size. It lends itself well to uncomplicated layout, fits easily into a file folder, and usually is economic in terms of paper (stock) costs. (Stock comes from the mill in any one of several large, precut sizes. The more pieces of paper that can be cut from each large sheet, the less wastage and more economy.)

8¾ × 11¼ Inches. The 8¾ × 11¼ brochure is almost identical to the 8½ × 11. The reason for the slight size difference is a pocket in the inside rear cover (cover No. 3) to hold additional information you may wish to include with your brochure. If the brochure pocket is to hold pieces of paper sized 8½ × 11 and not bind when closed, the slightly increased size is necessary.

9 × 12 Inches. Some prefer a 9 × 12 brochure because they feel the increased size has an effect upon the reader. While this may or may not be true, the fact is that a 9 × 12 brochure is not easily kept in a file folder, which typically is sized 9 × 11¾ or 9 × 12. In addition, this size sometimes causes paper wastage, especially when a pocket is included on cover 3. (Some firms that use this size cut the brochure cover into the shape of a file folder and print the name of the company on the tab. While this may be utilitarian, it sometimes looks somewhat unprofessional.)

11 × 8½ Inches. This is the same as 8½ by 11, with the exception that the fold is on the 8½ inch edge. While such an approach makes for a brochure that is somewhat out of the ordinary, it also creates some potential problems. As examples, a heavier weight, and thus more expensive, cover stock must be employed to prevent the brochure from becoming too floppy. Illustrations that demand strong vertical emphasis, such as a photo of a high-rise building, must be reduced in size to fit, thereby losing some of the impact when contrasted with the same illustration on an 8½ × 11 page. Also, it makes the use of a cover No. 3 pocket very difficult, usually confining inserts to precut, special-use items only.

Square. Typical sizes for a square brochure are 7 × 7 inches or 8 × 8 inches. The shape is atypical and thus, like other unusual shapes, may have the effect of being remembered somewhat more easily (although such a factor cannot be given too much credence in terms of a design-professional selection process). Square brochures usually limit use of cover No. 3 pockets and sometimes can be lost in a file folder. In addition, special envelopes sometimes must be ordered.

4 × 9 Inches. The 4 × 9 brochure also is referred to as No. 10 size, this being the most common business size envelope (9½ × 4⅛ inches) used for correspondence. A brochure of this size can be very economical in terms of printing costs, but it could have a negative impact in terms of firm evaluation based on brochure evaluation. Because of its small size, this brochure is easily lost in a file folder or even in a pile of papers on a crowded desk. Use of a pocket is virtually out of the question.

Other. Brochure sizes and shapes are virtually unlimited. You can use rectangles, squares, triangles, trapezoids, or practically any shape in just about any size imaginable. The more the size or shape differs from the ordinary, the more it will be remembered, which is not necessarily a positive factor. Before deciding on one specific size or shape, and especially on an unusual size or shape, consider who the readers of your brochure will be, what they are looking for, costs for special cuts and papers, costs for special bindings, and costs for specialized design and layout. Also, specially cut sizes and shapes sometimes create unanticipated problems in handling, filing, etc.

Bindings

There is a variety of bindings to choose from. Some permit you to add specialized information with your brochure; others do not. Some of the most common are described below.

Saddle Wire. Saddle wiring involves placing two staples in the unfolded center of a brochure that consists of four-page signatures. (A signature is the printed sheet of paper that is folded to form four or more pages. For example, by folding a printed sheet, sized 17×11, down the middle, you get four $8\frac{1}{2} \times 11$ pages. Thus, you have a four-page signature.) This is the most common binding method and usually results in a completely acceptable appearance for your brochure. If you are considering development of a brochure or a family of brochures that requires a custom make-up for each or each type of prospective client, be advised that saddle wiring limits flexibility. The change of one page necessitates the change of four pages.

Plastic Spiral Spine. Use of a plastic spiral spine also is a very common binding method. The major difference between the plastic spiral and saddle wire is that signatures comprise two pages only and are not folded. There is no significant difference in cost between spiral binding and saddle wiring. One of the purposes cited most frequently for a plastic spiral binding is the supposed ability to insert additional sheets or change certain pages. Unless you have the proper equipment to open and close this particular binding, however, changing pages can be a very difficult, time-consuming procedure. In addition, many graphic designers feel that the spiral binding diminishes the attractiveness and professional appearance of a brochure, and limits what can be done with the layout because the plastic spiral binding and the page punches take up valuable space inside the brochure.

Screw-Together. The screw-together binding usually involves two holes being punched in the margin of the brochure pages for insertion of screws and receptacles that hold the brochure together. This binding is especially well suited for brochures that require custom make-up for particular types of clients, families of brochures, brochures for use in branch offices, and so on. This type of binding works best when at least twenty pages are involved. Care should be taken in specifying page size and layout because a quarter-inch or more of each page will be hidden. Like the plastic spiral binding, the screw-together approach involves two-page signatures only, facilitating changes, additions, and so forth. Only the cover involves a four-page signature that, when applied, gives the brochure the appearance of having a perfect binding (see below). One graphic consideration to bear in mind is the appearance of the two screws on the cover.

Plastic Slip Binders. The plastic slip binder is a very inexpensive binding method. It involves slipping a tapered plastic gutter widest at the base over the spine edge of pages, holding the contents of the brochure together by pressure and friction. (This approach works well for custom assembled brochures, and it precludes the extra step of punching.) Assembling is easy, but we strongly advise that at least two staples be inserted in the pages before applying the slip binder to prevent pages from scattering if the binder falls off. Be advised that this binding method can give an air of the temporary to something that, among other things, is designed to establish an organization's permanence.

Glued. A simple glued method is sometimes employed for brochures that are composed of nothing more than two or three four-page signatures. In such a case, gluing is an alternative to saddle wiring (costs are comparable). This approach should be used carefully because not all printers have the required equipment (necessitating that the procedure be done by hand, a very costly approach), and because some glues have a tendency to dry out after a while. A glue-bound brochure that has been packaged for a year or so may very well have to be stapled together before it is used.

Perfect Binding. A perfect binding is employed usually for very large brochures, which are not recommended. Typical of perfect binding are those brochures that are composed of several clusters of signatures. In other words, rather than having one set of signatures where the signature bearing the first page also is the signature holding the last page, several nests of signatures are involved. Signatures are usually either stapled or glued together before the cover is glued in place. The result is very attractive in that no staples, screws, or other devices are visible. It is a costly approach, however, but one that which, even on a 12- or 16-page brochure, adds a certain degree of class. It should be noted that perfect binding machines are now available that enable you to insert pages and cover in one end and receive a completed, perfectly-bound brochure at the other end. This is a very effective device if you intend to utilize custom brochures that differ from prospect to prospect, or prospect type to prospect type. Cost for the device is $800 or so new. They are available from several manufacturers, one of whom is General Binding Corporation.

Plastic Punch and Press. A relatively new binding method involves two narrow strips of plastic placed on the spine edges of covers 1 and 4; these strips are connected to hold the brochure together by small plastic pins. Some large firms use this method primarily to prepare reports and proposals. Using this method for a brochure is not highly recommended. The two pieces of plastic have a tendency to come apart with usage and the spine itself is left bare.

Three-Ring Binder. A three-ring binder is not recommended for publication of a brochure. It can be very costly and, it generally is agreed, is not as attractive as many of the other methods available.

Folds. A brochure that involves no binding is necessarily a folder. Various basic folds are possible (see Figure 30), some of which are suitable only for pages of a certain size. While folds certainly are acceptable, they have several drawbacks. First, no matter how well prepared, they look somewhat insubstantial when contrasted with other brochures. Second, large folders can be awkward to handle when fully opened. In fact, some folders can become somewhat confusing and certain pages actually will not get read. Third, folders do not work too well with pockets. The pocket either will be flimsy and items in it will drop out, or the items contained will block sections of the brochure, which, as a result, never will be seen.

Library Binding. Some organizations have gone to the extent of preparing a brochure in book form, utilizing a typical library binding. This is, of course, a very costly method. While it lends an undisputable degree of permanency to the brochure, it may be perceived as being too much, giving some readers the impression that the firm involved is, like the brochure, overly elaborate and overly costly.

Boxes. A box brochure uses stiff paper (Bristol, index or double-weight cover) to form large pockets in covers No. 2 and No. 3 or No. 3 alone. In some cases copy will be printed on the pockets or, when only a pocket on cover 3 is involved, on one or two four-page signatures glued into the spine. This technique is particularly effective when the brochure is intended to carry its message primarily through illustration. As such, it is used most frequently by architects, landscape architects, and interior designers to illustrate building façades, interiors, and so on. In some cases black and white

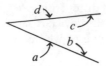

a = cover (cover No. 1)
b = page 1
c = page 2
d = back cover (cover No. 4)

Single fold, most suited for 17 × 11 folded to 8½ × 11.

a = cover No. 1
b = page 1
c = page 2
d = page 3
e = page 4
f = cover No. 4

Six-panel bi-fold, suited for a 25½ × 11 sheet folded to 8½ × 11 or a 12 × 9 sheet folded to 4 × 9 (No. 10 size).

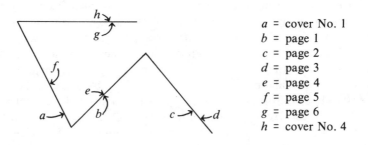

a = cover No. 1
b = page 1
c = page 2
d = page 3
e = page 4
f = page 5
g = page 6
h = cover No. 4

Eight-panel parallel fold, most suited for a 16 × 9 sheet folded to 4 × 9 (No. 10 size).

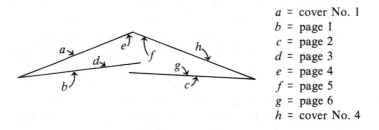

a = cover No. 1
b = page 1
c = page 2
d = page 3
e = page 4
f = page 5
g = page 6
h = cover No. 4

Eight-panel trifold, most suited for a 16 × 9 sheet folded to 4 × 9 (No. 10 size). This fold often is clumsy and is *not* recommended.

Figure 30. Typical folds and folding patterns.

illustrations are used, in other cases, color. In all cases, however, a variety of different illustrations can be inserted—sometimes up to fifty or more—enabling the firm to provide the reader with a specific selection in light of his particular interests. We recommend, in all cases, that firm identification be placed on or in the illustration itself, in the margin of the illustration, or on the back. (Case history data also can be included on the back.) Identification is suggested to overcome a major drawback of the box approach, namely, the possibility that the contents may get scattered and lost. In fact, the more a brochure depends on inserts to be meaningful, the greater the danger that the brochure could become meaningless after the first person sees it and perhaps does not return the inserts to the pocket. For this reason we recommend that, when the box approach is used, a cover No. 3 pocket only be used, and that four or eight pages of copy with at least a few illustrations be included to ensure at least some usability of the brochure in case its inserted contents do not remain with it.

Other. New binding procedures are being developed continually, but by far the bulk of them are directed toward office assembly of materials, and they involve purchasing the necessary equipment. A major criterion to consider in selecting any binding method is the image the method may create. Those that appear to be less than permanent may convey the impression that, regardless of what the brochure may say, the company is not stable enough to produce a permanent brochure. Other considerations must include the effectiveness of the binding method over a period of time and the versatility of the method (or the versatility that can be built into the brochure itself, e.g., saddle wired with pocket). Your printer can also give you advice on binding methods and costs.

Pockets

Regardless of the size, shape, or binding of your brochure, a pocket (see Figure 31) will add a degree of flexibility otherwise unobtainable. In most cases a pocket will cost only a few dollars more (for folding), although more expense is involved when using a pocket means fewer covers cut from a sheet of cover stock or hand operations such as gluing or stapling.

A pocket most frequently is used in connection with cover No. 3. In some cases, an additional pocket is placed on cover No. 2 (inside front cover) and, on occasion, extra covers are printed to create a presentation folder. Pockets also can be used on folders, most often (when a three-panel bi-fold is involved) under the center panel.

It is important to note that the pocket should not be overburdened. In other words, it should not contain more than four or five inserts. Any more than that and there is the risk that important material may be removed and not replaced, as already noted.

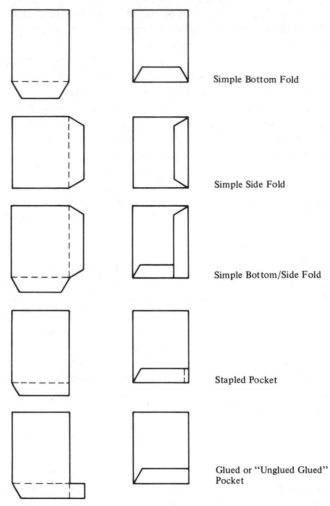

Simple Bottom Fold

Simple Side Fold

Simple Bottom/Side Fold

Stapled Pocket

Glued or "Unglued Glued" Pocket

Figure 31. Typical folds to create a pocket for cover No. 3.

Simple Bottom Fold. A simple bottom fold involves a two- or three-inch tab under the full width of a panel, folded up to create the pocket. When placed on cover No. 3, the left-hand edge of the pocket is cut on a 60 or so degree angle from bottom to top to allow for easier closing. (The right-hand edge often is cut as well.) Note that inserts can fall out of this kind of pocket.

Simple Side Fold. A simple side fold involves use of a two-inch or so tab along the outside margin of the brochure. This kind of pocket is not recommended because it allows materials to fall out too easily.

Simple Bottom/Side Fold. Used most frequently on cover No. 3 of 8¾ × 11¼ inch brochures, this pocket involves the use of a bottom fold and a side fold that, when folded into place, create a pocket that holds material very well. (See also "unglued glued.")

Stapled. A stapled pocket usually involves a bottom fold three to four inches high, angle cut on the left edge and stapled on the right. While it holds materials well, it detracts from the appearance of the piece. Also, stapling involves extra cost.

Glued. A glued pocket achieves the same effect as a stapled pocket, in terms of ability to hold materials, without having the drawback of having staples driven through a cover. Gluing is a hand operation, however, and is, therefore, somewhat expensive. In addition, the glue has a tendency to dry up after a few months of storage, sometimes making a second gluing process mandatory before issuance.

Unglued Glued. An "unglued glued" pocket is the same as the glued described above but no glue is applied. It compares favorably with a simple bottom/side fold.

Segmentation

For ease of reference we recommend that your brochure be segmented into specific, headlined sections, each beginning at the top of a page. Below is a brief discussion of the segments you should consider. This subject is discussed in greater detail in the pages following; at this point it is necessary to determine how segmentation is to be handled for purposes of an initial rough layout.

Table of Contents. A table of contents is seldom necessary because a brochure is usually not long enough to warrant one. It certainly doesn't hurt to have one regardless of length, but it always involves some slight extra cost.

Title Page/Fly Sheet. A title page or fly sheet sometimes is used as the first page of a brochure to indicate the logo and name of the company, plus various addresses and phone numbers. This is most applicable if the cover of the brochure is given graphic treatment so that only the name or logo of your company appears on it. The same information can be, and often is, placed on the back cover (cover No. 4) or on the inside front cover (cover No. 2). If you have several branch locations, and if these branch locations change addresses and phones with some degree of regularity, it probably will be best to print only the address and phone of the headquarters office, noting elsewhere in the copy only that several branches exist. An insert page then can be used to provide updated information as needed.

Letter from the President. A letter from your company's president, when used, appears as the first page of a brochure, sometimes printed to simulate a letterhead. It works especially well for very large organizations that have many officers, perhaps too many to list fully in the brochure itself. Note that such a device should not be used instead of an accompanying, personal letter, which should be sent with each brochure.

Introduction. An introductory statement (instead of, or in conjunction with, a letter from the president) is always advisable for several purposes, discussed below. Briefly, it serves to sum up what follows and to convey what the firm considers to be its major selling points in a manner felt to be effective for the type of prospects involved.

History of the Firm. Such information as would be contained in a history section is usually very important and sometimes fascinating to the company president or founder. The fact is, however, that such information usually is best included briefly in the introduction. There is the very real possibility that it will not be read if carried as a separate section.

Management Techniques/Organization. If you happen to have a project management method that is somewhat out of the ordinary, or that somehow provides the client with better service, you may wish to have a separate segment to identify it. You also could use this section to illustrate how your company is organized in terms of departmental interrelationships.

Officers. You should include information about the active officers or principals of your company. This is a simple matter for relatively small companies that have only three or four principals actively involved in certain aspects of the firm's work. In such cases each officer can be pictured with accompanying biographical materials.

In the case of firms that have more than four officers, most of whom are not involved in design aspects, either less space should be devoted to each (if all are to be shown and written up) or only a few key officers should be pictured. As far as the prospect is concerned, he knows that he will come into contact with only one or two of those involved and so he may consider it a time-consuming (and easily avoidable) chore to read through several pages of biographies.

Key Personnel. Regardless of the size of a firm, there will be certain key personnel who deserve mention. The way you handle this element is important. We recommend strongly that no paid staff members be written up in the brochure itself, for several reasons. First, the loyalty to a firm felt by employees is far different from that felt by partners, principals, or officers. An employee may leave if he has a better offer or to start a firm of his own. When that happens, if he has been written up in the brochure, the brochure automatically becomes outdated. Even when the brochure has been designed for easy changing of pages, you must still develop and print new pages, eliminate the old, insert, etc. Second, a personnel relations problem may be involved, especially when an employee not written up feels he was slighted. It could lead to bad feelings or to a situation that requires you to list "Smith" because you listed "Jones". Third, including employees in a brochure may preclude listing a new and very valuable staff member. For example, if a new man comes on board, how will he be written up at least on a par with others? Can his biography be inserted easily into your brochure? Perhaps not as easily as you think when you consider that even easily changed brochures utilize a two-page signature. How would it look to insert a page that contains a half-page write-up on one side and is blank on the other side?

Two alternatives are recommended for handling employee write-ups. The first recommended approach involves using a pocket on the inside back cover (cover 3) of your brochure, and developing a standard format for employee biographies and photos. Each employee's biography then could be written up, preferably one to a page, and inserted as appropriate. In this manner, should an employee leave or another be hired, a write-up can be discarded or added without the least difficulty. The alternative recommendation, applicable only to brochures that are easily customized, is to insert employee biographies as final pages, perhaps two or three to each side of a page or, preferably, one to a page.

Service/Project Types. Most prospects are probably concerned about what you can do for the specific kind of project involved. In many cases it will be best to utilize a series of segments that break out each general kind of project in which the firm has experience or is adept. In order to keep copy as brief as possible, we suggest that each of these project-type segments include, perhaps boxed on the page or highlighted in copy, an outline listing of the various services it can perform for each type or project.

An alternative to this approach involves using minibrochures in a pocket of the brochure. Each minibrochure describes a certain project type and the service related to it. In some cases minibrochures are staggered in size, and often each is produced in a separate color. In this way, when placed together in a pocket, one can see the title of each one, or at least, by color differentiation, that there is more than one minibrochure (see Figure 32). We do not recommend this approach strongly. It is costly in the first place, and the minibrochures can easily become lost.

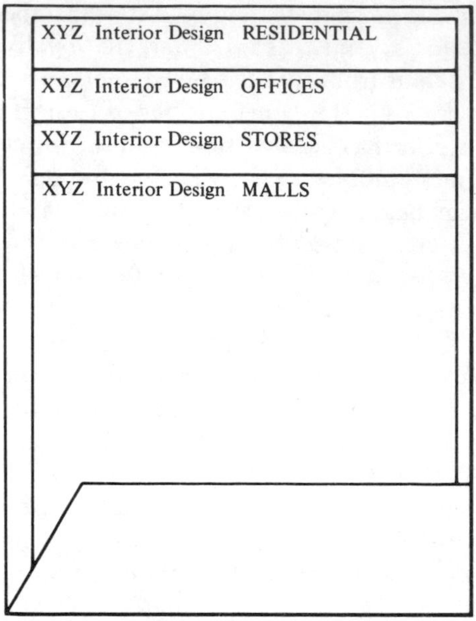

Figure 32. An example of the minibrochure approach. Each minibrochure is staggered in height. Color also can be used to differentiate.

Another approach to the same situation is to prepare a separate brochure for each service or project type, repeating the same general information (introduction, officers, etc.) in each. This is even more costly and can result in a prospect believing that the only thing the firm does is the kind of work discussed in a given brochure, assuming he does not see the other brochures.

Experience. Factors relating to experience in different sorts of projects should be included as an element of copy under project services.

Facilities. It is sometimes effective to describe the facilities your company has, such as drafting area, data terminals, surveying equipment, special drill rigs, etc.

Clients. It is a good idea, in our opinion, to list the various clients you have served. In most cases this is done best by an insert, which enables you to update your list every six months or so, especially if you happen to do a major job for an important client who should be referenced.

Back Matter. We have already noted that, in most cases, biographies of key employees and lists of clients, for the most part, should be included as insertable back matter to help ensure that such material can be changed without affecting the overall brochure. Other back matter to consider includes experience listings and case histories.

Experience listings involve an alphabetical or chronological listing of projects by type. The extent of type definition is up to you. For example, you may list commercial projects or commercial/high-rise and commercial/malls, etc.

Case histories are designed to provide in-depth information about how your company approached a certain kind of project, how it performed, etc., giving the prospect an in-depth view of the way in which your company works.

Others. There may be other segments you want to include. In all cases recognize that the more you have, the longer your brochure will be. The longer your brochure, the less likely that it will all be read. Therefore, consider what else you have to say and, being highly critical, determine if it is really essential. If it is, determine if it could possibly be included in one of the segments already discussed.

Segment Ordering and Space Allocation

Once you have determined which segments should be included in your brochure and how each should be handled, establish the order in which they should appear in the brochure and how insert material is to be prepared. These do not have to be hard and fast decisions at this point. Rather, they should be working decisions that will help development of the brochure. In essence, you can't get anywhere unless you start somewhere. Even if the ultimate production is different from what is decided upon at this point, the decisions and thought that went into making and implementing them will have served their purpose.

Once a tentative order is decided upon, determine the amount of space to be dedicated to each segment, including illustrations. If you have decided to utilize a saddle wiring, or any other binding method that requires the use of four-page signatures, remember that *the total number of pages involved must be a multiple of four.* A typical ordering and space allocation is given below.

Cover 1—Name of firm and logo
Cover 2—Lower left corner, firm name and address
Page 1—Introductory copy
Page 2—Photo of partners
Page 3—Biographies of partners
Page 4—Aerial shot, cars traveling over cloverleaf
Page 5—Highways (copy)

Page 6—Photo of suspension bridge
Page 7—Bridges (copy)
Page 8—Frontal view of commercial jet lifting off from runway
Page 9—Airports (copy)
Page 10—Subdivision layout
Page 11—Land planning (copy)
Page 12—Photo of tennis players, top half/skiers bottom half
Page 13—Recreational facilities (copy)
Page 14—Photo of sewage treatment plant
Page 15—Water and waste water treatment (copy)
Page 16—Copy: listing of facilities
Cover 3—Pocket, no copy
Cover 4—Logo centered on page

First Rough Layout

The preparation of a first rough layout is intended to help you visualize the decisions made up to this point. Development of the first rough layout is relatively easy. The steps listed below can be followed.

1. If necessary, cut to the size and shape of the brochure at least one and a half times the number of pages planned, including covers, inserts, and so on.

2. Examine the ordering of segments tentatively decided upon. For each page indicated in the tentative ordering/space allocation, prepare a rough sketch of what the page might look like. If it's a photo only, so indicate, and write down what the photo will be, even though the photograph may not yet exist.

3. Photocopy pages of type from a brochure, book, magazine, or whatever. Cut and tape them into place where you will have copy in the brochure. Likewise, photocopy photographs from a construction magazine or advertisements that are approximately the size you have in mind, and tape them into place.

4. Prepare a front cover, using either the firm's letterhead (cut and pasted) or a sketch. Indicate any special treatments such as stamping or embossing.

5. Prepare other covers (Nos. 2, 3, and 4), even if they are to be left blank. If cover No. 3 is to have a pocket, so indicate.

6. Prepare pocket inserts as appropriate.

7. Using a heavy marker or press-type (a form of type with a waxed back that can be purchased in an art supply store), indicate segment titles and where they will appear. For example, the word introduction may be inscribed in the upper right corner of page one.

8. If desired, prepare alternatives. For example, if four principals are involved, consider two versions of handling the segment, perhaps one showing a full-page photograph on the left-hand page with copy on the right-hand page, or two pages of copy with good size photographs inset into copy.

9. Tape or glue together pages as they will appear in the brochure. For example, page 2 would be taped or glued to the back of page 1.

Once the first rough layout of the brochure is prepared, with alternatives separate, begin to analyze the proposed layout, the segmentation, and other factors. Once you reach firmer decisions, the writing can begin. (Note: To an extent, the ordering of steps above is based on developing the format first and the writing second. Others prefer preparation of copy first, then development of the format. While either way is acceptable, and the decision is yours alone, do bear in mind that your brochure may be judged after only a glance and, therefore, how it looks may be more important than what it says.)

Perform Prewriting Research

While it is not necessary to complete all research for all subjects before writing, it is necessary, or at least advisable, to compile all research pertaining to a given segment prior to preparing copy for it. The following material indicates the type of research material required for each segment. For some firms it will be too much; for others, too little. Because of the various ways in which a given brochure segment or subject can be approached, research from several areas may be necessary.

Introduction (includes Letter from the President)

firm's original name, founding date, first and subsequent locations, founders, original fields of practice

names of owners added and/or deleted, and related dates of action, since founding to present

locations of main office since founding, dates moved

location of satellite operations, methods of affiliation (wholly owned, partially owned, partnership, etc.) dates opened, moved, closed original services; dates additional services established types of projects in general (industrial, commercial, residential, and so forth, as well as special projects)

projects or types of projects with which the firm may not have had experience, but with which certain key members of staff or officers may have had in-depth experience

current construction or replacement value of buildings/structures for which the firm and/or its current employees provided services

special capabilities

affiliations of firm (i.e., prominent organizations of which the *firm* is a member, charter member, etc.)

awards won by firm (or personnel engaged in firm projects)

keywords re philosophy, such as: establish close relationship with customer; in-budget, on-time; integrity; capable of handling large assignments and small; and so on.

other general and pertinent information

Officers/Key Employees:

name

title

location during formative years

education, degrees held and from where, dates of degrees awarded

work experience prior to affiliation with firm

amount and types or projects for which in responsible charge, prior to joining firm and since

special experience, talent or capabilities

profession-related awards or citations

professional and trade association affiliations, including positions held

articles published, where, when, subjects

military service

nonprofession-related awards and affiliations

Services:

subdivide services by specific headings, such as architecture, mechanical engineering, airport design, mass transit system design, and so on

list those services applicable to each project type, as already discussed

Projects:

list the name, thumbnail description, location, client, and year for each project with which the firm has been involved (from data developed during organizational research)

for new firms, all projects in which officers (and key personnel, if desired) have acted as responsible charge, with other data as above

where necessary, identify those projects that will be discussed either in narrative copy, or case histories or to which special attention may be given

for each project that will or may be discussed in detail, gather information relating to special problems or considerations of the project, work portion assigned to the firm, method of handling the project, special techniques used or developed, plus any other extraordinary factors or other factors deemed important, such as time involved, actual cost in relation to budget, etc.

Clients:

list all clients for whom the firm has performed work, indicating what type is involved

if desired, list type of work performed for each client type

Organize and Evaluate Research

Organize your raw research material by segments. For example, if services are to be discussed with narrative copy that also discusses project types, research data for the segment involved would include services and case history project data together. If separate case histories are to be used also, this research may then be duplicated for case history sections.

Once organized, research should be evaluated to determine that everything pertinent has been included; then evaluate it again to determine what elements should not be mentioned, what *may* be mentioned if space permits, what preferably *should* be mentioned, and what *must* be mentioned.

It may be good policy to have at least several key members of the company evaluate research independently. Once done, conduct a meeting to examine any subjects about which there is a difference of opinion. This method will help prevent giant steps backward later on in the development process.

Writing

A professional writer can usually prepare a first draft written approximately to the required length, but the amateur writer probably will achieve best results by writing without regard to the space allocated to a given segment or other factors. In this way, everything that is believed worthy of being stated can be stated; selective weeding can come later, should copy be over-written.

Although there should be a certain stylistic sameness unifying all copy, each segment must be approached in the manner most suited to it, as discussed below.

General. A few general considerations should be mentioned before getting into specifics. First, a page of a copy should be prepared for each page and each cover in the brochure. For example, cover 1 would be typed in draft as "Cover No. 1, logo only," if, in fact it were to have only a logo. If it were to have logo, firm name, address, and telephone number, the copy then would indicate logo, name and address of the firm, etc. Likewise, a page that is to have a full page photo only would indicate what the photo would be and its approximate size.

Another consideration that will make the task somewhat easier is the page identification placed on draft copy. It is suggested that the upper left corner of each draft page have on it the corresponding page number of the brochure.

Introduction. The introduction to the brochure is one of its most important elements. It is usually the first segment read and, in some cases, the only one read. Some firms title this segment "Introduction"; others title it with the name of the firm; some give it no title at all.

The purpose of the introduction is not to tell the reader everything management feels he should know about the firm; rather, it is to summarize much of what follows, establish the credibility of the firm, and leave an impression in accord with the image the firm wishes to convey.

The introduction is best kept relatively brief. The way to present topics should be based on evaluation and rating of research. Those elements considered to be most important, in light of the firm's own self-evaluation and what it deems to be the interest of readers, deserve either early mention or full coverage, or both.

When writing, refer to section 7.5 of this chapter which provides some in-depth guidance. In general, try to make sentences as brief as possible. Avoid long, run-on sentences that try to say too much. Also, try to make the ordering of sentences and paragraphs as logical as possible so that one thought leads to the next. It may be best to note each item to be discussed on a 3 by 5 card, e.g., one card would say, "fields of practice—commercial, industrial, etc.," another might say, "opening of branch offices," and so on. Once all elements are so covered, place the cards in various orderings until it appears that you have achieved a flow of thought that will make the copy easy to follow, while also conforming (to as great an extent as possible) to evaluation of research. Once cards are in a good order, prepare an outline and use it in preparing your first rough draft. A typical outline appears below:

Name of firm—first mention
Founding
Growth
Fields in which service offered—industrial, governmental, etc.
Typical types of projects
Reference to personnel
Stress cost-effectiveness and innovation
Stress close relationship with client

A typical introduction is given below:

XYZ Architects, Inc., was established in 1956 to provide a full range of architectural services for governmental, commercial, industrial, institutional, and multifamily residential projects.

Since its founding, a primary objective of the firm has been establishment of a close working relationship with clients to help ensure responsiveness to requirements and coordination of effort with other professionals assigned to a project. The success of this approach can be measured in terms of loyalty of clients, many of whom have utilized XYZ for ten or more projects through the years.

Since 1967 the firm has been engaged in a program of controlled expansion to fulfill increased requests for its services. While the firm's complement of personnel has been expanded, the scope of its services has changed little, better enabling concentration on continued advancements in the state of the art and innovations applicable to clients' projects.

The following pages are devoted to a capsulized summary of the firm's activities and projects. Because a brochure such as this cannot accurately convey all that must be known before a company is retained, you are invited to contact John Jones, President, for further information.

Officers. What is said about each officer depends, to an extent, on his relationship to the firm. For example, if an officer is involved in the actual production of design, stress his experience. If, on the other hand, he serves primarily as a go-between, soliciting a client's business and keeping him happy, emphasize activities that suggest how others rely on his capabilities. Generally, a write-up should not exceed 350 words. Even 250 is a bit long. As in other cases, bear in mind that the intent is to provide a glimpse. Materials provided later will serve to fill in any blanks that may exist.

Note: Be careful in certain cases where you mention current service. For example, if the subject is serving as president of the state NSPE chapter at the time of the writing, cite that service in the past tense: ". . . and served as president of the organization" or ". . . was elected president for 1975–1976." *Do not* state "is serving as president" or "will serve." This tends to date the brochure prematurely.

Two typical biographies are given below. Read brochures in your field for others.

John Doe, President

John Doe began his career in interior design in 1952, shortly after graduating from State University. Employed first as a designer in a large architectural firm, his responsibilities increased until, in 1955, he was appointed director of the firm's 12-man interior design department. He established XYZ Interior Design in 1957. Today his company employs more than 40 persons involved with more than 100 different projects annually. Active in community affairs, Mr. Doe is Past President of Anytown Jaycees, and is an active member of various fraternal organizations. In 1968 he was named Anytown Jaycee's Young Man of the Year.

Peter Smith, Vice President

Peter Smith, XYZ's vice president since 1971, is responsible for project coordination. A 1962 civil engineering graduate of City College, he earned a master's degree in business management from State University in 1965. He had been employed by XYZ since graduation, and has developed highly effective management approaches to projects of various sizes and types. His assignments with the firm have ranged from individual project management to customer relations and marketing. He not only brings to bear training and experience in his specialty, but also an intimate awareness of other concerns that must be addressed for successful development of each project.

Personnel. Write-ups for supervisory personnel can follow any one of several forms: the one used for officers; a form similar to the one used for officers, plus an additional listing of all projects for which the individual involved has served as responsible charge; or an outline listing, indicating name, date of birth, education, projects for which the individual involved has served as responsible charge, organizations and positions held, awards, and so on. Many regard the listing method as most effective in terms of providing full, easily read details, especially when personnel descriptions are included as inserts for a cover No. 3 pocket. Whatever method is selected should be applied uniformly for all personnel.

Services. In many cases, the service segment—alone or as an element of a project segment—needs no copy other than that used to formulate a skeletal outline of services. In other cases, however, services may be presented as a narrative element of project descriptions. It is important that the various service elements be indicated clearly, especially if a service outline is not used. A typical service listing is shown in Figure 33.

Projects. We suggest that, when preparing copy for projects, you first separate research data by means of project types. While the interests of the prospects should give you some clues on the way to go, evaluate your own experience. For example, if you define five types of bridges, but the firm is active and highly experienced in only three, it may be best to lump facts and statistics together. Otherwise, you may be put in the position of having to say, about one of the remaining two, "XYZ has designed only three suspension bridges."

We advise that you do not get into too many specifics in the copy, leaving them to be covered by illustrations or back matter. Accordingly, consider the following sample project write-ups (assuming that a service listing would be boxed on the page) and caption.

Roadway Design

XYZ Engineers has designed more than 1000 miles of roadways, including dual-lane, four-lane, interstates, interstate cloverleafs, etc. Estimated replacement value exceeds one billion dollars. XYZ personnel have made substantial innovations in the field of roadway design and materials specification, as well as various construction methods.

Interstate Highways

XYZ Engineers has designed more than 650 miles of interstate highways, including 80 miles of I-95 and 50 miles of I-66. The company also is experienced in smaller interstate projects, and was responsible for the widening and resurfacing design of 25 miles of Route 1 between Smith City and Anytown.

(caption)

Smith City Cloverleaf, I-95, designed to handle more than 4,500 vehicles daily. Despite substantial unanticipated subsurface conditions, the project was completed only one week behind schedule.

Note that the caption, in addition to identifying the illustration, describes favorable facts about the company that cannot be illustrated, namely, ability to expedite.

services

electrical engineering

Design and evaluation of systems for:

Power Generating Plants
Interior Lighting
Exterior Lighting
Athletic Lighting
Electrical Distribution
Transmission
Communication
Sound
Alarm
Security
Television Antenna Systems
Utility Master Planning
Computer Facilities
Temperature Controls

water supply and sewage systems

Studies and design of:

Sewage Collection Systems
Solid Waste Disposal Systems
Packaged Waste-Water
Treatment Plants
Water Treatment Plants
Water Supply and Storage Facilities
Water Distribution Systems
Pumping Stations
Sanitary Sewer Systems
Storm Sewer Systems

construction management

Design for Turnkey Projects
Design/Construct Projects
Fast Track Design
Construction Management
Construction Supervision
Construction Inspection
Cost Estimating
Budget and Forecast Preparation

systems analysis

Performance Specifications
Systems Design
Modular Systems
Construction Trade-Off Analysis
Life-Cycle Costing

energy conservation

The Company is thoroughly experienced in the area of energy conservation consultation and design. Typical services include:

Mechanical System Survey
Electrical System Survey
Evaluation of Operating Procedures
Evaluation of Maintenance Procedures
Utility Rate Studies
Life Cycle Costing
Fuel Selection Studies
Conversion Feasibility Studies
Systems Design for Energy Conservation
Systems Monitoring
Instructional Programs for Maintenance
Personnel
Preparation of Systems Manuals
Solar Energy Systems

general

In addition to other specific services listed, the Company also provides these general services:

Feasibility Studies
Cost Studies
Preliminary Engineering Studies
Preliminary Design Drawings
Cost Estimating
Construction Management
Construction Supervision
Inspection
As-Built Drawings
Modular Housing Design

Figure 33. Typical service listing (courtesy Shefferman & Bigelson Company).

mechanical engineering

Design and evaluation of systems for:

Heating
Ventilation
Airconditioning
Environmental Control
Plumbing
Steam Distribution
Compressed Air
Gas
Fuel Handling
Coal Burning and Handling Systems
Solar Energy Systems

Industrial Exhaust
Pollution Control
Interior Transportation
Conveying
Low Temperature Facilities
Clean Rooms
Laboratories

fire protection systems

Sprinkler Systems
Fire Standpipes
Chemical Extinguishing Systems
Booster Systems

Figure 33. (*Continued*)

Case Histories. Case histories could be used as an element of a project description. It is usually best to separate them and use them for back matter, thus permitting you to insert case histories applicable to the particular prospect. In addition, case histories usually take at least a page each. Since several case histories can be used to describe each project type, we think it best that only general copy be used for projects.

Assuming you do decide to use case histories, we suggest that you prepare them after the brochure is complete, and that you develop a standard format, not only for graphics, but also for presenting information (name of project first, name of client second, etc.) For easy reference, each case history could be given a number. In some cases you may want to differentiate among them by the color of paper used.

A typical case history could read as follows:

XYZ RECREATIONAL DESIGN
CASE HISTORY NO. 5

Name of Project: City Tennis and Squash Club

Client: City Tennis and Squash Club Associates

Project Description: Design six tennis courts for extended season use, and manage construction

Problem: For the tennis courts to be profitable, an XYZ economic analysis showed, they would have to be open for play between March 15 and November 15 of each year, resulting in an extended season. Most courts in the project area normally are playable only from April 15 to September 15. A study of historical weather conditions and a report prepared by a soil and foundation engineer indicated that courts could be subject to frost heaves beginning in early November through mid-March unless protective measures were taken. The protective measures suggested initially would have precluded play, making the extended season impossible. In addition, because of delays caused by a special zoning appeal, the anticipated start of construction—designed to have the courts open for play on March 15—would be impossible to meet.

Solution: After meeting with the owners, XYZ staff specialists decided that the frost heave problem could be solved by increasing the depth of excavation, lining the excavation with asphaltic material (rather than plastic material originally specified), and relying on full-depth construction to significantly minimize possible damage done by frost heaves. In addition, XYZ suggested applying two coats of an advanced polymer-based paint over the asphalt surface.

Outcome: Through its management procedures, XYZ was able to select a contractor to begin construction in as short a time as possible. This ability, combined with the use of overtime labor and rented floodlights, allowed construction to be completed on time. The additional, unanticipated costs associated with the techniques ultimately used were paid back within two years because protective and maintenance procedures, given the construction methods used, were far less complex and costly than those required originally, and because the extended period was extended still more—from March 1 through December 1. Cost of overtime labor was recovered through funds received because of timely completion; had completion been delayed, those funds would have been lost.

Whether or not you wish to use cost data is up to you. In most cases, however, we recommend against it, as the client may object. In addition, inflation quickly distorts cost factors. Cost factors could possibly be supplied on request.

Facilities and Equipment. Information about facilities can be carried partially through illustration, such as a photograph of your firm's computer room. Do not go overboard, and do not use a montage, which tends to create confusion. We suggest that you use introductory copy such as:

XYZ has invested more than $2 million in sophisticated data processing equipment and facilities. A partial list is given below.

The listing that follows such an introduction can be very general, somewhat general, specific, or very specific. The best approach probably is to be highly specific about the most important items and less specific about others. The more specific you are, of course, the more your listing is subject to change. (You may wish to include only a general listing in the brochure, being specific only about items not subject to change, and to provide specifics on a separate sheet for back matter.)

Back Matter. Additional back matter items include, primarily, a listing of clients and experience.

A listing of clients can be presented in several ways. You can include all those ever served, all those served within a past number of years, a selective listing (with or without a time frame), etc. The ones you actually name can be listed alphabetically or subdivided by governmental, commercial, etc., or by state governments, county governments, municipal governments, private developers, and so on, with clients being listed alphabetically within subdivisions.

An experience listing can be handled in several ways. The method recommended is this:

a. Segregate projects by type using either general categorization (such as industrial plants) or general categorizations with specific subcategories, (auto assembly plants) or specific categories without the general.

b. List projects within categories or subcategories in logical sequence, usually by date of project or alphabetical listing. Using time as the basis makes it easier to add to the list.

c. For each project listed, include relevant material, for example:

Interstate I-95, 6 miles, eight lanes, City, State. Estimated current replacement cost, $3.5 million

You may want to include more or less. Note that estimated replacement values are included instead of original cost.

d. Establish a presentation method. Since in most cases a prospect is interested only in that specific kind of project related to what he is preparing to undertake, it seems wasteful to provide him with the complete list. Accordingly, we suggest that you prepare an overall summary sheet describing the number of various types of projects handled, and overall estimated replacement value, along with a complete listing for the specific kind of project involved. You could also include just a listing of typical projects within a category—instead of the whole listing—with summary information. In other words, list ten projects of a given type, but indicate the total number of projects handled (from when to when), total replacement value, etc.

Illustration

Once the first draft of copy has been prepared, you can begin to consider illustrative materials. While it is not a case of "the more illustrations the merrier," do recognize that illustrations can serve to make your brochure far more attractive and effective. We recommend that your illustrations be kept to photographs only. They depict what actually exists and can back up what is said in copy. (You can call a job highly complex, but showing a photo of it proves its complexity.) Second, photos can be used very effectively at relatively low cost. Third, and most important, photos are highly flexible. To understand how to use them, therefore, it is necessary first to discuss flexibility.

Illustrations can be placed just about anywhere in your brochure, mingled in with copy, above it, below it, to the side, on a page of illustrations only, or on a page with only one illustration. For the most part, this discussion concentrates on the "page opposite," because an effective but simple format often involves illustrations being placed on left-hand pages and copy on the right-hand pages.

The larger the illustration the more the effect achieved. Illustrations shown full page usually are referred to as full-page bleeds. (In printing, the photo is bled around the edges of the page, meaning that it will be shot at 8-9/16 × 11-1/16 and the page will then be trimmed to its final size of 8-1/2 11 inches.) An alternative to the full-page bleed is to use an almost full-page photo, leaving an unprinted frame or border on all sides. It should be emphasized that only good illustrations deserve to be presented in this manner. If enlargement causes fuzziness, obtain a better illustration.

Putting several photos on a page usually requires a degree of artistic ability. Probably not more than five photos per page should be used. Captions can be placed either adjacent to each photo or in a key somewhere on the page. One simple method of getting around the problems connected with several illustrations per page is to make all the photos the same size, and limit them to, perhaps, three per page. This can be achieved easily through cropping.

You may wish to use photos in the body of the text itself, rather than having them on a separate, preferably left-hand, page only. In such cases it is often best to make the photo self-explanatory, as with a photo of an officer. As there is no need for a caption, the layout will not become awkward or difficult to follow.

Photos can be adjusted easily in terms of size, either by enlargement or reduction. The printer can take care of this and you should have to mark only the percentage of reduction or increase. For example, if the photo you have is 2 × 2½ inches, and it must be used for a space 7 × 8¾ inches, it would be marked "350% of original." Likewise, you can determine how large the length must be if the width of the space allocated is 2 inches, and the original width is 4 inches. In other words, at 50% of original width, correct space allocation for length would be 50% of original.

A less common adjustment is cropping, the cutting out of portions of the photograph, usually around the edges. For example, if the photograph of an individual is off center, it can be centered simply by cropping from one side or the other. This technique is especially important for enlargements. For example, assume you have a 2 × 3 photo that must be used for a bleed on an 8¾ × 11¼ page. When the 2-inch edge is enlarged to fit the 8¾-inch space (438% of original), it would make the 3-inch edge 13.123 inches, which means something would have to be cropped. You would have to determine where the cutting will take place—from the top, bottom, or both.

Another way of cropping is to work inside the borders. For example, you may have an illustration of two persons standing behind a table. When enlarging the photo to the desired size, you find that centering the photo on the page will result in each person "losing" half an arm. One solution is to cut right up the middle of the photo, removing a portion of it, then putting the two pieces back as one. Be advised that this is a risky operation. Backgrounds usually do not match correctly, the desk may look strange, and so on. Further, it may require retouching. The advice, therefore, is to simply reshoot the photo or use something else.

Retouching is an adjustment process that usually involves painting a photo to delete certain items. This is very expensive, time-consuming work. In most cases it is best to use another photo.

Greeking is a far simpler retouching method. Usually it is used to make unintelligible certain signs or wording. For example, assume you have a photograph of a completed parking lot you want to use. In the background there is a site sign you prefer that the client not see. Very often the printer or free-lance talent can add slight bits of touch-up paint to the sign so it becomes unreadable.

Silhouettes have been used very well to achieve a bit of artistic effect at low cost. Silhouetting involves posing a subject against a white background and lighting so no shadows exist. The resulting photo is then retouched by hand or is machine-processed to create the silhouette. The silhouette can then be placed on another photo, on a photo of a set of plans, or on an overlay sheet for a full page photo of a complete project.

Line conversions and quasi line conversions are used to create special effects you probably have seen. Typically, they make photos book as though they are composed of concentric circles or many dots, or that they have little shading (being mostly black and white without grays), etc. These effects are usually the result of line conversion performed with special development equipment by or through a printer. It creates a very artistic effect (maybe too artistic for your tastes and the purpose of the brochure) at a minimal cost. It often achieves good effects for photographs that are not too good to begin with.

One thing to bear in mind: if you do it for some photographs, you may have to do it for all in that it "sticks out like a sore thumb" in comparison with conventional photos.

Quasi line conversion can be achieved by using overlays obtainable from art supply stores. These are clear plastic sheets of dots and circles which are placed over the photo for effect. In some cases they work well, but in others they can be detrimental. Experimentation and critical judgment are advised before a final decision is made.

Some persons favor use of a collage of photos, as many as ten, fifteen or more, some actually lying across others. In most cases this technique comes across as amateurish and does little to enhance an image.

In certain cases you may want to use line drawings, as for a semiportrait of certain people. Such line drawings are made relatively easily, just by tracing a photograph, something done best by a professional, usually at little expense. If a line drawing is used to illustrate one item, however, it should be used to illustrate similar items. For example, one officer should not be depicted by a line drawing and another by a photograph. Line drawings can be used for certain evocative illustrations scattered throughout the brochure but, we suggest, only with competent professional guidance.

Research. Once you are familiar with what can be done with illustrations, what options are open to you, and so forth, perform some research to determine what illustrative materials are available to you. This includes research of files to obtain a list of all photographs and slides available, regardless of subject matter, as well as project-related items that can be photographed and reproduced easily in the brochure. Also review the copy to determine which of the projects discussed should be illustrated. You also may wish to call other companies involved in certain projects to determine what they have available. (Do not at this time prepare any new illustrations. Merely see what is available and, through the next step, what you want to use.)

Determining What To Use. To determine what photos to use, examine your first rough layout and create a list of possibilities or suggestions (for review by key personnel or whomever is involved in the brochure production process). Some possibilities, segment-by-segment, are discussed below:

Introduction: The introduction is very often the first right-hand page, facing cover 2. As a result, an illustration may not be needed. (If you have the introduction on a left-hand page, reconsider your layout. The natural tendency is for right-hand pages to be read first.) When the first page is a flysheet bearing the firm's logo, name, and address (es), resulting in the introduction being placed on what amounts to page 3, page 2 then could be left blank, used for a table of contents, or for photographic illustration. A typical photo could be a shot of the headquarters building (providing it is an impressive building), an evocative interior scene (conference in progress), a typical site scene, etc.

Officers: Simple head shots of officers, whether used on full pages, half-pages, or mixed in with descriptive copy, leave much to be desired. In fact they serve little purpose except to show a head and what the person looks like. We recommend that you use a typical scene that not only illustrates the person involved, but also tells the reader something about him. For example, in the case of two partners, consider a left-hand page illustration of the two standing in shirtsleeves examining a set of plans, or in hard hats at a construction site, or sitting in a conference room with other staff members. By using this technique, you convey a certain extra something to indicate that the key men get involved.

Personnel: Personnel can be illustrated in the same manner as officers. When pocket inserts are used, as suggested, you may consider using two descriptions per page. In such a case, the two involved could be shown in a long photographic strip, down the left or right margin, depicting them working together; alternatively, good photos of each may be used in the body of the text. Recognize that it is usually unnecessary to include photos when biographical sheets are included.

Projects: Nothing is more barren than a long stretch of empty roadway or a large warehouse surrounded by a huge empty parking lot. Photos used to illustrate projects should have "snap." For roadways, consider an aerial shot of a cloverleaf at rush hour. Show a warehouse with trucks loading and unloading. Illustrate a factory by showing workers in action. In other words, where applicable, use something that symbolizes the subject. Also consider using good site photos; close-ups (as of a workman's face), etc.

Use an actual photo of a project as completed only when it has visual appeal or when the façade of the project is what really counts, as often is the case for an architect. Consider client interests. If yours is an inter-professional mechanical engineering firm, for example, it is pointless to use ten photos of boiler rooms. Rather, show the buildings for which mechanical engineering systems have been designed. This is what relates best to the architect who wants to know the types of projects for which your firm has been retained.

Basic Mechanical Specifications

We are now at the point in brochure development where decisions must be made concerning basic mechanical specifications. As mentioned earlier, these particular decisions are best made with outside assistance, especially those tasks that involve measuring type and copy and selecting typefaces.

Determine Basic Layout for Type. The first step toward a more definitive rough layout of the brochure begins with developing a format for each page of primarily textual matter (see Figure 34). For example, a page that dis-cuses officers and combines photos with copy would be considered primarily textual. A page of two or three photos of officers and captions would be primarily illustrative. There are a variety of different layouts that can be selected. It is not necessary for a layout to remain consistent from segment to segment (provided that there is a reason for change).

Determine and Draw in Margins. Once you have determined basic layout(s), draw in the top, bottom, and side margins of each page, ignoring (for the time being) any illustrations. A line of type in single column layout probably should not exceed six inches. Double column layout lines should not exceed three-and-one-half inches.

In determining top margins, bear in mind that each segment headline should generally be the same distance from the top of the page and from the first line of copy. (A left-hand page segment head should either be centered or flushed left so it starts at the left margin. Right-hand page segment heads should be either centered or flushed right, so the last letter is flush with the right margin.) Bottom margins probably should allow at least one-half inch to the bottom of the page, perhaps more if page numbers are to be used there.

When drawing in marginal lines, recognize that the lines should indicate boundaries for textual copy only, not heads.

Indicate Illustrations. Indicate illustrations or tentative illustrations to be interspersed with type on the various textual pages. In so doing you will also

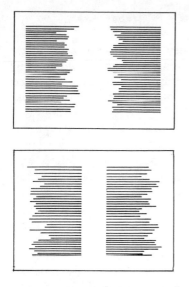

Left pages flush left; right pages flush right

Left pages flush right; right pages flush left

Justified left and right

Double columns justified left and right

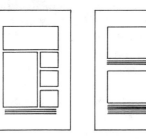

On left, five photos covered in one keyed caption; on right, one caption per photo

Figure 34. Some typical formats for brochure pages.

have to adjust the margins or perhaps add new ones, such as a rectangle within a column if an illustration is to be inserted. Remember that copy will not abut illustrations. It is best to allow for at least one-eighth inch of space between illustration and type. Indicate space when drawing marginal lines.

Select Text Type Size and Leading: The next step is to select the text type size measured in points, size being measured from the bottom of a letter to the top. We recommend that you select a type no smaller than nine or ten points, and no larger than twelve. If a type is too small it can be difficult to read. If it's too large, it can look "horsey."

You must also select the leading (the amount of space between the lines), which also has a great bearing on readability and appearance. Typical leading is two points; thus the expression "ten on twelve" means that a ten point typeface will be used in a space large enough for twelve point type, resulting in two points of space, or leading, between the lines. Leading should remain uniform throughout the brochure, despite changes in the margins.

Select Typeface. Once you have selected the size and the leading of your text type, it is as good a time as any to determine what typeface will be used for the text, as well as what typefaces in what sizes will be used for other elements of the brochure.

The face selected for the text type should be very legible. Some of the more common faces available include Schoolbook, Melior, Helvetica, Garamond, Optima, and similar "old standards" that, regardless of the particular name ascribed to them, are available from most printers and even office type-setting equipment such as IBM's MT/ST/SC and others. Typesetters usually have twenty or more basic faces (many of which are relatively new).

The face chosen for the text can be used for pagination (numbers should be at least the same size, perhaps set in a bold or italic version of the face), for captions (either the same size or slightly smaller, perhaps in italics), and, occasionally, for subheadings (usually bold, set in 18 or 20 points).

Special typefaces (there are about 100 or more of them) can be used for special effects for major heads (such as the cover, usually set up to 36 points or larger) or for subheads. Printers seldom have any great variety of these faces available. Typesetting charges for these special faces often are $2 or more per word. In selecting these special typefaces, remember that they should be somewhat compatible with the text type, and should represent the firm's image. A firm striving to portray a modern image, for example, would con-sider using, among others, the Avant Garde typeface. In some cases, especially with some of the newer standard faces, major heads can be set in large, bold versions of text type. Use of a special face adds an extra dimension to the brochure, however.

Measuring Type and Copy. Once you have determined margins, typefaces, and other factors, you can determine the maximum amount of copy that can fit on a page. If you get a sample of the type you want to use set in the size and leading you intend to use, you can determine approximately how many characters (including spaces) can fit on a line of the length you have selected. (Length varies with face.) Otherwise use an outside source to make the determination for you.

The total number of lines per page can be determined approximately by dividing the space between top and bottom margins by the inch equivalents of the type size and leading. Size 10 on 12 would mean dividing the space between the top and bottom margins by the inch equivalent of 12 points, or approximately 5/32 inch. A fourteen-point line (12 on 14) equals approximately 3/16 inch. This information, too, is best obtained from an outside source.

The purpose of these figures will be seen later.

Editing

All copy, including that for cover, captions, heads, and subheads, should by now have been reviewed by everyone involved. Some outside talent should have been included, too, if only someone who, though not a professional writer, will not be afraid to offer comments that seemingly could be interpreted as criticizing "the boss."

Once the editing has been performed, type the copy for each segment in accordance with the beginning of the second rough layout, which indicates margins. For example, if you have selected a layout that allows for 110 characters per line, you should set the margins of your typewriter so that—on the average—you have 110 characters per line. In most cases, this will require that typewriter paper be inserted on the 11-inch edge, with the margins set to allow for that average amount of characters per line that will result when copy is set in type. Be sure to use a standard typewriter that does *not* have variable spacing.

If copy is kept within the limits created by the layout, fine. If not, you have several choices.

The first, and the one most often used, is to re-edit, cutting and condensing until the copy fits. This function is best performed by a professional who can usually do the job quickly without losing the substance.

The second choice is to change column widths to allow for more characters per line, leaving the copy untouched. Such a step should be taken with great care to ensure that you do not harm the appearance or readability of the brochure.

As a third choice, you could use a smaller type size (in no case should this be smaller than nine point). This would affect all other type in the brochure.

Once the matter is resolved, even if no change is required, review the copy once again as closely and as critically as possible. Are all dates correct? Are all names spelled correctly? Are all verbs in the correct tense? Are sentences kept relatively brief and uninvolved? Is everything that should be said mentioned? Is everything important stressed somehow? Remember, changes after this stage will be much harder and costlier to make, and you will be reluctant to make them. Be sure now that everything you want to say is said and said right.

Illustrations Finalization

Once copy is complete, finalize the illustrations. For the most part this will mean obtaining photographs or other illustrations you do not now have. (Usually the printer can shoot photos of plans, renderings, and other materials prior to printing.) For shots of your office or staff, try to pose as naturally as possible. If it is a relatively informal firm, a group shot of a conference should not depict seven wooden Indians dressed in suits sitting stiffly around a table. Be conscious of details, too. This might mean removing certain items from the walls if they are not to be seen, or clearing a particularly messy desk or table.

It is usually advisable to have several views of each prospective illustration, enabling you to select the one you think best. A photographer can supply you with contact prints (small prints reproduced directly from the film and best examined with a magnifying glass).

Once you have made your selection order a 7 × 9 glossy (preferably with a negative) of each chosen. Place these with all other illustrative materials and prepare the captions.

Determine where illustrative materials are going to be placed and how they are to be composed. For example, one illustration may be composed of two illustrative elements, such as a layout of a plan and a silhouette of a paving machine both to be prepared from your materials by the printer. This will entail indicating whether full page bleeds are involved, which means you will have to make a rough layout of all the other pages of the brochure.

In laying out illustrative pages with more than one photograph, determine whether captions are to be placed adjacent to photos or in a key. A key at the bottom of the page of four photos may preface each caption with a place indicator, such as "top left," "lower right," and so forth. Also determine if type size selected allows enough room. Using the size type selected, count characters to ensure that captions are not too long. The layout should indicate where the captions are to go, line length, and other factors. Also, with full page bleeds, indicate whether you want a caption to be indicated in a cut-out box or in reverse printing (see discussion below) over the illustration itself.

Paper Selection

There are literally hundreds of different kinds of paper stock. A good printer probably will be able to supply you with the broadest range of papers, collected from a variety of different paper houses that distribute papers for the various paper mills.

Quality. The quality of paper depends on a variety of different factors, primarily on what the paper consists of. The more rag or linen in the paper, for example, the more expensive it usually will be. There is a general rule of thumb to consider. In small quantities, such as 500 brochures, the cost of using the best paper is just slightly more than the cost of cheap paper. In some cases genuine bargains can be obtained if the printer has some good stock left over from a previous job. Be sure to ask to see samples.

Finish. There are two basic finishes, smooth and textured. Smooth is most commonly seen as enameled or slick stock, similar to that used in magazines. Textured or felt or other finish stock comes in a great many varieties. There also are several different types of special purpose stocks such as tissues and plastics used primarily for overlay work, as well as foils (metallic papers sometimes used for covers). The finish selected has a great deal to do with establishing your image. A firm trying to establish a very modern image, for example, should give greatest consideration to enamel stock and foils.

Weight. Weight of paper is determined by the weight of a standard package of paper cut in certain standard sizes. There are two distinct weights: cover weight and text weight. A 70-pound cover is heavier and stiffer than 80-pound text.

Selecting the Paper for Your Brochure. To select paper for your brochure, start with the cover. What image are you trying to convey? Modern? Then consider using an enamel or metallic cover. If you choose an enamel cover you also may want to use enamel text. If that is the case, then be sure to specify enamel cover coated on both sides. If you do not want shiny enamel text, consider an enamel cover coated on one side only. You also may want to have a few insert pages of textured paper if you have one particular segment that is far longer and far more important than any other.

If you prefer one of the many textured papers, then consider selecting a text stock from the same family as the cover. (Many special finish papers come in both cover and text weights.)

Recognize that certain paper characteristics may be required. If a plastic spiral spine is to be used, for example, you may wish to select heavier paper to prevent accidental tear-outs. If you are to be dealing with conservation-related clients, you may wish to select paper made from recycled fibers (be sure to note this fact somewhere in the brochure, as on cover 4 or lower right cover 3 if there is no pocket). If the shape is to be horizontal (such as 11 × 8½), you will need a stiffer cover. If you are using a pocket, you cannot select a cover stock so stiff and heavy that it will crack when the pocket is folded into place. Be certain that stocks are compatible with one another. A foil cover used with a heavily textured text may create a study in contradiction.

Coloration

A rule of thumb has it that the more colors you use in a brochure, the more expensive it will be. In fact, you can use a variety of colors without spending a cent extra or, in some cases, with only a slight additional cost.

Compatibility: Before getting into the specifics of coloration, it is important that you bear one thing in mind—compatibility. The inks (your printer can show you varieties) should be compatible with one another. For the most part only two papers will be involved—cover stock and text stock. In most cases, an enamel cover will require white enamel text, and a felt finish cover will require felt finish text of a compatible color. If you choose an earth color cover, such as brown or brownish red, slightly off-white cream or ivory felt text may be best. Before making any decision, however, read the following materials.

Reverse Printing: Reverse printing is the term applied when the ink being printed is printed around the letters invoked. In other words, if the color of the paper is white, the lettering would come out white. The ink would create background color. Reverse printing, if desired, is suggested for the cover only. (When used for small type, reverse printing can tend to get somewhat muddy.) Reverse printing offers several benefits. First, assuming that you are not using duplex paper (see below), it enables you to have cover stock that appears to be one color on one side and a different color on the other. For example, assume that you have selected a dark brown cover with an off-white, ivory text. Instead of having dark brown facing an ivory first and last page, you could reverse print an ivory cover with dark brown on one-side, resulting in the inside front and back covers being the same color as the text.

Duplex Cover Stock. Duplex cover stock is one color on one side and another color on the other side. It actually is two different colored papers glued together at the mill. It usually comes in high quality paper only, and is somewhat more expensive than others. It is most applicable for box-type brochures.

Screens. The screening process can result in the effect of several colors. It involves an ink not being printed at full intensity, which leaves small spaces as if printed through a screen. The larger the spaces, the lighter the ink will appear. In other words, a black ink printed at a 50% screen will look gray. Another factor involved, however, is the color of the paper. The more the screen, the more the color of the paper involved shows through. Screens are especially effective if you want certain heads in the brochure to stand out. For example, all subheads may be printed at 50% intensity making them stand out even more. (The alternative is simply to use another color ink.)

Two Colors. Using two colors of ink is preferred in some cases but, for the most part, it is not necessary. If you do decide to use two colors, however, bear in mind that several other colors can be derived by overprinting one color on the other, or through using overprinted screens, etc. Usually there is just a slight extra charge to use one color ink for the cover and another for the text.

Other. There are many other alternatives available in coloration. We advise that you consult outside talent, perhaps the printer, who will be able to provide sound guidance.

Special Cover Effects

Two special cover effects often used and worth mentioning are embossing and stamping.

Embossing. Embossing involves the preparation of a special die, expensive in and of itself, plus the actual embossing process. In terms of printing cost, embossing acts as the printing of a color. If you decide to use embossing on a cover, plus other printing, the cost will be the equivalent of using two colors, exclusive of the cost of the die. Note that embossing affects both sides of a page. Often the inside front cover (cover 2) will show the reverse of the embossment. One way of getting around this is to have another piece of paper glued to the cover after embossing, but this is a very costly operation.

Stamping. An alternative to embossment is hot stamping. A comparatively inexpensive die is prepared and then struck onto the page through a piece of treated foil, usually seen in gold or silver. The appearance usually is very attractive, and it does not leave a mark on the other side of the paper if the stock so stamped is relatively heavy.

Final Rough Layout

Once copy has been prepared, the second rough layout has been completed, and specific papers and colors have been selected, order through your printer or paper house at least two "dummies" of your brochure. These are nothing more than mock-ups of your brochure cut to the correct size and bound according to your specifications.

Transfer the second rough layout directly to the dummy or onto tissue paper to be taped to the dummy, indicating exactly what goes where. Colored pencils should be used to indicate colors involved, illustration placement, copy placement, heads, cover arrangement and special treatment, and all other pertinent elements. Needless to say, it should be reviewed carefully.

Mark-up for Type

Marking up copy for type is almost an art form in itself. Whoever is setting the type can do it perfectly in a matter of minutes and, for this reason, we recommend strongly that you do not even attempt to do it yourself. Rather, take him your copy (be sure to have the copy photocopied for your files "just in case") and explain what you want done, what type faces, line measurements, and other factors are involved. Bring your rough dummy, too, or an equivalent, in case there are questions.

In submitting the copy, be sure that it is ready for setting. This means that any changes, insertions, corrections or what have you are noted through use of proofreader's marks. (Proofreader's marks usually are shown in a dictionary.) All handwritten changes should be printed clearly and neatly. Be certain that at least two people proofread the material prior to submission. Be sure to explain to the typesetter what any underlines you may have used mean. (Single underlines mean "italicize" to the typesetter.)

Galley Proofs/Rough Layout

Galley proofs, usually called galleys, are the long pages of type you will receive from the typesetter. (Be certain that they are not the originals of the type. If so, photocopy them and handle them with care.) Galleys should be proofread by at least two people, who should note any errors with red ink. (There should be no charge for correcting typesetter's errors.) It is not too late at this time to make changes to copy if you so wish. (Changes *should* have been made earlier. They are more expensive now.)

Before sending galleys back, take one set of them and paste them up as they will appear in the brochure. Make sure that they take up just the amount of space planned. (Overage at this time means costly change.) Be sure you are happy with line length and other factors.

Assuming that everything is working out well, return a set of corrected galleys to the typesetter who should, in a few days, supply you with a new set of galleys plus the originals.

Paste-up/Printer Preparation

If you decide to perform paste-up in house, here are the steps necessary.

Obtain Paste-Up Paper. Obtain paste-up paper, usually good quality white paper or board, such as Bainbridge Board, available from an art supply house.

Indicate Page Size. Using a light blue pencil, which will not reproduce when photographed, draw the lines needed on the layout paper to indicate the size of the pages. Usually you can draw the outline of two pages on each board or piece of paper.

Protect Originals. Protect originals of type by spraying on a light coat of plastic. (Sprays are available from an art supply house.)

Paste-up. Utilizing the final rough layout and dummy as a guide, cut out the type and paste it on each page, using rubber cement. (Cement either the paper or the type only. Cementing both type and paper will result in a fix so strong that any changes will result in cutting the paper or perhaps damaging the type, which will require expensive resetting.)

Be certain that all heads are at uniform distances, that all copy is straight and so on. In fact, what you see is what you will get.

Indicate Photos. Leave space for the illustrations. For each space, indicate what illustration is involved, such as No. 1, No. 2, etc. The corresponding photo then must be marked up to indicate exactly what will be done with it: reduction, line conversion, silhouette, etc.

Review. The result of paste-up is camera-ready copy, in other words, ready for photo-offset printing. Review everything carefully several times. If possible, photocopy the results to ensure that all pasting-up has been done correctly. Have several people review the results.

Confer with the Printer

Take the camera-ready art to the printer and, page for page, go over with him exactly what you want done in terms of color, special photo or illustrative techniques, etc. In fact, directions should be written out on a page-by-page basis, with a copy for the printer and one for yourself. Any corrections or modifications to these instructions should be written. In this way, should an error be committed, you will provide yourself with protection. Under no circumstances should you submit these instructions without a conference first to ensure that everyone understands who should be responsible for what.

Blueline

The printer, within a week or so, should present you with a blueline, or blueprint, a proof that shows you exactly how the finished product will look except for coloration and stock. All the photos will be in place, reduced or changed as necessary, and so on.

Review the blueline with utmost care. Any little marks or scratches that appear should be circled in red and brought to the printer's attention to ensure that they will not appear on the finished product. Once you sign off and approve the blueline, with or without changes, it is out of your hands. The next time you see your brochure, it will be complete.

Quantities

One question that arises is, "How many brochures should we order?" The answer usually depends on the size of your company, the number of sales calls made, etc.

Do not base your decision on cost per copy. When you do that you can suddenly realize that a brochure costs, let us say, $4 per copy. As such you treat it like gold and distribute it very sparingly. It should be distributed widely, regardless of per-copy cost.

In many cases 500 copies will last for a year or more. Per-copy cost probably will be $3 or more, including outside talent (not just printing). The more you order, the lower your per-copy cost. The more you order, the more wastage there is likely to be. Some companies order too many and have to revise the brochure while they still have a large quantity. Some compound the error by distributing the outdated brochure instead of the new one as an "economy" move. Usually it's false economy.

Printing usually is not the most expensive part of putting a brochure together. The costs of writing, design, photography, typesetting and paste-up usually are more. When reprinting, however, you pay only for the cost of the printing.

Get as many brochures as you think you can use. Reorder as necessary. Consider making revisions when you reprint if revisions are in order.

Updating

Having a pocket in your brochure makes it relatively easy to update materials regarding clients, jobs, personnel, and so on, thereby leaving the rest of the brochure intact. If there is a change in top management, however, or some other significant event, consider redoing the brochure, preferably when your supply is running out. In many cases you can salvage much of what you have done and then substitute what you have to. Do not miss an opportunity for significant improvement by attempting to salvage where new work is advised.

In the case of certain minor changes, such as address or phone number, and perhaps even others of more major consequence, consider having self-adhering labels printed. These can easily be affixed to the appropriate places before the brochure is distributed. It is far less expensive than reprinting. Nonetheless, if you have to use several of these, consider a reprint or, where possible, a reprint of only those pages or signatures involved.

7.9   SLIDE SHOWS AND OTHER AUDIO-VISUAL TECHNIQUES

Slide shows are excellent vehicles to use in a presentation, serving to expand upon the firm's capabilities. In essence, they pick up where the brochure leaves off. We suggest the following simple steps for preparing slide shows.

Collect Photos. Make it a practice to obtain photographs of all or most projects in which your firm is involved in any way. Whoever takes the photographs should be experienced, be he a professional or someone on staff. Photographs should show aspects of projects that are most relevant to your practice. In most cases, you should have on hand at least five or six different photos of each project, each showing something different, something you feel merits attention. We advise taking all photos in slide form, preferably in color. It is easier to store slides for quick reference, as in notebooks with slide pouch pages. Also, any color slide can be made into either a color or black and white photo, for use with a news release, magazine article, brochure, or whatever.

Customize Shows. Do not make up any set slide show. Rather, prepare each in terms of the prospect involved. In this way, you can pick and choose and select those that best fit individual requirements. For example, an industrial client probably will want to see what you have done by way of various plants and systems.

The presentation should be made with a live speaker, not a cassette recorder, so that any slide can be examined as the prospect desires, and further explanation can be made. Such shows also are excellent in presenting talks to various groups.

Be Prepared. We strongly suggest that the slide projector you obtain be one that will permit either rear screen or wall projection. Several such machines are now on the market, one of which certainly will meet your needs. Also, be certain to carry with you—perhaps inside the projector case—an extra projection bulb and one or more extension cords, for obvious reasons.

Other Audio-Visual Techniques

There are numerous other audio-visual techniques that can be used in making presentations of one sort or another, including slide films, video tape, and motion pictures. There are numerous ramifications that can be brought into play as well, including multiscreen presentations, multimedia presentations, etc. Some consultants recommend that firms—usually the very large ones—prepare some of the more elaborate A-V shows as part of proposals.

As far as we are concerned, the majority of persons actually involved in selection procedures have become somewhat more sophisticated in recent years. They are interested in what you have done, how well you have done it, and other basic facts. In almost all cases, you can communicate this information through simple means as easily as through more elaborate ones. In other words, there is every reason to believe that if you prepare a good slide show, which tells your story well, you will probably get very little extra credit for a promotional piece that costs 20 times as much. Moreover, there is every reason to believe that, in some cases at least, an elaborate A-V presentation can turn off some prospects by promoting an image of being too large, too slick, or perhaps too eager to spend money on unnecessary frills.

Because the A-V field is so broad, encompasses so many variations, and in large measure—other than slide shows—represents a realm of sophistication applicable to relatively very few design professional firms, we are not supplying any how-to's. There are numerous books on the subject which may be obtained, as well as excellent periodicals covering A-V (e.g., *Audio-Visual Communications*, United Business Publications, Inc., 750 Third Avenue, New York, New York 10017).

7.10 PRESENTATION FOLDERS

The firm should have on hand a supply of presentation folders or proposal binders. While you can use ready-made folders available from most stationers we suggest that, for more impact, you have your own prepared. The folder can feature, as a cover, a near duplicate of your brochure cover, with space to add "PROPOSAL FOR THE JOHN DOE CORPORATION." While a variety of formats is available, perhaps the most easily used is that involving a 17½ × 11¼ inch page that, when folded, forms an 8¾ × 11¼ inch cover. Materials can be inserted by use of a plastic spine, which holds contents together by friction. For larger proposals, or for proposals going out to large organizations, a more sophisticated approach may be in order. There are numerous different types, including those that use a screw and post binding method (contents are held in place by two screws), plastic spiral binder, plastic punch-and-press, and do-it-yourself perfect binding, all discussed in Section 7.8 of this chapter.

7.11 MAGAZINE ARTICLES

Having magazine articles published can be a very effective promotional technique whose importance cannot be overemphasized. There are a variety of different kinds of articles to consider.

The first is the article written by you or a member of your firm to discuss a particular technical subject or a particular job. Most often it is placed in a technical magazine, either a journal of a professional society or one similar to it. While there is nothing wrong with this kind of article, you are in essence communicating only with fellow professionals, often the competition. You can reach potential clients with it only when you reprint the article and distribute it to your own mailing list, which, in most cases, will be minimal.

The second kind of article is the one written about a certain given project or a problem intrinsic with a certain project, but placed in a magazine relating to a client or prospective client group. For example, let us assume that you devise an innovative new pollution control device for an asphalt plant. Rather than writing the article for an engineering magazine, you submit it to a magazine devoted to those involved in asphalt plants. In this way you reach a huge public of potential clients at the time of publication, and a secondary public through reprinting and distribution to your own mailing list.

The third article is basically the same as the second, and even has implications for the first. The main difference is that the article is written about your firm or its activities by someone who is not a representative of the firm. The basic advantage of this method is that it allows the author to inject his own comments. In cases where you have no control over the author, if he is a staff member of a magazine, for example, this can lead to problems, but, if you hire a free-lance author or a PR firm to do the work, control is simple and some reasonably flattering things can be said. Since you're not saying them about yourself, they're not "self-laudatory."

Review Publications

You already should be subscribing to all magazines that relate both to your own activities and to those of various client and prospective client groups.

To determine whether you have all of them on hand, review a publications directory such as the *Ayer Directory of Publications*. Obtain copies of magazines you do not now have on hand.

Determine Subjects

Focusing on one particular public at a time, determine what you could write that would interest each, be it a recent project, new technological developments in the field, or what have you. Often you can get material for articles simply by utilizing some technical materials that have appeared in other magazines. Create a list of possible subjects for each publication or type of publication.

Prepare An Outline

Prepare a very general outline of the article, listing primarily what you think will be the main points covered.

Query

Select the magazine that has the largest circulation among the prospective client public you wish to reach. Determine the editor's name (from the magazine itself or from the publications directory), and send him a query. A typical query reads as follows:

Dear Mr. Jones:

I'm writing to determine if SUGAR NEWS has any interest in an article describing how utilization of a new structural steel component in the design of a sugar refinery was responsible for saving some $250,000 in construction costs.

Briefly, our firm was responsible for development of this new component, which replaces a traditional sugar refinery design methodology established in 1938. The points I feel would be worthwhile covering would be:

1. Brief history of former method and purpose.
2. Statement of the problem as presented to us by Acme Sugar Company.
3. How we researched the problem and came up with several possible solutions.
4. Analysis of each possible solution and selection of the one ultimately developed.
5. Development of the new system, early problems encountered, modifications required for specific application.

6. Selection of fabricators and problems encountered.
7. Installation of the new component.
8. Brief discussion of actual performance of the component to date.
9. Advice on utilizing the new concept for new and existing refineries.

We have available complete design specs and plans for the new component, as well as numerous photographs (color and black and white) depicting the component in fabrication stages, complete as fabricated, and complete as installed. We also have schematics of the plant showing the component in place.

I would very much like to hear from you to learn if you are interested in this article and, if so, if there are any particular aspects of the story you might want stressed, deleted, or so on.

Sincerely,

If you do not receive a reply within three weeks, write the editor again, or call to determine if he has received your letter and, if so, what his reaction is. If the article is rejected, either sooner or later, examine the reasons given, if any, or perform your own analysis. If you feel it advisable, change those elements to be covered, and query another magazine in the field until one accepts. If none accepts, go on to another idea you think appropriate. Submit one query at a time. *Under no circumstances submit a query for the same article to more than one magazine at a time.*

If you intend to have the article written about your firm by a free lance or PR firm, whoever does the writing should handle the queries. Any payment received from the magazine for the article should be deducted from whatever writing fee is decided upon. Few competent writers are willing to work on a contingency basis, that is, payment only if the article is published.

Writing the Article

Assuming you receive a favorable response to your query, the next step is to begin writing the article or to have it written for you. If you undertake the writing function in-house, the general rules of writing already given are applicable. Some magazines have styles of their own, however, so it is suggested that you read a variety of articles published in recent numbers of the magazine involved. In most cases it is advisable to include as much case-history information as possible, usually including cost data. Approvals from clients should be obtained. When the article is written about your firm, it usually is advisable to include some complimentary quotations from the client. Client approval for use of such quoted materials is mandatory.

Submitting

When typing the article in final form for submission to the magazine:

1. be sure typewriter characters are clean;

2. use a new fabric or carbon ribbon;

3. type on 8½ × 11 inch white paper;

4. leave an inch margin on either side;

5. double space;

6. number pages, and

7. place your name on the top right-hand corner of each page.

In addition, prepare a title page, which will include the name of the article and the author, and an author biography, such as:

John Smith is a principal of the architectural firm of Smith, Jones, Doe and Miller. A 1954 graduate of State University, he entered the practice of architecture in 1955 with XYZ and Associates. Ten years later he established his own firm, which recently has completed six major projects for various sugar companies in four countries.

Be certain to submit the originals of the article. Keep copies for your own files.

Afteruse

Be sure to reprint all magazine articles written by firm members or written about the firm. Obtain the publisher's permission and have the printing done either by your own printer or, if the price is acceptable, by the magazine's printer. Reprints should be distributed to clients and prospects with whom you have had some form of contact, with letters and brochures, in proposals, and wherever else appropriate. You also may wish to submit copies to your congressmen, and enlist their support—if it's something you want—in getting the article into the hands of potential foreign clients. For more information on what is required here, contact the national office of ACEC, AIA, and similar organizations.

Recognize that often the same article can be rewritten for other magazines, usually working the three main elements, technical, professional, public. For example, an article on a new structural component for a sugar plant could be prepared for the sugar industry publication, for a publication detailing professional activities, for example working for sugar companies, and for a magazine that specializes in articles about steel fabrication. In each case, a similar query could be made. Little effort will be required to redirect the emphasis of the article to the audience involved.

7.12   BOOKS

It is not out of the realm of possibility to write a book on a technical subject, or to have several staff members write such a book, or to have the book professionally edited or ghosted based on your technical input or that of others.

The advantages of having a book with your name on it are obvious. If you are going after a centralized building automation system design project, and you have written a book on the fundamentals of centralized building automation design, the prospect cannot help but be impressed.

If you have an idea for a book, first determine which publishers typically handle such subjects. Pick the one you consider to be best and send a query with a complete outline much as required for a magazine article. If you get a refusal, keep plugging. You should usually send out at least fifteen queries—always one at a time—before you start getting despondent.

You could also go to a vanity publisher—one who charges you a fee for publishing your book—and have the book designed and developed. Also, you can sometimes go to a major publisher and offer to buy 5,000 or so copies of the book, which, in many cases, will be enough to generate a significant degree of interest. While these latter two approaches obviously involve some expense, the rewards can be gratifying—to your ego as well as to your bottom line.

7.13   PRINT PUBLICITY

For our purposes, publicity can be described as coverage in a news-oriented medium, such as a newspaper, newsletter, TV or radio news program, etc., as well as news-related columns of various magazines.

It is doubtful that anyone will elect to use your services because you or your firm is mentioned in a brief item in a newspaper or some other medium. However, by having your name frequently before the public—including specific prospective client publics—you will become much better known, and so will increase chances of at least being considered for certain jobs.

Look at it this way. If you happen to walk into a prospective client's office precisely when he is seeking a firm such as yours to provide a needed service, chances are excellent that you will be able to land the project. The chances of this ever happening, of course, are somewhat remote. However, if you obtain publicity in various sources that prospects read, and if that publicity appears with a fair degree of regularity, chances are excellent that at any given time when services such as yours are needed, the prospect involved will just have seen an article about your firm or is about to read such an article. In other words, by obtaining frequent publicity—just as by making frequent sales calls—you greatly increase the odds that your firm will be recognized as one able to fill an immediate need.

The vehicle by which you obtain publicity is, for the most part, the news release.

Release Subjects

The first thing to establish is a general framework for determining which subjects are newsworthy and which are not. An old PR axiom has it that news is what an editor thinks is news. Consequently, something you feel is very important may be considered meaningless by one editor, but very significant by another. Conversely, what you feel may be relatively insignificant could be deemed very important by someone else. As a result, do not try to evaluate beforehand. Rather, develop general guidelines that you feel are satisfactory. Here are some typical subjects worthy of a news release.

Personnel Changes
  New staff members
  Promotions

Contracts/Projects
  Announcement of new contracts
  Completion of design
  Preparation of rendering
  Start of construction
  Topping out
  Completion of project/occupancy

Activities of Staff Members
  Association positions
  Winning of awards

Civic Involvement of Firm

Awards to Firm

Opening Branch Offices

All the above fall into the category of hard news, that is, they are related to events and happenings. In fact, every event and happening that occurs in your firm should be considered in terms of a potential news release.

Not all releases fall into the hard news category. As an example, consider the opinion release, which can come from the head of a firm, and be based on virtually anything to do with design or construction. Assume that a bill pending before the United States Congress calls for bidding by design professionals. Based on your own analysis of the bill, or on others', you can write a release praising the bill, damning it, offering changes, etc., simply by saying that you have "issued a statement." Every quotation in the news release could then be based on that "statement." Once the release is complete, write the statement, which could be issued along with the release.

Similar to the above is the tie-in release based on material or a release from an association or other source. Your release would cite your opinions coupled with those of the source, with the source's statement or news release included along with your own. In a similar manner, you could modify an item regarding national statistics or developments to take your own community into consideration.

Still another type of release centers on statistics, involving development of figures regarding the number of projects undertaken in the past year, amount of employees added, the total amount of square footage designed, and so forth.

To go into all the possibilities regarding such events would take a full book, but it would not be necessary really. The best sources of ideas are newspapers and organization newsletters. Read as many as possible and clip articles you feel could serve as guides for your own releases.

Developing a News Media List

Essential to developing an effective news release system is compilation of a comprehensive news media list, which includes pertinent information about each listed medium on individual 3 by 5 cards. Media to be listed and pertinent information to be covered for each, in addition to name and address, are discussed below.

Daily Newspapers. At the vert least, you should have a complete listing of all daily papers in your area including, for each, time of publication (morning or evening—morning papers are staffed most heavily in the evening; evening papers in the morning) and names of pertinent editors or reporters in real estate, architecture, construction, etc.

Weekly Newspapers. The easiest way to establish a listing of local weekly papers is to consult the *Ayer Directory*, your area Chamber of Commerce, state newspaper association, or Yellow Pages.

Periodicals. Under the heading of periodicals, include all magazines related to your own and clients' interests. The easiest way of compiling such a list is to contact either your local or national office of AIA, ACEC, or other group, and request its release list from the director of PR. If he is not willing to oblige, use the *Ayer Directory*.

Related Professions' Publications. Include a listing of newsletters of all organizations to which you, other key staff members, and your firm belong, as well as related organizations. Information should include the name of the person responsible for writing the publication and its date of issuance.

Wire Services. Include names and local addresses of national wire services, such as Associated Press, United Press International, and others. Frequently they will be located at the offices of a major daily in your area.

Selected Writers. Your list should also include certain free-lance writers whom you know to be active in your field. You probably will see their names mentioned frequently in various trade publications. Contact the publication's offices for the writer's address.

Your 3 by 5 cards can be filed alphabetically, alphabetically within media categories (dailies, weeklies, etc.), or in any other manner convenient and usable for you.

Writing the Release

News releases require a unique format and writing style, which we discuss immediately below.

Follow Basic Steps. Basic to almost all forms of writing are the following steps: know your subject; assemble research material; read all research material at least twice; make reflective notes, and categorize.

Evaluate Categories. A news release must be organized on the basis of the most important subject first, second most important second, etc., much as a regular news article is written. This style—called "inverted pyramid"— is used for two reasons. First of all, editors receive a steady stream of news releases every day that they must evaluate quickly. If the major point is buried somewhere in the body of the release, chances are that the editor may never get to it before he decides that the release is worthless. Second, the inverted pyramid style is typical of that used in news media or news columns of magazines. There are two reasons why news media use the inverted pyramid style. First, they want to grab readers' or prospective readers' attention. Readers, after all, must determine whether or not any article is of interest and—if it is—chances are they will purchase the publication. Second, and perhaps more important, the person who writes the article usually cannot know beforehand what the layout of the publication will be. If there is an advertisement that must be placed, and if space is limited, the news item will be cut. The cut is made as late in the item as possible. Therefore, if the key points are covered in early paragraphs only material least vital to the item is deleted.

Write the Lead. The lead, or first paragraph, is the most important part of the release. It should be a terse summary of the major elements of the story listing the most important facts. It usually should answer the questions who, what, why, when, and where. To find examples of leads, pick up any daily newspaper and read the first paragraphs of hard news items.

Write the Rest of the Release. In writing the balance of the release, keep sentences as short as possible. Do not use any adjectives such as "wonderful," "terrific," etc., unless they are contained in quoted material. Such adjectives call for qualitative judgment, as compared to facts, and must be attributed.

Examine First Draft. In examining your first draft, ask yourself these questions: "Have I said everything I want to say?" "Is all key information contained in the lead?" "Do subsequent paragraphs elaborate on the lead, most important item first?" Rewrite and reorganize until each question can be answerd with an unqualified "yes."

Prepare Final Draft. In preparing your final draft, examine the release critically to ensure that sentences are as short as possible, that adjectives are limited and qualitative adjectives are in attributed quotes, that those quoted have given their permission to be quoted, and that all numbers, names, and titles (including Miss and Mrs., college degrees, etc.) are absolutely correct.

Putting the Release on Paper

There is a definite format you should use when typing a release for submission. Examine the model release in Figure 35. The letters in parentheses below refer to letters in the release:

(A) *Stationery:* The release should be issued either on your firm's letterhead or on special news release stationery, which can have a large "NEWS RELEASE" or "NEWS FROM..." printed across the top, centered, below which your firm's name and address appear.

YOUR FIRM'S LETTERHEAD OR SPECIAL
RELEASE STATIONERY   (A)

(B)

FOR MORE INFORMATION, CONTACT: (D)

John Doe
Smith & Doe Associates
123 Main Street
City, State 12345
Phone: 123-4567

FOR IMMEDIATE RELEASE   (E)

SMITH & DOE AWARDED MAJOR CONTRACT   (F)

(C)   *City, September 7 —*   (G)   Smith & Doe Associates, a consulting engi-   (H)
neering firm with offices here, today announced that it has been awarded a
contract to undertake the mechanical and electrical design portions of the
new <u>Garbetti</u> (N) widget factory. Announcement was made by firm
president, Joseph Smith.

(MORE)   (J)

ADD ONE   (K)   JOHN DOE   (L)

According to Mr. Smith, the new factory will involve some 250,000   (I)
square feet of interior space and will take approximately two   (I)   years
to design and build. "This will be one of the larger factories in the area and
we intend it to be one of the most modern of its kind," Smith said. He
added: "The Garbetti Company has stated that it not only wants this factory to be modern to boost productivity, but also to take advantage of all
available technological advances in energy conservation and optimization
and pollution abatement and control." Smith noted that his firm is "very
experienced" in that field.

According to Mr. Smith, the factory will be located on a six-acre site on
Second Street, approximately one mile north of U.S. 123 in City. Total
construction cost is estimated at $7 million.

Smith & Doe Associates was established in 1965. It currently employs
some thirty technical and nontechnical personnel. A branch office was
opened in Town in 1972.

(M)

Figure 35. News release.

For best results, type the original on a blank piece of paper and duplicate onto your own stationery, *one side only*. This can be done with Xerox, Itek, Pitney Bowes, Cannon, 3M, or similar equipment. If you do not have such equipment, contact a local printer.

(B) *Top margin:* The top margin should begin no less than one and one-half inches below the masthead.

(C) *Side margins:* The side margins should be one and one-half inches from their respective edges throughout.

(D) *Contact:* "FOR MORE INFORMATION, CONTACT," should be the first line typed in all capital letters. Below it should appear the name, address, and telephone number of at least one person who can answer questions for a reporter. You may wish to use two names or include a home phone for evening calls.

(E) *Release date:* In most cases, the material you send can be published or reported at any time, which can be indicated by "FOR IMMEDIATE RELEASE." In some instances, as in the case of an award to an employee, you may wish to indicate that the release cannot be used until the event transpires. In such cases, indicate the day on which the story can be reported, and the time (AM or PM), for example, FOR RELEASE NOVEMBER 8, AM. In the case of daily news media be sure the release is timed to arrive no more than three days before the release date.

(F) *Headline:* A headline on a release serves to identify the subject of the release. While supplied headlines seldom are used by a paper, it is good practice to include one for identification purposes.

(G) *Dateline:* If you do use a dateline, which seldom is necessary, indicate the location and the date of the action, with time references in the body of the release being based on the dateline time reference (today, yesterday, tomorrow) and location reference (here).

(H) *Spacing:* All copy should be double- or triple-spaced.

(I) *Numbers:* Spell out numbers one through ten, and use numerals for 11 and above. Never begin a sentence with a numeral.

(J) *More than one page:* If the release is more than one page long, try to avoid ending any page in the middle of a paragraph, even if it means leaving an unusual amount of space at the bottom of the page. Be certain to include the word "MORE" in all caps and centered or to the right indicating that there is more copy. This should be done at the bottom of *every* page except the last.

(K) *Second page:* In the upper left-hand corner of the second page type the words "ADD ONE," indicating that it is the first additional page after the first. On the third page would appear "ADD TWO," and so on.

(L) *Release identification after page one:* At the top of each additional page, type in the name of your firm's contact.

(M) *End symbol:* Indicate the end of the release by using, on the center of the page, the symbol ###, or –30–, or –end–.

(N) *Proofread:* Before the release is duplicated it should be proofread by at least two people. All numbers should be checked carefully, as well as spelling of names. In cases of complicated names or unusual spellings of common names, underline to indicate to the editor that the name is spelled correctly, e.g., Adamopolous or Smithe.

Mailing the Release

Attention must be given to who gets the release and how and when he gets it.

Determine Who Should Receive the Release. Examine your release list to determine which media should receive the release. Not all will be interested, but realize that some releases can be rewritten to have greater interest for certain media that otherwise would not care. You should differentiate among those media that *will* be interested, those that *may* be interested, those that *will* be interested *if* the release is changed, those that *may* be interested *if* the release is changed, and those that *will not* be interested under any circumstances. Do not mail releases to those media that will not be interested under any circumstances, and do not bother to rework the release if rewriting will net only a handful of maybes in relatively unimportant media.

Fold and Stuff the Release with Care. How you fold the release and stuff it into the envelope can be important, especially when dealing with editors and writers who are in a hurry, as most usually are.

Fold the release so the letterhead will be on top. In other words, place the release copy side down; fold the bottom edge to about three and two-thirds inches from the top edge, then place the folded bottom on the top edge, and fold again. When stuffing into the envelope, the letterhead should be on the flap side, the first thing seen when the flap is opened. If a large photograph accompanies your release, leave the release (and of course the photo) unfolded. Give extra support to the large photo by including a piece of stiff cardboard with it and the release in a 9 by 12-inch envelope marked "Do Not Bend."

Address Carefully. Address envelopes to media so each is desk- or person-directed. Each envelope should have on it either the name of a reporter or editor, or a title (e.g., Attn: Metro Editor) or both. This is especially important for daily papers.

Note: If you mail the same release to two persons at the same medium, be certain to indicate on each release—handwritten if necessary—"also sent to ..." Do not try to get coverage of the same subject in two sections of the same medium (for example, real estate and business). If it works, it will work against you. The editors involved will be somewhat embarrassed and will make it a point to not cover your material in the future unless unavoidable, and then who knows what biases long memories may establish.

Mailing/Delivery. Once you have sealed the envelopes, determine when the materials should be mailed by observing deadlines indicated on media list cards. If the release is particularly important, it may be best to deliver it in person. Otherwise, allow enough time for the mailing process to ensure that the release will arrive when it is supposed to.

Photographs

Whenever possible submit a photograph with your release. It heightens the chance of improved coverage, e.g., story plus photo plus caption versus story only, or captioned photo versus no coverage. Caption the photograph for identification purposes. To learn how, examine captioned photos in local newspapers. In cases where rather long captions are used in a newspaper, but no general article accompanies the photo, chances are that only the photo has been used, and the caption is the only story to tell. In such cases the newspaper staff writes the caption, which is why yours should be utilitarian only.

Once you are certain that the caption is in complete accord with the photo; that all names are spelled correctly, and that all titles, especially Miss, Mrs. or Ms., are correct, duplicate as many captions as there are photos.

Affix the caption to the photo by placing both face up, sliding the caption under the photo so the top of the sheet on which the caption is printed is approximately one-half inch above the bottom of the photo, taping the top of the caption sheet to the back of the photo, and folding the caption up so it covers the photo.

Tricks of the Trade

Here follow a few "tricks of the trade" that will improve your news release program.

Make the Release Fit the Media. As mentioned above, not all media will be interested in the same story, but many stories can be rewritten to fit the medium. For example, assume that a staff member has been promoted. The story given to a daily paper will be brief. The same story rewritten for the staff member's home-town weekly or daily newspaper could be much longer, including details on his past life in the local community.

Extra Mileage. Extra mileage can be gained from a release concerned with one particular person by issuing the release to media concerned with the person involved, such as a country club newsletter, a church bulletin, an alumni magazine, etc. This is not only a valued service, which the person, such as a new staff member, appreciates, but also one that will generate even more mention and knowledge of your firm.

Quotations. To emphasize a particular point, or to use adjectives that you would not ordinarily use in the body of a news release, create a quote. Make it interesting, and say it aloud to be sure it can be spoken without difficulty. Once you have the quote written, contact the person quoted to get permission to use it.

Exclusive. If you have what you feel to be an excellent story, contact an editor and offer him an exclusive. Chances are he will send out a reporter to get the story, an investment he may have been unwilling to make if other news media also were covering the event. Make sure he does have an exclusive, but also be sure to issue releases on the same story once the first article appears.

Specials. A special is not an exclusive. A special simply means that one particular version of a release is sent to one particular medium. Be sure that such a release is: substantially different from any other on the same subject; marked on the top "SPECIAL TO THE (Name of Medium)", and is the original typewritten version of the release.

Notes to the Editor. If an event is felt to be particularly newsworthy, send with the release a personal note to the editor to tell him why the material described is particularly important. You also can invite the editor to attend a certain function. Also, consider the possibility of contacting an editor before an event transpires to offer an exclusive or ideas about a possible feature story. For example, if you have been awarded a contract to restore an historical site in the area, the editor may want to cover the story in depth—from beginning to end. Remember, all that it takes to inquire is a note or call.

Statistics. Statistics can be made very interesting and human with little effort. For example, supposing your firm designed six large factories last year. While it may sound like a somewhat large amount of work, consider how it sounds when stated as "six factories with total square footage of 19 football fields laid end-to-end." Suddenly a flat statistic becomes much more active, alive, and interesting by presenting it in a different light.

Before and After Release. To get extra mileage out of a good story, prepare a release to announce an event, such as a ground breaking, and where and when it will take place. Once the event has occurred, send out a "wrap-up" release describing what happened.

Added Materials. In certain cases, you will have available brochures and other material that, even though not pertinent to the release, can be included for the editor's use in whatever manner. If you are quoting from a prepared statement, enclose the full text to all media.

Interviews. In granting an interview to a reporter, keep several things in mind. First, know what you're talking about. If you are unsure of a name or a figure, don't mention anything until you check it out. Second, do not preface any remark with, "Off the record." By doing this you annoy the reporter and, if he wants to, he may state in his article, "Mr. Smith told this reporter, off the record, that . . ." If you want something off the record, simply do not say it. Third, do not tell the reporter what to include in the article. If there are items you think should be covered, merely state that there are some other facts he may want to know about and indicate what some are. If he says he doesn't want them, so be it. If you force the issue you may be the loser because of it.

Photographs. Consider sending two or three captioned photographs with a story instead of one. It increases the chances that at least one photo will be used, either along with, or instead of, a story. Also, if you have several acceptable shots and several local newspapers, consider sending a different photo to each paper with still one other different photo sent to all other area print media. With each of the one-of-a-kind photos include a note indicating that the photo is exclusive to the paper involved. When having prints of a photo made, as from a slide, have a title block developed right into the print itself. (This is particularly appropriate for architects.) In this way, if the photo is used, the name of the firm appears in the photo itself, in the caption, and possibly in an accompanying article as well. (Do not use title blocks when the photo is used for a brochure or similar purpose.)

7.14 BROADCAST PUBLICITY

Broadcast publicity relates primarily to your GMA public, rather than to specific prospective clients or client types. It involves the same guidelines suggested for obtaining print publicity, in that news releases should also be sent to radio and television stations, which should be included on your news release mailing list. There are some basic differences, however, that should be observed.

Lists

You should have on file the names of radio and television stations that have their own news crews (in other words, a staff that does more than merely rewrite material as it comes off the AP or UPI wire) and their respective news assignment editors. Also determine and list those that have locally-originated panel discussion or call-in talk shows and the respective program producers, personalities, or talent coordinators. (This information can be obtained easily, just by calling the various stations.)

Procedures/News

Just as you would give an exclusive to a newspaper, so may you consider giving an exclusive to a radio or television station. First, you must determine if the story really is worthwhile. You will quickly ruin your credibility (and wear out your welcome) if you call a television or radio station every time you have a release ready to issue. A worthwhile story, for example, would be a major project that might have significant local impact. To attempt to obtain coverage, call the news assignment editor of what you consider to be the best local television station. Introduce or reintroduce yourself and tell him that you think you have a story that would be of interest, and that you would be happy to give him the exclusive if he indicates interest. Inform him of the nature of the story and possibilities for visual coverage, such as a rendering or a model. If he shows interest, call no more stations and issue no releases to any other television station. Do prepare a release, however, for use of print media or radio, as well as a data summary sheet for use by the TV news crew. If no interest is indicated, try the next station.

The same procedure will work for radio stations, except visual criteria do not apply.

Of course, if you feel the story is "big," you may wish to send a release to all area TV and radio stations. If this tack is used, be certain to include a personal note to each news assignment editor indicating why the story is felt to be so important. Two days after you issue the release, call each editor to ask if the release was received and, if so, if there is any interest. Expand on any comments made in the personal note, trying to excite the editor's imagination as much as possible. Do not go overboard; a news assignment editor is especially wary of overglamorized subjects or people, and you may very well run the risk of overdoing it. Therefore, show your own enthusiasm but stick closely to reality.

Procedures/Nonnews

Some of your best publicity may come from what is known as the nonnews category, which, for the most part, hinges on your own ingenuity as applied to radio and TV talk programs.

First assess each of the talk programs in your area to determine the kinds of people and subjects they like to cover and what audience is involved. It then will be up to you to come up with ideas, which you should submit to the producer or talent coordinator in a personal letter. For example, you may be able to get together with other local design professionals to discuss problems of growth, pollution, energy, etc. In some cases you may volunteer to appear on a program with someone who holds an opposite point of view. Read the newspapers and watch some of these programs for ideas. Whenever an idea occurs to you, write it down and follow it up with a letter. If you have no response in a week's time, call the person to whom you wrote. If there is no interest, keep trying.

You also may note that a particular reporter on a TV or radio station usually does a certain variety of story. If there is a way in which you can somehow develop a story in his line, let him know of your suggestion.

As a last word, don't forget national news and talk shows. If you have what you feel to be a particularly interesting story, do not hesitate to mail out a release or note. You never can tell what returns the investment of a postage stamp may bring.

7.15 EMERGENCY PRESS RELATIONS

A lifetime of image building can be eradicated all too quickly as the result of a calamity, such as the collapse of a building under construction, especially when handled incorrectly by the press, or when someone says something that he absolutely should not. Take the following steps before a calamity actually occurs.

1. *Determine communicators:* At the time of signing a contract, determine who should be the spokesman for the design/owner team in the event of press contact due to emergency.

2. *Refer questions:* Until such time as key design team personnel can get together, refer all questions to the spokesman.

3. *Meet:* As soon as possible after the calamity or emergency situation, representatives of all members of the design/ownership team should meet to review everything that has been said. If possible, a general statement should be prepared, or statements for each design team member should be prepared. The statement may be no more than, "Smith & Doe Associates feels it inappropriate at this time to make any statement other than to reiterate its belief that only a thorough investigation of all circumstances will lead to defining the causes of the tragic event." In some cases it may be best to have an attorney present as well, although the attorney alone should not be responsible for the statement. All too often their news statements are hobbled by legalese, which immediately casts suspicion on the issuer. Very often the same intent can be fulfilled by using more effective language that, of course, the attorney could check for applicability.

4. *Giving interviews:* In the event that you decide to give an interview to a reporter: clear it with other members of the group; give it in your office only, *never* by phone or in the field; and have a tape recorder running or a stenotypist on hand to protect yourself against misquotation. (If the reporter objects, do not give the interview.)

5. *Instruct employees:* Instruct employees, on an ongoing basis, perhaps in the employees' policy handbook, that no one is to make any statement of any kind unless fully cleared by whomever provides clearance.

7.16 PROJECT CREDIT TECHNIQUES

There are numerous techniques available to obtain credit for participating in a given project, as discussed below. The question many firms will ask, however, is "Why make the effort?" The answer is relatively straightforward. If you obtain credit often enough, on a regular basis, and in as many ways possible for each given project, sooner or later you will become recognized as a firm that is actively involved in GMA construction activity. The thought behind this answer, as with much promotional activity or PR, is to keep the name of the firm continually before the public and, more specifically, the prospective client public.

Planning

Before getting into specific techniques, a few words should be said about project credit planning.

In most cases, promotional activity will be a relatively jumbled affair. Releases typically come from builders, design professionals, contractors, and so on, none tied in with the other, but all relating to the same project. To an extent this is unfair because a given medium usually will limit the amount of exposure given to any one project. If, for example, the owner and architect prepare a release to be issued with the rendering, the consulting engineer will find it difficult to obtain any mention by issuing a copy of the rendering and a release at about the same time, unless different media are involved. (Typically, the different media are engineering-oriented publications, not those directed toward prospective clients.) If a site sign goes up indicating the name of the owner-contractor, it will be difficult to have additional signs for other project participants. In some jurisdictions, in fact, site signs are tightly regulated by government.

What we're saying is, in essence, everyone should get his own fair share of credit. For this reason, we suggest that rules for promotional activity be incorporated into the contract, or as an addendum, with one or several persons acting as one, being given authority to approve or disapprove various activities. Obviously, rules would expand as the design team grows, as contractors are brought in, and so forth. In this manner, for example, the project could be named in a release announcing the owner's intention to build. The owner and architect would be mentioned in a release announcing the architect's selection. The owner, architect, and consulting engineer(s) would be mentioned when consulting engineers are selected, and so on. Also, a joint method for payment for such PR activities could be established, if need be. Should special individual promotional activities be desired, the concept first would have to be approved as well as the actual program or product. In this way there are no hard feelings and usually all participants obtain more coverage.

If this method cannot be utilized for one reason or another, make it a point to obtain as much coverage of your own involvement as possible, still properly clearing activities before undertaking them. If, for example, your story with photo is issued and published a week before the realtor handling the project gets his story out, and your story effectively kills his and so hurts opening sales, your successful attempt to gain coverage can prove to be very harmful in terms of ill will created with the owner and realtor alike. In a similar manner, when uncoordinated action is involved, you must be very conscious of taking only credit that is rightfully yours.

Techniques

News Releases. News releases have been discussed at length already.

Site Signs. Know, and be familiar with, local regulations regarding site signs. If, for example, only one sign is allowed, determine who will be putting it up and be sure to have your firm's name included. If you can put up your own, obtain permission to do so, determine where it can be placed, how large it can be, and whether or not you want to include other firm names and so diminish your share of the cost. In most cases site signs will be read from passing vehicles, so the larger and less complicated the sign, the more likely it will be seen and read. As in all such activities, be certain to utilize the same company logo and colors to reinforce recognition.

Brochures. In many cases brochures of various kinds will be prepared for a building. In nonspeculative construction, the brochure will often be used as a grand opening piece. In speculative building, the brochure is more significant and is used as a selling tool. Make every attempt to ensure that your firm's name is included in the brochure with credit given for activities you undertook. Note that in some speculative building brochures that contain loose floor plans, it makes sense to have your name on the floor plans as well, especially when prospective building occupants are business organizations that might need your services someday. In fact, these floor plans will be kept, reprinted, and redistributed many times during the life of the building, and so have a degree of permanency far longer than that of the brochure itself.

Permanent Notice. Permanent notice includes having the firm's name on the building cornerstone or, as seen in some cases, actually carved neatly somewhere in the façade of the building. Usually credit is given only to the architect in such cases, but no doubt an enterprising consulting engineer also could make it feasible to have the name of his firm included, perhaps as partial recompense for the all-too-common, uncompensated last minute changes which have to be designed.

Other. Other methods of obtaining credit for work on a project are limited only by imagination. For soil and foundation engineers or surveyors, for example, whose services seldom receive any credit, some consideration should be given to utilizing general purpose temporary site signs. For example, a geotechnical engineering firm's drill rig may have placed on it a large sign reading, to the effect: "SOIL AND FOUNDATION ENGINEERING SERVICES BEING PERFORMED BY JONES & ASSOCIATES."

7.17 AWARDS

Every attempt should be made to go after as many design awards as possible. Winning awards, in the view of many clients and prospective clients, can be very important. Just a few of the organizations that sponsor awards include:

American Association of Community Junior Colleges
American Association of Nurserymen
American Association of School Administrators
American Consulting Engineers Council (and its chapters)
American Institute of Architects (and its chapters)
American Institute of Steel Construction
American Library Association
American Society of Church Architecture
Architectural Record magazine
Association of Medical Clinics
College & University Business magazine
Design in Steel Awards Program (AISI)
Electrical Consultant magazine
National Conference on Religious Architecture
Prestressed Concrete Institute
Reynolds Aluminum Awards
U.S. Department of Housing and Urban Development/Federal Housing
    Administration

Nor is this by any means a complete listing.

Also not to be overlooked are the many local organizations that give awards for design and for personal involvement. NSPE chapters, for example, give out annual Engineer and Architect of the Year awards. Several ACEC chapters give Man of the Year awards as well as Draftsman of the Year.

As discussed earlier, personnel résumés should be reviewed to determine what, if any, awards individuals on staff have received, or what projects in which they have been involved may have won awards.

7.18 NEWSLETTER

A newsletter is an excellent way to keep the firm in contact with, and before the eyes of, a variety of publics including clients, prospective clients, governmental personnel, and so on.

For the most part, newsletter should be attempted only if the firm will be able to put it out on a fairly regular basis and if it has something to say each time, not merely articles designed to tell readers how wonderful the firm is. In fact, a self-glamorizing newsletter can boomerang and cause negative image impact every time it is seen.

A newsletter does not have to be very expensive to produce. Assuming a mailing list of 500, and a competent staff member who can write or edit the material each month, total production costs probably can be kept to less than $1,800 per year, including postage.

Format

There are a variety of formats from which you can choose. These range from an 8½ × 11-inch page printed on both sides and folded to 5½ × 8½ to obtain four pages, to a multipage 8½ × 11 production complete with typeset columns, photographs, etc. The format should be a function of both budget and amount of material available each issue. Also, consider that you may run the risk of turning off some clients or prospects if the publication is too elaborate. After all, overhead is usually a factor when it comes to fees, and some may not particularly like the idea that they have to pay for an elaborate publication that, in fact, they very easily could live without. Also, the larger the format, the more material you have to use. For example, if you come out with a standard format that requires X-much verbiage or illustration to fill it up, then you must come up with the X-amount each time. If X is too large, it means that some low-grade material will have to be included. As a result, the publication is apt to lose readership appeal because it is filled with too much pap. Therefore, if you are considering developing a newsletter, we suggest that you begin small and expand as appropriate.

Design

The newsletter should have a basic design, i.e., standard masthead and other features. We recommend that a professional do the basic design to ensure that it relays the image you want conveyed. Do not try to skimp. For the most part you will not have to spend an overly great sum of money for design and, in most cases, it will be used for at least several years.

Articles

The key concern is what to include. Review newsletters of other firms for ideas. Typical items include:

Commentary of a principal, usually addressing himself to some current issue of interest to reader.

Design innovations, either achieved by firm personnel or capable of being handled by firm personnel.

Interesting projects, primarily those of the firm, but only if very interesting.

Round-up of news events that are germane to readers.

Quirks in the news that are interesting regardless of audience.

Brainteasers.

It is important to note that the newsletter, in our opinion, should be both multifaceted and light. Your newsletter will not be must reading, so if it is to be read, it must be "want" reading. One of the best ways of achieving this is to have something for everyone, as well as items that will bring a smile.

We suggest that someone on staff be assigned responsibility for turning out the newsletter, or that a staffer act as liaison with an outside writer. Any items of interest observed in any other publication should be clipped and filed for later reference and possible use. Also, staff members should be encouraged to jot down notes about any article they feel worthy of publication in the newsletter, just as they should do for news releases.

Type

Options available for type are varied. Either the newsletter can be set in type, as this book is, by a professional typesetter, which is costly, or you may have, or know, someone with office typesetting equipment such as the IBM MT/ST-MT/SC system, or you can simply use a typewriter. If the latter approach is selected, you can use type at 100% size, or can reduce it to about 75% of size and type it at widths that, when reduced, will enable you to get two columns to the page.

Paper

There are hundreds of different kinds of paper (stock) available. Obviously, you should select one that is light in color, to permit easy reading, and good quality, so it doesn't look cheap. You may wish to investigate recycled paper. Your printer should have numerous paper samples available.

Ink

Ink comes in all colors under the sun. Whatever color is chosen, make it compatible with the color of the newsletter stock. You may wish to use two colors of ink, which is a more expensive printing process. Is it worth it? Bear in mind that you can screen ink, that is, use it at different intensities, thus achieving the effect of several different colors usually for the price of one.

Printing Method

There are several printing methodologies available. Mimeograph is not suggested, nor is any other that does not give high quality and economy. We suggest utilization of Itek equipment or regular photo-offset. Itek is the less expensive of the two, but can run only one color and does not do too well with photographs.

Printers

Talk with printers to get their ideas. Chances are they can show you a variety of formats, styles, etc., and can possibly provide such services as typesetting, art, design, and so on. Check prices carefully, and also obtain bids for services.

Mailing

Many firms and printers can mail for you, that is, stuff newletters (or other materials) into envelopes, seal, address, stamp, and send. You can also do it in-house. If you plan to mail news releases frequently on your own, it is advisable to have in-house mailing equipment. One of the most effective systems utilizes the small hand-operated Addressograph-Multigraph imprinter. Plates and frames can be supplied by A-M usually at a cost of 55 cents each. The imprinter itself is relatively inexpensive, and often can be found used for under $100. Another system is provided by Pitney-Bowes. Xerox also has a system involving photocopying a list onto labels, but of course there are drawbacks in terms of keeping the list current and alphabetical. Other systems also are available, many of them low in cost and high in ease of utilization and maintenance.

7.19 PUBLIC SPEAKING

Public speaking is a very effective communications technique, especially when the audience you address represents a significant potential client public.

In most cases, the biggest drawback to public speaking is fear: fear of actually speaking in public; fear of having nothing good to say; fear of being unable to get a speaking engagement. Nonetheless, you have nothing to fear but fear itself, because public speaking is not difficult; having something to say is not difficult, and obtaining speaking engagements is not difficult either.

Possible Subjects

Divide your public into specific publics, ranging from specific client and prospective client publics, to peer group publics, GMA business publics, and so on.

Because the idea is to hunt where the ducks are, consider first your client and prospective client publics and the various organizations that represent their interests. For each organization, prepare a list of possible topics on which you could speak, much as you would begin to select subjects for possible magazine articles. In fact, magazine articles are an excellent source of subjects, and serve as a basis for research and an indication of how subjects can be applied for the audience involved.

Obtaining Speaking Engagements

To obtain speaking engagements, list the various organizations in which you are interested.

The second step is to develop a list of contacts. In some cases you will belong to some of the organizations listed. In other cases friends or other contacts belong. It may even be necessary to ask friends of friends, until contact is made, and you learn the name of an organization's president or program committee chairman.

The third step is to make contact and make known your availability as a speaker. First, of course, determine what you will talk about. If you have little experience as a public speaker, it is advised that you start on the most friendly territory first, such as organizations you belong to or those in which friends hold office.

With other groups, simply contact the appropriate individual in person, by phone, or letter, and state that you would like to speak before the group if they do on occasion have guest speakers. In cases where speaking programs are solid, find out when an appropriate time would be to make application to deliver a talk during the next year.

Finalizing Arrangements

Once you do get a speaking engagement, be certain to finalize arrangements. This includes knowing exactly where and when the talk is to be given, how much time should be taken, whether or not a question-and-answer session will follow, whether or not you can distribute materials, etc. Also, you should inform the organization about your needs, including a microphone, podium (if you have notes), a light (for reading the speech if you are not familiar enough with it to work from memory or hand-held cards), projection equipment, easel, flip charts, and so forth.

Preparing the Talk

It has been said that, when delivering a talk, you should tell the audience what you are about to tell them, tell them, then tell them what you told them. In essence, this means introduction, main material, summary. For the most part, you can follow writing instructions already given. Recognize, however, that written English and spoken English are almost two different languages. Therefore, once you write your talk, read it aloud to make all changes necessary to make the talk a talk, and not just a reading of a written document. More specifically, follow these guidelines when preparing a talk from scratch or personalizing a model.

Don't Use Big Words. A "big word" does not have to be long and poly-syllabic, but very often it is. Many people like to use big words because they are convinced it shows how educated they are. But that is not what the audience came to find out. To be sure that your audience understands what you are talking about, use as many commonplace words as possible: do not use "albeit" and "wherefore" when "but" and "why" will do; don't "disseminate information" when you can just "give the facts." If you have to use terms germane to the profession, explain them first—in detail.

Keep Sentences Short. When writing a document, long sentences are some-times acceptable—one can always hunt back to find the verb, subject, etc.—but one cannot hunt when listening to a talk. Keep the sentences short and clear. If an audience has to figure out what you just said, it means they've totally lost what you're saying now.

Remention What You're Referring To. If you have to refer back to some-thing, avoid "it," "which," "who," etc., because their use may tend to confuse the audience. Do not be afraid to remention names or statistics. When written, such things may look foolish, but a live audience will appreciate your care. If you are dealing with a variety of different names or statistics, so that even rementioning may become confusing, it may be best to use an easel and some handwritten charts, just to ensure that the audience is with you all the way.

Use Visuals When Appropriate. Visuals, such as slides you may have on file, always add interest to a talk. If you are going to use them throughout, as opposed to using them just during certain segments, be sure you have enough on hand to prevent one slide from being on screen too long.

Be Specific about an Action Request. If you ask your audience to do some-thing, be specific about your request without "pussyfooting." For example, "Those are the statistics. So I want each one of you to sign this petition now to avoid what easily could be a calamity for this community."

Localize Facts. Many prepared speeches will come with facts pertaining to the nation. To heighten audience interest, include or substitute related statistics pertinent to your region, state, or community.

Sum Up without Summing Up. The last point in your speech should sum up, in as few words as possible, the entirety of what you have said. To emphasize the point, don't clutter it up with "And in conclusion," "In summation," or similar phrases. Make it a hard-hitting declarative sentence.

Delivering Your Talk

The manner in which a talk is delivered is important. If it is too smooth, it can make your audience feel as though you do not necessarily believe in what you are saying. If it is too ragged, even the most powerful talk can turn into a confusing mess. For best results, keep in mind the following brief guidelines.

Type the Speech. Ideally you should be able to deliver your talk without using notes of any kind. If you are not familiar enough with it to do that, however, the second best method is to use 3 by 5 note cards with key words written on each. If you are not familiar enough with the talk to do that, then by all means type the speech so you can avoid mistakes.

When typing, use an IBM Orator font (if you have an IBM Selectric typewriter available). Otherwise, use all capital letters, and triple space, making it easy to find your place when looking back to the page after looking up at the audience. Do not end a line with a hyphenated word. Do not end a page in the middle of a paragraph. Indicate emphasis by underlining in red, or by leaving extra space between words. For example: WE CAN, AND WE SHALL, MAKE THIS COMMUNITY A BETTER PLACE TO LIVE.

Be as Familiar with the Speech as Possible. Even though you may have to use the typed speech before the audience, be familiar with it so you can look up at the audience as much as possible. Familiarize yourself with the speech by reading it aloud at least seven times. Read it before your family or others, and ask for frank criticism. Also, read it before a mirror, and tape record what you have said. Listen to the recording critically and, if there are parts of the speech you wish to change or emphasize, make markings on the typed pages for your reference while speaking.

Don't Be Lifeless. Do not act like an automaton before your audience, merely standing there and reading. Put life into your talk. Move around on the podium. Mention names of people in the audience when appropriate. Talk to the audience, rather than lecture them.

Don't Say "Uh!"

Ad-Libbing

To ad-lib, according to Webster, means to "deliver spontaneously." This means that your ad-libs, which help to emphasize a point or to insert some comic relief if it is needed, should be delivered in a casual manner, and cannot be read.

Select with Care. Select your ad-libs with care, especially when jokes are involved. Be especially careful not to tell any story that in any way could cause an ethnic backlash. (In many cases you can change the butt of an ethnic joke. For example, an engineer may like to tell a story about two "dumb architects" (rather than "Polacks") or an architect may tell "engineer" jokes.) Avoid profanity or nonprofane descriptions of possibly obscene circumstances, especially if there are women in the audience. (The women may love it, but certain males attending may feel you to be totally inconsiderate.)

Be Familiar with Your Ad-Lib(s). Know the story well before attempting to tell it. Be sure it is germane to the topic being discussed at the time of its introduction. Merely indicate an ad-lib in the following manner: THAT OCCURRED IN 1970, AND IT REMINDS ME OF A STORY. *AFTER WILSON AD-LIB COME IN HERE:* SO YOU SEE, NONE OF US IS. . . .

Use Ad-Libs Sparingly. Remember that even when used to emphasize a point, an ad-lib is a digression, and as such a sidetrack. The more you use, the more sidetracked your talk becomes. Use ad-libs sparingly, however, and they can help balance your talk and make it far more enjoyable for all concerned. Be sure each ad-lib is relevant. Be sure you are familiar with each one.

Mechanical Considerations

When delivery of the talk will depend on more than just speaking, be certain that everything else needed has been taken care of. For example, if you will be using slides, be certain that:

> the room has an electrical outlet;
>
> the room has blinds, drapes, or other means of blocking out daylight;
>
> equipment needed will be on hand, including the slides, a projector compatible with the slides, a mechanism for advancing slides (or someone to advance them for you on cue), an extension cord, an extra projection lamp, a table on which to place the projector, and a screen of sufficient size.

Likewise, if you will be using a large flip chart, be certain that you will have the tablet, sufficient writing implements, an easel, proper illumination, and so on. Knowing that if something can go wrong it will, you must be certain to prepare for just about any reasonable eventuality.

Some PR Considerations

While public speaking is an excellent PR tool, as already mentioned, it can be made even more worthwhile through several gambits.

News Release. Determine a month or so prior to the talk if the group you will address has PR staff or PR capabilities. If not, you should handle issuing news releases. Regardless of who assumes the responsibility, the following should be done.

> *Issue a news release prior to the talk*, including a photograph of the speaker with caption. The release should detail when and where the talk will be given, whether or not the public is invited, how to make reservations, etc. Be sure to time the release effectively, especially for weekly papers, which should have the release in time to publish it before the talk is given.

> *Invite the press, if appropriate*, by contacting appropriate editors several days prior to sending out the release. For weekly papers, an invitation to the editor-in-chief is correct. For dailies, choose the editor most appropriate.

> *Issue a news release following the talk*, based primarily on a summary of the speech text. A photograph also should accompany this release. For weeklies, mail the release prior to the talk, so it will be published immediately after the talk; for dailies, mailing on the day of the talk is suitable.

Distribution Materials. When appropriate, have materials on hand for distribution to the audience. These could include reprints of a magazine article, an outline of key points you intend to make, forms for making surveys, etc. Be certain to staple a business card to materials distributed.

Texts. Just as reprints of magazine articles are excellent vehicles for establishing you as an authority in your field in the eyes of those who did not read the article when it was published, so does the text of a speech, edited, set in type and printed, help to establish you as an authority in the eyes of those who did not hear your talk. To have the text printed, first edit it or have it edited, and bring it to the printer, who should use large bold type across the top of an $8\frac{1}{2} \times 11$ inch page to indicate the title of the talk and italics below that for wording such as "Text of an address delivered before the (name of the group, date), by (name, title)." The text can be set in ten point type, such as Century or Schoolbook, in double columns. Have the material printed on quality, enamel stock, and distribute and use just as you would a magazine reprint.

7.20 SCRAPBOOKS

A scrapbook is an excellent, low-cost promotional tool. While its use usually is confined to being leafed through by those in your office waiting area, it can create a very favorable impression.

Contents

Your scrapbook should contain all appropriate news clippings relating to your firm and its employees; articles relating to opening of projects in which you have been involved; initial advertisements and possibly brochures relating to projects in which you have been involved; magazine articles by firm members or about the firm, and other germane items.

Type of Book

There are a variety of different scrapbooks on the market. The one that seems easiest to use and most practical utilizes a clear plastic cover over a sticky page, enabling easy placement and replacement of photos and other items and appropriate captions without glue or photo corners. A three ring binder to hold such material makes it easier to store and leaf through.

Keeping the Book Current and Clean

A scrapbook program is easy to undertake and maintain, providing someone is assigned responsibility for doing it, and does it. The book should be cleaned from time to time as needed.

7.21 GREETING CARDS

Although not dynamic promotion, regularly mailing personal greeting cards to various people on their birthdays, religious and lay holidays, and other specific occasions, such as anniversaries, bereavement, etc., can serve to maintain, if not foster and improve, good will. It also keeps the name of the firm and/or its personnel before those you deem important.

Establish a List

You and other members of the firm should establish a list of occasions when cards should be sent and a list of persons to whom cards should be sent on each occasion. Some of the occasions and typical recipients follow.

Birthdays. Compile a list of birthdays, where known, of all employees (from records), clients and members of their firms, officials with whom you work frequently, associates, suppliers, manufacturers' representatives, fellow professionals, etc. Obtain a calendar of the coming year and mark down appropriate birthdates. Naturally, those sending the card, or at least signing it, should know the recipient. Do not send a card to someone you do not know well. When that happens, the person getting the card is forced to conclude that the greeting is completely contrived, resulting in a feeling exactly opposite to the one you wish to engender.

Christmas/New Year. For these holidays just about everyone sends cards to just about everyone else. If at all possible, try to develop your own card, which should be unique. Consider those that emphasize "Season's Greetings" rather than "Merry Christmas," at least for those whose religions do not celebrate the birth of Christ.

Valentine's Day. Cards are particularly suitable for mailing to females, such as secretaries of firms you are in contact with frequently, and others.

St. Patrick's Day. Primarily for those of Irish ancestry.

Rosh Hashana. For those of the Jewish faith.

Other. There are numerous other occasions, including other holidays, anniversaries, and so on.

Mechanics

Obviously, don't go overboard. One person should not receive more than two or three cards per year. Do be imaginative as the occasion befits. For example, you may wish to send anniversary cards to employees on the anniversary of their first coming to work with you, possibly with a token gift.

By all means, and for all cards—including those mailed in large quantities, such as New Year's cards—be certain that each card is signed by hand, and add some sort of personal comment if possible. Do not send cards that have nothing more on them than the imprinted name of the firm or an individual. It merely emphasizes the fact that your greetings are "mass produced."

7.22   ADVERTISING

While design professionals can advertise, ethical restrictions limit such activity to "business card advertising," more aptly referred to in the advertising industry as "tombstone advertising."

Most design professionals advertise in the Yellow Pages. While the cost usually is small, in most cases it is a waste to purchase more space than that to which you are entitled free by virtue of having a phone, unless your clientele includes consumers, such as homeowners who require inspection services of one type or another. An owner looking for an architect to design a multistory structure simply does not "let his fingers do the walking." In fact, due to Yellow Pages advertising, many design professionals receive calls that they do not wish to receive in the first place.

Some larger firms have seen fit to advertise on a regular basis in various business publications and trade journals. Such advertising usually is effective only when one to two specific services are advertised, along with the name of the firm, and then only when the ads appear on a regular basis. If such advertising is to be effective at all, it must not only be relatively large—to ensure that it is seen and read—but it must be repetitive, appearing in issue after issue after issue, constantly keeping the name of the firm before the readers. If your marketing budget is limited, so you have to choose between such advertising and retaining a public relations firm to generate publicity in the form of articles and news releases, we highly recommend the latter approach. In fact, if an effective marketing program is in operation, a firm should be able to reach exactly the prospective clients targeted in an advertising program, but in a far more effective manner, and probably at less cost.

7.23 COMPLETING THE MARKETING PLAN

Completing the marketing plan (begun in Chapter 4) involves inserting materials relative to promotional tactics. The methodology is relatively simple.

Consider major tactics, such as establishing a company identification program, creating magazine articles, developing brochures and a newsletter, etc.

Based on marketing plans for the first two future years, determine when major supplementary tactics should be implemented. For example, if you will need your company identification program completed by March 1979, you can assume you will need four months to develop it and you will have to begin no later than December 1978. Given holidays during that month, and allowance for the unexpected, November 1978 may be a more appropriate "launch" date.

Note that having a marketing plan will permit you to consider the future design of various tactic approaches. For example, if relatively rapid change is projected in terms of management reorganization, the brochure should be designed so that major elements of it can be included in the expanded version, which will be required shortly after the change is implemented.

Smaller tactics, such as giving talks, issuing releases, and so on, can be stated in terms of a frequency pattern. Thus, if you know that a firm representative should give at least twelve speeches a year, you can pick arbitrary dates (such as third Friday of each month) for delivering talks.

Given the pattern you intend to follow for MU penetration, you can also include ideas for prospective audiences. Knowing that you have to give a speech means that you also should be issuing at least one and perhaps two releases for each. In many cases magazine articles (or at least printed texts) can stem from talks.

Specific tactics, by and large, will tend to suggest themselves, based on business and marketing activities. A review of the preceding promotional tools, therefore, coupled with logical projection of when they will be needed, suggests all planning required.

One important consideration is this: promotional tactics are generally very easy to implement and often can be highly productive. The problem is, usually, that they get overlooked. Never miss an opportunity to promote what the firm has done, is doing, and will be doing. Someone must be assigned responsibility not only to see to it that promotional tactics are implemented, but also that the various departments and individuals within them realize the importance of promotion and so keep open the lines of communication which, in almost all cases, is essential for promotional success.

Once promotional strategies and tactics are included in the basic marketing plan, the firm's initial plan is complete. Nonetheless, be sure to perform review to ensure that projected cash flow will be sufficient to support all planned activities. Allow slack. Be certain that, as strategy and tactics come due for implementation, everything is going as planned. When differences are noted, alter your plans or timing as necessary.

IMPLEMENTING THE MARKETING PLAN

The only element of marketing plan implementation not already discussed is the active pursuit of prospects. This is a multifaceted process that entails, to a great extent, the concept of "marketing your services," that is, selling them. The activities suggested in this chapter should, of course, be undertaken in concert with the various promotional tools and image development and control programs already discussed.

8.1 PREPARATION OF A PROSPECT LIST

At this time you are ready to prepare a list of prospects. The list serves four purposes.

First, it enables you to visualize the various different kinds of prospects or client types you can approach.

Second, being comprehensive, it enables you to establish whom you want to contact and approximately when you want the contact to be made.

Third, it provides you knowledge of the general approaches that should be taken for development of promotional programs.

Fourth, and most obviously, it enables you to undertake a program of client contact which is essential to your overall marketing program.

Primarily for the sake of direct contact, your list should be divided into two parts: prospects who are already approachable, and those who are not.

In all cases, prepare a separate file on each prospect. In this file store all information already on hand about him, which may have been picked up through marketing research, plus all new information gleaned from qualification procedures. In addition, indicate information on sales calls, identifying when the call was made, who made it, who was contacted, what was discussed, and so on. It is possible to develop standardized forms for this procedure, but the problem with such forms is that they can become tedious. Sales personnel may wind up spending more time doing paperwork than making contact. Therefore, we recommend that you prepare guidelines on the type of information needed so your sales staff can dictate or write memoranda that answer the pertinent questions in the easiest manner for the person involved.

Review all files periodically, perhaps as frequently as every three months, depending on the size of your firm.

Already Approachable

Prospects who are already approachable should have been identified through organizational research. These include:

Past and current clients of the firm.

Clients of principals of the firm or key personnel prior to joining your firm.

Those with whom certain staff members have worked when with another firm, acting in responsible charge or as team captain of certain projects.

Indirect clients of the firm or its personnel.

Those people you, principals, key staff members, and others know on a personal basis who are prospects, but who have never utilized services of the firm.

All those contacted through your marketing research activities.

Not Yet Approachable

Under the heading of prospects who are not yet approachable list all those with whom you would like to make contact. This can be done in several ways.

Using Research Information. Utilizing mostly information you should already be familiar with through marketing research, prepare a list of all those firm names you have come across, either in *Dodge Reports*, *Commerce Business Daily*, magazine articles, and so on. For example, if yours is an architectural firm specializing in hospitals, you obviously would want to contact a contractor who has been involved in hospital construction, assuming, of course, that hospitals are one of your priority MUs.

In a similar manner, examine MUs identified for penetration during the next five years, and determine who should be contacted when an MU involves providing typical services to a new client type. In the case of government, for example, ascertain exactly whom to contact, at least in terms of department, agency, and title.

Other methods of developing lists of names include examining membership directories of various state and national associations (including engineers, architects, builders of all types, owners, etc.) and using telephone Yellow Pages listings. To obtain Yellow Pages for other cities, simply call the business office of the telephone company.

Using Contacts

A conscious effort should be made to expand contacts within given areas. For example, if you do not have what you feel to be enough prospects in a given MU, you may urge principals and staff members to speak with clients, association acquaintances, and so on, to ask if they know of particular people in certain fields. An employee at an ASHRAE meeting, for example, may inquire of a friend employed by a noncompetitive firm or government if he happens to know anyone connected with a certain firm with which you would like to touch base. Likewise, you may tell an acquaintance that you want to get into a particular MU and ask if he knows anyone who represents a firm in this area. If he doesn't know of someone, perhaps he can put you on to someone who does. Some people are reluctant to do this and will use a variety of reasons to mask what very often is nothing more than embarrassment. In fact, however, you will find that most successful firms do not at all mind undertaking such "prospecting" activities. The results can be impressively worthwhile.

In most cases, you will find that many prospects can be identified through contacts you or other firm members have at associations. A review of association memberships, as revealed in staff résumés, will be very helpful. Be certain to speak with the executive directors of the various associations as well. In many cases they have a "handle" on many of their members and can identify quickly and precisely those firms with which you should make contact.

8.2 CLIENT TYPES

Assuming that you now have a fairly comprehensive list of prospects, you must indicate—in light of your five-year plan—specifically which should be contacted during the first year, which during the second, and so on.

In all probability you will have listed many more prospects than can be contacted directly. You, therefore, should establish a selection process to determine which prospects you would most like to have as clients.

The first element to consider, of course, is client mix. In other words, you do not want to be in a position of relying on just one or two client types, such as petroleum refiners or the state roads commission. Should something happen to a predominant client or client type, your firm could be dealt a severely damaging blow. (In fact, this method of defining client type is closely akin to defining project type, and should already have been considered in establishing your five-year plan.)

There is another way of defining client types, namely, in terms of what field they are in rather than what they build. For example, a governmental client could be involved in airways, colleges, office buildings, etc., just as a professional client could be. In these terms, each client type has characteristics of which new firms in particular must be aware. If financing capabilities are limited, for example, you may wish to avoid or delay contacting those who probably will be slow to pay. Therefore, review the following client-type characteristics—bearing in mind that they are generalities subject to the shortcomings of all generalities—to determine which prospects are most desirable in terms of providing the firm with the business and conditions necessary for achievement of goals.

Professionals

Professionals include those with whom you deal on an interprofessional basis, such as a consulting engineer acting as a subcontractor to an architect. Fellow professionals share your concerns. They usually are very conscious of time and quality of service, at least to the extent that such consciousness is present in their own dealings with clients. For example, in some cases they may be interested in having a job performed well, but not so meticulously that it will cost more than the budget will allow. In other words, the professional client or prospective client understands your position well, and knows precisely what he is looking for.

New firms in particular may find the prospective professional client type most rewarding because, among other things, many are sympathetic to the problems of starting up. Moreover, they can eliminate what others might perceive as risks of dealing with a new firm by checking into backgrounds of principals. In many cases they know well those for whom principals of a new firm have worked in the past, and so can establish in their own minds the qualifications of the new firm. Regardless of a firm's longevity in business, however, qualifications are essential because, in most cases, the professional client must be responsible for the quality of your services. In other words, how well you perform has a direct bearing on the professional client's relationship with his client.

There are two primary drawbacks to working with professionals. First, in terms of their being a prospective client group, they will often have just one or two firms on which they rely to provide a given service. This limits your access to them in light of certain ethical considerations. Therefore, planning your contact is important. General contacting methods, such as sending them a newsletter, brochure, etc., are no problem, but they have only limited appeal. Therefore, specific contacting methods must be geared to developing a working knowledge of the people involved, as through association functions and direct contact when you hear that they are looking for specific services or experience that they feel current sources are unable to provide.

The second drawback concerns payment. In most cases you will not be paid until your professional client is paid (and sometimes not until a while after that), so it often will be necessary to have working capital to carry you through the work performance-payment gap.

Contractors

Many contracting firms, even some of the smaller ones, are aggressively pursuing design/build services either using their own in-house design professionals or retaining or joint venturing with independent firms. Their aggressive marketing efforts have rewarded them with many jobs, particularly those in the modernization and renovation segments of various markets. Accordingly, contractors not only are potential clients but also potential competitors. As a result, contractors have a significant position in your GMA.

One of the key elements in working with contractors is communication. Unlike other groups, contractors are likely to see professionals as more like one another. As a result, they often elect to work with the firm they feel most comfortable with. Accordingly, those from your firm who would be working with contractors should be able to speak their language. For the most part, this means more of a layman's approach than that used in professional-to-professional communication. This is not to say that contractors are not as intelligent or as business-oriented as professionals. Rather, they are more likely to place emphasis on personalities, provided they feel that a firm is fully competent and its representatives show proper deference when it comes to a contractor's ability in procurement, installation, and mangement of construction.

Those Who Build, Occupy and Manage

This client group includes the majority of industrial/manufacturing groups, some commercial elements (such as department stores, grocery stores, drug stores, etc.) as well as institutional clients such as hospitals, colleges, universities, and so on. While there are numerous specific differences between the various types of clients in this group, even from one client to another in a specific type, they have much in common.

First, they all demand extensive experience in the specific kind of project involved. For example, those involved in a hospital project demand that the design professionals be fully aware of the special equipment involved and hospital operation; how equipment and personnel differ from department to department, but interrelate in terms of overall patient care or hospital function; how process and environmental considerations must be involved in planning; layout and design of the facilities, and so on. Similarly, an industrial concern prefers to deal only with firms that have personnel who have extensive experience in the particular kind of industrial process involved.

Second, because this group is not as short-term profit oriented as some others, it is more apt to take advantage of benefits indicated by life-cycle costing as well as innovative techniques that are within budget. Studies also indicate that they are more likely to undertake major improvements for existing facilities, which speculative builders are reluctant to undertake. For example, shortly after general awareness of the energy crisis, industrial, institutional, and commercial clients (in that order) were looking for ways to establish meaningful energy conservation and optimization measures within their facilities.

Third, a majority of these prospects are corporate entities, usually meaning that several layers of personnel within the organization must be satisfied before you can get a job. Your firm must be able to relate to the various personalities who might be involved, and especially to the one or two persons who have the greatest say-so. In many cases these one or two persons will have final say on smaller jobs and will be providing usually-heeded advice to the board of directors or president on major undertakings. It is essential that any marketing strategy be aimed at determining who these key individuals are and relating to them in terms most relevant.

While the chain of command aspect of dealing with a corporate client can at times be tiring, it also can work to your advantage. Once a provider of services is found to be acceptable to a variety of people, he is likely to be kept. Especially when expanding organizations such as department store chains are involved, your firm can be presented with excellent opportunities for establishing satellite operations in new areas with relatively little risk.

A few cautionary notes: many large organizations will utilize a standard purchase order when obtaining professional services. Be certain you understand exactly what the purchase order entails. In most cases it will be more to your advantage to utilize a standard contract form, such as those available from AIA, ACEC, NSPE, or one developed for your firm by your own attorneys. Also be aware that in working with large organizations, corporate or otherwise, you will often be dealing with the "corporate mentality." In other words, you will be working with those who have a penchant for planning and organizing. Work within their plans. Try to meet schedules and be prepared to offer explanations when you cannot. Prepare progress reports. If you determine that there is room for innovation or improvement, put your ideas in a memorandum and submit it through the chain of command. Remember that you are dealing with an organization. It is far better, in terms of business, to have someone else take credit for your idea, or for pursuing your idea, than for you to take all the glory. After all, who would you rather have working for you? Someone competent who makes you look good? Or someone competent who makes you look bad?

Government

Governments—federal, state, county, municipal, district, departments, agencies, and so on—are concerned primarily about the same features that concern the private sector, namely, quality, cost, performance, reliability, maintainability, etc. There are many dissimilarities, too.

First of all, dealing with the government means dealing with red tape. This can be not only frustrating and aggravating, but also more costly in terms of time involved.

Another dissimilarity: services are usually procured on a piecemeal basis. For example, construction inspection will often be provided by separate contract, not necessarily by those who provided the original design services. By the same token, contractors and suppliers are not likely to be involved during the early stages of project development.

Another major difference concerns procurement procedure. Usually a preselection board prequalifies a certain number of firms on the basis of a standard form, such as a Form 251 or Forms 254 and 255. To stand the best possible chance of being considered prequalified, submit a separate form to each agency or a similar form that goes into detail about those specific projects that most reflect work usually undertaken by the agency or department involved. Your wording should be specific, simple, clear, and emphasize your strong points. Also, be sure to include projects not performed by your firm, but for which firm personnel have acted as responsible charge. Such projects can be footnoted or asterisked to indicate that they were not performed by your firm.

Government Forms

There are a variety of different government forms that may have to be used depending on the agency or work involved. The most prevalent forms used by design professionals are SF (standard form) 251, 254, and 255.

SF251. SF 251 (Figure 36) is now all but phased out at the federal government level, replaced by SF254 and 255, as discussed below. Nonetheless, numerous state agencies still use SF251 and probably will continue to do so for a while to come. If you do have to complete an SF251, consider the following pointers:

1. If the firm has undertaken a variety of projects, break them down into project types, such as office buildings, shopping malls, health care facilities, etc. Put a heading above each section. If many projects are involved, list only those under each category that are fairly recent and show a full range of the firm's capabilities. (Be certain to indicate that those listed are representative only and so do not constitute all firm, or key personnel, projects.)

2. Include in your listing all projects for which principals and key employees assumed responsible charge while in previous employment. Be certain to asterisk these projects and explain that they were not done by the firm sending in the SF251, but rather by people now with the firm. (This is an especially useful tactic if the firm involved is just starting out.)

3. Break up listings. If, for example, you are listing 20 different manufacturing plants, skip a space after each five entries. Also, keep verbiage to a minimum and try to keep sentences short and to the point.

4. Customize the form for the sorts of projects and offices (departments, agencies, etc.) involved. In other words, if you are seeking hospital work, place the hospital and other health care facilities projects first.

5. Insert pages as needed. For example, there is very little room for a large firm to indicate and describe the complete scope of its services. Therefore, consider adding an insert following page two. (Be sure to indicate in the form that an insert is being used. Indicate on the insert to which question the inserted material relates.)

STANDARD FORM 251. JUNE, 1961
GENERAL SERVICES ADMINISTRATION
FED. PROC. REG. (41 CFR) 1-16.803

U. S. GOVERNMENT
ARCHITECT-ENGINEER QUESTIONNAIRE

See explanatory notes on page 9. DATE (Month, day, and year)

1. FIRM NAME

2. ESTABLISHED — A. YEAR — B. STATE

3. TYPE OF ORGANIZATION (Check one)
- [ ] INDIVIDUAL
- [ ] PARTNERSHIP
- [ ] CORPORATION
- [ ] JOINT VENTURE
- [ ] OTHER (Explain in item 22)

4. FORMER FIRM NAME(S), IF ANY, AND YEAR(S) ESTABLISHED

5. HOME OFFICE BUSINESS ADDRESS AND TELEPHONE NO.

6. PRESENT BRANCH OFFICE(S)
A. ADDRESS
NAMES
B. TELEPHONE NO.
C. NAME OF PERSON IN CHARGE

7. PRINCIPALS OF FIRM
NAMES

8. ASSOCIATE MEMBERS OF FIRM
NAMES

9. KEY PERSONNEL OF FIRM (Names)

A. ARCHITECTS

D. STRUCTURAL ENGINEERS

G. ELECTRICAL ENGINEERS (Indicate Specialty)

B. LANDSCAPE ARCHITECTS

E. SANITARY ENGINEERS (Indicate Specialty)

H. PLANNERS (Indicate Specialty as Site, City, Town, Community, etc.)

C. CIVIL ENGINEERS

F. MECHANICAL ENGINEERS (Indicate Specialty)

I. OTHER KEY PERSONNEL (Indicate Specialty)

10. NUMBER OF PERSONNEL IN YOUR PRESENT ORGANIZATION

LOCATED AT	a. PRINCIPALS & KEY PERSONNEL*				b. OTHER PERSONNEL										TOTALS
	ARCH. (1)	ENG- (2)	OTHER (3)	ARCH. (4)	ENGINEERS				DRAFTS-MEN (9)	SPEC. WRITERS (10)	ESTIMA-TORS (11)	INSPEC-TORS (12)	SURVEY-ORS (13)	BALANCE (14)	(15)
					(5)MECH.	(6)ELEC.	(7)CIVIL	(8)OTHER							
A. HOME OFFICE															
B. BRANCH OFFICE IN															
C. TOTALS															

11. NUMBER OF PERSONNEL IN YOUR ORGANIZATION DURING LAST 5 YEARS
A. MAXIMUM NO. — B. YEAR — C. NORMAL STRENGTH

* (Total of items 7 and 9)

- 1 -

251-101

Figure 36. SF251.

12.

OUTSIDE ASSOCIATES AND CONSULTANTS USUALLY EMPLOYED BY YOUR FIRM
(Furnish a separate completed questionnaire for each firm or individual listed below but see note c, page 9)

a. CATEGORY	b. NAME OF FIRM OR INDIVIDUAL AND ADDRESS	a. CATEGORY	b. NAME OF FIRM OR INDIVIDUAL AND ADDRESS
A. ARCHITECTS		F. MECHANICAL ENGINEERS	
B. LANDSCAPE ARCHITECTS		G. ELECTRICAL ENGINEERS	
C. CIVIL ENGINEERS		H. PLANNERS	
D. STRUCTURAL ENGINEERS		I. ESTIMATORS	
E. SANITARY ENGINEERS		J. OTHER CONSULTANT AFFILIATIONS	

13. INDICATE IN ORDER OF PRECEDENCE, USING "1," "2," "3," ETC., THE TYPES OF PROJECTS IN WHICH YOUR FIRM SPECIALIZES *(Work specialties not sufficiently identified by the printed general categories are to be listed separately in the spaces provided)*

____ ACOUSTICS - SOUND SUPPRESSION	____ HOSPITALS	____ PUBLIC BUILDINGS
____ AIRFIELD FACILITIES	____ HOUSING	____ SURVEYS AND REPORTS
____ AIR COND. - REFRIG. - VENT.	____ INDUSTRIAL BUILDINGS	____ UTILITIES
____ BRIDGES	____ IRRIGATION OR DRAINAGE	____ WATER - SEWAGE
____ CHANNEL IMPROVEMENTS	____ LABORATORIES	____
____ CHEMICAL FACILITIES	____ MANUALS	____
____ COMMUNICATIONS	____ MASTER PLANNING - SITE DEVELOP.	____
____ COMMERCIAL BUILDINGS	____ MILITARY STANDARD DESIGN	____
____ EARTH FILL DAM WORK	____ MISSILES - FACILITIES - FUELS	____
____ ELECTRONIC FACILITIES	____ NUCLEAR FACILITIES	____
____ HARBOR FACILITIES	____ PETROLEUM FACILITIES	
____ HIGHWAYS	____ POWER - HEATING PLANTS	

14. INDICATE THE SCOPE OF SERVICES PROVIDED BY YOUR FIRM WITHOUT USE OF OUTSIDE ASSOCIATES OR CONSULTANTS ON TYPES OF PROJECTS INDICATED IN ITEM 13 *(i.e. Architectural, Mechanical, Electrical, Structural, etc.)*

STANDARD FORM 251
JUNE 1961

- 2 -

Figure 36. (Continued)

15. PERSONAL HISTORY STATEMENT OF PRINCIPALS AND ASSOCIATES WITHIN YOUR FIRM
(Furnish complete data but keep to essentials)

A. NAME *(Last-first-middle initial)*

DATE OF BIRTH *(Month-day-year)*	YEARS OF EXPERIENCE	AS PRINCIPAL IN THIS FIRM	AS PRINCIPAL IN OTHER FIRMS	OTHER THAN PRINCIPAL

EDUCATION *(College, degree, year, specialization)*

MEMBERSHIP IN PROFESSIONAL ORGANIZATIONS

REGISTRATION *(Type, year, State)*

B. NAME *(Last-first-middle initial)*

DATE OF BIRTH *(Month-day-year)*	YEARS OF EXPERIENCE	AS PRINCIPAL IN THIS FIRM	AS PRINCIPAL IN OTHER FIRMS	OTHER THAN PRINCIPAL

EDUCATION *(College, degree, year, specialization)*

MEMBERSHIP IN PROFESSIONAL ORGANIZATIONS

REGISTRATION *(Type, year, State)*

C. NAME *(Last-first-middle initial)*

DATE OF BIRTH *(Month-day-year)*	YEARS OF EXPERIENCE	AS PRINCIPAL IN THIS FIRM	AS PRINCIPAL IN OTHER FIRMS	OTHER THAN PRINCIPAL

EDUCATION *(College, degree, year, specialization)*

MEMBERSHIP IN PROFESSIONAL ORGANIZATIONS

REGISTRATION *(Type, year, State)*

D. NAME *(Last-first-middle initial)*

DATE OF BIRTH *(Month-day-year)*	YEARS OF EXPERIENCE	AS PRINCIPAL IN THIS FIRM	AS PRINCIPAL IN OTHER FIRMS	OTHER THAN PRINCIPAL

EDUCATION *(College, degree, year, specialization)*

MEMBERSHIP IN PROFESSIONAL ORGANIZATIONS

REGISTRATION *(Type, year, State)*

E. NAME *(Last-first-middle initial)*

DATE OF BIRTH *(Month-day-year)*	YEARS OF EXPERIENCE	AS PRINCIPAL IN THIS FIRM	AS PRINCIPAL IN OTHER FIRMS	OTHER THAN PRINCIPAL

EDUCATION *(College, degree, year, specialization)*

MEMBERSHIP IN PROFESSIONAL ORGANIZATIONS

REGISTRATION *(Type, year, State)*

F. NAME *(Last-first-middle initial)*

DATE OF BIRTH *(Month-day-year)*	YEARS OF EXPERIENCE	AS PRINCIPAL IN THIS FIRM	AS PRINCIPAL IN OTHER FIRMS	OTHER THAN PRINCIPAL

EDUCATION *(College, degree, year, specialization)*

MEMBERSHIP IN PROFESSIONAL ORGANIZATIONS

REGISTRATION *(Type, year, State)*

STANDARD FORM 251
JUNE 1961

- 3 -

Figure 36. *(Continued)*

15. CONTINUED   PERSONAL HISTORY STATEMENT OF PRINCIPALS AND ASSOCIATES WITHIN YOUR FIRM
(Furnish complete data but keep to essentials)

G. NAME (Last-first-middle initial)

DATE OF BIRTH (Month-day-year)	YEARS OF EXPERIENCE	AS PRINCIPAL IN THIS FIRM	AS PRINCIPAL IN OTHER FIRMS	OTHER THAN PRINCIPAL

EDUCATION (College, degree, year, specialization)

MEMBERSHIP IN PROFESSIONAL ORGANIZATIONS

REGISTRATION (Type, year, State)

H. NAME (Last-first-middle initial)

DATE OF BIRTH (Month-day-year)	YEARS OF EXPERIENCE	AS PRINCIPAL IN THIS FIRM	AS PRINCIPAL IN OTHER FIRMS	OTHER THAN PRINCIPAL

EDUCATION (College, degree, year, specialization)

MEMBERSHIP IN PROFESSIONAL ORGANIZATIONS

REGISTRATION (Type, year, State)

I. NAME (Last-first-middle initial)

DATE OF BIRTH (Month-day-year)	YEARS OF EXPERIENCE	AS PRINCIPAL IN THIS FIRM	AS PRINCIPAL IN OTHER FIRMS	OTHER THAN PRINCIPAL

EDUCATION (College, degree, year, specialization)

MEMBERSHIP IN PROFESSIONAL ORGANIZATIONS

REGISTRATION (Type, year, State)

J. NAME (Last-first-middle initial)

DATE OF BIRTH (Month-day-year)	YEARS OF EXPERIENCE	AS PRINCIPAL IN THIS FIRM	AS PRINCIPAL IN OTHER FIRMS	OTHER THAN PRINCIPAL

EDUCATION (College, degree, year, specialization)

MEMBERSHIP IN PROFESSIONAL ORGANIZATIONS

REGISTRATION (Type, year, State)

K. NAME (Last-first-middle initial)

DATE OF BIRTH (Month-day-year)	YEARS OF EXPERIENCE	AS PRINCIPAL IN THIS FIRM	AS PRINCIPAL IN OTHER FIRMS	OTHER THAN PRINCIPAL

EDUCATION (College, degree, year, specialization)

MEMBERSHIP IN PROFESSIONAL ORGANIZATIONS

REGISTRATION (Type, year, State)

L. NAME (Last-first-middle initial)

DATE OF BIRTH (Month-day-year)	YEARS OF EXPERIENCE	AS PRINCIPAL IN THIS FIRM	AS PRINCIPAL IN OTHER FIRMS	OTHER THAN PRINCIPAL

EDUCATION (College, degree, year, specialization)

MEMBERSHIP IN PROFESSIONAL ORGANIZATIONS

REGISTRATION (Type, year, State)

STANDARD FORM 251
JUNE 1961

- 4 -

Figure 36. (Continued)

16. PRESENT ACTIVITIES ON WHICH YOUR FIRM IS DESIGNATED ARCHITECT OR ENGINEER OF RECORD

NAME AND TYPE OF PROJECT	LOCATION	NAME AND ADDRESS OF OWNER	ESTIMATED CONSTRUCTION COST	PERCENT COMPLETED	
				DESIGN	FIELD SUPV.

TOTAL NUMBER OF PRESENT PROJECTS:

TOTAL ESTIMATED CONSTRUCTION COST:

STANDARD FORM 251
JUNE 1961

- 5 -

Figure 36. (*Continued*)

17.
PRESENT ACTIVITIES ON WHICH YOUR FIRM IS ASSOCIATED WITH OTHERS
(Indicate phase of work for which your firm is responsible)

NAME OF PROJECT AND PHASE OF WORK	LOCATION	OWNER	ESTIMATED CONSTRUCTION COST OF		PERCENT OF ENTIRE PROJECT COMPLETED		FIRM ASSOCIATED WITH
			ENTIRE PROJECT	WORK FOR WHICH YOUR FIRM IS RESPONSIBLE	DESIGN	FIELD SUPV.	

TOTAL NUMBER OF PRESENT PROJECTS:

TOTAL ESTIMATED CONSTRUCTION COST OF WORK FOR WHICH YOUR FIRM IS RESPONSIBLE:

STANDARD FORM 251
JUNE 1961

- 6 -

Figure 36. (*Continued*)

18. COMPLETED WORK ON WHICH YOUR FIRM WAS DESIGNATED ARCHITECT OR ENGINEER OF RECORD DURING THE LAST 10 YEARS

NAME AND TYPE OF PROJECT	LOCATION	YEAR YOUR WORK CON-PLETED	NAME AND ADDRESS OF OWNER	ESTIMATED CONSTRUCTION COST	CON-STRUCTED (Yes or No)

TOTAL NUMBER OF COMPLETED PROJECTS:

TOTAL ESTIMATED CONSTRUCTION COST:

- 7 -

STANDARD FORM 251
JUNE 1961

Figure 36. *(Continued)*

19. COMPLETED WORK ON WHICH YOUR FIRM WAS ASSOCIATED WITH OTHER FIRMS DURING THE LAST 10 YEARS
(*Indicate phase of work for which your firm was responsible*)

NAME OF PROJECT AND PHASE OF WORK	LOCATION	OWNER	YEAR YOUR WORK COMPLETED	ESTIMATED CONSTRUCTION COST OF		CONSTRUCTED (*Yes or No.*)	FIRM ASSOCIATED WITH
				ENTIRE PROJECT	WORK FOR WHICH YOUR FIRM WAS RESPONSIBLE		

TOTAL NUMBER OF COMPLETED PROJECTS:

TOTAL ESTIMATED CONSTRUCTION COST OF WORK FOR WHICH YOUR FIRM WAS RESPONSIBLE:

- 8 -

STANDARD FORM 251
JUNE 1961

Figure 36. (*Continued*)

20. EXHIBITS OF COMPLETED WORK

Unless specifically requested, submission of photographs is optional. Where submitted, furnish one exterior and one interior photograph of five examples of completed architectural work that are listed in items 18 and 19. (Photographs of models, renderings, sketches, etc., are NOT desired.) Size of photographs not to exceed 8½"x11". On the back of each photograph give the following information: (1) Name and address of client; (2) Name and address of your firm; (3) Type of structure; (4) Location of structure; (5) Cost of specific structure. Photographs of electrical or mechanical facilities and other components of a decided engineering character are not necessary.

21. SECURITY CLEARANCE (See Note d)

A. CURRENT STATUS (Check one)

☐ ACTIVE ☐ INACTIVE ☐ NONE

B. DEGREE OF CLEARANCE

C. DATE OF CLEARANCE

D. CLEARED BY

E. HAVE PRINCIPALS BEEN CLEARED?

☐ YES ☐ NO

22. IN THE EVENT SPACES PROVIDED ON THE FORM ARE NOT SUFFICIENT FOR ENTRIES, OR IF YOU WISH TO FURNISH ADDITIONAL INFORMATION, IT MAY BE INSERTED HERE, ON THE REVERSE OF THIS PAGE, OR ON SEPARATE SHEETS, WITH APPROPRIATE REFERENCES.

23. PURPOSE OF SUBMITTING THIS QUESTIONNAIRE (Check A or B, not both)

A. I/We wish to be considered for architectural or engineering services in connection with the ☐ design, ☐ inspection, ☐ supervision (check applicable box or boxes) of construction projects for Federal Agencies.

B. This completed questionnaire is submitted as evidence of employment as outside associate or consultant. (See item 12.)

NAME OF FIRM ASSOCIATED WITH

As of this date: _____ the foregoing is a true statement of facts.

NAME OF FIRM OR INDIVIDUAL SUBMITTING QUESTIONNAIRE	TYPE NAME AND TITLE OF PERSON SIGNING	SIGNATURE

NOTES:

(a) Form is to be completed by typewriter. Completed forms may be reproduced in any quantity deemed necessary to meet distribution requirements.

(b) It will be to a firm's advantage to maintain its experience record on a current basis. This may be accomplished by periodically forwarding current data.

(c) It is NOT necessary for individuals or firms who check item 23B to furnish separate questionnaires for their outside associates and consultants.

(d) Item 21 is for consideration only with respect to classified projects.

STANDARD FORM 251
JUNE 1981

- 9 -

☆ GPO 1981 O-572738-88

Figure 36. (Continued)

6. Consider having the information you want to include set in type. The appearance is far neater and you can get more words into the space provided. As an alternative, consider having the form reproduced at double the original size, type in information, and then have the whole thing reduced to normal size. In this way you can fit twice the information in the same space.

7. Include relevant photographs. They should be captioned to emphasize the point even more, e.g., "The fountain illustrated also serves as a cooling tower, thereby adding to the aesthetic appeal of the project while also lowering costs."

8. Rather than copying SF251s in-house, consider having them produced by a printer using photo-offset (if photographs are to be copied along with everything else), or Itek (if no photos are being used or if individual photos are inserted to illustrate only those projects that the office to which you are submitting may be interested).

9. Consider having the SF251 bound by a plastic spiral spine or in-house, perfect binding method. Some firms even have special covers designed for the form, along with a table of contents and dividers. Now that the form has been substantially replaced, such extremes may not be cost effective.

10. Before finalizing the form, be certain to check it to ensure that everything that should have been filled out has been.

Be sure to file SF251s with all agencies and offices that use them. Do not expect one office to provide your form to another. Likewise, resubmit a new form each year where appropriate, and more frequently if important changes have been made, such as completion of several important projects. Also, be certain to review the specific form you are asked to complete. A state agency, for example, may have based its form on the 251, but there may be important differences.

SF254 and 255. Most agencies of the federal government have replaced SF251 with SF254 and SF255 (obtainable from Regional GSA (Government Services Administration) offices (listed in telephone white pages under "United States Government") or from the Superintendent of Documents, U.S. Government Printing Office, Washington, D.C. 20402). It is too early to tell at this stage how many state and local government entities will follow suit, but most probably will eventually.

In essence, Form 254 (Figure 37) is the one that has replaced the 251. It is far more streamlined and allows for precious little expansion or glamori-

STANDARD FORM (SF)
254

Architect-Engineer and Related Services Questionnaire

Standard Form 254
General Services Administration,
Washington, D.C. 20405
Fed. Proc. Reg. (41 CFR) 1-16. 803
Armed Svc. Proc. Reg. 18-403

Purpose:

The policy of the Federal Government, in procuring architectural, engineering, and related professional services, is to encourage firms lawfully engaged in the practice of those professions to submit annually a statement of qualifications and performance data. Standard Form 254, "Architect-Engineer and Related Services Questionnaire" is provided for that purpose. Interested A-E firms (including new, small, and/or minority firms) should complete and file SF 254's with each Federal agency and file SF 254's with each Federal agency and with appropriate regional or district offices for which the A-E is qualified to perform services. The agency head for each proposed project shall evaluate these qualification resumes, together with any other performance data on file or requested by the agency, in relation to the proposed project. The SF 254 may be used as a basis for selecting firms for discussions, or for screening firms preliminary to inviting submission of additional information.

Definitions:

"**Architect-engineer and related services**" are those professional services associated with research, development, design and construction, alteration, or repair of real property, as well as incidental services that members of these professions and those in their employ may logically or justifiably perform, including studies, investigations, surveys, evaluations, consultations, planning, programming, conceptual designs, plans and specifications, cost estimates, inspections, shop drawing reviews, sample recommendations, preparation of operating and maintenance manuals, and other related services.

"**Parent Company**" is that firm, company, corporation, association or conglomerate which is the major stockholder or highest tier owner of the firm completing this questionnaire; i.e. Firm A is owned by Firm B which is, in turn, a subsidiary of Corporation C. The "parent company" of Firm A is Corporation C.

"**Principals**" are those individuals in a firm who possess legal responsibility for its management. They may be owners, partners, corporate officers, associates, administrators, etc.

"**Discipline**", as used in this questionnaire, refers to the primary technological capability of individuals in the responding firm. Possession of an academic degree, professional registration, certification, or extensive experience in a particular field of practice normally reflects an individual's primary technical discipline.

"**Joint Venture**" is a collaborative undertaking by two or more firms or individuals for which the participants are both jointly and individually responsible.

"**Consultant**", as used in this questionnaire, is a highly specialized individual or firm having significant input and responsibility for certain aspects of a project and possessing unusual or unique capabilities for assuring success of the finished work.

"**Prime**" refers to that firm which may be coordinating the concerted and complementary inputs of several firms, individuals or related services to produce a completed study or facility. The "prime" would normally be regarded as having full responsibility and liability for quality of performance by itself as well as by subcontractor professionals under its jurisdiction.

"**Branch Office**" is a satellite, or subsidiary extension, of a headquarters office of a company, regardless of any differences in name or legal structure of such a branch due to local or state laws. "Branch offices" are normally subject to the management decisions, bookkeeping, and policies of the main office.

Instructions for Filing (Numbers below correspond to numbers contained in form):

1. Type accurate and complete name of submitting firm, its address, and zip code.

1a. Indicate whether firm is being submitted in behalf of a parent firm or a branch office. (Branch office submissions should list only personnel in, and experience of, that office.)

2. Provide date the firm was established under the name shown in question 1.

3. Show date upon which all submitted information is current and accurate.

4. Enter type of ownership, or legal structure, of firm (sole proprietor, partnership, corporation, joint venture, etc.)

4a. Check appropriate box indicating if firm is minority-owned. (See 41 CFR 1-1.13 or ASPR 1-332.3(a) for definitions of minority ownership.)

5. Branches or subsidiaries of larger or parent companies, or conglomerates, should insert name and address of highest-tier owner.

5a. If present firm is the successor to, or outgrowth of, one or more predecessor firms, show name(s) of former entity(ies) and the year(s) of their original establishment.

6. List not more than two principals from submitting firm who may be contacted by the agency receiving this form. (Different principals may be listed on forms going to another agency.) Listed principals must be empowered to speak for the firm on policy and contractual matters.

7. Beginning with the submitting office, list name, location, total number of personnel and telephone numbers for all associated or branch offices, (including any headquarters or foreign offices) which provide A-E and related services.

7a. Show total personnel in all offices. (Should be sum of all personnel, all branches.)

8. Show total number of employees, by discipline, in submitting office. (If form is being submitted by main or headquarters office, firm should list total employees, by discipline, in all offices.) While some personnel may be qualified in several disciplines, each person should be counted only once in accord with his or her primary function. Include clerical personnel as "administrative."

Standard Form 254 July 1975
Prescribed by GSA Fed. Proc. Reg. (41 CFR) 1-16.803

254-101

1

Figure 37. SF254.

STANDARD FORM (SF) 254

Architect-Engineer and Related Services Questionnaire

Standard Form 254
General Services Administration,
Washington, D. C. 20405
Fed. Proc. Reg. (41 CFR) 1-16. 803
Armed Svc. Proc.. Reg. 18-403

Write in any additional disciplines — sociologists, biologists, etc. — and number of people in each, in blank spaces.

9. Using chart (below) insert appropriate index number to indicate range of professional services fees received by submitting firm each calendar year for last five years, most recent year first. Fee summaries should be broken down to reflect the fees received each year for (a) work performed directly for the Federal Government (not including grant and loan projects) or as a sub to other professionals performing work directly for the Federal Government; (b) all other domestic work U.S. and possessions, including Federally-assisted projects, and (c) all other foreign work.

Ranges of Professional Services Fees

INDEX

1. Less than $100,000
2. $100,000 to $250,000
3. $250,000 to $500,000
4. $500,000 to $1 million

INDEX

5. $1 million to $2 million
6. $2 million to $5 million
7. $5 million to $10 million
8. $10 million or greater

10. Select and enter, in numerical sequence, **not more than thirty** (30) "Experience Profile Code" numbers from the listing (next page) which most accurately reflect submitting firm's demonstrated technical capabilities and project experience. **Carefully review list.** (It is recognized some profile codes may be part of other services or projects contained on list; firms are encouraged to select profile codes which best indicate type and scope of services provided on past projects.) For each code number, show total number of projects and gross fees (in thousands) received for profile projects performed by firm during past five years. If firm has one or more capabilities not included on list, insert same in blank spaces at end of list and show numbers in question 10 on the form. In such cases, the filled-in listing **must** accompany the complete SF 254 when submitted to the Federal agencies.

11. Using the "Experience Profile Code" numbers in the same sequence as entered in item 10, give details of at least one recent (within last five years) representative project for each code number, up to a **maximum** of thirty (30) separate projects, or portions of projects, for which firm was responsible. (Project examples may be used more than once to illustrate different services rendered on the same job. Example: a dining hall may be part of an auditorium or educational facility.) Firms which select less than thirty "profile codes" may list two or more project examples (to illustrate specialization) for each code number so long as total of all project examples does not exceed thirty (30). After each code number in, question 11, show: (a) whether firm was "P", the prime professional, or "C", a consultant, or "JV", part of a joint venture on that particular project (New firms, in existence less than five (5) years may use the symbol "IE" to indicate "Individual Experience" as opposed to firm experience.); (b) provide name and location of the specific project which typifies firm's (or individual's) performance under that code category; (c) give name and address of the owner of that project (if government agency indicate responsible office); (d) show the estimated construction cost (or other applicable

cost) for that portion of the project for which the firm was primarily responsible. (Where no construction was involved, show approximate cost of firm's work); and (e) state year work on that particular project was, or will be, completed.

12. The completed SF 254 should be signed by a principal of the firm, preferably the chief executive officer.

13. Additional data, brochures, photos, etc. should not accompany this form unless specifically requested.

NEW FIRMS (not reorganized or recently-amalgamated firms) are eligible and encouraged to seek work from the Federal Government in connection with performance of projects for which they are qualified. Such firms are encouraged to complete and submit Standard Form 254 to appropriate agencies. Questions on the form dealing with personnel or experience may be answered by citing experience and capabilities of individuals in the firm, based on performance and responsibility while in the employ of others. In so doing, notation of this fact should be made on the form. In question 9, write in "N/A" to indicate "not applicable" for those years prior to firm's organization.

Standard Form 254 July 1975
Prescribed By GSA Fed. Proc. Reg. (41 CFR) 1-16.803

2

Figure 37. (Continued)

Experience Profile Code Numbers
for use with questions 10 and 11

001 Acoustics; Noise Abatement
002 Aerial Photogrammetry
003 Agricultural Development; Grain Storage; Farm Mechanization
004 Air Pollution Control
005 Airports; Navaids; Airport Lighting; Aircraft Fueling
006 Airports; Terminals & Hangars; Freight Handling
007 Arctic Facilities
008 Auditoriums & Theatres
009 Automation; Controls; Instrumentation
010 Barracks; Dormitories
011 Bridges
012 Cemeteries (Planning & Relocation)
013 Chemical Processing & Storage
014 Churches; Chapels
015 Codes; Standards; Ordinances
016 Cold Storage; Refrigeration; Fast Freeze
017 Commercial Buildings (low rise); Shopping Centers
018 Communications Systems; TV; Microwave
019 Computer Facilities; Computer Service
020 Conservation and Resource Management
021 Construction Management
022 Corrosion Control; Cathodic Protection; Electrolysis
023 Cost Estimating
024 Dams (Concrete; Arch)
025 Dams (Earth; Rock); Dikes; Levees
026 Desalinization (Process & Facilities)
027 Dining Halls; Clubs; Restaurants
028 Ecological & Archeological Investigations
029 Educational Facilities; Classrooms
030 Electronics
031 Elevators; Escalators; People-Movers
032 Energy Conservation; New Energy Sources
033 Environmental Impact Studies, Assessments or Statements
034 Fallout Shelters; Blast-Resistant Design
035 Field Houses; Gyms; Stadiums
036 Fire Protection
037 Fisheries; Fish Ladders
038 Forestry & Forest Products
039 Garages; Vehicle Maintenance Facilities; Parking Decks
040 Gas Systems (Propane; Natural; Etc.)

041 Graphic Design
042 Harbors; Jetties; Piers; Ship Terminal Facilities
043 Heating; Ventilating; Air Conditioning
044 Health Systems Planning
045 Highrise; Air-Rights-Type Buildings
046 Highways; Streets; Airfield Paving; Parking Lots
047 Historical Preservation
048 Hospitals & Medical Facilities
049 Hotels; Motels
050 Housing (Residential, Multi-Family; Apartments; Condominiums)
051 Hydraulics & Pneumatics
052 Industrial Buildings; Manufacturing Plants
053 Industrial Processes; Quality Control
054 Industrial Waste Treatment
055 Interior Design; Space Planning
056 Irrigation; Drainage
057 Judicial and Courtroom Facilities
058 Laboratories; Medical Research Facilities
059 Landscape Architecture
060 Libraries; Museums; Galleries
061 Lighting (Interiors; Display; Theatre, Etc.)
062 Lighting (Exteriors; Streets; Memorials; Athletic Fields, Etc.)
063 Materials Handling Systems; Conveyors; Sorters
064 Metallurgy
065 Microclimatology; Tropical Engineering
066 Military Design Standards
067 Mining & Mineralogy
068 Missile Systems (Silos; Fuels; Transport)
069 Modular Systems Design; Pre-Fabricated Structures or Components
070 Naval Architecture; Off-Shore Platforms
071 Nuclear Facilities; Nuclear Shielding
072 Office Buildings; Industrial Parks
073 Oceanographic Engineering
074 Ordnance; Munitions; Special Weapons
075 Petroleum Exploration; Refining
076 Petroleum and Fuel (Storage and Distribution)
077 Pipelines (Cross-Country — Liquid & Gas)
078 Planning (Community, Regional, Areawide and State)
079 Planning (Site, Installation, and Project)
080 Plumbing & Piping Design
081 Pneumatic Structures; Air-Support Buildings
082 Postal Facilities

083 Power Generation, Transmission, Distribution
084 Prisons & Correctional Facilities
085 Product, Machine & Equipment Design
086 Radar; Sonar; Radio & Radar Telescopes
087 Railroad; Rapid Transit
088 Recreation Facilities (Parks, Marinas, Etc.)
089 Rehabilitation (Buildings; Structures; Facilities)
090 Resource Recovery; Recycling
091 Radio Frequency Systems & Shieldings
092 Rivers; Canals; Waterways; Flood Control
093 Safety Engineering; Accident Studies; OSHA Studies
094 Security Systems; Intruder & Smoke Detection
095 Seismic Designs & Studies
096 Sewage Collection, Treatment and Disposal
097 Soils & Geologic Studies; Foundations
098 Solar Energy Utilization
099 Solid Wastes; Incineration; Land Fill
100 Special Environments; Clean Rooms, Etc.
101 Structural Design; Special Structures
102 Surveying; Platting; Mapping; Flood Plain Studies
103 Swimming Pools
104 Storm Water Handling & Facilities
105 Telephone Systems (Rural; Mobile; Intercom, Etc.)
106 Testing & Inspection Services
107 Traffic & Transportation Engineering
108 Towers (Self-Supporting & Guyed Systems)
109 Tunnels & Subways
110 Urban Renewal; Community Development
111 Utilities (Gas & Steam)
112 Value Analysis; Life-Cycle Costing
113 Warehouses & Depots
114 Water Resources; Hydrology; Ground Water
115 Water Supply, Treatment and Distribution
116 Wind Tunnels; Research/Testing Facilities Design
117 Zoning; Land Use Studies
201 _____
202 _____
203 _____
204 _____
205 _____

Standard Form 254 July 1975
Prescribed By GSA Fed. Proc. Reg. (41 CFR) 1-16.803

Figure 37. (Continued)

3

OMB Approval No. 29-RO234

STANDARD FORM (SF)
254
Architect-Engineer and Related Services Questionnaire

1. Firm Name / Business Address:

1a. Submittal is for ☐ Parent Company ☐ Branch Office

2. Year Present Firm Established:

3. Date Prepared:

4. Type of Ownership:
4a. Minority Owned ☐ yes ☐ no

5. Name of Parent Company, if any:

5a. Former Firm Name(s), if any, and Year(s) Established:

6. Names of not more than Two Principals to Contact: Title / Telephone
(1)
(2)

7. Present Offices: City / State / Telephone / No. Personnel Each Office

7a. Total Personnel _____

8. Personnel by Discipline:

___ Administrative	___ Electrical Engineers	___ Oceanographers
___ Architects	___ Estimators	___ Planners: Urban/Regional
___ Chemical Engineers	___ Geologists	___ Sanitary Engineers
___ Civil Engineers	___ Hydrologists	___ Soils Engineers
___ Construction Inspectors	___ Interior Designers	___ Specification Writers
___ Draftsmen	___ Landscape Architects	___ Structural Engineers
___ Ecologists	___ Mechanical Engineers	___ Surveyors
___ Economists	___ Mining Engineers	___ Transportation Engineers

9. Summary of Professional Services Fees Received: (insert index number)

Last 5 Years (most recent year first)

19____ 19____ 19____ 19____ 19____

Direct Federal contract work, including overseas
All other domestic work
All other foreign work*

*Firms interested in foreign work, but without such experience, check here: ☐.

Ranges of Professional Services Fees
Index
1. Less than $100,000
2. $100,000 to $250,000
3. $250,000 to $500,000
4. $500,000 to $1 million
5. $1 million to $2 million
6. $2 million to $5 million
7. $5 million to $10 million
8. $10 million or greater

Standard Form 254 July 1975
Prescribed By GSA Fed. Proc. Reg. (41 CFR) 1-16.803

4

Figure 37. (Continued)

10. Profile of Firm's Project Experience, Last 5 Years

Profile Code	Number of Projects	Total Gross Fees (in thousands)	Profile Code	Number of Projects	Total Gross Fees (in thousands)	Profile Code	Number of Projects	Total Gross Fees (in thousands)
1)			11)			21)		
2)			12)			22)		
3)			13)			23)		
4)			14)			24)		
5)			15)			25)		
6)			16)			26)		
7)			17)			27)		
8)			18)			28)		
9)			19)			29)		
10)			20)			30)		

11. Project Examples, Last 5 Years

Profile Code	"P", "C", "JV", or "IE"	Project Name and Location	Owner Name and Address	Cost of Work (in thousands)	Completion Date (Actual or Estimated)
		1			
		2			
		3			
		4			
		5			
		6			
		7			

Standard Form 254 July 1975
Prescribed By GSA Fed. Proc. Reg. (41 CFR) 1-16.803

5

Figure 37. (Continued)

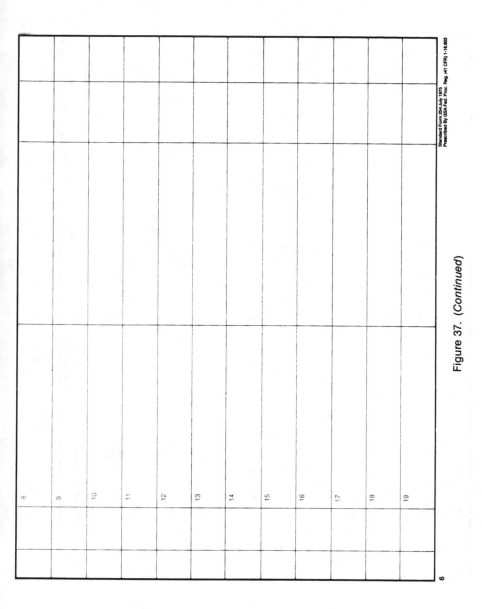

Figure 37. *(Continued)*

20											
21											
22											
23											
24											
25											
26											
27											
28											
29											
30											

12. The foregoing is a statement of facts

Signature: _____ Typed Name and Title: _____ Date: _____

7

Standard Form 254 July 1975
Prescribed By GSA Fed. Proc. Reg. (41 CFR) 1-16.803

Figure 37. (*Continued*)

zation. Nonetheless, several of the packaging techniques suggested for the 251 can be applied.

In that the 254 is a relatively new form, you should expect to have questions about it over the next several years. For this reason you should contact your closest GSA regional office, other federal agency offices, and state or local governmental entities (where it is adopted locally) to determine if certain specific things can be done, such as:

including photographs,

indicating with an appropriate footnote those projects not performed by the firm, but for which professional staff members and principals served as responsible charge while with another firm,

including as services provided by the firm those services provided by it from regularly retained consultants,

updating construction cost figures in terms of current dollar amounts (a project completed five years ago at a cost of $4 million would have a replacement value today of probably close to $5 to $6 million).

Remember these important factors:

1. Keep track of those agencies, departments, etc., to whom you send Form 254 so you can update as needed (see below).

2. Update whenever there is any substantial change, but always send in a new form at least once a year, even if it represents no change at all.

3. Select the projects you itemize on the basis of the needs of the agency you send to. For example, if you send in a 254 to EPA, those projects indicated, wherever possible, should be the kind in which EPA is most interested.

SF255 (Figure 38) is the form to be used for submitting qualifications regarding a specific project. It is more or less self-explanatory.

There is, unfortunately, no way of providing some highly specialized "tricks of the trade" on how to work with those forms because there is not yet enough experience. However, one of the things you should attempt to do is obtain copies of other firms' forms 254 and 255 from the agencies or firms involved. National associations may have samples on file. In addition, contact your national associations to obtain whatever advice and continuing experience information they have available.

Other Forms. SF254 and 255 are not the only forms used by the federal government that may interest you. For example, if you want to attempt

STANDARD FORM (SF)

255

Architect-Engineer
and Related Services
Questionnaire for
Specific Project

Standard Form 255
General Services Administration,
Washington, D. C. 20405
Fed. Proc. Reg. (41 CFR) 1-16 . 803
Armed Svc. Proc. Reg. 18-403

Purpose:

This form is a supplement to the "Architect-Engineer and Related Services Questionnaire" (SF 254). Its purpose is to provide additional information regarding the qualifications of interested firms to undertake a specific Federal A-E project. Firms, or branch offices of firms, submitting this form should enclose (or already have on file with the appropriate office of the agency) a current (within the past year) and accurate copy of the SF 254 for that office.

The procurement official responsible for each proposed project may request submission of the SF 255 "Architect-Engineer and Related Services Questionnaire for Specific Project" in accord with applicable civilian and military procurement regulations and shall evaluate such submissions, as well as related information contained on the Standard Form 254, and any other performance data on file with the agency, and shall select firms for subsequent discussions leading to contract award in conformance with Public Law 92-582. This form should only be filed by an architect-engineer or related services firm when requested to do so by the agency or by a public announcement. Responses should be as complete and accurate as possible, contain data relative to the specific project for which you wish to be considered, and should be provided, by the required due date, to the office specified in the request or public announcement.

This form will be used only for the specified project. Do not refer to this submittal in response to other requests or public announcements.

Definitions:

"**Architect-engineer and related services**" are those professional services associated with research, development, design and construction, alteration, or repair of real property, as well as incidental services that members of these professions and those in their employ may logically or justifiably perform, including studies, investigations, surveys, evaluations, consultations, planning, programming, conceptual designs, plans and specifications, cost estimates, inspections, shop drawing reviews, sample recommendations, preparation of operating and maintenance manuals, and other related services.

"**Principals**" are those individuals in a firm who possess legal responsibility for its management. They may be owners, partners, corporate officers, associates, administrators, etc.

"**Discipline**", as used in this questionnaire, refers to the primary technological capability of individual in the responding firm. Possession of an academic degree, professional registration, certification, or extensive experience in a particular field of practice normally reflects an individual's primary technical discipline.

"**Joint Venture**", is a collaborative undertaking of two or more firms or individuals for which the participants are both jointly and individually responsible.

"**Key Persons, Specialists, and Individual Consultants**", as used in this questionnaire, refer to individuals who will have **major** project responsibility or will provide **unusual or unique** capabilities for the project under consideration.

Instructions for Filing (Numbers below correspond to numbers contained in form):

1. Give name and location of the project for which this form is being submitted.

2. Provide appropriate data from the *Commerce Business Daily* (CBD) identifying the particular project for which this form is being filed.

2a. Give the date of the *Commerce Business Daily* in which the project announcement appeared, or indicate "not applicable" (N/A) if the source of the announcement is other than the CBD.

2b. Indicate Agency identification or contract number as provided in the CBD announcement.

3. Show name of the individual or firm (or joint venture) which is submitting this form for the project.

3a. List the name, title, and telephone number of that principal who will serve as the point of contact. Such an individual must be empowered to speak for the firm on policy and contractual matters and should be familiar with the programs and procedures of the agency to which this form is directed.

3b. Give the address of the specific office which will have responsibility for performing the announced work.

4. Insert the number of personnel by discipline presently employed (on date of this form) at work location. While some personnel may be qualified in several disciplines, each person should be counted only once in accord with his or her primary function. Include clerical personnel as "administrative." Write in any additional disciplines—sociologists, biologists, etc.—and number of people in each, in blank spaces.

5. Answer only if this form is being submitted by a joint venture of two or more collaborating firms. Show the names and addresses of all individuals or organizations expected to be included as part of the joint venture and describe their particular areas of anticipated responsibility, (i.e., technical disciplines, administration, financial, sociological, environmental, etc.)

5a. Indicate, by checking the appropriate box, whether this particular joint venture has successfully worked together on other projects.

Each firm participating in the joint venture should have a Standard Form 254 on file with the contracting office receiving this form. Firms which do not have such forms on file should provide same immediately along with a notation

255-101

Standard Form 255 July 1975
Prescribed By GSA Fed. Proc. Reg (41 CFR) 1-16.803

Figure 38. SF255.

STANDARD FORM (SF)

255

Architect-Engineer and Related Services Questionnaire for Specific Project

Standard Form 255
General Services Administration,
Washington, D. C. 20405
Fed. Proc. Reg.(41 CFR) 1-16 . 803
Armed Svc. Proc. Reg. 18-403

regarding their association with this joint venture submittal.

6. If respondent is not a joint venture, but intends to use outside (as opposed to in-house or permanently and formally affiliated) consultants or associates, he should provide names and addresses of all such individuals or firms, as well as their particular areas of technical/professional expertise, as it relates to this project. Existence of previous working relationships should be noted. If more than eight outside consultants or associates are anticipated, attach an additional sheet containing requested information.

7. Regardless of whether respondent is a joint venture, an individual or an independent firm, provide brief resumes of key personnel expected to participate on this project. Care should be taken to limit resumes to only those personnel and specialists who will have major project responsibilities. Each resume must include: (a) name of each key person and specialist and his or her title, (b) the project assignment or role which that person will be expected to fulfill in connection with this project, (c) the name of the firm or organization, if any, with whom that individual is presently associated, (d) years of relevant experience with present firm and other firms, (e) the highest academic degree achieved and the discipline covered (if more than one highest degree, such as two Ph.D.'s, list both), the year received and the particular technical/professional discipline which that individual will bring to the project, (f) if registered as an architect, engineer, surveyor, etc., show only the field of registration and the year that such registration was first acquired. If registered in several states, do not list states, and (g) a synopsis of experience, training, or other qualities which reflect individual's potential contribution to this project. Include such data as: familiarity with Government or agency procedures, similar type of work performed in the past, management abilities, familiarity with the geographic area, relevant foreign language capabilities, etc. Please limit synopsis of experience to directly relevant information.

8. List up to ten projects which demonstrate the firm's or joint venture's competence to perform work similar to that likely to be required on this project. The more recent such projects, the better. Prime consideration will be given to projects which illustrate respondent's capability for performing work similar to that being sought. Required information must include: (a) name and location of project, (b) brief description of type and extent of services provided for each project (submissions by joint ventures should indicate which member of the joint venture was the prime on that particular project and what role it played), (c) name and address of the owner or that project (if Government agency, indicate responsible office), (d) completion date (actual or estimated), (e) total construction cost of completed project, (or where no construction was involved, the approximate cost of your work) and that portion of the cost of the project for which the named firm was/is responsible.

9. List only those projects which the A-E firm or joint venture, or members of the joint venture, are currently performing under direct contract with an agency or department of the Federal Government. Exclude any grant or loan projects being financed by the Federal Government but being performed under contract to other non Federal governmental entities. Information provided under each heading is similar to that requested in the preceding Item 8, except for (d) "Percent Complete." Indicate in this item the percentage of A-E work completed upon filing this form.

10. Through narrative discussion, show reason why the firm or joint venture submitting this questionnaire believes it is especially qualified to undertake the project. Information provided should include, but not be limited to, such data as: specialized equipment available for this work, any awards or recognition received by a firm or individuals for similar work, required security clearances, etc. Respondents may say anything they wish in support of their qualifications. When appropriate, respondents may supplement this proposal with graphic material and photographs which best demonstrate design capabilities of the team proposed for this project.

11. Completed forms should be signed by the chief executive officer of the joint venture (thereby attesting to the concurrence and commitment of all members of the joint venture), or by the architect-engineer principal responsible for the conduct of the work in the event it is awarded to the organization submitting this form. Joint ventures selected for subsequent discussions regarding this project must make available a statement of participation signed by a principal of each member of the joint venture. ALL INFORMATION CONTAINED IN THE FORM SHOULD BE CURRENT AND FACTUAL.

Standard Form 255-July 1975
Prescribed By GSA Fed. Proc. Reg. (41 CFR) 1-16.803

2

Figure 38. (Continued)

OMB Approval No. 29–RO235

STANDARD FORM (SF) **255**
Architect-Engineer Related Services for Specific Project

1. Project Name / Location for which Firm is Filing:

2a. *Commerce Business Daily* Announcement Date, if any:

2b. Agency Identification Number, if any:

3. Firm (or Joint-Venture) Name & Address

3a. Name, Title & Telephone Number of Principal to Contact

3b. Address of office to perform work, if different from Item 3

4. Personnel by Discipline:

___ Administrative	___ Electrical Engineers	___ Oceanographers
___ Architects	___ Estimators	___ Planners: Urban/Regional
___ Chemical Engineers	___ Geologists	___ Sanitary Engineers
___ Civil Engineers	___ Hydrologists	___ Soils Engineers
___ Construction Inspectors	___ Interior Designers	___ Specification Writers
___ Draftsmen	___ Landscape Architects	___ Structural Engineers
___ Ecologists	___ Mechanical Engineers	___ Surveyors
___ Economists	___ Mining Engineers	___ Transportation Engineers
		___ Total Personnel

5. If submittal is by Joint-Venture list participating firms and outline specific areas of responsibility (including administrative, technical and financial) for each firm: (Attach SF 254 for each if not on file with Procuring Office.)

5a. Has this Joint-Venture previously worked together? ☐ yes ☐ no

Standard Form 255 July 1975
Prescribed By GSA Fed. Proc. Reg. (41 CFR) 1-16.803

3

Figure 38. (Continued)

6. Outside Key Consultants/Associates Anticipated for this Project (Attach SF 254 for Consultants/Associates Listed, if not already of file with the Procuring Office)

Name & Address	Specialty	Worked with Prime before (Yes or No)
1)		
2)		
3)		
4)		
5)		
6)		
7)		
8)		

Standard Form 255 July 1975
Prescribed By GSA Fed. Proc. Reg. (41 CFR) 1-16.803

Figure 38. *(Continued)*

7. Brief Resume of **Key** Persons, Specialists, and Individual Consultants Anticipated for this Project

a. Name & Title:	a. Name & Title:
b. Project Assignment:	b. Project Assignment:
c. Name of Firm with which associated:	c. Name of Firm with which associated:
d. Years experience: With This Firm ____ With Other Firms ____	d. Years experience: With This Firm ____ With Other Firms ____
e. Education: Degree(s) / Year / Specialization	e. Education: Degree(s) / Years / Specialization
f. Active Registration: Year First Registered/Discipline	f. Active Registration: Year First Registered/Discipline
g. Other Experience and Qualifications relevant to the proposed project:	g. Other Experience and Qualifications relevant to the proposed project:

Standard Form 254 July 1975
Prescribed By GSA Fed. Proc. Reg. (41 CFR) 1-16.803

5

Figure 38. (*Continued*)

7. Brief Resume of **Key** Persons, Specialists, and Individual Consultants Anticipated for this Project

a. Name & Title:	a. Name & Title:
b. Project Assignment:	b. Project Assignment:
c. Name of Firm with which associated:	c. Name of Firm with which associated:
d. Years experience: With This Firm _____ With Other Firms _____	d. Years experience: With This Firm _____ With Other Firms _____
e. Education: Degree(s) / Year / Specialization	e. Education: Degree(s) / Years / Specialization
f. Active Registration: Year First Reg stered/Discipline	f. Active Registration: Year First Registered/Discipline
g. Other Experience and Qualifications relevant to the proposed project:	g. Other Experience and Qualifications relevant to the proposed project:

6

Standard Form 255 July 1975
Prescribed By GSA Fed. Proc. Reg. (41 CFR) 1-16.803

Figure 38. (*Continued*)

7. Brief Resume of **Key** Persons, Specialists, and Individual Consultants Anticipated for this Project

a. Name & Title:	a. Name & Title:
b. Project Assignment:	b. Project Assignment:
c. Name of Firm with which associated:	c. Name of Firm with which associated:
d. Years experience: With This Firm_____ With Other Firms_____	d. Years experience: With This Firm_____ With Other Firms_____
e. Education: Degree(s) / Year / Specialization	e. Education: Degree(s) / Years / Specialization
f. Active Registration: Year First Registered/Discipline	f. Active Registration: Year First Registered/Discipline
g. Other Experience and Qualifications relevant to the proposed project:	g. Other Experience and Qualifications relevant to the proposed project:

Standard Form 255 July 1975
Prescribed by GSA Fed. Proc. Reg. (41 CFR) 1-16.803

7

Figure 38. *(Continued)*

7. Brief Resume of **Key** Persons, Specialists, and Individual Consultants Anticipated for this Project

a. Name & Title:

b. Project Assignment:

c. Name of Firm with which associated:

d. Years experience: With This Firm _____ With Other Firms _____

e. Education: Degree(s) / Year / Specialization

f. Active Registration: Year First Registered/Discipline

g. Other Experience and Qualifications relevant to the proposed project:

a. Name & Title:

b. Project Assignment:

c. Name of Firm with which associated:

d. Years experience: With This Firm _____ With Other Firms _____

e. Education: Degree(s) / Years / Specialization

f. Active Registration: Year First Registered/Discipline

g. Other Experience and Qualifications relevant to the proposed project:

Standard Form 255 July 1975
Prescribed By GSA Fed. Proc. Reg. (41 CFR) 1-16.803

8

Figure 38. (*Continued*)

8. Work by Firm or Joint Venture Members which Best Illustrates Current Qualifications Relevant to this Project   (List not more than 10 Projects)

a. Project Name & Location	b. Nature of Firm's Responsibility	c. Owner's Name & Address	d. Completion Date (actual or estimated)	e. Estimated Cost (in thousands)	
				Entire Project	Work for which Firm was/is responsible
(1)					
(2)					
(3)					
(4)					
(5)					
(6)					
(7)					
(8)					
(9)					
(10)					

Standard Form 255 July 1975
Prescribed By GSA Fed. Proc. Reg. (41 CFR) 1-16.800

9

Figure 38. (Continued)

9. All work by firms or Joint Venture members **currently being performed directly for Federal agencies**

a. Project Name & Location	b. Nature of Firm's Responsibility	c. Agency (Responsible Office) Name & Address	d. Percent complete	e. Estimated Cost (In Thousands)	
				Entire Project	Work for which firm is responsible

Standard Form 25C July 1975
Prescribed By GSA Fed. Proc. Reg. (41 CFR) 1-16.603

10

Figure 38. (*Continued*)

10. Use this space to provide any additional information or description of resources supporting your firm's qualifications for the proposed project

11. The foregoing is a statement of facts.

Signature: _____ Typed Name and Title: _____

Date: _____

Standard Form 255 July 1975
Prescribed By GSA Fed. Proc. Reg. (41 CFR) 1-16.803

11

Figure 38. (Continued)

penetration of the often lucrative R&D (research and development) field, a special form will probably be required. In all cases ask to see samples of others' completed forms and determine by asking a contract or project officer what can and cannot be done (such as including illustrations).

Agencies

All government agencies who need or might need your services should be contacted. Lists of local offices and officials can be obtained easily from local and state GSA government offices. Federal agencies that utilize A-E services include the following:

BUREAU OF INDIAN AFFAIRS

Division of Contracting Services
Department of the Interior
1951 Constitution Avenue, N.W.
Washington, D.C. 20245
Phone: 202-343-2141

AREA OFFICES

Bureau of Indian Affairs
115 Fourth Avenue, S.E.
Aberdeen, South Dakota
Phone: 605-255-7343

Department of Indian Affairs
5301 Central Avenue
Albuquerque, New Mexico 87108
Phone: 505-766-3055

Department of Indian Affairs
Federal Building
Anadarko, Oklahoma
Phone: 405-247-6231

Department of Indian Affairs
316 N. 26th Street
Billings, Montana 59101
Phone: 406-245-6315

Department of Indian Affairs
831 2nd Avenue, South
Minneapolis, Minnesota 55402
Phone: 612-725-2904

Department of Indian Affairs
Box 3-8000
Juneau, Alaska 99801
Phone: 907-596-7177

Department of Indian Affairs
Federal Building
Muskogee, Oklahoma 74401
Phone: 918-693-3431

Department of Indian Affairs
Navajo Area Office
Window Rock, Arizona 86515
Phone: 602-871-4368

Bureau of Indian Affairs
124 W. Thomas Road
Phoenix, Arizona 85011
Phone: 602-261-4101

Bureau of Indian Affairs
1425 Irving Street, N.E.
Portland, Oregon 97208
Phone: 503-234-3361

Bureau of Indian Affairs
Federal Office Building
Sacramento, California 95825
Phone: 916-484-4682

Bureau of Indian Affairs
1951 Constitution Avenue, N.W.
Washington, D.C. 20245
Phone: 202-343-5582

BUREAU OF RECLAMATION

Department of the Interior
Washington, D.C. 20240
Phone: 202-343-4157

PACIFIC NORTHWEST REGION

Bureau of Reclamation
Box 043
550 W. Fort Street
Boise, Idaho 83724
Phone: 208-343-2101

MID-PACIFIC REGION

Bureau of Reclamation
2800 Cottage Way
Sacramento, California 95825
Phone: 916-484-4571

LOWER COLORADO REGION

Bureau of Reclamation
P.O. Box 427
Nevada Highway and Park Street
Boulder City, Nevada 89005
Phone: 702-293-8411

UPPER COLORADO REGION

Bureau of Reclamation
P.O. Box 11568
125 S. State Street
Salt Lake City, Utah 84111
Phone: 801-524-5592

SOUTHWEST REGION

Bureau of Reclamation
Box H-4377
Herring Plaza
137 E. 3rd Street
Amarillo, Texas 79101
Phone: 806-376-2401

UPPER MISSOURI REGION

Bureau of Reclamation
P.O. Box 2553
316 North 26th Street
Billings, Montana 59103
Phone: 406-245-6214

LOWER MISSOURI REGION

Bureau of Reclamation
Building 20
Denver Federal Center
Denver, Colorado 80225
Phone: 303-234-4441

**CORPS OF ENGINEERS
(CIVIL WORKS)**

Department of the Army
Office of the Chief of Engineers
Forrestal Building
Washington, D.C. 20314
Phone: 202-693-7154

**U.S. ARMY ENG. DIV.,
LOWER MISSISSIPPI VALLEY**

P.O. Box 80
Vicksburg, Mississippi 39180

U.S. Army Engr. Dist., New Orleans
P.O. Box 60267
New Orleans, Louisiana 70160

U.S. Army Engr. Dist., St. Louis
210 North 12th Street
St. Louis, Missouri 63101

U.S. Army Engr. Dist., Vicksburg
P.O. Box 60
Vicksburg, Mississippi 39180

**U.S. ARMY ENGR. DIV., MISSOURI
RIVER**

P.O. Box 103, Downtown Station
215 North 17th Street
Omaha, Nebraska 68106

**U.S. ARMY ENGR. DIST., KANSAS
CITY**

700 Federal Bldg.
601 East 12th Street
Kansas City, Missouri 64106

U.S. ARMY ENGR. DIST., OMAHA

6014 USPO and Courthouse
215 North 17th Street
Omaha, Nebraska 68102

U.S. ARMY ENGR. DIV., NEW
ENGLAND

424 Trapelo Road
Waltham, Massachusetts 02154

U.S. ARMY ENGR. DIV., NORTH
ATLANTIC

90 Church Street
New York, New York 10007

U.S. Army Engr. Div., Baltimore
P.O. Box 1715
Baltimore, Maryland 21203

U.S. Army Engr. Dist., New York
26 Federal Plaza
New York, New York 10007

U.S. Army Engr., Dist., Norfolk
803 Front Street
Norfolk, Virginia 23510

U.S. Army Engr. Dist., Philadelphia
U.S. Custom House
2nd & Chestnut Street
Philadelphia, Pennsylvania 19106

U.S. ARMY ENGR. DIV., NORTH
CENTRAL

536 South Clark Street
Chicago, Illinois 60605

U.S. Army Engr. Dist., Buffalo
1776 Niagara Street
Buffalo, New York 14207

U.S. Army Engr. Dist., Chicago
219 South Dearborn Street
Chicago, Illinois 60604

U.S. Army Engr. Dist., Detroit
P.O. Box 1027
Detroit, Michigan 48231

U.S. Army Engr. Dist., Rock Island
Clock Tower Building
Rock Island, Illinois 61201

U.S. Army Engr. Dist., St. Paul
1210 USPO & Custom House
St. Paul, Minnesota 55101

U.S. ARMY ENGR., DIV., NORTH
PACIFIC

Room 210, Custom House
Portland, Oregon 97209

U.S. Army Engr. Dist., Alaska
P.O. Box 7002
Anchorage, Alaska 99510

U.S. Army Engr., Dist., Portland
P.O. Box 2946
Portland, Oregon 97208

U.S. Army Engr. Dist., Seattle
1519 Alaskan Way South
Seattle, Washington 98134

U.S. Army Engr. Dist., Walla Walla
Building 602, City-County Airport
Walla Walla, Washington 99362

U.S. ARMY ENGR. DIV. OHIO RIVER

P.O. Box 1159
550 Main Street
Cincinnati, Ohio 45201

U.S. Army Engr. Dist., Huntington
P.O. Box 2127
Huntington, West Virginia 25721

U.S. Army Engr. Dist., Louisville
P.O. Box 59
Louisville, Kentucky 40201

U.S. Army Engr. Dist., Nashville
P.O. Box 1070
Nashville, Tennessee

U.S. ARMY ENGR. DIV., PACIFIC
OCEAN

Building 96
Fort Armstrong
Honolulu, Hawaii 96813

U.S. ARMY ENGR. DIV., SOUTH
ATLANTIC

510 Title Building
30 Pryor Street, S.W.
Atlanta, Georgia 30303

U.S. Army Engr. Dist., Charleston
P.O. Box 919
Charleston, South Carolina 29402

U.S. Army Engr. Dist., Jacksonville
P.O. Box 4970
Jacksonville, Florida 32201

U.S. Army Engr. Dist., Mobile
P.O. Box 2288
Mobile, Alabama 36628

U.S. Army Engr. Dist., Savannah
P.O. Box 889
Savannah, Georgia 31402

U.S. Army Engr. Dist., Wilmington
P.O. Box 1890
Wilmington, North Carolina 29401

U.S. ARMY ENGR. DIV., SOUTH PACIFIC

630 Sansome Street, Room 1216
San Francisco, California 94111

U.S. Army Engr. Dist., Los Angeles
P.O. Box 2711
Los Angeles, California 90053

U.S. Army Engr. Dist., Sacramento
650 Capitol Mall
Sacramento, California 95814

U.S. Army Engr. Dist., San Francisco
100 McAllister Street
San Francisco, California 94102

U.S. Army Engr. Div., Southwestern
1114 Commerce Street
Dallas, Texas 75202

U.S. Army Engr. Dist., Albuquerque
P.O. Box 1580
Albuquerque, New Mexico 87103

U.S. Army Engr. Dist., Forth Worth
P.O. Box 17300
Forth Worth, Texas 76102

U.S. Army Engr. Dist., Galveston
P.O. Box 1229
Galveston, Texas 77550

U.S. Army Engr. Dist., Little Rock
P.O. Box 867
Little Rock, Arkansas 72203

U.S. Army Engr. Dist., Tulsa
P.O. Box 61
Tulsa, Oklahoma 74102

CORPS OF ENGINEERS
(MILITARY CONSTRUCTION)

Department of the Army
Office of the Chief of Engineers
Forrestal Building
Washington, D.C. 20314
Phone: 202-693-6435

U.S. ARMY ENGR. DIV., NORTH ATLANTIC

Division Engineer (New York, Norfolk and Baltimore Districts)
U.S. Army Engr. Div., North Atlantic
90 Church Street
New York, New York 10007

District Engineer (Connecticut, Maine, Massachusetts, New Hampshire, New Jersey, New York, Rhode Island, Vermont)
U.S. Army Engr. Dist., New York
26 Federal Plaza
New York, New York 10007

District Engineer (Delaware, District of Columbia, Kentucky, Maryland, Ohio, Pennsylvania, northern part of Virginia, West Virginia)
U.S. Army Engr. Dist., Baltimore
31 Hopkins Plaza
Federal Building
P.O. Box 1715
Baltimore, Maryland 21203

District Engineer (Southern Virginia)
U.S. Army Engr. Dist., Norfolk
803 Front Street
Norfolk, Virginia 23510

U.S. ARMY ENGR. DIV., SOUTH
ATLANTIC

District Engineer (Savannah and Mobile
Districts)
U.S. Army Engr. Div., South Atlantic
510 Title Building
30 Pryor Street, S.W.
Atlanta, Georgia 30303

District Engineer (Georgia, North Caro-
lina, South Carolina)
U.S. Army Engr. Dist., Savannah
200 East, St. Julian Street
P.O. Box 889
Savannah, Georgia 31402

District Engineer (Alabama, Florida,
Mississippi, Tennessee)
U.S. Army Engr. Dist., Mobile
2301 Airport Boulevard
P.O. Box 2288
Mobile, Alabama 36628

U.S. ARMY ENGR. DIV., MISSOURI
RIVER

Division Engineer (Omaha District)
U.S. Army Engr. Div., Missouri River
U.S. Post Office and Court House
215 North 17th Street
P.O. Box 103, Downtown Station
Omaha, Nebraska 68101

District Engineer (Colorado, Illinois,
Indiana, Iowa, Kansas, Michigan, Min-
nesota, Missouri, Nebraska, North
Dakota, South Dakota, Wisconsin,
Wyoming)
U.S. Army Engr. Dist., Omaha
U.S. Post Office and Court House
215 North 17th Street
Omaha, Nebraska 68102

U.S. ARMY ENGR. DIV.,
SOUTHWESTERN

Division Engineer (Fort Worth District)
U.S. Army Engr. Div., Southwestern
1114 Commerce Street
Dallas, Texas 75202

District Engineer (Arkansas, Louisiana,
New Mexico, Oklahoma, Texas)
U.S. Army Engr. Dist., Fort Worth
819 Taylor Street
P.O. Box 17300
Forth Worth, Texas 76102

U.S. ARMY ENGR. DIV., SOUTH
PACIFIC

Division Engineer (Sacramento and Los
Angeles Districts)
U.S. Army Engr. Div., South Pacific
630 Sansome Street, Room 1216
San Francisco, California 94111

District Engineer (California, Idaho, Montana, Nevada, Oregon, Utah, Washington, less those areas listed under Los
Angeles District)
U.S. Army Engr. Dist., Sacramento
650 Capitol Mall
Sacramento, California 95814

District Engineer (Arizona, California,
southern part including counties of San
Luis Obispo, Kern and Inyo; Nevada,
counties of Lincoln and Clark)
U.S. Army Engr. Dist., Los Angeles
300 North Los Angeles Street
P.O. Box 2711
Los Angeles, California 90053

U.S. ARMY ENGR. DIV., ALASKA
AREA

Division Engineer (Alaska District)
U.S. Army Engr. Div., North Pacific
210 Custom House
Portland, Oregon 97209

District Engineer (Alaska)
U.S. Army Engr. Dist., Alaska
P.O. Box 7002
Anchorage, Alaska 99510

U.S. ARMY ENGR. DIV., MEDITER-
RANEAN AREA

APO (Leghorn, Italy)
New York, New York 09019

U.S. ARMY ENGR. DIV., PACIFIC OCEAN AREA

Division Engineer (Hawaii)
U.S. Engr. Div., Pacific Ocean
Building 96, Fort Armstrong
Honolulu, Hawaii 96813

U.S. ARMY LIAISON DETACHMENT

26 Federal Plaza
New York, New York 10007

DEPARTMENT OF THE AIR FORCE

Engineering Division
USAF—PREE
Boiling Air Force Base
Washington, D.C. 20332
Phone: 202-767-4180

Note: For the most part, Air Force construction programs are handled either by the Naval Facilities Engineering Command (NAVFAC) or the Corps of Engineers (Military Works). District offices of NAVFAC and the Corps are listed elsewhere in this section. Note that direct contact should be made with Air Force Base procurement officers if your firm is interested in obtaining relatively minor projects, such as development of maintenance programs and design of plans for repair and renovation of base facilities, including housing. Direct A-E contracts are not awarded at the Engineering-Division headquarters office shown above.

DEPARTMENT OF COMMERCE

U.S. Department of Commerce
Office of Administrative Services and
  Procurement
Procurement Division, Room 6511
14th & Constitution Avenue, N.W.
Washington, D.C. 20230

DEPARTMENT OF STATE—OFFICE OF FOREIGN BUILDINGS

Department of State, A/FBO, SA-6
Washington, D.C. 20520
Phone: 235-9445

ECONOMIC DEVELOPMENT ADMINISTRATION

Department of Commerce
Washington, D.C. 20230
Phone: 202-967-5081

ATLANTIC REGIONAL OFFICE

Suite 10424, William J. Green, Jr. Building
600 Arch Street
Philadelphia, Pennsylvania 19106
Phone: 215-597-4603

MIDWESTERN REGIONAL OFFICE

32 West Randolph Street
Chicago, Illinois 60601
Phone: 312-353-7706

ROCKY MOUNTAIN REGIONAL OFFICE

Suite 505, Title Building
909 17th Street
Denver, Colorado 80202
Phone: 303-837-4714

SOUTHEASTERN REGIONAL OFFICE

Suite 555, 1401 Peachtree Street, N.E.
Atlanta, Georgia 30309
Phone: 404-526-6401

SOUTHWESTERN REGIONAL OFFICE

702 Colorado Street
Austin, Texas 78701
Phone: 512-397-5461

WESTERN REGIONAL OFFICE

Suite 500, 1700 Westlake Avenue North
Seattle, Washington 98109
Phone: 206-442-0596

ENERGY RESEARCH AND DEVELOPMENT ADMINISTRATION

Engineering and Facilities Branch
Division of Administrative Services
Washington, D.C. 20545
Phone: 202-973-3658

ALBUQUERQUE OPERATIONS OFFICE

U.S. Energy Research and Development
  Administration
P.O. Box 5400
Albuquerque, New Mexico 87115

Amarillo Area Office
U.S. Energy Research and Development
  Administration
P.O. Box 1086
Amarillo, Texas 79105

Burlington Area Office
U.S. Energy Research and Development
  Administration
P.O. Box 561
Burlington, Iowa 52601

Dayton Area Office
U.S. Energy Research and Development
  Administration
P.O. Box 66
Miamisburg, Ohio 45342

Kansas City Area Office
U.S. Energy Research and Development
  Administration
P.O. Box 202
Kansas City, Missouri 64141

Los Alamos Area Office
U.S. Energy Research and Development
  Administration
Los Alamos, New Mexico 87544

Pinellas Area Office
U.S. Energy Research and Development
  Administration
P.O. Box 11500
St. Petersburg, Florida 33733

Rocky Flats Area Office
U.S. Energy Research and Development
  Administration
P.O. Box 928
Golden, Colorado 80401

Sandia Area Office
U.S. Energy Research and Development
  Administration
P.O. Box 5400
Albuquerque, New Mexico 87115

CHICAGO OPERATIONS OFFICE

U.S. Energy Research and Development
  Administration
9800 South Cass Avenue
Argonne, Illinois 60439

Batavia Area Office
U.S. Energy Research and Development
  Administration
P.O. Box 2000
Batavia, Illinois 60510

Brookhaven Area Office
U.S. Energy Research and Development
  Administration
Upton, New York 11973

Argone National Laboratory Contracts
U.S. Energy Research and Development
  Administration
P.O. Box 2528
Idaho Falls, Idaho 83401

Harvard-MIT Contracts
U.S. Energy Research and Development
  Administration
Contracts Division
Cambridge Massachusetts Institute of
  Technology
Room 20-D-224
77 Massachusetts Avenue
Cambridge, Massachusetts 02139

Princeton University Contracts
U.S. Energy Research and Development
  Administration
Princeton Office—Chicago Operations
  Office
P.O. Box 102
Princeton, New Jersey 08540

GRAND JUNCTION OFFICE

U.S. Energy Research and Development
  Administration
P.O. Box 2567
Grand Junction, Colorado 81501

IDAHO OPERATIONS OFFICE

U.S. Energy Research and Development
  Administration
550 Second Street
Idaho Falls, Idaho 83401

NEVADA OPERATIONS OFFICE

U.S. Energy Research and Development
  Administration
P.O. Box 14100
Las Vegas, Nevada 89114

Pacific Area Support Office
U.S. Energy Research and Development
  Administration
P.O. Box 9186
Honolulu, Hawaii

OAK RIDGE OPERATIONS OFFICE

U.S. Energy Research and Development
  Administration
P.O. Box E
Oak Ridge, Tennessee 37830

Cincinnati Area Office
U.S. Energy Research and Development
  Administration
P.O. Box 39188
Cincinnati, Ohio 45239

New Brunswick Laboratory
U.S. Energy Research and Development
  Administration
P.O. Box 150
New Brunswick, New Jersey 08903

Paducah Area Office
U.S. Energy Research and Development
  Administration
P.O. Box 1150
Paducah, Kentucky 42001

Portsmouth Area Office
U.S. Energy Research and Development
  Administration
Piketon, Ohio 45661

Puerto Rico Area Office
U.S. Energy Research and Development
  Administration
P.O. Box BB
Hato Rey, Puerto Rico 00919

PITTSBURGH NAVAL REACTORS
OFFICE

U.S. Energy Research and Development
  Administration
P.O. Box 109
West Miffin, Pennsylvania 15122

RICHLAND OPERATIONS OFFICE

U.S. Energy Research and Development
  Administration
P.O. Box 550
Richland, Washington 99352

SAN FRANCISCO OPERATIONS OFFICE

U.S. Energy Research and Development
  Administration
1333 Broadway
Oakland, California 94612

Office of Program Coordination &
  Management-SLAC
U.S. Energy Research and Development
  Administration
P.O. Box 4349
Stanford, California 94305

SAVANNAH RIVER OPERATIONS
OFFICE

U.S. Energy Research and Development
  Administration
P.O. Box A
Aiken, South Carolina 29801

SCHENECTADY NAVAL REACTORS
OFFICE

U.S. Energy Research and Development
  Administration
P.O. Box 1069
Schenectady, New York 12301

**ENVIRONMENTAL PROTECTION
AGENCY**

Chief of Engineering and Architectural
  Services
Office of Facilities Management Section
401 M Street, S.W.
Washington, D.C. 20460
Phone: 202-755-0367

REGIONAL ADMINISTRATOR, I
(CONNECTICUT, MAINE, MASSA-
CHUSETTS, NEW HAMPSHIRE, RHODE
ISLAND, VERMONT)

U.S. Environmental Protection Agency
Room 2303, John F. Kennedy Federal
    Building
Boston, Massachusetts 02203
Phone: 617-223-7210

REGIONAL ADMINISTRATOR, II
(NEW JERSEY, NEW YORK, PUERTO
RICO, VIRGIN ISLANDS)

U.S. Environmental Protection Agency
Room 908, 26 Federal Plaza
New York, New York 10007
Phone: 212-264-2525

REGIONAL ADMINISTRATOR, III
(DELAWARE, MARYLAND, VIR-
GINIA, WEST VIRGINIA, DISTRICT
OF COLUMBIA, PENNSYLVANIA)

U.S. Environmental Protection Agency
Curtis Building, 6th & Walnut Streets
Philadelphia, Pennsylvania 19106
Phone: 215-597-9801

REGIONAL ADMINISTRATOR, IV
(ALABAMA, FLORIDA, GEORGIA,
KENTUCKY, MISSISSIPPI, NORTH
CAROLINA, SOUTH CAROLINA,
TENNESSEE)

U.S. Environmental Protection Agency
1421 Peachtree Street
N.E., Atlanta, Georgia 30309
Phone: 404-526-5727

REGIONAL ADMINISTRATOR, V
(ILLINOIS, INDIANA, MICHIGAN,
MINNESOTA, OHIO, WISCONSIN)

U.S. Environmental Protection Agency
1 North Wacker Drive
Chicago, Illinois 60606
Phone: 312-353-5250

REGIONAL ADMINISTRATOR, VI
(ARKANSAS, LOUISIANA, NEW
MEXICO, TEXAS, OKLAHOMA)

U.S. Environmental Protection Agency
1600 Patterson Street, Suite 1100
Dallas, Texas 75201
Phone: 214-749-1962

REGIONAL ADMINISTRATOR, VII
(IOWA, KANSAS, MISSOURI,
NEBRASKA)

U.S. Environmental Protection Agency
1735 Baltimore Avenue
Kansas City, Missouri 64108
Phone: 816-374-5493

REGIONAL ADMINISTRATOR, VIII
(COLORADO, MONTANA, NORTH
DAKOTA, UTAH, WYOMING, SOUTH
DAKOTA)

U.S. Environmental Protection Agency
Suite 900, Lincoln Tower
1860 Lincoln Street
Denver, Colorado 80203
Phone: 303-837-3895

REGIONAL ADMINISTRATOR, IX
(ARIZONA, CALIFORNIA, HAWAII,
NEVADA, AMERICAN SAMOA, GUAM,
TRUST TERRITORIES OF PACIFIC
ISLANDS, WAKE ISLAND)

U.S. Environmental Protection Agency
100 California Street
San Francisco, California 94111
Phone: 415-556-2320

REGIONAL ADMINISTRATOR, X
(ALASKA, IDAHO, OREGON,
WASHINGTON)

U.S. Environmental Protection Agency
1200 Sixth Avenue
Seattle, Washington 98101
Phone: 206-442-1220

FARMERS HOME ADMINISTRATION

Note: The Farmers Home Administration makes no direct A-E contract awards. It participates in construction by awarding grants and loans exclusively to communities of 10,000 or less population, primarily for water-sewer projects, for community facilities such as libraries and parks, and for business and industrial developments. Obviously, the potential recipient communities must have design professionals prepare the plant for these projects. Likewise, it is possible that some communities may be unaware of the assistance available. Accordingly, design professionals should learn about opportunities available through the Farmers Home Administration. For a listing of state administrators, contract forms, and other informative materials, contact:

Data Division
Office of the Administrator
Farmers Home Administration
U.S. Department of Agriculture
Washington, D.C. 20250
Phone: 202-447-2211

FEDERAL AVIATION ADMINISTRATION

Department of Transportation
800 Independence Avenue, S.W.
Washington, D.C. 20590
Phone: 202-426-8181

MAINE, NEW HAMPSHIRE, VERMONT, MASSACHUSETTS, RHODE ISLAND, CONNECTICUT

Airports Division
Federal Aviation Administration
12 New England Executive Park
Burlington, Massachusetts 01803
Phone: 617-273-7237

NEW YORK, NEW JERSEY, PENNSYLVANIA, DELAWARE, MARYLAND, VIRGINIA, WEST VIRGINIA, DISTRICT OF COLUMBIA

Airports Division
Federal Aviation Administration
Federal Building Room 329
John F. Kennedy International Airport
Jamaica, New York 11430
Phone: 212-995-8543

NEW YORK, NEW JERSEY

Airports District Office
Federal Aviation Administration
Colonial Building
181 South Franklin Avenue
Valley Stream, New York 11581
Phone: 212-995-9528

PENNSYLVANIA, DELAWARE

Airports District Office
Federal Aviation Administration
Terminal Building
Capital City Airport
New Cumberland, Pennsylvania 17070
Phone: 717-782-4531

MARYLAND, VIRGINIA, D.C.

Airports District Office
Federal Aviation Administration
900 South Washington Street
Falls Church, Virginia 22046
Phone: 703-557-2431

WEST VIRGINIA

Airports Field Office
Federal Aviation Administration
600 Neville Street
Beckley, West Virginia 25801
Phone: 304-252-7335

GEORGIA, NORTH CAROLINA, SOUTH
CAROLINA, FLORIDA, PUERTO RICO,
VIRGIN ISLANDS, TENNESSEE, KEN-
TUCKY, MISSISSIPPI, ALABAMA

Airports Division
Federal Aviation Administration
P.O. Box 20636
Atlanta, Georgia 30320
Phone: 404-526-7288

GEORGIA, NORTH CAROLINA,
SOUTH CAROLINA

Airports District Office
Federal Aviation Administration
Suite C, Room 116
1568 Willingham Drive
College Park, Georgia 30337
Phone: 404-526-7639

FLORIDA, PUERTO RICO, VIRGIN
ISLANDS

Airports District Office
Federal Aviation Administration
P.O. Box 2014, AMF Branch
Miami, Florida 33159
Phone: 305-526-2540

TENNESSEE, KENTUCKY

Airports District Office
Federal Aviation Administration
3400 Democrat Road
Memphis, Tennessee 38118
Phone: 901-534-3495

MISSISSIPPI, ALABAMA

Airports District Office
Federal Aviation Administration
FAA Building-Municipal Airport
P.O. Box 6111-Pearl Branch
Jackson, Mississippi 39208
Phone: 601-969-4628

ILLINOIS, INDIANA, MICHIGAN,
WISCONSIN, MINNESOTA, OHIO

Airports Division
Federal Aviation Administration
2300 East Devon Avenue
Des Plaines, Illinois 60018
Phone: 312-694-4500 ext. 2771

ILLINOIS, INDIANA

Airports District Office
Federal Aviation Administration
2300 East Devon Avenue
Des Plaines, Illinois 60018
Phone: 312-694-4500 ext. 3335

WISCONSIN, MINNESOTA

Airports District Office
Federal Aviation Administration
6301 34th Avenue South
Minneapolis, Minnesota 55450
Phone: 612-725-3346

OHIO

Airports District Office
Federal Aviation Administration
Westview Building
21010 Center Ridge Road
Rocky River, Ohio 44116
Phone: 216-333-6432

KANSAS, MISSOURI, IOWA,
NEBRASKA

Airports Division
Federal Aviation Administration
Federal Building
601 East 12th Street
Kansas City, Missouri 64106
Phone: 816-374-5278

ARKANSAS, TEXAS, OKLAHOMA,
NEW MEXICO, LOUISIANA

Airports Division
Federal Aviation Administration
P.O. Box 1689
Fort Worth, Texas 76101
Phone: 817-624-4811

ARKANSAS, NORTHEAST TEXAS

Airports District Office
Federal Aviation Administration
Federal Building, Room 4A07
819 Taylor Street
Fort Worth, Texas 76102
Phone: 817-334-3541

OKLAHOMA

Airports District Office
Federal Aviation Administration
FAA Building, Room 204
Wiley Post Airport
Bethany, Oklahoma 73008
Phone: 405-789-2905

NEW MEXICO, WEST TEXAS

Airports District Office
Federal Aviation Administration
5301 Central Avenue, N.E., Suite 900
Albuquerque, New Mexico 87108
Phone: 505-706-2687

LOUISIANA, SOUTH TEXAS

Airports District Office
Federal Aviation Administration
Bradley Building
8345 Telephone Road
Houston, Texas 77017
Phone: 713-643-0661

COLORADO, WYOMING, UTAH,
SOUTH DAKOTA, MONTANA, NORTH
DAKOTA

Airports Division
Federal Aviation Administration
Park Hill Station
P.O. Box 7213
Denver, Colorado 80207
Phone: 303-837-3855

COLORADO, WYOMING

Airports District Office
Federal Aviation Administration
Park Hill Station 7213
Denver, Colorado 80207
Phone: 303-837-4397

SOUTH DAKOTA

Airports District Office
Federal Aviation Administration
P.O. Box 1037
Pierre, South Dakota 57501
Phone: 605-224-8243

NORTH DAKOTA

Airports District Office
Federal Aviation Administration
FAA Building
Bismarck Municipal Airport
Bismarck, North Dakota 58501
Phone: 701-255-4385

UTAH

Airports District Office
Federal Aviation Administration
116 North 24th West Street
Salt Lake City, Utah 84116
Phone: 801-524-4260

MONTANA

Airports District Office
Federal Aviation Administration
FAA Building, Room 2
Helena County Airport
Helena, Montana 59601
Phone: 406-442-3271

MICHIGAN

Airports District Office
Federal Aviation Administration
Room 25, Landy Taylor Building
16647 Airport Road, Route 4
Lansing, Michigan 48906
Phone: 517-487-3711

WASHINGTON, IDAHO, OREGON

Airports Division
Federal Aviation Administration
FAA Building, Boeing Field
Seattle, Washington 98108
Phone: 206-767-2740

CALIFORNIA, ARIZONA, NEVADA

Airports Division
Federal Aviation Administration
P.O. Box 92007, Worldway Postal Center
Los Angeles, California 90009
Phone: 213-536-6240

SOUTHERN CALIFORNIA, ARIZONA

Airports District Office
Federal Aviation Administration
5885 West Imperial Highway
Box 45018, Westchester Station
Los Angeles, California 90045
Phone: 213-536-6580

NORTHERN CALIFORNIA, NEVADA

Airports District Office
Federal Aviation Administration
831 Mitten Road
Burlingame, California 94010
Phone: 415-692-2441 ext. 281

ALASKA

Airports Division
Federal Aviation Administration
Headquarters Building
632 Sixth Avenue
Anchorage, Alaska 99501
Phone: 265-4446

HAWAII TRUST TERRITORIES OF
THE PACIFIC ISLANDS, AMERICAN
SAMOA, GUAM

Airports Division
Federal Aviation Administration
Room 808, 1833 Kalakaua Avenue
P.O. Box 4009
Honolulu, Hawaii 96813
Phone: 808-955-0293

FEDERAL ENERGY ADMINISTRATION

New Post Office Building
12th and Pennsylvania Avenue, N.W.
Washington, D.C.
Phone: 202-961-8251

REGION I (MAINE, NEW HAMPSHIRE,
VERMONT, RHODE ISLAND, MASSA-
CHUSETTS, CONNECTICUT)

Department of Labor
150 Causeway Street
Boston, Massachusetts
Phone: 617-223-5195

REGION II (NEW YORK, NEW JERSEY,
VIRGIN ISLANDS, PUERTO RICO)

General Services Administration
26 Federal Plaza
New York, New York 10007
Phone: 212-264-1021

REGION III (PENNSYLVANIA, DELA-
WARE, VIRGINIA, WEST VIRGINIA,
MARYLAND, DISTRICT OF
COLUMBIA)

Department of Housing & Urban
    Development
Federal Office Building
1421 Cherry Street, Room 1009
Philadelphia, Pennsylvania 19106
Phone: 215-597-3890

REGION IV (NORTH CAROLINA,
SOUTH CAROLINA, GEORGIA,
FLORIDA, ALABAMA, MISSISSIPPI,
TENNESSEE, KENTUCKY, CANAL
ZONE)

Office of Petroleum Allocation
1720 Peachtree Street, North
Atlanta, Georgia 30309
Phone: 404-876-2492

REGION V (MICHIGAN, ILLINOIS,
WISCONSIN, MINNESOTA, INDIANA,
OHIO)

Internal Revenue Service
Federal Office Building
175 West Jackson Street
Chicago, Illinois 60605
Phone: 312-353-8421

REGION VI (ARKANSAS, LOUISIANA, NEW MEXICO, OKLAHOMA, TEXAS)

212 North St. Paul Street
Dallas, Texas 75201
Phone: 817-387-5811

REGION VII (IOWA, NEBRASKA, MISSOURI, KANSAS)

Federal Office Building
811 Grand Street
Kansas City, Missouri 64106
Phone: 816-374-2064

REGION VIII (MONTANA, WYOMING, NORTH DAKOTA, SOUTH DAKOTA, COLORADO, UTAH)

P.O. Box 25487, Denver Federal Center
Denver, Colorado 80225
Phone: 303-234-2420

REGION IX (CALIFORNIA, NEVADA, ARIZONA, HAWAII, AMERICAN SAMOA, GUAM, TRUST TERRITORY OF THE PACIFIC ISLANDS)

Fox Plaza Building, Suite 250
1390 Market Street
San Francisco, California 94102
Phone: 415-556-7651

REGION X (WASHINGTON, ALASKA, OREGON, IDAHO)

Federal Office Building
909 First Avenue, Room 3098
Seattle, Washington 98104
Phone: 206-442-7261

FEDERAL HIGHWAY ADMINISTRATION

Department of Transportation
Nassif Building
400 7th Street, S.W.
Washington, D.C. 20591
Contracts and Procurement Division
Phone: 202-426-0724

REGION I

Federal Highway Administration
4 Normanskill Boulevard
Delmar, New York 12054
Phone: 518-472-6476

REGION III

Federal Highway Administration
Room 1633
George H. Fallon Federal Office Building
31 Hopkins Plaza
Baltimore, Maryland 21201
Phone: 301-962-2361

REGION IV

Federal Highway Administration
Suite 200
1720 Peachtree Road, N.W.
Atlanta, Georgia 30309
Phone: 404-526-5078

REGION V

Federal Highway Administration
18209 Dixie Highway
Homewood, Illinois 60430
Phone: 312-799-6300

REGION VI

Federal Highway Administration
819 Taylor Street
Fort Worth, Texas 76102
Phone: 817-334-3232

REGION VII

Federal Highway Administration
P.O. Box 7186
Country Club Station
Kansas City, Missouri 64113
Phone: 816-926-7563

REGION VIII

Federal Highway Administration
Room 230
Building 40
Denver Federal Center
Denver, Colorado 80225
Phone: 303-234-4051

REGION IX

Federal Highway Administration
450 Golden Gate Avenue
Box 36096
San Francisco, California 94102
Phone: 415-556-3851

REGION X

Federal Highway Administration
Room 412, Mohawk Building
222 S.W. Morrison Street
Portland, Oregon 97204
Phone: 503-221-2065

**FEDERAL INSURANCE
ADMINISTRATION/HUD**

Department of Housing and Urban
  Development
451 7th Street, S.W.
Washington, D.C. 20410
Phone: 202-755-6770

FEDERAL POWER COMMISSION

Office of Administrative Operations
825 North Capitol Street, N.E.
Washington, D.C. 20426
Phone: 202-386-5585

**FEDERAL RAILROAD
ADMINISTRATION/DOT**

Office of Installation and Logistics 9104A
Department of Transportation
400 7th Street, S.W.
Washington, D.C. 20590
Phone: 202-426-4244

The Alaska Railroad
P.O. Box 7-2111
Anchorage, Alaska 99510
Phone: 206-442-0150

**GENERAL SERVICES
ADMINISTRATION**

Public Buildings Service
F bet. 18th and 19th Sts., N.W.
Washington, D.C. 20405
Phone: 202-343-4731

REGION I (MAINE, VERMONT, NEW
HAMPSHIRE, CONNECTICUT, MASSA-
CHUSETTS, RHODE ISLAND)

General Services Administration
Construction Management Division
PO & Courthouse
Boston, Massachusetts 02109
Phone: 617-223-3271

REGION II (NEW YORK, NEW JERSEY,
VIRGIN ISLANDS, PUERTO RICO)

General Services Administration
Construction Management Division
26 Federal Plaza
New York, New York 10007
Phone: 212-264-4245

REGION III, OFFICE OF OPERATING
PROGRAMS (DISTRICT OF
COLUMBIA, MARYLAND,
DELAWARE, PENNSYLVANIA,
WEST VIRGINIA, VIRGINIA)

General Services Administration
Construction Management Division
F betw. 18th & 19th Sts., N.W.
Washington, D.C. 20405
Phone: 202-343-7944

REGION IV (NORTH CAROLINA,
SOUTH CAROLINA, TENNESSEE,
MISSISSIPPI, ALABAMA, GEORGIA,
FLORIDA, KENTUCKY)

General Services Administration
Construction Management Division
1776 Peachtree Street, N.W.
Atlanta, Georgia 30309
Phone: 404-526-5648

REGION V (ILLINOIS, WISCONSIN,
MICHIGAN, INDIANA, OHIO,
MINNESOTA)

General Services Administration
Construction Management Division
219 Dearborn Street
Chicago, Illinois 60604
Phone: 312-353-5897

REGION VI (MISSOURI, KANSAS, IOWA, NEBRASKA)

General Services Administration
Construction Management Division
Federal Building
1500 E. Bannister Road
Kansas City, Missouri 64131
Phone: 816-926-7431

REGION VII (TEXAS, LOUISIANA, ARKANSAS, OKLAHOMA, NEW MEXICO)

General Services Administration
Construction Management Division
819 Taylor Street
Fort Worth, Texas 76102
Phone: 817-334-2561

REGION VIII (COLORADO, WYOMING, UTAH, NORTH DAKOTA, SOUTH DAKOTA, MONTANA)

General Services Administration
Construction Management Division
Denver Federal Center
Building 41
Denver, Colorado 80225
Phone: 303-234-2639

REGION IX (CALIFORNIA, NEVADA, ARIZONA, HAWAII)

General Services Administration
Construction Management Division
525 Market Street
San Francisco, California 194105
Phone: 415-556-3252

REGION X (WASHINGTON, OREGON, IDAHO, ALASKA)

General Services Administration
Construction Management Division
GSA Center
Auburn, Washington 98002
Phone: 206-833-5233

HUD OFFICE OF POLICY DEVELOPMENT AND RESEARCH

Department of Housing and Urban
   Development
451 7th Street, S.W.
Washington, D.C.
Phone: 202-755-5600

For information pertaining to Housing and Community Development Act [Block Grant Program]; contact your local or regional office.

REGION I (MAINE, VERMONT, CONNECTICUT, RHODE ISLAND, NEW HAMPSHIRE, MASSACHUSETTS)

U.S. Department of HUD
800 John F. Kennedy Federal Building
Boston, Massachusetts 02203
Regional Administrator: James J. Barry
Phone: 617-223-4066

REGION II (NEW YORK, NEW JERSEY, PUERTO RICO)

U.S. Department of HUD
26 Federal Plaza, Room 3541
New York, New York 10007
Phone: 212-264-8068

REGION III (PENNSYLVANIA, WEST VIRGINIA, MARYLAND, DELAWARE, WASHINGTON, D.C., VIRGINIA)

U.S. Department of HUD
Curtis Building
6th and Walnut Streets
Philadelphia, Pennsylvania 19106
Phone: 215-597-2560

REGION IV (SOUTH CAROLINA, NORTH CAROLINA, TENNESSEE, ALABAMA, MISSISSIPPI, GEORGIA, KENTUCKY, FLORIDA)

U.S. Department of HUD
Peachtree-Seventh Building
50 Seventh Street, N.E.
Atlanta, Georgia 30323
Phone: 404-526-5585

REGION V (MINNESOTA, WISCONSIN, MICHIGAN, ILLINOIS, INDIANA, OHIO)

U.S. Department of HUD
300 South Wacker Drive
Chicago, Illinois 60606
Phone: 312-353-5680

REGION VI (NEW MEXICO, TEXAS, OKLAHOMA, LOUISIANA, ARKANSAS)

U.S. Department of HUD
Room 14B35, New Dallas Federal
  Building
1100 Commerce Street
Dallas, Texas 75202
Phone: 214-749-7401

REGION VII (KANSAS, MISSOURI, IOWA, NEBRASKA)

U.S. Department of HUD
Federal Office Building, Room 300
911 Walnut Street
Kansas City, Missouri 64106
Phone: 816-374-2661

REGION VIII (MONTANA, SOUTH DAKOTA, NORTH DAKOTA, WYOMING, COLORADO, UTAH)

U.S. Department of HUD
Federal Building
1961 Stout Street
Denver, Colorado 80202
Phone: 303-837-4881

REGION IX (NEVADA, ARIZONA, CALIFORNIA)

U.S. Department of HUD
450 Golden Gate Avenue
P.O. Box 36003
San Francisco, California 94102
Phone: 415-556-4752

REGION X (WASHINGTON, IDAHO, OREGON, HAWAII, ALASKA)

U.S. Department of HUD
Arcada Plaza Building
1321 Second Avenue
Seattle, Washington 98101
Phone: 206-442-5415

NATIONAL AERONAUTICS AND SPACE ADMINISTRATION

300 7th St., S.W.
Washington, D.C. 20546
Phone: 202-755-3394

AMES RESEARCH CENTER

National Aeronautics and Space
  Administration
Moffett Field, California 94035
Phone: 415-965-5820

FLIGHT RESEARCH CENTER

National Aeronautics and Space
  Administration
P.O. Box 273
Edwards, California 93523
Phone: 805-258-2526

GODDARD SPACE FLIGHT CENTER

National Aeronautics and Space
  Administration
Greenbelt, Maryland 20771
Phone: 301-982-6474

JET PROPULSION LABORATORY

4800 Oak Grove Drive
Pasadena, California 91103
Phone: 213-354-2970

LYNDON B. JOHNSON SPACE CENTER

National Aeronautics and Space
  Administration
Houston, Texas 77058
Phone: 713-483-5473

JOHN F. KENNEDY SPACE CENTER

National Aeronautics and Space
  Administration
Kennedy Space Center, Florida 32899
Phone: 305-867-7210

LANGLEY RESEARCH CENTER

National Aeronautics and Space
  Administration
Langley Station
Hampton, Virginia 23665
Phone: 804-827-2321

LEWIS RESEARCH CENTER

National Aeronautics and Space
  Administration
21000 Brookpark Road
Cleveland, Ohio
Phone: 216-433-6500

GEORGE C. MARSHALL SPACE
FLIGHT CENTER

National Aeronautics and Space
  Administration
Marshall Space Flight Center
Huntsville, Alabama 35812
Phone: 205-453-3334

NASA PASADENA OFFICE

4800 Oak Grove Drive
Pasadena, California
Phone: 213-354-5359

WALLOPS STATIONS

National Aeronautics and Space
  Administration
Wallops Island, Virginia 23337
Phone: 804-824-2277

NATIONAL BUREAU OF STANDARDS

Department of Commerce
Procurement Division
Room 6511
14th Street & Constitution Avenue, N.W.
Washington, D.C. 20230
Phone: 202-967-4248

NATIONAL PARK SERVICE

Department of the Interior
Denver Service Center
755 Parfet Street
P.O. Box 25287
Denver, Colorado 80255
Phone: 303-234-4500

NAVAL FACILITIES ENGINEERING
COMMAND

Department of the Navy
Naval Facilities Engineering Command
200 Stovall Street
Alexandria, Virginia 22332
Attn: Contractor Liaison Officer
Phone: 202-325-8550

NORTHERN DIVISION (COLORADO,
CONNECTICUT, DELAWARE,
ILLINOIS, INDIANA, IOWA, KANSAS,
MAINE, MASSACHUSETTS, MICHI-
GAN, MINNESOTA, MISSOURI,
NEBRASKA, NEW HAMPSHIRE, NEW
JERSEY, NEW YORK, NORTH
DAKOTA, OHIO, PENNSYLVANIA,
RHODE ISLAND, SOUTH DAKOTA,
VERMONT, WISCONISN, WYOMING)

Commanding Officer
Northern Division
Naval Facilities Engineering Command
Building 77, Naval Air Engineering Center
Philadelphia, Pennsylvania 19112

CHESAPEAKE DIVISION (DISTRICT OF
COLUMBIA, THE COUNTIES OF ANNE
ARUNDEL, PRINCE GEORGES,
MONTGOMERY, ST. MARYS, CALVERT
AND CHARLES IN MARYLAND; AND
THE COUNTIES OF ARLINGTON,
FAIRFAX, STAFFORD, KING GEORGE,
PRINCE WILLIAM, WESTMORELAND,
AND THE CITY OF ALEXANDRIA IN
VIRGINIA)

Commanding Officer
Chesapeake Division
Naval Facilities Engineering Command
Washington Navy Yard
Washington, D.C. 20390

ATLANTIC DIVISION (MARYLAND, WEST VIRGINIA, VIRGINIA, KENTUCKY, AND EASTERN PARTS OF NORTH CAROLINA, INCLUDING COUNTIES OF GATES, CHOWAN, WASHINGTON, BEAUFORT, CRAVEN, JONES, ONSLOW, AND ALL COUNTIES EAST THEREOF; LESS AREAS LISTED UNDER CHESAPEAKE DIVISION)

Commander
Atlantic Division
Naval Facilities Engineering Command
U.S. Naval Base
Norfolk, Virginia 23511

SOUTHERN DIVISION (ALABAMA, ARKANSAS, FLORIDA, GEORGIA, LOUISIANA, MISSISSIPPI, NEW MEXICO, NORTH CAROLINA, EXCEPT AREAS LISTED UNDER ATLANTIC DIVISION, OKLAHOMA, SOUTH CAROLINA, TENNESSEE, TEXAS)

Commanding Officer
Southern Division
Naval Facilities Engineering Command
2144 Melbourne Street
Charleston, South Carolina 29811

WESTERN DIVISION (ARIZONA, CALIFORNIA, IDAHO, MONTANA, NEVADA, OREGON, WASHINGTON AND ALASKA)

Commanding Officer
Western Division
Naval Facilities Engineering Command
Sneath Lane and El Camino Real
P.O. Box 727
San Bruno, California 94067

PACIFIC DIVISION (PACIFIC AREA)

Commander
Pacific Division
Naval Facilities Engineering Command
Pearl Harbor, Hawaii
FPO San Francisco, California 96610

ATLANTIC DIVISION (ATLANTIC AREA)

Commander
Atlantic Division
Naval Facilities Engineering Command
U.S. Naval Base
Norfolk, Virginia 23511

HEW OFFICE OF FACILITIES ENGINEERING AND PROPERTY MANAGEMENT

Department of Health, Education, and
Welfare
330 Independence Avenue, S.W.
Washington, D.C. 20201
Phone: 202-245-1914

REGION I (CONNECTICUT, MAINE, MASSACHUSETTS, NEW HAMPSHIRE, RHODE ISLAND, VERMONT)

Department of Health, Education, and
Welfare
John F. Kennedy Federal Building
Boston, Massachusetts 02203
Phone: 617-223-6641

REGION II (NEW JERSEY, NEW YORK, PUERTO RICO, VIRGIN ISLANDS)

Department of Health, Education, and
Welfare
26 Federal Plaza
New York, New York 10007
Phone: 212-246-3600

REGION III (DELAWARE, MARYLAND, PENNSYLVANIA, VIRGINIA, WASHINGTON, D.C., WEST VIRGINIA)

Department of Health, Education, and
Welfare
P.O. Box 13716
Philadelphia, Pennsylvania 19101
Phone: 215-597-6888

REGION IV (ALABAMA, FLORIDA, GEORGIA, KENTUCKY, MISSISSIPPI, NORTH CAROLINA, SOUTH CAROLINA, TENNESSEE)

Department of Health, Education, and Welfare
50 Seventh Street, N.E.
Atlanta, Georgia 30323
Phone: 404-526-3352

REGION V (ILLINOIS, INDIANA, MICHIGAN, MINNESOTA, OHIO, WISCONSIN)

Department of Health, Education, and Welfare
300 South Wacker Drive, 33rd Floor
Chicago, Illinois 60606
Phone: 312-353-6595

REGION VI (ARKANSAS, LOUISIANA, NEW MEXICO, OKLAHOMA, TEXAS)

Department of Health, Education, and Welfare
1114 Commerce Street
Dallas, Texas 75202
Phone: 214-749-2115

REGIONAL VII (IOWA, KANSAS, MISSOURI, NEBRASKA)

Department of Health, Education, and Welfare
601 East 12th Street
Kansas City, Missouri 64106
Phone: 816-374-2387

REGION VIII (COLORADO, MONTANA, NORTH DAKOTA, SOUTH DAKOTA, WYOMING, UTAH)

Department of Health, Education, and Welfare
Federal Office Building, Room 9017
19th and Stout Streets
Denver, Colorado 80202
Phone: 303-837-3119

REGION IX (ARIZONA, CALIFORNIA, GUAM, HAWAII, NEVADA)

Department of Health, Education, and Welfare
50 Fulton Street
San Francisco, California 94102
Phone: 415-556-7934

REGION X (ALASKA, IDAHO, OREGON, WASHINGTON)

Department of Health, Education, and Welfare
The Arcade
1319 Second Avenue
Seattle, Washington 98101
Phone: 206-442-0406

UNITED STATES COAST GUARD
DEPARTMENT OF TRANSPORTATION

Chief, Office of Engineering
Washington, D.C. 20590

HEADQUARTERS:

Commandant (G-ECV / 61)
U.S. Coast Guard Headquarters
Washington, D.C. 20590

DISTRICT OFFICES:

Commander
First Coast Guard District
150 Causeway St.
Boston, Massachusetts 20114

Second Coast Guard District
Federal Building
1520 Market St.
St. Louis, Missouri 63103

Third Coast Guard District
Govenors Island
New York, New York 10004

Fifth Coast Guard District
Federal Bldg.
431 Crawford St.
Portsmouth, Virginia 23705

Seventh Coast Guard District
Federal Bldg. Room 1012
51 S.W. 1st Ave.
Miami, Florida 33130

Eighth Coast Guard District
Customhouse
New Orleans, Louisiana 70130

Ninth Coast Guard District
1240 East 9th St.
Cleveland, Ohio 44199

Eleventh Coast Guard District
Heartwell Bldg.
19 Pine Ave.
Long Beach, California 90802

Twelfth Coast Guard District
630 Sansome St.
San Francisco, California 94126

Thirteenth Coast Guard District
618 2d Ave.
Seattle, Washington 98104

Fourteenth Coast Guard District
P.O. Box 48
FPO San Francisco, California 96610

Seventeenth Coast Guard District
FPO Seattle, Washington 98771

ACADEMY:

Superintendent
U.S. Coast Guard Academy
New London, Connecticut 06320

YARD:

Commanding Officer
U.S. Coast Guard Yard
Curtis Bay
Baltimore, Maryland 21226

TRAINING CENTER:

Commanding Officer
U.S. Coast Guard Training Center
Governors Island
New York, New York 10004

TRAINING CENTERS:

Commanding Officer
(Cape May)
U.S. Coast Training Center
Cape May, New Jersey 08204
(Alameda)
U.S. Coast Guard Training Center
Government Island
Alameda, California 94501

RESERVE TRAINING CENTER:

Commanding Officer
U.S. Coast Guard Reserve Training
Center
Yorktown, Virginia 23490

AIRCRAFT REPAIR AND SUPPLY
CENTER:

Commander:
U.S. Coast Guard Aircraft Repair &
Supply Center
Elizabeth City, North Carolina 27909

ACTIVITIES EUROPE:

Commander
Coast Guard Activities, Europe
Box 50
c/o Fleet Post Office
New York, New York 09510

UNITED STATES FOREST SERVICE

Department of Agriculture
12th and Independence Avenue, S.W.
South Building
Washington, D.C. 20250
Phone: 202-447-6661

INTERMOUNTAIN FOREST STATION

Forest Service, USDA
507 25th Street
Ogden, Utah 84401

NORTH CENTRAL FOREST STATION

Forest Service, USDA
Folwell Avenue
St. Paul, Minnesota 55101

NORTHEASTERN FOREST STATION

Forest Service, USDA
6816 Market Street
Upper Darby, Pennsylvania 19082

PACIFIC NORTHWEST FOREST
STATION

Forest Service, USDA
1960 Addison Street
P.O. Box 3141
Portland, Oregon 97208

PACIFIC SOUTHWEST FOREST
STATION

Forest Service, USDA
1960 Addition Street
P.O. Box 245
Berkeley, California 94701

ROCKY MOUNTAIN FOREST STATION

Forest Service, USDA
240 West Prospect Street
Fort Collins, Colorado 80521

SOUTHEASTERN FOREST STATION

Forest Service, USDA
Post Office Building
P.O. Box 2570
Asheville, North Carolina 28802

SOUTHERN FOREST STATION

Forest Service, USDA
T-10210 Federal Building
701 Loyola Avenue
New Orleans, Louisiana 70113

UNITED STATES POSTAL SERVICE

Real Estate and Building Department
475 L'Enfant Plaza, West, S.W.
Washington, D.C. 20260
Phone: 202-245-4372

CENTRAL REGION

Real Estate and Buildings
U.S. Postal Service
Main Post Office Building
Chicago, Illinois 60690

EASTERN REGION

Building Analysis and Design Division
U.S. Postal Service
P.O. Box 8601
Philadelphia, Pennsylvania 19101

SOUTHERN REGION

Real Estate and Buildings
U.S. Postal Service
Memphis, Tennessee 38166

WESTERN REGION

Real Estate and Buildings
U.S. Postal Service
631 Howard Street
San Francisco, California 94106

NORTHEAST REGION

Real Estate and Buildings
U.S. Postal Service
Main Post Office Building
New York, New York 10098

**URBAN MASS TRANSPORTATION
ADMINISTRATION**

Procurement Operations Division TAD43
Office of Administrative Operations
Department of Transportation
400 7th Street, S.W.
Washington, D.C. 20590
Phone: 202-426-0028

VETERANS ADMINISTRATION

Office of Construction (08),
Attention: Chairman Architect-Engineer
    Evaluation Board
811 Vermont Ave., N.W.
Washington, D.C. 20420

Note: VA hospitals may contract directly
with A-Es for repairs and improvements to
their facilities. For a list of hospitals in
states in which you have offices, contact
the office indicated above.

In addition to those agencies and offices indicated above, the following organizations are involved—and have considerable weight—in qualifying A-E firms for international assignments. Most have their own forms and procedures, and will forward them, along with other informative materials, on request.

AFRICAN DEVELOPMENT BANK (AFDB)
Operations Department
B.P. No. 1387, Adibjan
Ivory Coast, Africa

AGENCY FOR INTERNATIONAL DEVELOPMENT (AID)
Director of Engineering/AID
New State Department Building
21st and Virginia Avenue, N.W.
Washington, D.C. 20523

ASIAN DEVELOPMENT BANK (ADB)
United States Director of ADB
P.O. Box 789
Manila, Philippines

EXPORT-IMPORT BANK (EXIM)
Office of Engineering
811 Vermont Avenue, N.W.
Washington, D.C. 20571

INTER-AMERICAN DEVELOPMENT BANK (IDB)
Office of Project Planning
808 Seventeenth Street, N.W.
Washington, D.C. 20577

INTERNATIONAL BANK FOR RECONSTRUCTION AND DEVELOPMENT (IBRD)
Consultant Service Officer
1818 H Street, N.W.
Washington, D.C. 20433

Obtaining Pertinent Information

In almost all cases, government officials who can provide answers to key questions are readily accessible. Information regarding forms, already discussed, is easily obtained. Likewise, be sure to get details on general precautions. For example, how much emphasis does a particular agency or office put on a letter of intent? What does the agency want to see included in a letter of intent? What kind of brochures are most important? Who should attend interviews and briefing sessions? What capabilities are most sought? Should joint ventures apply? What weighting system will be employed? How will various factors be weighted? The answers to these and numerous other questions generally will be answered candidly by someone in the A-E design services procurement office of local government entities, as well as by contracting and project officers at the federal level. While in many cases requirements and suggested approaches will be similar, they are seldom identical. In fact, it may be wise to keep a "poop sheet" on each government entity you are interested in, including names of your contacts. The more you know about what is sought, the greater your ability to present facts to support contentions that your firm has what it takes.

Working with Government Agencies

As implied by procurement arrangements, there is a great deal of impersonality in government. At times one gets the feeling that it is the red tape that holds everything together and that people are subservient to the process. This is perhaps best reflected in dealings with the contract officer, who is responsible for doling out funds based on the reports of the project officer, who is responsible for determining technical competence. While governmental contracting officers are fair, typically they expect you to perform to the very letter of the agreement. If you have misunderstood something, if you have agreed to a change that is not fully authorized, if you do not do what the contract says you are supposed to do, even if the contract is wrong, you often will get little sympathy and even less compensation. By the same token, of course, development of a good working relationship with the contracting officer, crossing of all T's and dotting of all I's, can lead to development of an excellent source in terms of obtaining information about future projects and related matters.

Also, unlike working with other groups, previous experience with a certain government entity is no guarantee of future business. While it certainly is a positive element, each new project usually begins with a clean slate.

Here are a few other tips and comments about working with government entities.

Obtain and Follow Suggested Practices. As already mentioned, determine what interview, proposal, and submission practices are suggested by the entity involved. This can be done by obtaining whatever literature they have, by meeting with project officers, and so on. Follow all suggestions to the letter. In essence, they're telling you how to win contracts. If at all possible, review originals or obtain copies of typical proposals submitted for projects. Look at those of the winners and the losers. This should give you some excellent insights.

Use Realistic Pressure. Government at all levels is now beginning to resort to more objective and public evaluation and selection proceedings. As such, in many cases it is of little value to ask your congressmen or state or local representatives to do something on your behalf when there is nothing they can do. In fact, application of pressure in such circumstances actually may backfire.

If under some circumstances it is possible that using some political clout will help, determine who to contact and how to do it. Consider these suggestions:

Federal: You usually have three or four elected representatives serving you in the government, and sometimes more. These include two senators, the representative from the district in which your office is located, the representative from the district in which your home is located (if different from your office), representatives of areas in which certain key firm personnel live, representatives of branch office locations, etc. Determine from this list which one or two have the most clout with the agency or department involved, something usually determined by committee positions. Obviously, if you are talking about a contract with the Department of Defense, and one of your representatives serves on a Senate or House committee or subcommittee that oversees DoD, he's the man to contact.

If you happen to know the representative on a personal basis, fine. Chances are you don't, and you have three ways of contacting him to urge support.

You can write him a letter. You probably will get a standard reply along with a copy of a standard letter sent to whomever the owners may be in the agency or department involved.

You can call him. Chances are he won't be in and you will get a call back from someone on staff. Therefore, the best bet when telephoning is to determine the name of the representative's administrative assistant (or AA) and ask to speak with him. (AA's run most of Capitol Hill anyway.) Explain your situation to him and explain why your getting the job will be good for the district or state involved.

Ask for suggestions and assistance. Follow up with a comprehensive letter. If you hear nothing for several weeks, or if all you get is a perfunctory letter to whatever agency is involved, write a strong letter of complaint.

Another method—and far and away the best—is to call and make an appointment with the representative and go in and see him. If he helps you get the contract, and if you do get it, it's good for the home district, it's good for him, and it's good for you.

State: If you have a state legislature with elected representatives, proceed the same way, keeping everything strictly above board. You may have some problems in this regard, of course, in that other firms going after the same contract are highly likely to have the same representative.

Local: The same as for state, with the chances of local competition being even greater, thus making any suggestion by the representative of your selection over someone else highly circumspect.

Whenever you ask a representative to do something for you, you are likely to receive later on a request for a political contribution. This opens up a tremendous bag of worms, which still is a matter of debate. Accordingly, we won't even begin to address the subject, but we will make this observation.

It is the job of an elected government official to represent the best interests of the people he was elected to represent. If he does not do a good job when you ask him for assistance, if he does a better job for those people who worked for him or contributed most to his campaign funds, then he is not doing a good job. He should be told so. Others should be told so. Some will say this is idealistic and overlooks "the way things are." But "the way things are" certainly is not the way things have to be. In five years consumers shook off an age-old yoke because they believed things as they were were not the way things had to be. Women did the same. Environmentalists did the same. And so on ad infinitem. If more design professionals would be willing to speak up, perhaps they, too, would be listened to.

Follow the Drifters. Government, especially the federal government, is noted for job drift. A person will be in one department on Tuesday and another on Wednesday. Be sure to know who has replaced whom. Be sure to follow up on the old contact at his new position. A shift could result in your suddenly having a contact in an agency or administration you've been trying to get into.

Learn Local Considerations. Don't go after a state or local project if you are not located in the state or locality, and such location will be used as a criterion, unless a degree of highly rarefied expertise is involved. In the event that a locality will be issuing a series of contracts, then consider opening a branch office that will be more than just a front; consider developing a relationship with a local firm, etc.

Get Experience. If at all possible, obtain some practical experience in working with government (if you haven't done it before) by working as an associate with others who do have government contracts.

Get Advice. Get competent advice on working with the federal government in particular. ACEC, NSPE, AIA, and numerous other management-based professional associations have excellent materials. Numerous books also are available on the subject, as are seminars. One of the leaders in this field, incidentally, is Federal Publications, Inc., a Washington, D.C.-based organization that publishes books and sponsors seminars that reportedly comprise excellent advice.

Speculative Builders

Speculative builders are typified by commercial clients whose main concern is first cost and return on investment. The key is not so much quality of work as cost. Innovation and other attributes of top firms are of relatively little concern unless they show up on the bottom line.

Most speculative builders themselves are very much involved in marketing. For them to make a living they must know what kind of building is needed where and when. As a result, they often look favorably on those design firms that also are sensitive to marketing, that understand who will be occupying the building, what their needs are, and how these needs can be met.

In many cases speculative building organizations are run by one individual, hence it is necessary to have his ear or favor. In larger organizations, with subsidiary divisions each involved with a different building type, it is often necessary to contact the division director before contacting the top man. In certain cases, even though a speculative builder will not be the direct client, he can determine who his design team will be. For example, an engineer may contact a speculative builder, who in turn notifies his architect that he wants to have a particular engineer involved on a certain project.

Internationals

When you are talking in terms of international prospects, you are talking about thousands of different possibilities depending on the person involved, the country involved, etc. In other words, it is generally very difficult to make any valid general statements. However, you definitely should contact the U.S. Department of Commerce (either in Washington, D.C. or a regional office) to determine what literature can be provided; what assistance can be provided, etc. You can usually contact specialists of one kind or another who can provide highly usable insights into the programs involved, customs of the nation involved, etc. Also contact national associations of which you are a member for advice. ACEC, for example, has an enviable record of accomplishment in the international field. In many cases even smaller firms can get involved in international work by forming joint ventures, consortia, etc. In all cases be circumspect, especially in terms of payment.

Membership in the various professional organizations such as ACEC and AIA enable you to discuss pursuit of international business (among other things) with your peers, most of whom share information, tips, etc., willingly. Additional information can come from contacting embassies of various foreign nations (especially the oil-rich). You can learn what their countries' needs are, what industries the government is supporting most, contracting methods, biases, etc. Information can also come from reading articles in general, financial, and trade publications, from attending seminars, from U.S. Department of Commerce and other publications, and so on. Information on foreign jobs available can come from reporting services already noted.

To emphasize: even small firms can become involved in foreign markets through methods such as joint venturing. If the first steps are not taken, however, the experience required to penetrate these new markets never will be obtained. In other words, if pursuit of MUs in other nations fits your marketing plans, then by all means try.

8.3 QUALIFYING THE PROSPECT

Given the amount of time necessary to actively pursue a prospect, it is first necessary to determine whether or not he is worth pursuing. If he has a reputation for slow payment, for example, don't waste your time.

The amount of effort to be spent in pursuit depends on the answers to the following questions:

Does the prospect need the service?

If you offer services that are relatively specialized or new, and the prospect currently has no source known to you for obtaining such services, obviously he is an excellent prospect. If he is already obtaining the services you offer, you must determine if you can offer something better or something of equal quality but perhaps at less cost. In other words, does the prospect need the service and, if so, can you supply it in a way that makes the prospect need you?

Does the prospect have the ability to pay?

It is self-defeating to pursue a prospect who does not have the ability to pay. Check the prospect's financial status from sources such as:

1. Dun and Bradstreet and other credit bureaus;
2. the prospect's bank, which should be able to supply a general statement as to the condition of the prospect's business account;
3. suppliers, who can inform you of how well he pays his accounts, and
4. trade allies and fellow professionals who can inform you of how well the prospect has paid his accounts.

What is the prospect's business history?

If your services are geared to involve modernization or related activities, determine if the prospect is progressive. A visual inspection of the outside of the facility may give some indication. If you have a stock broker, he may know something. If the company issues an annual report, obtain one. From these and other sources you will be able to determine whether the prospect leans more toward "things are fine as they are" or "I may be interested if you can prove the advantages." If it is obvious that the prospect likes to be an innovator, then you have a better chance of selling your ideas.

What is the prospect's law suit record?

If at all possible, determine how often the prospect in the past has brought suit against design professionals he has retained directly or indirectly.

In all too many cases, a client will sue his design professionals on shaky claims of errors or omissions primarily to achieve an out-of-court settlement that effectively reduces the fee. In fact, it is rumored that one hotel magnate used to brag that he never paid a design professional full fee because of this relatively simple tactic. Try to protect yourself as much as possible. Do not undertake work for someone who in the past has shown no compunction about suing at the drop of a hat.

Does your contact have the authority to buy?

In smaller operations, your contact is probably your prospect, such as the owner of a building. If the prospect is a large business entity, learn where your contact fits into the scheme of things. If he does not have the authority to buy, you should ask him who has, or you may work with him at the outset and then go with him to the buyer. This latter approach may work best if the buyer is usually one source, as discussed below. Note that a *Fortune* magazine article tends to indicate that chief executive officers of many large corporate structures tend to become most involved in image-making facilities. For example, it was found that corporate involvement in energy, chemical, and other manufacturing projects is left primarily to middle-management. If the structure is a bank, headquarters office, or some other nonmanufacturing facility, however, the person in charge usually is the company president or vice president and the project team will report directly to him.

What is the prospect's reputation?

Whether or not your contact is the buyer, your recommendations have to be geared to the buyer's way of doing things. Check with suppliers and others, such as manufacturers' representatives, to determine whether the buyer prefers price or quality. This will have a great deal to do with the proposal you make and the way you make it.

Is he a one-source buyer?

If you are dealing with a one-source buyer, you may have a difficult time convincing him to deal with you. Pursue the one-source buyer only if you feel it is worthwhile, perhaps because you have heard rumors that he is dissatisfied with his current sources, has on occasion used another source, or if you can supply something that a current source cannot.

8.4 CONTACTING COLD TURKEY

For the purposes of this book, we shall assume that you will have little difficulty contacting past and current clients, or prospects you already know, whether through personal, business, professional, or other relationships. The trick is contacting those you do not know.

General contact, of course, comes about through general promotional activities such as news releases, magazine articles, speeches, and so on. More specific approaches can be made by mailing reprints of articles, texts of talks, and other materials that, while certainly promotional, are also informative.

Specific contact, however, can come about only through a direct approach tempered by professionalism and a concern for ethics.

The following method is considered workable and effective in most cases. Naturally, it can be modified to fit the concerns of your firm and those of the prospect.

First Overture

We suggest that your first official contact be by letter. This is preferable to the telephone because it allows the prospect to hear from you at his leisure, rather than being interrupted in the midst of a conference or whatever. Besides, as will be seen, it allows for more effective telephone contact later on.

The letter, to be effective, must be worded carefully. The following is a suggestion.

Dear Mr. Jones:

A mutual friend of ours, John Miller, suggested that I contact you to tell you a bit about our firm's services. He noted that you were getting involved in areas where he felt services such as we offer could be helpful.

At John's request, therefore, I am enclosing herewith some material that you may find of interest, including a brochure and lists of projects and clients. I also am including a few recent articles written by members of our staff.

Rather than go into any great detail at this time, I would greatly appreciate being given the opportunity of discussing our services at somewhat greater length, and providing you with more specific information pertaining to the type of work you are undertaking.

I look forward to your response.

Sincerely,

Note that the opening paragraph of the letter could just as easily have read: "John Miller, a member of your firm, happened to be talking with me at a recent ASHRAE meeting. He suggested that you may be interested in services that our firm provides."

It is imperative that the basis of contact be completely legitimate. If you are told that so-and-so needs services that you offer, you have no basis for contact. However, if the response to "Do you mind if I use your name when I give him a call" is "yes," then you do have a basis for contact.

If you get a call or letter from the prospect inviting you to come in for a visit, fine. By all means do so. And if you are told by the prospect that he is not interested in your services, cease active pursuit, but do continue forwarding materials of general interest, such as magazine article reprints, speech texts, revised brochures, newsletters, and so on. You never can tell when circumstances may change.

If you do not get any response within two or three weeks, however, you should make the second overture.

Second Overture—Telephone

The second overture is made by telephone. By placing the call after having written a letter, you have a reason for calling; the prospect probably knows who you are, and chances are he will speak to you because he has not given you the courtesy of a reply.

It is just about impossible to give you examples of "typical" telephone conversations because you not only have to consider the individuality of each person, but also the particular mood he is in at the time you happen to call. If you reach him ten minutes after he has dismissed a design professional, and you happen to offer the same services, you would be in an excellent position to set up a meeting to discuss pertinent matters. The chances of such serendipity are slim indeed. Therefore, your goal should be to set up an appointment for some time in the future to talk with the individual, show him who you are, who your company is, what it does, and so on. The correct method of going about this will vary from person to person but, in essence, the best method is the one that will promote a good image for the firm (whether or not an appointment is ever made) and result in an appointment.

If the person contacted tells you that he absolutely never will have a need for your services, there's very little you can do except to obtain his permission to forward materials of general interest published by or about your firm. If, however, the person indicates that "at some time in the future" he will be able to meet, ask when you should call back. Two weeks? A month? Be professional, but be persistent. Surveys have shown that most sales are made after the seventh call. So if you call back and are told to wait another month, wait and call again. Eventually you will get through. If you give up, however, you never will get through and will never make the sale.

8.5 THE INITIAL PRESENTATION

Your initial presentation must be used primarily to establish the firm in light of the client's concerns, as follows.

Experience. The prospect is concerned about the types of projects handled by your firm which are most similar to his own. He wants to know who the owners were, where the buildings are, when they were built, and so on. It takes more than just listing projects. It takes the knowledge required to provide details about each project and specific answers to specific questions. In other words, the salesman must prepare before he makes the call.

Concept of the Problem. The prospect wants to be sure your firm is fully aware of his specific problems and how to solve them. In most cases some general material can be prepared, but specifics should be stated only after some careful study.

Competence. The prospect needs to know that your firm has the capability of turning out high quality technical work. The salesman must convince him of this by highlighting technical competence in various projects.

Local Knowledge. The client also wants to make sure that your firm is fully aware of all specific local conditions involved, meaning all local codes, zoning restrictions, et al., as well as all federal and state restrictions also applicable. The salesman can manifest his own understanding of local conditions easily when he is familiar with such local conditions.

Staff. The client, in most cases, realizes that your firm is no better than the specific personnel who would be assigned to his project. The salesmen better know who probably will be assigned and have résumés and backgrounds handy, as well as personal insights to help humanize the biographical data.

Responsiveness. The client wants to know how responsive your firm will be to his needs. The salesman, therefore, should be capable of explaining relevant firm organization and how responsiveness is maintained. Specific examples would be good, as well, indicating how the firm can at least try to meet all client demands.

Reputation. The client also will want to know the reputation of the firm in terms of references from clients, particularly those in a line similar to his own. For this reason you should have available a client listing, as well as names and phone numbers of persons who can be contacted directly. Recitation of involvement of key personnel in various professional, industry, civic, and other organizations also will be of assistance.

Due to marketing and other research, it is expected that you already are familiar with the industry in which the prospect is involved and its problems. You also should know something about the prospect/contact as a person, as well as the projects in which the prospect currently is involved or is about to become involved.

Gather Materials

When preparing to "make your pitch," gather together clean copies of all relevant materials, including: several copies of your firm's brochure; business cards; copies of project and client sheets; copies of personnel résumés, particularly of those who probably would be involved in the prospect's project; case histories of projects in which you feel the client would be interested; projection equipment plus slides of projects that indicate both the firm's capabilities and services, as well as projects similar to those in which the client is involved; magazine articles and other reprints, and other information you consider germane. Try to anticipate questions that might be asked and be ready to supply answers for those that should be answered. (Always guard against revealing information given to you in confidence, perhaps by a competitor of the prospect. While the prospect may appreciate the information received, he probably would better appreciate knowing that you can keep a confidence.)

Prepare to Meet

The meeting itself usually will take place at one of two locations—your offices or the offices of the prospect. If you are particularly proud of your facilities you may suggest that the prospect come to you, but don't force the issue. His wish in this matter should be your command.

Your Office. If the meeting is to take place at your office, be certain that everything is as clean and neat as practical. This does not mean that you must sterilize the office, nor does it mean that all employees should come in dressed to kill. Chances are the prospect has been around somewhat and knows what the usual state of affairs is in many design offices. If yours is artificially neat and orderly with all employees performing like well-trained field mice, there is the possibility that the prospect may start thinking in terms of, "What is he trying to hide?"

If the prospect is coming in from out of town, offer to make all necessary arrangements for him. Also determine for how long he will be in town and whether or not he would like to have dinner with you (at home or in a restaurant), see the sights, etc. Naturally, this must be played by ear. If he prefers to make his own arrangements, so be it. If you can make some arrangements, and he makes others, that's all right, too. In most cases, however, the very least you should offer to do is to pick him up at the airport or train station, and—assuming he is leaving after your meeting—return him.

Double check all arrangements you are making for the prospect. If he is not met on time, if he does not have the hotel room you told him he would have, etc., you are starting out with 2.9 strikes against you.

There are numerous gimmicks you can put into play when the meeting is on your "turf." You can have the person chauffered around in a limousine. You can have a fruit basket and champagne waiting for him in his hotel room. You can arrange for so-called escorts. The list goes on and on, including one suggestion that advises that a national celebrity who happens to be in the area can be paid to make a brief walk-on while the prospect is in your office. Some of these and other tactics, like the limousine and champagne, usually apply to those very few individuals who actually appreciate such nonsense. Do not simply assume that because a person is a very influential or highly-paid executive that he goes for this. Very often he will appreciate more the person who does the job well without unnecessary frills. In other cases, as with "escorts," you are courting disaster. In one or two very special circumstances, such a ploy is very marginally acceptable. In almost all cases, however, you should not jeopardize your professional reputation by becoming known as a pimp, nor should you pursue prospects who will evaluate your professional expertise on the basis of your ability to procure. As for gimmicks such as walk-ons by celebrities who indicate that they know you and so on, we advise against it. It is obviously dishonest and unethical. But if that doesn't bother you, consider how seriously it can backfire, especially if the star pumps the wrong hand or if the prospect's mind is taken completely off what you have to say.

Obviously, you do want to make sure that arrangements for the presentation itself are letter-perfect. Be certain that all necessary personnel will be on hand. Know the tour route to use when taking the prospect around your offices or perhaps to local buildings that you have been involved in. Be certain that all necessary projection equipment is on hand if you will be using it. Know when coffee will be brought in. Have all calls held. (If you are expecting one or two very important calls, notify the prospect beforehand that you may have to be interrupted.)

Prospect's Office. If the meeting will take place at the prospect's office, your main concern is any special equipment you may need. Inquire if it will be on hand. Also determine, if necessary, the size of the room and lighting conditions. If you intend to show slides, for example, but the room is sunlit and without blinds, you will have to be sure to have back-projection equipment with you.

In general, be sure to review your clothing for the day to ensure that it reflects an element of your own personality as well as the firm's. In most cases this will mean that your clothing should be clean and well pressed. Shoes should be polished. It sounds perhaps a bit too big brotherish, but the facts are that the prospect, like any human, may have certain beliefs, such as "you can tell whether or not a man is honest by looking at his eyes," or "you can tell whether or not a guy is successful by seeing if his shoes are shined." In other words, don't leave anything to chance. While you can't do anything about your eyes, you can at least shine your shoes.

And don't forget personal hygiene, meaning clean hands and nails, hair cut and combed, etc.

Meet

You should keep the presentation as brief as possible, but long enough to get your message across, adjusting and taking a reading by the responsiveness of the prospect. For example, if you are showing slides and he is exhibiting great interest, keep going at the same pace, inquiring if he has any questions. If, however, the contact starts fidgeting, and looks bored with the presentation, pick up the pace and get on to the next subject.

Obviously, there should be no set presentation where you say the same things over again with each new prospect. You can get bored with it yourself and show your own boredom to the prospect. "Playing it by ear" helps keep you on your toes so that, ideally, you can keep the prospect on his toes, or at least somewhere near the edge of his seat.

The main objective of this meeting is not only to make your initial presentation, so satisfying the seven major items of interest in the prospect's mind (as discussed above), but to find out more about an upcoming project so you can make a follow-up presentation or proposal. You should seek answers to the following questions:

1. What projects are involved?

2. How did the prospect determine what he wants to build?

3. Is the program well-defined or will a firm such as yours be responsible for closer definition?

4. What budget is involved?

5. How much flexibility is there in the budget?

6. Have performance specifications been prepared for the design team?

7. What particular concerns does the prospect have in terms of energy consumption, pollution abatement and control, life-cycle costing, and so on?

8. How are various projects or stages thereof currently scheduled?

9. When is the project supposed to be started and completed?

10. How much flexibility is there?

11. Who will lead the design team?

12. How many firms will be considered?

13. What factors will be considered in evaluation of various firms?

14. Who will be doing the evaluating?

15. Will the traditional selection/retention method be honored, i.e., no cost bidding either directly or indirectly?

16. Where will interviews/negotiations be held?

17. How long will they last?

18. Who will make the final decision?

In essence, you should prepare a list of questions for each prospective client with enough items covered to ensure that you have enough information to prepare an intelligent proposal. While it may be best to intersperse questions throughout the initial meeting, rather than asking them in the form of a barrage, do try to get them all answered. In fact, you might find it worthwhile to prepare a standard list of questions for such meetings, including room for specialized questions as the specific case may require.

In some cases you may seek permission from the prospect to view the site involved or, in the case of existing construction, walk through the facility involved and question certain individuals.

Follow-up

It always is in order, following an initial meeting, to write the prospect and thank him for his time and to express general interest in future projects. A typical brief letter may read something like this:

Dear Mr. Smith:

Thank you very much for the time accorded to me and other members of our firm on January 6. I hope we were able to convey our desire and ability to be of service to American General United.

We would most appreciate hearing from you in the future regarding any projects you may have in mind. I would be pleased to come to your offices to discuss project requirements in detail and to provide a comprehensive proposal.

I look forward to hearing from you in the not too distant future.

Sincerely,

If a specific project was discussed, and if a proposal will be forthcoming, consider a letter such as this:

Dear Mr. Smith:

Thank you very much for the time accorded to me and my associates on January 6. I trust we were able to convey our desire and ability to be of service to American General United.

With specific regard to AGU's planned expansion of the Sheboygan plant, I would like to make these recommendations.

A. If at all possible, obtain the original plans and specs of the plant as well as plans and specs relating to any subsequent additions/expansion that were completed.

B. Consider having a new soil and foundation engineering study performed. The last study, you indicated, was undertaken eight years ago. The site is subject to changed conditions that, given the nature of the proposed expansion, could have a significant bearing on design.

C. Although architectural capabilities of the design team are important, structural engineering capabilities are—in my opinion—paramount. Also, in light of your electric energy intensive processes and the current energy situation, the electrical consultant also should possess extensive background in electrical energy conservation techniques.

I anticipate that we shall have a proposal ready for your review in three weeks' time. I would be perfectly willing to return to your offices to make a presentation myself or, if you prefer, I would be delighted to act as your host.

I know how cramped your schedule is right now, so I will not expect a reply for two weeks or so. However, I will give you a call if I have not heard from you by the time our proposal is finalized.

Incidentally, we all were very much impressed by the obvious progress that AGU has made in the past five years, and we all have some very fond memories of our superb dinner at Angelo's. I look forward to having an opportunity to returning your generous hospitality.

Sincerely,

Similar letters should be sent to government officials you have met with, as well as anyone outside the firm who has helped arrange meetings, be they with private or public organizational representatives. Everyone likes to be thanked and treated with genuine respect.

8.6 THE PREPROPOSAL SURVEY

Whether a project involves new or existing construction, you should attempt to see the site and take photographs, either with a Polaroid or other camera. For purposes of the proposal, to be discussed later, we suggest that a 35-millimeter camera be used, that slides be made, and that prints be made from the slides.

New Construction

For new construction, the architect, when possible, should review the site involved and take photographs from various appropriate angles. It will help, of course, if a geotechnical consultant already has prepared a report on the site. (If he has not, this might be mentioned to the prospect, indicating that in most cases development of plans cannot take place until certain subsurface conditions are known.) Those who should be involved in the actual physical reconnoitering of the land include not only the salesman, but also any of the designers who will be involved in preparation of preliminary plans.

If the client already has some ideas about what he wants to build on the site, or certain performance specifications in mind, check them against the actual site. Will it be possible to do what the client wants? Will it be practical? Is the site perhaps more suited for something different? What else could be done? How could savings be made? Value increased? In other words, put your professional experience and judgment to work.

In terms of an engineer working on an interprofessional basis with an architect, every attempt should be made to review preliminaries to provide as much usable input as possible. A structural engineer, in fact, even may want to review the site himself. Again, however, the point is to evidence as much professional savvy as possible. Be careful, however, lest you exaggerate potential. If you do, the prospect either will disbelieve what you say or retain your services on a false premise. In other words, promise results based on your best efforts and be sure that, should you get the project, a best effort is made.

Existing Construction

Existing construction, considered in this sense primarily for systems modernization, energy use optimization, new interior design, and related work, is a rather involved undertaking. Ideally, you want to be able to undertake a survey that will be extensive but not so extensive that it becomes an item of major expense.

Assuming that we are talking about systems, a survey will be facilitated if you can obtain as-built drawings, maintenance schedules, records of service, power bills, and related items. These, for the most part, should be studied first with an eye toward achieving the prospect's main goals, be it pollution abatement, less energy usage/wastage, etc.

A visual inspection should be made of the site, again, with a camera. Interviews should be conducted with appropriate personnel, depending on the information you need established.

From studying existing materials, reviewing current conditions on the site, interviews, etc., you should be able to determine what services exactly will be required, what the alternatives are, and so on. All of this should be readied for preparation of a proposal.

8.7 PREPROPOSAL CONSIDERATIONS

There are two primary preproposal matters to consider. The first is to determine whether or not you should submit a proposal. The second involves setting a fee.

When To Submit a Proposal

A basic question you must answer is, "Should a proposal be made?" If you are going after a new client; if the project is relatively clearcut; if you feel you stand a good chance of obtaining the work (or at least of creating a favorable impression in the prospect's mind, opening up new avenues even if this job is not obtained), and if the proposal will not involve a great deal of time and expense, your answer obviously is, "Make the proposal." However, some proposals can run up into the thousands of dollars. In such cases, you must evaluate your chances of success very carefully. Who is the competition? How much will more or less competition qualify you? What previous experience do they have with the prospect? Will the fee play a role? (Remember, no matter how much you try to avoid a bid situation, in many cases the prospect will try to obtain some cost-comparative information before making an ultimate selection.) What are the chances of success? Is there another job, which also would fit your schedule, that offers more of an opportunity for success? Is obtaining this job going to develop an opportunity for obtaining more work from the same client? Is this job good for your service mix? Does it help you achieve goals? In other words, how important is the job to you? You should consider these and other factors before you develop a proposal that will take a substantial investment.

Setting a Negotiable Fee

Establishing a negotiable fee is a very important responsibility to which the firm must give thorough consideration. There are two main elements of concern, namely, method of charging the fee and amount of fee.

There are a variety of methods of establishing a fee, among them, percentage of construction costs, cost plus fixed fee, fixed fee, fee based on time (per diem, retainer, hour, etc.), combination of these plus—especially so in the emerging energy-consulting market—a percentage of savings obtained over a period of years, basically a contingency fee not dissimilar to that used by attorneys. The fee methodology established for attainment of any one objective should be the one most commonly used within that segment or by the client. Ideally, however, it should be as flexible as possible to provide what the client wants.

The second aspect—amount—is something else again. We do not recommend that anyone make a practice of loss-leading. However, one should bear in mind that it may be necessary to risk a short-term loss in an attempt to secure long-term profitability. For example, if we are talking about a prospect with whom you have not dealt before, and an MU in which you have not been active but wish to be, it may be wise strategy to lower your profit margin if you honestly feel that such a reduction will help you obtain the work. This is done easiest on smaller jobs where a net loss would be small. On larger projects, however, be very wary. In all cases recognize that a project involving both a new client and a new MU almost is certain to result in lower profits even when no "price break" is involved. Above all, realize that all projects should be performed with quality in mind. If you do take a project for which you've lowered your fee somewhat, do not try to enhance profitability by sacrificing quality. You may make a few more dollars in the short run but, in the long term, you will jeopardize future opportunities in the MU involved, and perhaps in other MUs as well. Also recognize that too low a fee could lead the prospect to believe that you are "lowballing," indicating that you may attempt overrun later, or that you do not understand the proposed scope of work, or just are not capable of handling the job. In other words, setting fees must be done with a great deal of sensitivity to overall goals, perceived client reactions, and prevailing charges for similar services.

Fee Bidding

Including a section on fee bidding in this book should not be taken to mean that the authors favor a bidding approach. Far from it. It is our belief that the interests of the client can be served best only when the choice of design professional is made through a traditional procedure, which calls for ranking of several "finalist" firms and negotiation with each—one at a time—until a satisfactory agreement can be reached. If an agreement can be obtained with the firm deemed most qualified, then no additional negotiation is called for.

Despite our opinion, there is a growing body of evidence to suggest that more and more governmental entities are turning to a lowest bid selection basis. In that most design professionals are rather naive when it comes to making a bid, and given that it is difficult to establish any specific objective rules of thumb, here follows discussion of a competitive bidding strategy that may be useful.

Note that the system outlined below cannot be implemented until you have had at least two or three years' experience in bidding against your competition, or at least twenty head-to-head bidding confrontations.

Probability. The bid pricing strategy proposed below is based on the laws of chance (probability theory). These laws state that if you throw a coin in the air 100 times, it will land "heads" 50 times and "tails" 50 times. Likewise, it you toss a die into the air 60 times, it will land 1 ten times, 2 ten times, etc.

Probability is measured on a scale of 0 to 1. Zero indicates impossibility. One indicates certainty.

Probability is determined by dividing the number of ways in which a desired event can occur by the number of outcomes possible. Thus, with the coin-tossing example, the number of ways the desired outcome ("heads" or "tails") can occur is one. Accordingly, the probability of the coin landing "heads" is shown as $1 \div 2$, or .5. In other words, there is a 50% chance of achieving the desired outcome. The chance of getting a six on a die in one throw is $1 \div 6$, or .166 on the probability scale, or a 16.6% chance.

Applying Theory to Bidding. The same laws of chance that govern coin tossing and dice throwing can also be implemented to provide guidance in bidding.

To begin with, it is essential that you keep extensive records on each competitor. The kind of general information needed is discussed throughout this book, and should be gathered whether or not there is a possibility of competitive bidding. For this particular purpose, the data required most are prices submitted by each competitor on jobs for which you also submitted bids.

To understand how the system works, we begin by isolating data for one competitior only—competitor A.

As can be seen in Figure 39, the competitor's bid is expressed in terms of a ratio: his price to your estimated *cost* (not including your profit). Thus, if the competitor bids $90,000 on a job you figured would cost you $100,000, the ratio would be 90,000:100,000, or 9:10 or .9.

Once all the competitor's bids are tabulated in that manner, determine the frequency distribution. As shown in Figure 39, competitor A's bids were .9 of your cost estimate once, the same as your cost estimates five times, 1.1 times your estimates nine times, and so on.

As can be seen in Figure 40, the chart has been expanded to include probability data. If one of Competitor A's 50 bids was .9 of your cost estimate, the chances of that occurring again are 1 out of 50, or .02 on the probability

Competitor A's Bid	
Your Cost Estimate	Frequency of Occurrence
0.9	1
1.0	5
1.1	9
1.2	14
1.3	12
1.4	5
1.5	3
1.6	1
	TOTAL 50

Figure 39. Competitor's bid vs. your cost estimates.

scale (2%). Looking at it another way, the chances of A bidding something other than .9 of your cost estimate are .98, or 98%. The chances of him bidding the same as your cost estimate are 5 out of 50, or .1 (10%).

Obviously, a cumulative factor also is involved. Thus, while there is a 2% chance that competitor A will bid .9 of your estimated cost, and a 10% chance that he will bid the same as your estimated cost, there is a 6 of 50 chance (.12 or 12%) that he will bid the same as your estimated cost or less.

As can be seen in Figure 41, cumulative probability is determined by determining how many times in the past the competitor has beaten your bid. For example, the competitor has never been lower than .9 of your cost estimate; thus, if you bid the project at .89 of your cost estimate, theoretically you would have to beat A. Likewise, A has been lower than 1.2 of your cost estimate 15 times. Thus, if you bid at 1.19 your cost estimate, chances are that you would be lower than A 35 (50-15) times, for a probability of .7 (70%).

To apply this theory, look at Figure 42, and assume that, for the project involved, you estimate your cost at $100,000.

Competitor A's Bid		
Your Cost Estimate	Frequency of Occurrence	Probability
0.9	1	.02
1.0	5	.10
1.1	9	.18
1.2	14	.28
1.3	12	.24
1.4	5	.10
1.5	3	.06
1.6	1	.02

Figure 40. Frequency distribution of competitor's bids/your cost estimates.

Competitor A's Bid Your Cost Estimate	Frequency of Occurrence	Probability	Your Bid Your Cost Est.	Cumulative Probability that Your Bid Will Be Lower than Competitor A's
.9	1	.02	.89	1.00
1.0	5	.10	.99	.98
1.1	9	.18	1.09	.88
1.2	14	.28	1.19	.70
1.3	12	.24	1.29	.42
1.4	5	.10	1.39	.18
1.5	3	.06	1.49	.08
1.6	1	.02	1.59	.02
			1.69	.00

Figure 41. Competitor's bid/your cost estimate frequency distribution and probabilities.

As can be seen, there is a new column in Figure 42, "Best Expected Profit." This is determined simply by multiplying the estimated profit you would obtain at a given bid by the probability of obtaining that bid. Accordingly, it can be seen that a bid of $119,000 would result in the best "best expected profit" of $13,300. If the chances of your getting the award at $129,000 were 46% (.46) rather than 42%, the best expected profit at that level would be $13,340, rather than $12,180. As such, your decision to bid at $119,000 or $129,000 would have to be made on the basis of subjective judgment.

Naturally, when compiling statistics, the competitor's bids will not fall precisely at .9 times your cost estimate, 1.1 your cost estimate, etc. In fact,

Your Bid Your Cost Estimate	Possible Bid	Profit (Loss)	Cumulative Probability that Your Bid Will Be Lower than Competitor A's	Best Expected Profit (Loss)
.89	$ 89,000	($11,000)	1.00	($11,000)
.99	99,000	($ 1,000)	.98	(980)
1.09	109,000	9,000	.88	7,920
1.19	119,000	19,000	.70	13,300
1.29	129,000	29,000	.42	12,180
1.39	139,000	39,000	.18	7,020
1.49	149,000	49,000	.08	3,920
1.59	159,000	59,000	.02	1,180
1.69	169,000	69,000	.00	0

Figure 42. Your bid/your cost estimate and best expected profit.

in most cases you probably will have very few at identical levels. Nonetheless, by using the cumulative techniques outlined above, you should be able to structure your bid well.

In most cases, of course, there will be more than one competitor involved. Accordingly, you must have accurate and up-to-date information—preferably in a ready-to-be-used format—on all known competitors. Thus, if your bid of 1.09 your estimated cost results in an 88% chance of beating Competitor A and a 92% chance of beating Competitor B, it would have a .81 chance (.99 $\times$ .92) of beating both A and B. If a third competitor were involved and your bid at 1.09 of estimated cost has only a .5 chance of success with it, the probability of your beating A and B and C at 1.09 your cost estimate would be .4 (.88 $\times$ .92 $\times$ .50).

The above system, of course, is not at all foolproof. It requires extended use for best results, plus complete and accurate information on the competition. If there has been a gradual shift toward lowered or raised prices, will the shift continue? Does the competitor customarily bid higher for one type of job or another? For one type of client? And by all means, be certain that your own cost estimates are accurate. If you merely rush through, you could overlook something crucial and submit a winning bid that turns out to be a "loser" for your company.

8.8   THE PROPOSAL AND ITS PRESENTATION

In some cases, as when dealing with most governmental entities, the proposal (sometimes just a letter of intent) should be a relatively spartan affair. If it is liked, then your firm, in most cases, will be one of several "semifinalists." If a negotiated procedure is used, separate interviews then will be held and, if your firm still is in the running, it will be one of, usually, three finalists. If ranked first, discussions will be opened to discuss fee. If your fee is within guidelines established by the governmental entity, your firm will be selected. In other cases, as when dealing with certain elements of the private sector, you will make a proposal at the same time as you hold an interview, and also may be called upon to discuss fee.

Note two things. First, determine exactly what type of selection procedure will be utilized during your initial presentation or discussions. Second, if proposal presentation, interview, and fee negotiation sessions are to be held all at once, you should feel perfectly within your rights to determine if this same approach will be used for several firms, thereby resulting in fee bidding. In other words, you can, if you want, state that you will be happy to make the proposal, go through an interview, answer any questions, and so on, but you will not provide any fee information until such time as you are assured that firms have been ranked and, if your price is found acceptable, you will be retained.

Proposal Contents

In some cases, especially with the government, a standard format is required or suggested. If one is given stipulations on how your proposal should be broken down, stick to them. In some cases deviation can sour the evaluators immediately, indicating inattention to requirements. In other cases, format either will not be outlined, or the prospect simply will indicate subject matter that should be included. In such a case, you should have prepared a standard format. We suggest the following.

Proposal Cover. You should have on hand a standard proposal cover that ties in with overall company image and graphics, as already discussed.

Covering Letter. Your proposal should have a covering letter typed on the company letterhead. Where applicable, it should cite the title and/or number of the project involved. The contents of the letter should be brief, not too dissimilar from the following model:

Re: Jones Building

Dear Mr. Jones:

Attached herewith is the proposal of Smith and Doe Associates for provision of architectural design services in conjunction with the above referenced project.

Our proposal contains information relative to the firm's capabilities and experience in the particular area of design involved; comments regarding results of a survey conducted of the intended site; comments relating to performance criteria you have specified; sketches of design possibilities; additional services we can supply, which will result in heightened cost efficiency, and other matters we feel are germane to the project.

On behalf of the firm, I would like to thank you for giving us the opportunity to become involved in this project. We look forward to working with you and your associates in the not too distant future.

Sincerely,

Table of Contents. This section should follow the covering letter, but should be prepared last, indicating various section heads and subheads and pages on which they begin.

Summary. The summary section should be kept to no more than two pages and should serve to summarize all that follows. A typical summary is as follows:

Smith & Doe Associates is an architectural firm with extensive experience and capabilities in the field of multistory condominium development. The firm and its staff have been involved in the design of more than forty such projects, three of which have received awards from various organizations, including the Metropolitan Chapter of the American Institute of Architects.

A review of the intended site by Smith & Doe staff members, coupled with analysis of soil and foundation engineering report A1654 (Miller Soiltech), indicates that the building should be sited as shown in Figure 4 to take maximum advantage of natural landform and solar radiation.

The firm has prepared two alternative basic designs. The first (Figure 8) takes initial cost into primary consideration. The second (Figure 9) is based primarily on long-term cost effectiveness, particularly as it regards energy costs and availability.

It is our understanding that, following award of the contract, the firm selected shall be given eight months to prepare a complete set of plans. Smith & Doe Associates can work within this time frame.

Staff members who would be assigned to this project include, among others, Frank Small and John Little, both of whom have extensive experience in the field of multistory condominium design.

Review of the intended project by Messrs. Small and Little has indicated that provision of certain additional services by the firm, including landscape architecture, signage graphics, and project management will result in substantially improved cost effectiveness and value.

In the event that Smith & Doe Associates is considered worthy of undertaking the project, we feel confident that a mutually satisfactory fee and payment method can be established.

Statement of Experience and Qualifications. The statement of experience and qualifications should be very brief. Depending on the nature of the project and the firm, you can indicate either the total experience (in number of projects and current construction value) of the firm, firm personnel, or both, and the total experience in the specific MU involved.

The experience and capabilities of your firm are at least equivalent to the experience and capabilities of your current manpower, including principals. A new firm, for example, would have to emphasize experience of staff, and even an older firm, with limited firm experience in the MU involved, would want to stress experience of its staff. This section should be backed up by Appendix

A. In Appendix A would appear lists of all projects undertaken by the firm (or its personnel), or lists of projects relating to certain segments or sub-segments, as well as case histories.

If possible, you may wish to include photographs of previous projects either in the experience section or in Appendix A. If you have preprinted case histories of projects that contain project photos, they would go in the Appendix.

Survey Results. Discuss some of the basic findings of your survey results, as well as any indications of need for additional preliminary work. In some cases, for example, it may be necessary to perform a new topographic survey for a site. If so, or in similar cases, be certain to explain why it is necessary and what, possibly, could result if it is not undertaken.

By all means, include photographs or line drawings (easily made by tracing photos) of the site. Illustrate particular points of reference, potential problem areas, potential areas of advantage, and so on. Indicate that your firm is interested enough in the project to have undertaken a comprehensive survey to ensure a knowledgeable discussion of the project involved.

Design Potential. You may wish to include preliminary rough sketches of design possibilities if applicable and desirable. For example, you may wish to discuss two basic types of design, one addressing itself primarily to first costs, another to long-term cost effectiveness. In addition, you may wish to supply sketches of design details, such as floor plans, unit layouts, and so on, each backed up in discussion.

Inclusion of design, while it can serve to make the proposal substantially more effective, also can have several drawbacks. First, it can add substantially to the cost of the proposal. Second, you may produce a design or designs that the prospect does not like. In other words, not including design sketches may leave more to the prospect's imagination. Third, you may produce a design that the prospect simply will turn over to another source for development. Unfortunately, little can be done to prevent this.

An alternative to actual inclusion of design is discussion of various elements in light of performance criteria. (If performance criteria are not established by the client, you may suggest their establishment as part of additional services, and reference some related elements in discussion of various design alternatives.) An excellent method to supplement such discussion is to use illustrations, preferably from your own files. For example, an engineer may suggest consideration of several alternative systems and brief discussions of what is involved. He can illustrate the systems through manufacturers' photos, as-installed photos, plans, and so on, as well as by photos from publications (best reproduced in the form of line drawings). Also, in this way, you are not giving the prospect free ideas.

Scope of Work. This should be a relatively tersely written statement of the exact scope of the work involved, often done through use of an outline. For example, a statement such as "Scope of work shall consist of design of:" followed below by an indented listing of elements to be designed, is acceptable. Then, at a margin equal to that of "Design of:" "Supervision of:" and so on, often just a repetition of scope of work established by the prospect.

Work Flow/Timing. This section should consist of the various separable elements of the scope of the work, broken down on the basis of design feasibility study, design, supervision, and so on, or design broken down by various design elements.

Each element should be discussed in terms of methodology, that is, how the company will undertake the work, when the work will begin, and timing involved in the various steps toward completion. Also, where applicable, you may discuss coordination of work with other elements of work, indicating that at a certain time copies of reports will be brought to a certain department, etc.

It would be a good policy to provide a flow chart of the intended project from the point of view of your firm.

Additional Work. This is a matter of selling up. The section should be as thorough as possible. It is suggested that each additional service be given a heading with discussion following describing exactly what the service is, how it would be applied to the project involved, and the benefits that would accrue to the prospect if such additional services were decided upon. As appropriate, prepare either one overall flow chart showing all additional work or, as necessary, flow charts showing the influence of only one or two services at a time. For example, you may discuss alternative services that cover the same work area but take different approaches, i.e., the prospect could not specify both.

If possible, this section should be accompanied by photographic or similar illustration.

Personnel. Describe the personnel who would be involved in the project and their respective responsibilities. If you have preprinted résumé forms, you may simply wish to provide a page listing names and respective responsibilities for the project, to be followed by pages of relevant resumes.

Organization. Provide an organizational chart indicating the organizational management/responsibility framework for handling the project as it fits into the overall firm framework.

Fee. If you provide information on fees and/or cost estimates, you may find that, depending on circumstances, you are putting yourself into a competitive bid situation. Therefore, you simply may wish to state that, because the proposal has alternatives and/or because the proposal cannot possibly cover all ramifications, you prefer to discuss the fee in person, on a negotiated basis, with the understanding that, if it is found to be acceptable, you will be given the project. This is a relatively touchy decision to make, and you must use your own best judgment.

Appendixes. We already have discussed some of the material that belongs in an appendix, including detailed lists of projects, case histories, and so on. In addition, include lists of clients, awards won, organizations of which the firm is a member, at least one code of ethics (as that of AIA, ACEC, ASCE, NSPE, etc.), company brochure, copies of testimonial letters, and other relevant material, including copies of magazine articles written by firm members or about the firm, and so on.

Proposal Mechanics

Usually one is required to submit the original of a proposal and a certain number of copies.

Given the importance of the proposal, we suggest strongly that it be reviewed thoroughly in terms of grammar, spelling, and so on, as well as the prospect's ability to understand it. In many cases, for example, the prospect will be unfamiliar with certain basic technical concepts and, therefore, they should be expanded upon. It is suggested that all, or a least the most important, proposals be closely reviewed, edited, and commented upon by a good editor, either someone on staff or retained for the purpose. In this way you can help ensure that what you have said will be understood. In addition, you may find that a competent writer will be able to give a proposal some flair, which will make it exceptional. For important prospects especially, we suggest that you spend the funds required to make the proposal a piece of excellent writing.

Once it is written, of course, the proposal must be put on paper. Use the same paper stock that you use for your stationery. If you wish, you can have a special imprint made, such as the name of the firm printed neatly in the upper left or right hand corner of the page. The mechanics of typing already have been discussed in general. For a proposal, it is suggested that you double space and leave at least three-fourths inch on either side and one inch top and bottom. Each page should be numbered, preferably at bottom center of the page.

Some firms have automatic typesetting equipment and prefer to produce proposals set in type. This makes an exceptionally nice appearance, but certain drawbacks are possible, given the nature of the prospect or prospect/contact involved. A major drawback: will the prospect think that the firm actually is too big or too sophisticated for the project involved?

Duplicating the proposal brings several considerations to bear. First, if the original is requested along with copies, obviously you have to present the original and copies, as stated. But if you do not have to present the original, then you can type on white paper and have the piece duplicated on your own paper by using either Xerox, Itek, or other equipment. This makes each copy look that much better. Also, when duplicating, we recommend that you use one side of the page only.

Proposal Presentation

In some cases you merely submit a proposal and cross your fingers. In other cases you have the opportunity to present the proposal in person, to discuss it at greater length, possibly to discuss fees as well. In the latter event, consider using slides, preferably to be projected onto a screen, to emphasize elements of the proposal. For example, each illustration could be made into a slide (if the illustrations, such as site photos, were not prepared from slides), allowing you to highlight and augment proposal discussion with a pointer. In addition, if you have made some preliminary designs that you do not want to leave with the prospect, you may have them made as slides only, whetting his appetite but taking them with you so that, in the event you are not chosen, you will not have performed free work.

Also, by having such a presentation, you may be able to make certain statements that cannot be put in writing. For example, if you present ten alternative services that could be selected, you obviously are talking about thousands of different combinations, each of which would have an effect upon the other and the overall project.

Proposal Intelligence

Save copies of all proposals. In many of them you will find elements that can be reused in other ways. In addition, you may be able to develop certain standard wording for certain sections, which will enable you to put together future proposals that much faster.

Keep track of all time/expense elements of putting together proposals so that you will be able to know approximately how much time it will take to put together certain types of proposals and, accordingly, approximately how much it will cost.

As mentioned earlier, proposals also serve as sources of operations research. On a regular, perhaps annual basis, examine the jobs you did not get.

Why didn't you get them? Are there areas of commonality? Failure often is the best teacher of all. In many cases you can send out a letter or make a phone call to determine why you did not get the job. A typical letter would look like this:

Dear Bob:

Thank you for letting me know that American General United has selected a firm to undertake design of its Sheboygan plant expansion. I know how thoroughly the qualifications of all of those who submitted proposals were reviewed, and I am certain that Miller Jones will be able to perform well.

Naturally, I am disappointed that our firm was not awarded the contract. I felt that the experience and expertise represented by those who would have been assigned made us eminently qualified. Since you and others on the selection committee obviously felt differently, I have a favor to ask.

If at all possible, could you please take a few minutes to call or write to identify what Miller Jones had that we did not have? This will provide us with a much-needed objective point of view. Such insights are required if we are to be as responsive as possible to your and similar companies' needs.

I look forward to hearing from you on this matter, and I do hope that our firm will be considered for future assignments. Best of luck with the project.

Sincerely,

8.9 CONTROLLING THE MARKETING EFFORT

If your marketing effort is to be successful, it must be controlled firmly. To control it, you must obtain complete knowledge of its strengths and weaknesses. Without this information you are restricted to guesswork, and there simply is too much at stake to allow for that.

Once established, one of the major functions of the marketing department—once initial marketing research is undertaken—is to continue marketing research by keeping in touch with various individuals, reading certain publications, and so forth, taking notes for each MU or client as appropriate, so that marketing research becomes almost an effortless operation.

Marketing research, to be effective, must be tested.

At the end of the first six months of operation with a marketing effort/plan in force, tally all the appropriate figures to determine how close you have come to meeting goals. Do not be content merely with examining goal-related information. Rather, break it down into terms of MUs to see how close you came to achieving goals in the manner in which you thought you would achieve goals. This is the key.

In cases where activity in various MUs has exceeded expectations, determine why. For example, was it because a client unexpectedly entered a new MU? Because a large new client was brought on board? Because activity in this MU increased due to certain uncontrollable conditions, such as the energy situation. Once you have isolated what you feel to be reasons, examine your reasoning in light of ongoing marketing research. Is there agreement? If not, is your marketing research in error and, if so, why? What effect will this have on anticipated activity in the MU next year and the year after? What effect will that have on overall goals? In other words, glean as much information as you can.

In a similar manner, examine MUs that were way below par for whatever reason. For example, if profit was down, why? Examine internal records to see who headed appropriate projects. What is their expectation? Can you obtain additional information by examining other projects in which certain firm members are involved? Are a person's talents being put to the wrong purpose? Is he simply not capable of doing the work required? On the other hand, is it the fault of marketing research or some uncontrollable element? Again, trace elements to the root causes; determine how situations can be remedied, and take appropriate action, in some cases meaning either obtaining different personnel or pursuing different types of clients.

Control is not simply a year-end function. Of particular importance at all times is failure analysis, particularly as it relates to lost jobs. In all cases, attempt to determine why you lost a job. This can be done informally by holding a conversation with a client or prospect, or formally through submission of a brief questionnaire. This will give you an excellent opportunity to determine your weak points as others see them. Also, in some cases, you will be able to obtain a copy of the winning proposal. For example, in most cases you can inspect what the winner presented to the federal government. See what is good about it in terms of the client involved, and bear it in mind for the next time. Such information really can be invaluable.

Your continuing and year-end analyses also should indicate where additional research effort should be placed. For example, if you continually are losing jobs to a certain set of competitors, try to determine why. What (or who) do they have that you don't? What do they do that you don't?

Be being conscious of the need for feedback, by obtaining as much as possible, by subjecting it to as many different analyses as possible, you will be able to provide more and more insights into your continuing research functions, which, of course, will continually be plugged into other elements of your ongoing marketing effort. The more you analyze discrepencies between plans and facts, the more you can get the feel for some of the "hunch" or "gut reaction" aspects of marketing research and planning. The more you can do this, the more accurate your forecasting can be. The more accurate your forecasting, the more prepared your firm will be, and the more successful. And success, after all, is the ultimate toward which all firms must strive.

INDEX